Psychology of Obesity

Psychology of Obesity

Samapika Das Biswas
Institute of Engineering and Management, Kolkata, West Bengal, India

ELSEVIER
ACADEMIC PRESS
An imprint of Elsevier

Academic Press is an imprint of Elsevier
125 London Wall, London EC2Y 5AS, United Kingdom
50 Hampshire Street, 5th Floor, Cambridge, MA 02139, United States

ISBN: 978-0-443-27797-9

For Information on all Academic Press publications
visit our website at https://www.elsevier.com/books-and-journals

Publisher: Megan Ball
Acquisitions Editor: Megan McManus
Editorial Project Manager: Khyati Vat
Production Project Manager: Aishwarya R.
Cover Designer: Mark Rogers

Typeset by MPS Limited, Chennai, India

Contents

Preface

Psychology of Obesity is written in response to the growing understanding that obesity cannot be explained or addressed through biological or medical perspectives alone. While physiological factors are important, research consistently shows that psychological, behavioral, social, and cultural influences play a central role in the development and experience of obesity.

This book focuses on the psychological dimensions of obesity, viewing it not simply as a health condition but as a lived human experience shaped by thoughts, emotions, motivation, identity, relationships, and social environments. It moves beyond simplified or deficit-based explanations and emphasizes evidence-based, ethical, and compassionate approaches to understanding body weight and well-being.

The volume brings together key psychological themes related to obesity, including eating behavior, body image, self-esteem, stigma, anxiety, depression, coping strategies, and family influence. The aim is to connect psychological theory with practical understanding that can inform research, clinical practice, education, and policy.

Psychology of Obesity is intended for psychologists, healthcare professionals, researchers, educators, and students who seek a deeper and more humane understanding of obesity. It is hoped that this book will contribute to reducing stigma and promoting psychologically informed, person-centered approaches that support long-term health and well-being.

Acknowledgments

The completion of *Psychology of Obesity* has been made possible through the guidance, support, and encouragement of many individuals and institutions, to whom I express my sincere gratitude.

I respectfully acknowledge the late Sri Debabrata Biswas, retired professor, Department of Psychology, University of Calcutta, my late father-in-law, for his unconditional support and scholarly influence, which continue to inspire my work.

I gratefully acknowledge the Honorable President Mrs. Banani Chakrabarti and Prof. Dr. Satyajit Chakrabarti, Director, Institute of Engineering & Management, for their academic support and encouragement. I also thank Mr. Prabir Kumar Das, Head, Department of Basic Science and Humanities, Institute of Engineering & Management, for his guidance.

I express my sincere gratitude to my teacher Prof. Dr. Sanjukta Das, Professor, Department of Psychology, University of Calcutta, for her academic guidance and encouragement, and to Prof. Dr. Prabal Kumar Chattopadhyay, Retired Professor and former Head, Department of Psychology, University of Calcutta, for his support and motivation.

On a personal note, I thank Dr. (Mrs.) Tanusree Biswas, my mother-in-law, for her academic guidance; my parents, Ms. Tanushree Das and Mr. Prabhat Kumar Das, for their unwavering support; and my husband, Mr. Shubhabrata Biswas, for his constant encouragement. I also acknowledge my daughter, Ms. Trariti Biswas, for her quiet motivation, and my PhD scholars, Ms. Shreejeeta Kargupta and Mrs. Susmita Bhakat, for their academic dedication.

I remain deeply thankful to all who contributed, directly or indirectly, to the completion of this book.

Chapter 1

Introduction to obesity

"Health is shaped not only by biology, but by the environments in which young people grow, learn, and live."

Learning objectives

Upon completing this chapter, readers will be able to:

Define and classify obesity in children and adolescents using WHO, CDC, and IOTF criteria, and critically evaluate the limitations of BMI for South Asian populations.

Describe the global and Indian epidemiological trajectory of adolescent obesity using CNNS (2016–18) and NFHS-5 (2019–21) data.

Explain the multilevel determinants of youth obesity across biological, psychological, familial, community, and digital-media domains.

Apply at least two integrative theoretical frameworks (biopsychosocial, ecological, life-course) to analyze the nature of obesity in adolescence.

Evaluate the physical, psychological, educational, and economic consequences of youth obesity with reference to key longitudinal studies.

Critically assess India's current policy response to youth obesity and identify key gaps.

1.1 Introduction

Over the last four decades, the global health scenario has witnessed a dramatic change with the onset of a major paradox, whereby while diseases of scarcity continue to plague the poor in many parts of the world, diseases of excess have simultaneously spread across the globe, transcending social groups, national boundaries, and age groups that were once believed to be immune. Among the youth, this is particularly significant. What was once believed to be a disease of affluence, obesity, today presents one of the biggest challenges in the health scenario of the 21st century. In fact, the World Health Organization (2022) states that over 390 million children and adolescents aged 5–19 years were overweight or obese worldwide. This dramatic change is not only seen in the high-income countries, but the scenario has now spread to the low- and middle-income countries, which face the added challenge of undernutrition and infections, a condition referred to as the "double burden of malnutrition" (WHO, 2016). In India, this epidemiologic transition has been vividly manifest, especially with the rapid economic liberalization, urbanization, and technological advances. The data from India's National Family Health Survey (NFHS-5, 2019-21), which is one of the largest surveys of its kind, reveals that the number of persons becoming overweight is increasing across all demographic groups, with states like Sikkim, Goa, and Chandigarh having childhood and adolescent overweight rates greater than 20%. At the same time, the data from the Comprehensive National Nutrition Survey (CNNS, 2016-18), which is the largest nutrition survey ever conducted in India, estimated that 4.8% of adolescents between the ages of 10 and 19 years were overweight or obese, with significantly higher rates in the urban areas and the households belonging to the highest quintile. These numbers, however, mask the alarming heterogeneity in the rates across the nation. By 2030, India is estimated to have over 27 million children and adolescents with obesity, accounting for 11% of the global pediatric obesity burden, unless preventive strategies are put in place (UNICEF, 2019).

This book is based on the assumption that obesity among the youth needs to be understood as a multidimensional phenomenon that cannot be explained by a simple energy balance or behavioral deficit approach. Rather, as argued by Ulijaszek and Lofink in their Annual Review of Anthropology article of 2006, obesity is largely a biocultural problem that results from a combination of genetic factors, personal development, and social and cultural environments that affect how people behave, what they like to eat, how they are active, and how they perceive themselves in different ways throughout their lives. This book will discuss these different aspects of youth obesity from different angles and perspectives, including practical examples, theories, and the social and cultural background of the Indians. This current chapter provides a

Psychology of Obesity. DOI: https://doi.org/10.1016/B978-0-443-27797-9.00007-5

background for the rest of the chapters in the book. It does more than simply provide statistical information on the epidemiology of youth obesity; it provides a broad understanding of the phenomenon of youth obesity that includes the relationships of biological, psychological, social, and environmental factors and therefore needs a research approach as complex as the problem itself. The chapter is subdivided into 12 main sections: obesity among children and how it is defined and classified; a look at how it has emerged over the years and across the world; a critical analysis of the complex nature of obesity as a disease and a social problem; a look at the causes of obesity from a biological, psychological, familial, social, and virtual perspective; a look at the consequences of obesity from a physical, psychological, educational, and economic perspective; a look at the integrative theories of obesity; a look at the methodological problems; a look at the Indian scene; and finally, a look at the practical implications and research directions. The chapter is written in a research-based, thought-provoking, and compassionate manner because it recognizes that the youth and adolescents are not simply objects of medical intervention but active human beings whose experiences, social and cultural backgrounds, and views need to have a substantial impact on how research and practice are done.

1.2 Defining and classifying obesity: metrics, growth standards, and critiques

The definition and classification of obesity in children and adolescents pose a set of complexities that are simply not found in adults, largely because of the normative and highly variable physiological changes that accompany growth and development in children and adolescents. Thus, while obesity in adults is generally classified according to a body mass index (BMI) of 30 kg/m² or greater (WHO, 2000), the classification of obesity in children and adolescents is based on age- and sex-specific reference standards that take into account the dynamic body composition changes that accompany growth and development in children and adolescents. The most widely used metric for classifying obesity in children and adolescents is BMI for age percentiles, which has been implemented in two forms: the World Health Organization's reference standards for growth WHO Growth Reference Study Group (2007) for children aged 5–19 years, wherein overweight is defined by a BMI for age greater than +1 standard deviation from the median value and obesity by a BMI for age greater than +2 standard deviations from the median value; and the Centers for Disease Control and Prevention's growth charts for children aged 2–20 years (Centers for Disease Control and Prevention, 2000), wherein overweight is defined by a BMI for age at or above the 85th percentile but less than the 95th percentile and obesity at or above the 95th percentile. The third system was developed by the International Obesity Task Force, which uses specific cut-offs for different ages and sexes by applying the adult BMI of 25 and 30 kg/m² to calculate what these would be for children and thus enable comparison of studies from around the world.

Despite their general acceptability, classifications based on the application of the BMI have come under serious scientific and ethical concerns due to various reasons. For instance, the BMI is only an estimation of body adiposity and not a direct measure of body fat; it equates fat and lean body mass and also fails to recognize regional fat distribution patterns. Furthermore, the relationship between the BMI and metabolic risks also differs across ethnic groups (Deurenberg et al., 2002). This is of serious concern for people of Asian descent, such as Indians, as their body fat and risks are already high at much lower BMIs than those of people of European descent and their obesity thresholds of 30 kg/m². As Misra et al. (2009) noted, Asian Indians develop insulin resistance, abnormal cholesterol levels, and metabolic syndrome at much lower BMIs than 30 kg/m² and thus prompted recommendations for different BMI thresholds of ≥23 kg/m² for overweight and ≥25 kg/m² for obesity in Asia. It is thus scientifically not easy to apply the same BMI for everyone as is done in the general population, and it needs constant updating of health data to suit their needs.

Anthropometric measurements such as waist circumference, waist-to-height ratios, skinfold thickness at specified sites of the body, and mid-upper arm circumferences also offer additional valuable information regarding central obesity and its metabolic risks and are now advocated as additional methods for body fat measurements in both clinical and population settings (Freedman et al., 1999; Wells & Fewtrell, 2006). More sophisticated methods of body composition measurements such as dual-energy X-ray absorptiometry, air displacement plethysmography (Bod Pod), and bioelectrical impedance analysis also exist and are much more accurate in measuring body fat and lean body mass and their distribution but are mostly used in research settings due to their high costs and need for highly skilled personnel to conduct the measurements—problems that are mostly experienced in low- and middle-income countries.

In addition, apart from their technical limitations, classification systems for obesity are based on a series of cultural, social, and economic beliefs, which have considerable psychosocial implications. For example, calling children "obese" without providing them with support measures may lead not only to an increase in bullying, but also to a lack of seeking support, dissatisfaction with their body image, and even a worsening of their weight problems because of stress and eating habits. Experts on obesity such as Brewis (2014) have already warned against "blindly" transferring Western perceptions of body image and classification systems into other cultures, where bigger body sizes may have entirely different meanings related to health, wealth, or being a successful parent. The staging systems, such as the Edmonton Obesity Staging System, which not only considers body mass but also functional status, psychological comorbidities, and metabolic problems, are considered a more sophisticated classification system, as evidenced by the fact that obesity is now being recognized as a chronic, "recurring, multifactorial disease" rather than a "simple anthropometric phenomenon" (American Medical Association, 2013; Sharma & Kushner, 2009). Most research on adolescents has used BMI-for-age according to WHO references, and mostly only this, but sometimes adding waist circumference when possible, but obviously recognizing its limitations.

1.3 Historical and epidemiological context: from thrifty genes to globalized calories

In order to understand the present obesity epidemic in all its dimensions, it is essential to comprehend its historical genesis in biological, ecological, and political-economic dimensions. Neel's "thrifty genotype" hypothesis, published in the American Journal of Human Genetics in Neel (1962), postulated that genetic variants that had been favored by natural selection in ancestral times of food scarcity now predispose human populations to efficient fat storage—an adaptation to feast-or-famine environments that has become profoundly maladaptive in the context of nutritional abundance. While genetic research, including large-scale genome-wide association studies that have identified over 900 genetic loci associated with BMI and fat-related traits, has refined and complicated this hypothesis (Locke et al., 2015), the basic point of evolutionary history is important to comprehend the present obesity epidemic: the present obesity epidemic reflects a huge disconnect between our old biological setup and the very different modern food and exercise environment. The overall social circumstances that have created this disconnect have been conceptualized through two distinct but complementary theories. Omran's "epidemiological transition theory," published in the Milbank Quarterly in Omran (1971), documented the epidemiological shift towards chronic diseases that accompanies industrialization and economic development. Popkin's "nutrition transition theory," published in Nutrition Reviews (Popkin, 1994), conceptualized the nutrition-related aspects of this overall social circumstance by describing the systematic shift towards diets with increasing proportions of energy-dense but nutrient-poor ultra-processed and processed foods that has been extensively documented in the Indian epidemiological literature. In a review published in the Journal of Diabetes in 2011, Misra et al. found that the nutrition transition in India over the period 1973–2004 resulted in a 7% reduction in energy derived from carbohydrates and a 6% increase in energy derived from fats, with a reduction in the intake of coarse cereals, pulses, fruits, and vegetables and an increase in the intake of meat, refined grains, and salt.

Global epidemiological data reveal the consequences, and the Noncommunicable Diseases (NCD Risk Factor Collaboration (NCD-RisC, 2017), in their landmark study pooling 2416 population-based measurement studies involving 128.9 million participants from 200 countries, reported the tenfold rise in the global prevalence of obesity among 5- to 19-year-olds from 1975 to 2016, rising from 0.7% to 5.6% in girls, and from 0.9% to 7.8% in boys. Perhaps the most worrying part of this study was the observation that, while the rise in BMI has leveled off in high-income countries (already at high levels), it has increased exponentially in East and South Asia, including India, where the rate of increase in BMI in this region exceeds the rate in any other region in the world. The GBD 2015 Obesity Collaborators (2017) reported that, in 2015, 107.7 million children and 603.7 million adults were obese, with high BMI causing 4.0 million deaths and 120 million disability-adjusted life years (DALYs) each year.

It is, however, worth emphasizing how economic globalization accelerates these trends. The economic liberalization of India, initiated in 1991, has opened doors for food and drinks companies from all over the world to penetrate India's market rapidly. These developments have made ultra-processed foods (UPFs) highly accessible, affordable, and attractive to populations worldwide. Swinburn et al. (2011), in their landmark study published in The Lancet, have emphasized how these are the primary causes of what they call a "global syndemic," or the phenomenon of obesity, undernutrition, and climate change, all of which have been caused by factors that call for sweeping measures rather than simply trying to change individual behaviors. The COVID-19 pandemic has further fueled the trends of obesity, particularly among youth, through school closures, increased screen time, reduced opportunities for physical activities, food delivery services, and psychosocial stress, all of which have been observed across nations and merit further epidemiological research (Nogueira-de-Almeida et al., 2020).

1.4 The complex nature of obesity: disease, diversity, and the energy balance paradigm revisited

The reductionist "energy balance" model of obesity, popularly expressed as "calories in/calories out," has dominated the way in which obesity is understood for most of the last century. This model holds individuals accountable for the accumulation of excess body weight due to their inability to control food intake and physical inactivity. Though the "calories in/calories out" model of obesity is supported by science, it is also increasingly being challenged for its failure to account for the complex biological, hormonal, developmental, and environmental influences on body weight regulation in living organisms. In fact, the science of obesity of the last few years has established the fact that the human brain, particularly the hypothalamus, limbic system, and prefrontal cortex, is a highly advanced and adaptable "energy regulatory system," which coordinates and balances the hormones secreted by the adipose tissue (leptin [LEP]), the gastrointestinal system (ghrelin, glucagon-like peptide-1, peptide YY), the pancreas (insulin), and the entire metabolic system to control food intake, hunger, satiety, food preferences, physical inactivity, and metabolic rate (Schwartz et al., 2017, in the Endocrine Society's Scientific Statement). Any disruptions in the complex "regulatory systems," whether through genetics, epigenetics, or environmental stressors such as stress, sleep deprivation, and endocrine disruptors, lead to positive energy balance, which is not easily influenced by behavioral changes, thereby accounting for the well-known fact that "dieting is not an effective way to reduce weight and keep it off" (Hall et al., 2012).

The formal definition of obesity as a chronic, relapsing, multifactorial neurobiological disease, as accepted by the American Medical Association in 2013 and subsequently by numerous professional medical societies, represents a paradigm shift in our thinking and has profound clinical, social, and policy implications. This new definition shifts the locus of moral responsibility from individual willpower to the disease process, provides the basis for the development of long-term treatment modalities such as pharmacotherapy and weight loss surgery in conjunction with behavioral therapies, and challenges the widespread stigmatization of obesity as a personal flaw or moral failing. In a landmark article in the American Journal of Public Health, Puhl and Heuer (2010) have demonstrated the widespread psychological and social consequences of the stigmatization of individuals with excess weight, such as increased rates of depression, anxiety disorders, disordered eating patterns, reduced healthcare-seeking behavior, employment discrimination, and paradoxically, weight gain as a result of cortisol dysregulation in response to stigmatization, thereby not only failing as a treatment strategy but also as a path to poor health outcomes.

At the same time, disability studies scholars and body positivity activists are promoting the concept of body diversity, which challenges the negative perception of body mass by suggesting that it is a result of societal preference for thinness driven by historical, racial, and weight loss industry factors. Any framework would also need to deal realistically with the ethical concerns that this perspective generates. Nevertheless, it coexists with a large body of scientific literature supporting the association of excessive body mass, particularly excessive visceral and ectopic fat deposits, with type 2 diabetes mellitus, cardiovascular diseases, nonalcoholic fatty liver disease, certain cancers, sleep apnea, and musculoskeletal disorders (GBD 2015 Obesity Collaborators, 2017; Weiss et al., 2004). Any sophisticated framework would also need to recognize biological risks without reducing a person to their body mass and focus on health-promoting behaviors and psychosocial well-being as primary intervention targets.

1.5 Determinants of youth obesity: a multilevel analysis

1.5.1 Biological and genetic determinants

The contribution of genetics to the variation in BMI among individuals has been estimated to be around 40%–70%, based on studies carried out on twins over the years. Recent large-scale studies have identified over 900 locations where the genetics of BMI and obesity have been linked, with the fat mass and obesity-associated gene (FTO gene) being the most commonly identified gene. However, the "missing heritability" problem, where the proportion of heritability estimated based on family studies exceeds the proportion of variation in the population attributed to the known genetic loci, points to the fact that the genetics of obesity, apart from the identified loci, is likely due to gene-environment interactions, epistasis, or structural genomic variations. The proportion of obesity cases due to mutations in the genes for LEP, the leptin receptor, melanocortin-4 receptor, or pro-opiomelanocortin is very rare. The more important mechanisms for obesity in the population include the epigenetic mechanisms whereby the prenatal or early postnatal environment influences the offspring's metabolic development, as outlined in the "developmental origins of health and disease" hypothesis, first outlined by Barker et al. (1995), and later developed into the concept whereby the prenatal environment, based on nutritional scarcity or excess, influences the offspring's metabolic development, leading to obesity or metabolic disorders in later life (Godfrey et al., 2017, The Lancet Diabetes & Endocrinology).

The microbiome of the gut has also been established as a further major biological factor influencing adiposity and metabolism. Changes in diversity, composition, and functional potential of the microbiome, which are affected by antibiotic use, mode of delivery, infant feeding patterns, and dietary habits, have been prospectively related to increased risk of overweight in children (Sonnenburg & Backhed, 2016, Nature). Endocrine-disrupting chemicals (EDCs), which include bisphenol A, phthalates, polychlorinated biphenyls, and organochlorine pesticides, are known to cause "obesogenic" effects by disrupting adipogenesis, lipid metabolism, thyroid hormones, and hypothalamic regulation of energy balance. These are increasingly regarded as a new group of environmental determinants of overweight and obesity distinct from behavioral pathways (Janesick & Blumberg, 2011, International Journal of Andrology). Such biological complexity means that youth obesity cannot be regarded solely as a behavioral issue but also as a multifactorial condition that is affected by a combination of genetic predispositions, changes in gene expression, the microbiome of the gut, and the presence of harmful substances, which are affected by different environments at different times of a person's life.

1.5.2 Psychological determinants

In the development and maintenance of obesity in adolescents, psychological factors have been recognized as playing a critical role, although not as prominently as biological and environmental factors. Emotional and volitional factors and mental health issues such as depression and anxiety contribute to eating and other health-related patterns of young people. Moreover, constructs such as self-esteem and body image are also highly related to young people's behavioral patterns, as young people are highly sensitive to social evaluation and identity issues during their adolescent period. Empirical studies have consistently shown that these psychological factors are related to young people's unhealthy eating patterns and low levels of physical activity and their vulnerability to weight gain and obesity. These issues will be discussed in later chapters of this book.

1.5.3 Family and peer environment

The family environment is the primary environment in which children develop their eating habits, their exercise and sedentary behavior patterns, and their weight-related attitudes from birth through to their teenage years. Parent feeding practices such as food restriction, pressure to eat, permissive or uninvolved feeding practices, and the use of food as a reward or as a means of providing comfort have been linked to overweight in children through their impact on the child's innate ability to regulate their food intake according to their internal hunger and fullness cues (Birch et al., 2003, American Journal of Clinical Nutrition). Family food environment factors such as home food availability, food preparation practices, family mealtimes, and portion sizes are key modifiable factors related to the quality of children's diets and have been strongly linked to weight outcomes in children (Story et al., 2008, Annual Review of Public Health). Parent modeling of children's eating and exercise behaviors is also a key factor in child weight outcomes through the observational effects of these modeling behaviors on children's development and health, as described by Bandura's (1986) social cognitive theory. Parents who model healthy eating and exercise habits have children who tend to exhibit healthier weight-related behaviors than those of parents who model unhealthy eating and exercise patterns. Peer relationships become more important as children enter their teenage years and gain independence from parental influence and control; peer norms and appearance-based social comparison effects have been linked to dietary and physical activity patterns in adolescents (Simpkins et al., 2013, Journal of Research on Adolescence).

1.5.4 Community and built environment

The built environment, such as the availability of food in the neighborhood, parks for play, and the availability of transportation and housing, influences the amount of physical activity and diet of young people by making them more accessible and easier to obtain. This happens without the need for individual motivation (Lovasi et al., 2009, Epidemiologic Reviews). A neighborhood without parks for play, working parks, sidewalks, and food stores with healthy food at reasonable prices makes it difficult for people to make healthy choices. This is more common in neighborhoods with low incomes. The prevalence of fast food and convenience stores and the relative absence of grocery stores in low-income neighborhoods, or the "food swamp," creates the "externalized responsibility for health outcomes," as defined by Walker et al. (2010), shifting the locus of control for health outcomes from structural conditions to individual behavior. Socioeconomic inequality is a structural cause of obesity. In middle- and high-income countries, socioeconomic status is inversely related to the prevalence of youth obesity through several pathways, such as food budgets promoting the consumption of high-energy, nutrient-poor foodstuffs (Drewnowski and Specter, 2004, American Journal of Clinical Nutrition), chronic psychosocial stress leading to cortisol-induced fat accumulation, and reduced availability of secure outdoor physical activity environments (Shrewsbury & Wardle, 2008, Obesity). The most stable environment for the majority of people is the school. The quality of the food in the school, the availability of competitive food in the school, the quality of physical education in the school, the availability of recess in the school, and the culture of the school in the context of body image and physical competence have a great impact on the amount of food and physical activity of the students (Story et al., 2008).

1.5.5 Digital media and technological determinants

Digital media technology is a new and rapidly expanding determinant of youth obesity that affects youth obesity through a range of different pathways simultaneously. Prolonged use of digital media technologies such as TV, gaming, social media, online streaming services, and education technology reduces the amount of time available for engaging in physical leisure activities, affects sleep patterns by suppressing melatonin production caused by blue light emitted from these devices, and increases the amount of passive exposure to targeted food and drink advertisements. The food and drink industry has also been found to target children and adolescents with personalized digital media advertisements, thereby creating a greater preference for the advertised food and drink products, which are often high in calories and low in nutrient content. Social media sites such as Instagram, TikTok, and YouTube have also been found to have a strong impact on body image and obesity among adolescents and young adults by creating social comparison environments that are often idealized and digitally manipulated, thereby consistently increasing body dissatisfaction among both female and male adolescents and promoting unhealthy dietary and exercise habits through social comparison processes based on body image concerns (Perloff, 2014, Sex Roles; Tiggemann & Slater, 2013, International Journal of Eating Disorders). In India, the use of smartphones has shown an extraordinary rate of growth in terms of subscriptions that have crossed the one billion mark by 2023, thereby creating unprecedented exposure to global digital food advertisements and social media body ideals for a vast population of adolescents who were previously insulated from these factors (Telecom Regulatory Authority of India TRAI, 2023).

1.6 Consequences of youth obesity: physical, psychological, educational, and economic dimensions

The consequences of youth obesity are far-reaching and multisystemic and can be felt across the lifespan. In the physical domain, youth obesity has been associated with a number of health problems that are thought of as being adult problems, such as type 2 diabetes, insulin resistance, high blood pressure, abnormal cholesterol levels, nonalcoholic fatty liver disease, polycystic ovary syndrome among teenage girls, sleep apnea, and problems with the skeleton, such as Blount's disease and slipped capital femoral epiphysis. In a long-term study of heart health by the Bogalusa Heart Study, it was found that health problems such as a high level of body mass index, bad cholesterol levels, and high blood pressure are closely related to health problems that adults face. In addition, the study found that being obese as a child is one of the surefire ways of being obese as an adult and facing health problems that accompany it. In addition to this, there is also the issue of metabolic syndrome that has been found to be prevalent among obese youth. In a landmark study by Weiss et al. (2004), it was found that there was a prevalence of metabolic syndrome in 50% of severely obese youth.

The psychological outcomes are equally as compelling and of clinical significance. Adolescents who experience obesity have been found to have substantially increased risks of depression, generalized anxiety disorder, low global self-esteem, and poor health-related quality of life outcomes, which are partly but not entirely mediated by weight stigmatization and social exclusion (Schwimmer et al., 2003, JAMA; Sutaria et al., 2019). Binge eating disorder and loss of control eating, defined as experiencing episodes of eating large amounts of food and having a feeling of loss of control over eating, are also substantially increased in adolescents experiencing obesity and are not amenable to conventional behavioral interventions without psychological interventions (Tanofsky-Kraff et al., 2009, International Journal of Eating Disorders). Weight-based internalized stigma, or the extent to which people accept and apply to their own lives the negative stereotypes and social perceptions projected onto their body type by society, has been identified as a major mediator of depression and anxiety outcomes, independent of actual BMI levels, and is heightened in the identity-sensitive period of development of adolescence (Puhl & Heuer, 2010).

Regarding the educational consequences, while not emphasized as extensively in medical literature, there are considerable long-term effects. Weight-based bullying and appearance-based teasing are well-linked to school avoidance, scholastic underinvolvement, physical education class withdrawal, and increased truantism (Puhl & Latner, 2007, Psychological Bulletin). It has been found that stigmatization-based stereotypes linking obese persons with laziness or scholastic disengagement may impact teacher perceptions and peer group inclusion in a manner that negatively affects scholastic performance; however, this also needs to be researched more extensively while incorporating adequate control variables. The psychosocial effects of bullying and teasing also form a vicious cycle wherein increased social anxiety and depression may cause obese adolescents to withdraw from school-based social interactions, leading to a reduction in physical activity opportunities while simultaneously causing emotional distress.

1.6.1 Economic consequences

Economic consequences are significant at both individual and societal levels. In the case of India, the World Obesity Federation has found that the economic burden of obesity was around USD 29 billion in 2019, which was equivalent to 1% of GDP. It was also projected that this burden would increase to USD 839 billion or 2.5% of GDP by 2060 if preventive strategies are not adopted (UNICEF, 2019). These economic costs include direct medical costs of treating comorbid diseases of obese persons, loss of economic productivity due to disability and premature death, and the significant economic burden of childhood obesity leading to adult obesity and related health complications. In addition to this economic burden at the societal level, obese adolescents also face a loss of future economic opportunities due to scholastic underachievement, labor market discrimination, and increased future medical costs. These economic effects are also concentrated at the individual level within disadvantaged populations and contribute to the continuation of socioeconomic disparities.

1.7 Integrative frameworks: biopsychosocial, ecological, and developmental models

The multifactorial nature of youth obesity necessitates the development of theories that integrate the various factors involved. Three such theories have proven to be particularly helpful in the attempt to understand the multifactorial nature of youth obesity. The biopsychosocial model, for instance, recognizes the importance of the combined role of biology, psychology, and social factors in the development of health outcomes. Ecological theories, on the other hand, acknowledge the role of the various environments in the development of behavior in young people. These environments include the family, the school, and the community. Developmental and life-course theories also acknowledge the role of the various stages of development in the development of youth obesity. These theories have been discussed in more detail in the subsequent chapters.

1.8 Methodological challenges: measurement, causality, culture, and ethics

The methodological challenges facing rigorous research on youth obesity are significant and interrelated, and their existence must be acknowledged to properly interpret the extant body of research and design better research for the future. Measurement validity is a methodological challenge at all levels of analysis. When it comes to dietary data, self-reported measures, whether through 24 hour recalls, food frequency questionnaires, or diet diaries, have been found to have significant biases, including social desirability, differential recall, misreporting of portion sizes, and food composition database problems, with significant underreporting found among overweight and obese individuals (Livingstone & Black, 2003, Journal of Nutrition). While doubly labeled water, used for measuring total energy expenditure, and accelerometry, used for measuring physical activity, are significantly more accurate, their cost renders them impractical for group-level studies, particularly in resource-scarce settings. As mentioned in Section 1.2, BMI classification of obesity has been found to have population-specific measurement error, particularly relevant to South Asians.

Establishing causality for youth obesity is a methodological challenge because of the interrelated nature of all the factors, making it difficult to establish their importance. Most of the factors of interest, such as screen time, dietary habits, feeding styles, and food environment, are correlated with socioeconomic factors, which are independent risk factors for obesity, making it imperative but impossible to adjust for all confounding variables. Mendelian randomization, a form of causal inference, has been useful in clarifying causal associations between nutrients and disease, including obesity, by using natural randomization from genetics, but its accuracy is based on untestable assumptions of pleiotropy. The randomized controlled trials of environmental and policy-level interventions are perhaps the highest priority of all, but are hindered by ethical and practical difficulties, such as the impracticability of randomizing children into obesogenic environments and the long-term follow-up period that would be necessary to assess outcomes. Longitudinal cohort studies of adequate duration, sample size, and control of confounders are considered the gold standard of methodologies for understanding the etiologic pathways of health problems in observational studies and are scarce in South Asia and particularly in India.

Cultural validity of the instruments and constructs being employed by the researcher is another level of methodological challenge of particular interest to studies conducted in the context of India and other postcolonial countries. It is possible that standardized instruments developed and validated for use in Western cultures might not effectively capture the food habits, body ideation, family relationships, and cultural nuances that are essential to understanding the issue of obesity in youth from India. It has been increasingly acknowledged that a combination of quantitative and qualitative methodologies of research is essential to understanding cultural complexity that cannot be captured by numerical data alone (Patton et al., 2016, Lancet). Ethical considerations while carrying out studies with children and adolescents include issues of obtaining informed assent from the child and parental consent, designing a data collection process that does not stigmatize the child by measuring weight, communicating the results of the study to the child, and addressing issues of power imbalance that might compromise voluntariness. Rights-based methodologies that involve young people as coresearchers, rather than merely respondents, which is in keeping with the spirit of the United Nations Convention on the Rights of the Child, not only meet the ethical imperative, it may also produce more valid data while simultaneously developing the capacity of the participant (UNICEF, 2019).

1.9 India in focus: national trends, cultural mores, and policy responses

India provides an important country setting for the study of youth obesity because it has a large, ethnically diverse population, rapid but uneven economic growth, ongoing social inequalities, both undernutrition and overnutrition problems, rich traditions in food, and changing health trends. The national surveillance trends reveal alarming trends in the rising prevalence of overweight and obesity among Indian children and adolescents, with large variations in urban-rural, socioeconomic, and geographic differences. The CNNS (2016-18), conducted by India's Ministry of Health and Family Welfare, with the help of UNICEF in 30 states and union territories, surveyed the height and weight status of over 112,000 children and young people. The study reported the prevalence of overweight or obesity among adolescents aged 10–19 years to be 4.8% nationwide, but the prevalence was higher in urban areas and among the wealthier population (Ministry of Health and Family Welfare (MoHFW), Government of India, UNICEF, & Population Council, 2019; Sethi et al., 2024). In their study on overweight and obesity among 38,296 urban Indian schoolchildren, Misra, Shah, et al. (2011), Misra, Singhal, et al. (2011) reported the prevalence of overweight to be 18.5% and obesity 5.3% in metropolitan school-going populations, thus highlighting the large rural-urban divide and the concentration of obesity risk factors among urban, affluent, private school-going adolescents. The NFHS-5 (2019-21) study reported rising trends in overweight and obesity among all age groups, with some states such as Sikkim, Goa, and Chandigarh recording childhood and adolescent overweight prevalence above 20% (IIPS & ICF, 2021). In the next decade, that is, by the year 2030, India will contribute to 11% of the world's childhood obesity cases, according to the projections made by UNICEF (2019).

The cultural factors related to youth obesity in India involve the familial, spiritual, and intergenerational aspects of food, which carry significant meaning beyond the nutritional. In the context of India, food is related to the selflessness of the mother, hospitality, spirituality, and the solidarity of the family. The culture of India glorifies obesity as an indicator of prosperity, health, and good parenting, especially in the case of young children and male children. Such glorification of obesity might delay the recognition of the seriousness of the condition by parents and reduce the motivation for dietary changes. The complex interrelation between gender roles and obesity in India is another factor. Girls, especially, face stringent scrutiny of their bodies, especially with regard to marriage and social status, from an early age. They develop unhealthy food habits, which might lead to obesity, poor self-esteem, and mental health problems. Boys, especially, are encouraged to eat more, which is related to their growth and strength. The culture of India imposes certain body configurations, which might put the individual in a psychological bind, especially in the case of girls, and might not be addressed by the mainstream obesity interventions, which focus only on dietary and exercise habits.

The rapid urbanization and penetration of global food systems have profoundly influenced the dietary environment of Indian youth. The widespread marketing of ultra-processed foods (UPFs), sugar-sweetened beverages, and fast foods through digital platforms and point-of-sale advertising has significantly transformed dietary habits among urban adolescents. Simultaneously, post-liberalization academic competition, characterized by the proliferation of coaching centres, intensive academic schedules, and examination-oriented education systems, has contributed to the marginalization of physical education within school curricula and reduced opportunities for physical activity and recreational play among children and adolescents. In addition, urban planning challenges, including limited access to parks and recreational spaces, inadequate pedestrian infrastructure, and increasing levels of environmental pollution, have further constrained physical activity among young people.

The policy responses to the youth obesity epidemic in India have undergone significant transformation over the past decade. Key initiatives include the National Programme for Prevention and Control of Non-Communicable Diseases (NP-NCD), the Rashtriya Bal Swasthya Karyakram (RBSK) school health screening programme, and the Ayushman Bharat Health and Wellness Centres initiative. The Eat Right India Movement and Poshan Abhiyaan have further strengthened nutritional awareness and healthy lifestyle promotion among children and adolescents. In addition, the Food Safety and

Standards Authority of India (FSSAI) has introduced measures such as front-of-pack labeling initiatives and restrictions on junk-food marketing in and around schools. Despite these efforts, the implementation and reach of such programmes remain uneven across regions and population groups.

The National Education Policy (NEP) 2020 has explicitly recognized holistic health, physical fitness, and mental well-being as important educational goals, creating new opportunities for school-based obesity prevention initiatives. However, most existing programmes still lack explicit psychosocial components addressing body image, weight stigma, emotional eating, and media literacy, which are critical considerations for comprehensive adolescent obesity prevention and intervention.This book is based on an empirical research study conducted in Kolkata that examined the psychological characteristics and adjustment styles of adolescents and young adults living with obesity.

1.10 Implications for policy and practice: multilevel levers of change

The implications of the evidence reviewed in the current chapter highlight the need for a holistic approach to the prevention and management of youth obesity. Given the multifactorial nature of obesity, it is important that effective responses target factors at the individual, familial, school, community, and policy levels while also considering psychological factors alongside behavioral and biomedical factors. Behavioral interventions such as self-regulation techniques, counseling, and family-based practices have shown promise for enhancing dietary habits and physical activity among adolescents, especially when age-specific needs are considered and implemented in a supportive environment. At the same time, evidence is emerging of the need to consider psychological factors such as body image, emotional factors, and weight stigma in obesity management.

The family and school contexts remain important venues for intervention, and research has shown that positive family practices, role models, and healthy school environments are important contributors to positive health outcomes. Beyond these venues, community and structural factors, including access to healthy food, opportunities for physical activity, and socio-cultural influences, are significant contributors to health behaviors among adolescents. In the context of India, community-based approaches grounded in culture and indigenous models, as well as existing public health systems, are important venues for intervention. At the policy level, addressing structural and environmental factors, which are often beyond individual control, will be critical, and this is addressed through the multiple levels of intervention, as mentioned previously.

1.11 Future directions: data science, precision prevention, and youth voices

The future of youth obesity research and intervention is being shaped by convergent advances in digital health technologies, data science, precision medicine, and youth participatory methods, all of which hold promise for furthering our understanding of and efforts to address this persistent and significant health challenge. Digital health technologies, including smartphone-based ecological momentary assessment, allow researchers to assess dietary intake, physical activity, emotional states, and social contexts in naturalistic settings, providing a significant advance over traditional measurement instruments, which are often plagued by retrospective recall biases and do not allow for a more ecologically valid understanding of within-person processes related to obesity and related behaviors (Shiffman et al., 2008, Annual Review of Clinical Psychology). Indeed, wearable biosensors, continuous glucose monitors, and multimodal activity monitors hold promise for providing rich, ecologically valid data streams, allowing researchers to identify patterns of eating, the relationship between sleep disruption and appetite, and emotional antecedents of eating, all of which are not accessible through conventional epidemiological methods.

Machine learning and artificial intelligence methods, if applied to large longitudinal data sets including genetic, dietary, activity, electronic health, and social determinant variables, have the potential to reveal complex interaction effects and nonlinear relationships, which conventional statistical methods cannot reveal. This advancement will allow for more accurate predictions of the obesity trajectory for individuals, thus helping to target preventive measures for the individuals who are at the most biological and environmental risk (Obermeyer & Emanuel, 2016, published in the New England Journal of Medicine). Precision medicine approaches, including the use of polygenic risk scores, metabolomics, gut microbiome, and epigenetic markers, have the potential to allow us to divide young individuals into distinct groups based on their unique biological risk factors for gaining unhealthy weight in unhealthy environments, but using such methods in areas where fewer resources exist, along with different economic circumstances, raises ethical issues such as unequal access to precision health technologies, the potential for the "genetic determinism fallacy," and the possibility of creating health inequalities instead of addressing them, which needs to be considered when conducting research.

Most importantly, and most consistently not prioritized in the biomedical and public health literature to date, future progress must prioritize youth voices and approaches as a methodological and ethical requirement, rather than an afterthought. Young people have highly developed and highly accurate understandings of their worlds, the structural barriers they must navigate, and the support systems they need to effectively support them. Participatory action research, youth codesign, photovoice, digital storytelling, and youth advisory boards represent several approaches for effectively and authentically incorporating youth voices in the development of intervention and prevention programs, outcomes, and policy, and in evaluation. Programs designed in collaboration with the young people they serve have been shown to be more culturally appropriate, more acceptable, and more likely to promote sustained engagement. Investing in the development of young people who understand, critique, and advocate for evidence-based health policy represents not only a necessary and powerful research methodology but also a fundamental strategy for achieving the systems change necessary to effectively address the scope and complexity of the youth obesity epidemic.

1.12 Summary and chapter takeaway

This chapter has provided the necessary foundation of concepts and evidence for a proper understanding of the complex, multidimensional, and critical nature of youth obesity as a global public health concern. The chapter started with the difficulties of definition and measurement of obesity in developing children and adolescents. This includes the limitations of BMI-for-age as a proxy measure of adiposity, the need for Asia-specific criteria for South Asian populations such as Indians, and the cultural acceptance of body size norms. It then proceeded to explain the history of the current obesity epidemic, analyzing it from different perspectives, such as evolutionary history, health history, and globalization history, and how the prevalence of obesity in children and adolescents across the world has increased 10 times from 1975 to 2016, according to a 2017 publication. The complexities of obesity were also examined by closely analyzing the simple energy balance concept and limitations, obesity as a long-term, recurring, and complex brain disorder, and the difficulties of medical perspectives and body diversity that require thoughtful and nonjudgmental approaches to youth obesity. The chapter then proceeded to explain the complexities of the determinants of youth obesity by analyzing genetic/epigenetic factors, the gut microbiome, EDCs, individual factors such as emotional eating and regulation, family/social factors such as peers and families, community/environmental factors such as communities and built environments, and media factors such as digital media, while considering the interrelation of factors at each level of analysis.

The impact of adolescent obesity—physical, psychological, educational, and economic—was clearly described through major longitudinal studies such as the Bogalusa Heart Study and Project EAT, emphasizing the need for prevention and the role of psychological factors in holistic care. Three integrative theoretical frameworks—the biopsychosocial model, Bronfenbrenner's ecological systems theory, and life-course perspectives—were discussed as having conceptual power and scope to capture the complex issues not addressed by reductive biomedical theories and models. The issues of measurement validity, causal inference from observational data, cultural validity, and ethical practice in working with adolescent populations were discussed as essential considerations for evidence-based scholarship and practice. The Indian scenario was discussed in detail from the empirical and cultural aspects of the issue, drawing on CNNS and NFHS-5 data and scholarship on food culture and gender issues in India, and the changing policy scenario. The chapter concluded by emphasizing the different levels of impact for intervention and future efforts in digital health, targeted prevention, and youth involvement.

The overall argument of the chapter is that the comprehension of youth obesity is not just a function of the acquisition of more facts, but the integration of knowledge across disciplines, levels of analysis, and epistemologies. The following chapters extend this base of knowledge to examine the psychological attributes, adaptation strategies, and social experiences of late adolescents and young adults with obesity in the context of India, not in order to cure bodies, but to comprehend, and ultimately enhance, lives.

1.12.1 Ancillary teaching resources

1.12.1.1 Suggested class activity: multistakeholder policy simulation

This activity is intended to help students refine their capacity for multiperspective analysis of youth obesity policy, which is relevant for the application of the ecological/systemic approach discussed in this chapter for the comprehension of the topic. Divide the student group into seven groups, each representing one of the following stakeholders:

(1) A group of urban Indian teens aged 15–17 who have personally experienced stigma related to weight.

(2) Parents with different socioeconomic backgrounds are trying to juggle competing food culture and food science imperatives.
(3) School administrators with mandates related to curriculum, budget, and food vendor contracts.
(4) Public health officials with the responsibility of implementing the FSSAI restrictions related to food marketing in proximity to schools.
(5) Representatives of a multinational food company with operations in India.
(6) Mental health professionals concerned with the potential effects of weight stigma.
(7) Urban planners with responsibility for creating environments that promote youth exercise.

Each group is allocated specific readings from the chapter, which are directly relevant to their role in the simulation, such as 1.5.5 for the adolescent group and 1.9 for the policy official group. Each group is then asked to discuss their opinions on one of the proposed policy options, such as the requirement to make it mandatory to restrict the sale of UPF in school canteens and within 200 meters of schools in Indian cities. Following individual group work, the groups then present their opinions in a structured forum. The discussion should then explore the following in the facilitated session:

where there is consensus among the stakeholder groups;
where there is conflict and the conflict cannot be resolved without compromise;
the impact of power relationships among the various stakeholder groups on the policy process;
the potential legal, economic, and social instruments required to support consensus to action.

Students should also be required to individually write a 500-word reflection on the way in which one of the theoretical approaches in 1.7 of the chapter best explains the stakeholder group relationships in the simulation.

AI disclosure

During the preparation of this work, the author(s) used Chat GPT, PaperPal.com, Grammarly.com in order to edit & format. After using this tool/service, the author(s) reviewed and edited the content as needed and take(s) full responsibility for the content of the publication.

Key takeaways

Youth obesity is a growing public health concern globally and in India, which is influenced by biological, psychological, social, and environmental factors.
Among young people, the prevalence of obesity cannot be described by simple energy balance approaches and is considered a complex and multidimensional phenomenon.
The methods of measuring obesity, such as BMI, have significant limitations, especially for South Asians.
The factors that influence obesity are complex and involve different levels of influence, such as genetic factors, family factors, community factors, and influences of digital media.
Youth obesity is associated with significant physical, emotional, educational, and economic consequences over the life course.
The prevalence of youth obesity in India is a growing public health concern due to rapid urbanization and changing food environments.

Review questions

1. What is the effectiveness of the classification of obesity in Indian adolescents by the use of BMI-for-age percentiles as a classification tool for obesity in the country? What are the main scientific limitations of the classification of obesity in the South Asian population, as evidenced by the epidemiology of obesity in the country, as discussed in 1.2 and 1.9 of the chapter? What alternative anthropometric measures have been proposed to address the limitations of the BMI classification tool in the South Asian population, and what are the implications for the interpretation of the CNNS (2016-18) national prevalence data?
2. The chapter also refers to obesity as a "biocultural phenomenon" as per Ulijaszek and Lofink (2006). Using the factors discussed in the previous sections of this chapter, that is, 1.5.1 to 1.5.5, present an argument to explain why obesity among adolescents in contemporary urban India cannot be explained at any single level of analysis—genetic, behavioral, familial, or structural—and must be understood in terms of their interplay.

3. Using Bronfenbrenner's ecological systems theory of development, analyze the obesity of an individual adolescent in contemporary urban India. Choose a 15-year-old girl from a middle-income family in an urban Indian city, such as Mumbai, who is in a private school, spends at least four hours a day on social media sites, is involved in coaching sessions after school every day, and is classified as overweight by the school health team. Using Bronfenbrenner's ecological systems theory of development, describe the microsystem, mesosystem, exosystem, and macrosystem factors that influence her obesity, and then describe the leverage point at each level at which an intervention based on the best available evidence could be targeted.
4. Discuss the bidirectional relationship between psychological well-being and obesity in adolescence. Using the evidence reviewed in the previous sections of this chapter, that is, 1.5.2 and 1.6, explain how weight stigma, body image concerns, emotional eating, and depression interact to create cycles of obesity and poor psychological well-being, and what this means for the development of obesity interventions for school-based settings.
5. Critically analyze the response to youth obesity in India as presented in Section 1.9 of the chapter and identify the most important successes and omissions of the response to youth obesity in India. Using the material presented in Section 1.10 of the chapter, suggest three additional or modified aspects of the response to youth obesity in India that would be most beneficial to add to the comprehensive response to the obesity epidemic among adolescents in India and to strengthen the response to obesity and psychological well-being among adolescents in India.

Glossary

Adolescent obesity Excess body fat in individuals aged 10–19 years, assessed using age- and sex-specific growth standards
Body mass index (BMI) A ratio of weight to height (kg/m^2) used as a proxy for body fat, interpreted using age-adjusted percentiles in children and adolescents
Biopsychosocial model A framework explaining health as the interaction of biological, psychological, and social factors
Double burden of malnutrition The coexistence of undernutrition and overnutrition within the same population
Ecological systems theory A framework explaining how multiple environmental systems influence development and health
Epidemiological transition The shift from infectious diseases to chronic, NCD with socioeconomic development and urbanization
Nutrition transition Changes in dietary patterns toward energy-dense, processed foods associated with economic and lifestyle shifts
Weight stigma Negative attitudes and discriminatory behaviors directed at individuals based on body weight
Internalized weight bias The process by which individuals adopt and apply negative weight-related stereotypes to themselves
Built environment The physical surroundings, including infrastructure and food environments, that influence health behaviors
Obesogenic environment An environment that promotes excessive calorie intake and physical inactivity
Life-course perspective An approach examining how early-life experiences influence health outcomes across the lifespan

References

American Medical Association. (2013). Recognition of obesity as a disease (Resolution 420, A-13). American Medical Association House of Delegates.

Bandura, A. (1986). *Social foundations of thought and action: A social cognitive theory*. Prentice-Hall.

Barker, D. J. P. (1995). Fetal origins of coronary heart disease. *BMJ (Clinical Research ed.), 311*(6998), 171–174. https://doi.org/10.1136/bmj.311.6998.171.

Birch, L. L., Fisher, J. O., & Davison, K. K. (2003). Learning to overeat: Maternal use of restrictive feeding practices promotes girls' eating in the absence of hunger. *American Journal of Clinical Nutrition, 78*(2), 215–220. https://doi.org/10.1093/ajcn/78.2.215.

Brewis, A. A. (2014). Stigma and the perpetuation of obesity. *Social Science & Medicine, 118*, 152–158. https://doi.org/10.1016/j.socscimed.2014.08.003.

Centers for Disease Control and Prevention. (2000). CDC growth charts for the United States: Methods and development. *Vital and Health Statistics, Series, 11*(246). National Center for Health Statistics.

Deurenberg, P., Deurenberg-Yap, M., & Guricci, S. (2002). Asians are different from Caucasians and from each other in their body mass index/body fat per cent relationship. *Obesity Reviews, 3*(3), 141–146. https://doi.org/10.1046/j.1467-789X.2002.00065.x.

Drewnowski, A., & Specter, S. E. (2004). Poverty and obesity: The role of energy density and energy costs. *American Journal of Clinical Nutrition, 79*(1), 6–16. https://doi.org/10.1093/ajcn/79.1.6.

Freedman, D. S., Dietz, W. H., Srinivasan, S. R., & Berenson, G. S. (1999). The relation of overweight to cardiovascular risk factors among children and adolescents: The Bogalusa Heart Study. *Pediatrics, 103*(6), 1175–1182. https://doi.org/10.1542/peds.103.6.1175.

GBD 2015 Obesity Collaborators. (2017). Health effects of overweight and obesity in 195 countries over 25 years. *New England Journal of Medicine, 377*(1), 13–27. https://doi.org/10.1056/NEJMoa1614362.

Godfrey, K. M., Reynolds, R. M., Prescott, S. L., Nyirenda, M., Jaddoe, V. W. V., Eriksson, J. G., & Bhutta, Z. A. (2017). Influence of maternal obesity on the long-term health of offspring. *The Lancet Diabetes & Endocrinology, 5*(1), 53–64. https://doi.org/10.1016/S2213-8587(16)30107-3.

Hall, K. D., Heymsfield, S. B., Kemnitz, J. W., Klein, S., Schoeller, D. A., & Speakman, J. R. (2012). Energy balance and its components: Implications for body weight regulation. *American Journal of Clinical Nutrition, 95*(4), 989–994. https://doi.org/10.3945/ajcn.112.036350.

Janesick, A. S., & Blumberg, B. (2011). Obesogens, stem cells and the developmental programming of obesity. *International Journal of Andrology, 35*(3), 437–448. https://doi.org/10.1111/j.1365-2605.2012.01247.x.

Livingstone, M. B. E., & Black, A. E. (2003). Markers of the validity of reported energy intake. *Journal of Nutrition, 133*(3 Suppl), 895S–920S. https://doi.org/10.1093/jn/133.3.895S.

Locke, A. E., Kahali, B., Berndt, S. I., Justice, A. E., Pers, T. H., Day, F. R., & Speliotes, E. K. (2015). Genetic studies of body mass index yield new insights for obesity biology. *Nature, 518*(7538), 197–206. https://doi.org/10.1038/nature14177.

Lovasi, G. S., Hutson, M. A., Guerra, M., & Neckerman, K. M. (2009). Built environments and obesity in disadvantaged populations. *Epidemiologic Reviews, 31*(1), 7–20. https://doi.org/10.1093/epirev/mxp005.

Ministry of Health and Family Welfare (MoHFW), Government of India, UNICEF, & Population Council. (2019). Comprehensive National Nutrition Survey 2016–2018: National Report. Ministry of Health and Family Welfare.

Misra, A., Chowbey, P., Makkar, B. M., Vikram, N. K., Wasir, J. S., Chadha, D., & Munjal, Y. P. (2009). Consensus statement for diagnosis of obesity, abdominal obesity and the metabolic syndrome for Asian Indians and recommendations for physical activity, medical and surgical management. *Journal of the Association of Physicians of India, 57*, 163–170.

Misra, A., Shah, P., Goel, K., Hazra, D. K., Gupta, R., Seth, P., & Pandey, R. M. (2011). The high burden of obesity and abdominal obesity in urban Indian schoolchildren: A multicentric study of 38,296 children. *Annals of Nutrition and Metabolism, 58*(3), 203–211.

Misra, A., Singhal, N., Sivakumar, B., Bhagat, N., Jaiswal, A., & Khurana, L. (2011). Nutrition transition in India: Secular trends in dietary intake and their relationship to diet-related non-communicable diseases. *Journal of Diabetes, 3*(4), 278–292. https://doi.org/10.1111/j.1753-0407.2011.00139.x.

NCD Risk Factor Collaboration (NCD-RisC). (2017). Worldwide trends in body-mass index, underweight, overweight, and obesity from 1975 to 2016: A pooled analysis of 2416 population-based measurement studies in 128·9 million children, adolescents, and adults. *The Lancet, 390*(10113), 2627–2642. https://doi.org/10.1016/S0140-6736(17)32129-3.

Neel, J. V. (1962). Diabetes mellitus: A 'thrifty' genotype rendered detrimental by 'progress. *American Journal of Human Genetics, 14*(4), 353–362.

Nogueira-de-Almeida, C. A., Del Ciampo, L. A., Ferraz, I. S., Del Ciampo, I. R. L., Contini, A. A., & Ued, F. V. (2020). COVID-19 and obesity in childhood and adolescence: A clinical review. *Jornal de Pediatria, 96*(5), 546–558. https://doi.org/10.1016/j.jped.2020.08.006.

Obermeyer, Z., & Emanuel, E. J. (2016). Predicting the future — Big data, machine learning, and clinical medicine. *New England Journal of Medicine, 375*(13), 1216–1219. https://doi.org/10.1056/NEJMp1606181.

Omran, A. R. (1971). The epidemiologic transition: A theory of the epidemiology of population change. *The Milbank Quarterly, 49*(4), 509–538. https://doi.org/10.2307/3349375.

Patton, G. C., Sawyer, S. M., Santelli, J. S., Ross, D. A., Afifi, R., Allen, N. B., & Viner, R. M. (2016). Our future: A Lancet commission on adolescent health and wellbeing. *The Lancet, 387*(10036), 2423–2478. https://doi.org/10.1016/S0140-6736(16)00579-1.

Perloff, R. M. (2014). Social media effects on young women's body image concerns: Theoretical perspectives and an agenda for research. *Sex Roles, 71*(11–12), 363–377. https://doi.org/10.1007/s11199-014-0384-6.

Popkin, B. M. (1994). The nutrition transition in low-income countries: An emerging crisis. *Nutrition Reviews, 52*(9), 285–298. https://doi.org/10.1111/j.1753-4887.1994.tb01460.x.

Puhl, R. M., & Heuer, C. A. (2010). Obesity stigma: Important considerations for public health. *American Journal of Public Health, 100*(6), 1019–1028. https://doi.org/10.2105/AJPH.2009.159491.

Puhl, R. M., & Latner, J. D. (2007). Stigma, obesity, and the health of the nation's children. *Psychological Bulletin, 133*(4), 557–580. https://doi.org/10.1037/0033-2909.133.4.557.

Schwartz, M. W., Seeley, R. J., Zeltser, L. M., Drewnowski, A., Ravussin, E., Redman, L. M., & Leibel, R. L. (2017). Obesity pathogenesis: An endocrine society scientific statement. *Endocrine Reviews, 38*(4), 267–296. https://doi.org/10.1210/er.2017-00111.

Schwimmer, J. B., Burwinkle, T. M., & Varni, J. W. (2003). Health-related quality of life of severely obese children and adolescents. *JAMA: The Journal of the American Medical Association, 289*(14), 1813–1819. https://doi.org/10.1001/jama.289.14.1813.

Sethi, V., Bassi, S., Bahl, D., Kumar, A., Choedon, T., Bhatia, N., & Arora, M. (2024). Prevalence of overweight and obesity and associated demographic and health factors in India: Findings from the Comprehensive National Nutrition Survey (CNNS). *Maternal & Child Nutrition, 20*(1), e13585. https://doi.org/10.1111/mcn.13585.

Sharma, A. M., & Kushner, R. F. (2009). A proposed clinical staging system for obesity. *International Journal of Obesity, 33*(3), 289–295. https://doi.org/10.1038/ijo.2009.2.

Shiffman, S., Stone, A. A., & Hufford, M. R. (2008). Ecological momentary assessment. *Annual Review of Clinical Psychology, 4*(1), 1–32. https://doi.org/10.1146/annurev.clinpsy.3.022806.091415.

Shrewsbury, V., & Wardle, J. (2008). Socioeconomic status and adiposity in childhood: A systematic review of cross-sectional studies 1990–2005. *Obesity, 16*(2), 275–284. https://doi.org/10.1038/oby.2007.35.

Simpkins, S. D., Schaefer, D. R., Price, C. D., & Vest, A. E. (2013). Adolescent friendships, BMI, and physical activity: Untangling selection and influence through longitudinal social network analysis. *Journal of Research on Adolescence, 23*(3), 537–549. https://doi.org/10.1111/jora.12001.

Sonnenburg, J. L., & Backhed, F. (2016). Diet–microbiota interactions as moderators of human metabolism. *Nature, 535*(7610), 56–64. https://doi.org/10.1038/nature18846.

Story, M., Kaphingst, K. M., Robinson-O'Brien, R., & Glanz, K. (2008). Creating healthy food and eating environments: Policy and environmental approaches. *Annual Review of Public Health, 29*(1), 253–272. https://doi.org/10.1146/annurev.publhealth.29.020907.090926.

Sutaria, S., Devakumar, D., Yasuda, S. S., Das, S., & Saxena, S. (2019). Is obesity associated with depression in children? Systematic review and meta-analysis. *Archives of Disease in Childhood, 104*(1), 64–74. https://doi.org/10.1136/archdischild-2017-314608.

Swinburn, B. A., Sacks, G., Hall, K. D., McPherson, K., Finegood, D. T., Moodie, M. L., & Gortmaker, S. L. (2011). The global obesity pandemic: Shaped by global drivers and local environments. *The Lancet, 378*(9793), 804–814. https://doi.org/10.1016/S0140-6736(11)60813-1.

Tanofsky-Kraff, M., Yanovski, S. Z., Schvey, N. A., Olsen, C. H., Gustafson, J., & Yanovski, J. A. (2009). A prospective study of loss of control eating for body weight gain in children at high risk for adult obesity. *International Journal of Eating Disorders, 42*(1), 26–30. https://doi.org/10.1002/eat.20580.

Telecom Regulatory Authority of India (TRAI). (2023). *The Indian Telecom Services Performance Indicators October–December 2023*. TRAI.

Tiggemann, M., & Slater, A. (2013). NetGirls: The internet, Facebook, and body image concern in adolescent girls. *International Journal of Eating Disorders, 46*(6), 630–633. https://doi.org/10.1002/eat.22141.

Ulijaszek, S. J., & Lofink, H. (2006). Obesity in biocultural perspective. *Annual Review of Anthropology, 35*(1), 337–360. https://doi.org/10.1146/annurev.anthro.35.081705.123301.

UNICEF. (2019). Convention on the Rights of the Child: General comment No. 20 (2016) on the implementation of the rights of the child during adolescence. United Nations.

Walker, R. E., Keane, C. R., & Burke, J. G. (2010). Disparities and access to healthy food in the United States: A review of food deserts literature. *Health & Place, 16*(5), 876–884. https://doi.org/10.1016/j.healthplace.2010.04.013.

Weiss, R., Dziura, J., Burgert, T. S., Tamborlane, W. V., Taksali, S. E., Yeckel, C. W., & Caprio, S. (2004). Obesity and the metabolic syndrome in children and adolescents. *New England Journal of Medicine, 350*(23), 2362–2374. https://doi.org/10.1056/NEJMoa031049.

Wells, J. C. K., & Fewtrell, M. S. (2006). Measuring body composition. *Archives of Disease in Childhood, 91*(7), 612–617. https://doi.org/10.1136/adc.2005.085522.

WHO. (2000). Obesity: Preventing and managing the global epidemic (WHO Technical Report Series, No. 894). World Health Organization.

WHO. (2016). *Report of the commission on ending childhood obesity*. World Health Organization.

WHO Growth Reference Study Group. (2007). *WHO child growth standards: growth velocity based on weight, length and head circumference: Methods and development*. World Health Organization.

World Health Organization. (2022). Obesity and overweight. https://www.who.int/news-room/fact-sheets/detail/obesity-and-overweight.

Further reading

Austin, S. B. (2011). The blind spot in the drive for childhood obesity prevention: Bringing eating disorders prevention into focus as a public health priority. *American Journal of Public Health, 101*(6), e1–e4. https://doi.org/10.2105/AJPH.2011.300182.

Bacon, L., & Aphramor, L. (2011). Weight science: Evaluating the evidence for a paradigm shift. *Nutrition Journal, 10*(1), 9. https://doi.org/10.1186/1475-2891-10-9.

Bowleg, L. (2012). The problem with the phrase "women and minorities": Intersectionality: An important theoretical framework for public health. *American Journal of Public Health, 102*(7), 1267–1273. https://doi.org/10.2105/AJPH.2012.300750.

Bronfenbrenner, U. (1979). *The ecology of human development: Experiments by nature and design*. Harvard University Press.

Cargo, M., & Mercer, S. L. (2008). The value and challenges of participatory research: Strengthening its practice. *Annual Review of Public Health, 29*(1), 325–350. https://doi.org/10.1146/annurev.publhealth.29.091307.083824.

Cole, T. J., Bellizzi, M. C., Flegal, K. M., & Dietz, W. H. (2000). Establishing a standard definition for child overweight and obesity worldwide: International survey. *BMJ (Clinical Research ed.), 320*(7244), 1240–1243. https://doi.org/10.1136/bmj.320.7244.1240.

Davey Smith, G., & Hemani, G. (2014). Mendelian randomization: Genetic anchors for causal inference in epidemiological studies. *Human Molecular Genetics, 23*(R1), R89–R98. https://doi.org/10.1093/hmg/ddu328.

Dietz, W. H. (1994). Critical periods in childhood for the development of obesity. *American Journal of Clinical Nutrition, 59*(5), 955–959. https://doi.org/10.1093/ajcn/59.5.955.

Engel, G. L. (1977). The need for a new medical model: A challenge for biomedicine. *Science (New York, N.Y.), 196*(4286), 129–136. https://doi.org/10.1126/science.847460.

Epstein, L. H., Paluch, R. A., Wrotniak, B. H., Daniel, T. O., Kilanowski, C., Wilfley, D., & Finkelstein, E. (2007). Cost-effectiveness of family-based group treatment for child and parental obesity. *Annals of Behavioral Medicine, 34*(3), 251–256. https://doi.org/10.1007/BF02874551.

Farooqi, I. S., & O'Rahilly, S. (2006). Genetics of obesity in humans. *Endocrine Reviews, 27*(7), 710–718. https://doi.org/10.1210/er.2006-0040.

Garg, C., Sharma, S., & Bansal, R. D. (2012). Perception of weight, body image and weight control practices among urban adolescents. *Indian Journal of Community Medicine, 37*(3), 163–169. https://doi.org/10.4103/0970-0218.99919.

Graziano, P. A., Calkins, S. D., & Keane, S. P. (2010). Toddler self-regulation skills predict risk for pediatric obesity. *International Journal of Obesity, 34*(4), 633–641. https://doi.org/10.1038/ijo.2009.288.

Gupta, N., Goel, K., Shah, P., & Misra, A. (2012). Childhood obesity in developing countries: Epidemiology, determinants, and prevention. *Endocrine Reviews, 33*(1), 48–70. https://doi.org/10.1210/er.2010-0028.

Ho, M., Garnett, S. P., Baur, L., Burrows, T., Stewart, L., Neve, M., & Collins, C. (2012). Effectiveness of lifestyle interventions in child obesity: Systematic review with meta-analysis. *Pediatrics, 130*(6), e1647–e1671. https://doi.org/10.1542/peds.2012-1176.

International Institute for Population Sciences (IIPS) & ICF. (2021). National Family Health Survey (NFHS-5), 2019–21: India Volume I. International Institute for Population Sciences.

Krishnakumar, J., Thow, A. M., Singh, G., Kumar, P., & Krishnamurthy, K. (2020). Restricting unhealthy food marketing to children: A review of policy options and policy actions in India. *Public Health Nutrition, 23*(16), 2982–2995. https://doi.org/10.1017/S1368980019004051.

Kuh, D., & Ben-Shlomo, Y. (Eds.). (2004). *A life course approach to chronic disease epidemiology*(2nd ed.). Oxford University Press.

Lobstein, T., Jackson-Leach, R., Moodie, M. L., Hall, K. D., Gortmaker, S. L., Swinburn, B. A., McPherson, K., Gutta, S., & Boyd, D. (2015). Child and adolescent obesity: Part of a bigger picture. *The Lancet, 385*(9986), 2510–2520. https://doi.org/10.1016/S0140-6736(14)61746-3.

Maes, H. H., Neale, M. C., & Eaves, L. J. (1997). Genetic and environmental factors in relative body weight and human adiposity. *Behavior Genetics, 27*(4), 325–351. https://doi.org/10.1023/A:1025635913927.

Neumark-Sztainer, D., Wall, M., Guo, J., Story, M., Haines, J., & Eisenberg, M. (2006). Obesity, disordered eating, and eating disorders in a longitudinal study of adolescents: How do dieters fare five years later? *Journal of the American Dietetic Association, 106*(4), 559–568. https://doi.org/10.1016/j.jada.2006.01.003.

Ozer, E. J. (2017). Youth-led participatory action research. In In. M. Fine, & M. E. Torre (Eds.). *Handbook of critical and indigenous methodologies*. SAGE.

Pradeepa, R., & Mohan, V. (2015). Prevalence of type 2 diabetes and its complications in India and economic costs to the nation. *European Journal of Clinical Nutrition, 69*(10), 1095–1100. https://doi.org/10.1038/ejcn.2015.128.

Puhl, R. M., & Heuer, C. A. (2009). The stigma of obesity: A review and update. *Obesity, 17*(5), 941–964. https://doi.org/10.1038/oby.2008.636.

Resnicow, K., Taylor, R., Baskin, M., & McCarty, F. (2005). Results of go girls: A weight control program for overweight African-American adolescent females. *Obesity Research, 13*(10), 1739–1748. https://doi.org/10.1038/oby.2005.212.

Sahoo, K., Sahoo, B., Choudhury, A. K., Sofi, N. Y., Kumar, R., & Bhadoria, A. S. (2015). Childhood obesity: Causes and consequences. *Journal of Family Medicine and Primary Care, 4*(2), 187–192. https://doi.org/10.4103/2249-4863.154628.

van Strien, T., Konttinen, H., Homberg, J. R., Engels, R. C. M. E., & Winkens, L. H. H. (2016). Emotional eating as a mediator between depression and weight gain. *Appetite, 100*, 216–224. https://doi.org/10.1016/j.appet.2016.02.034.

Strings, S. (2019). *Fearing the black body: The racial origins of fat phobia*. NYU Press.

UNICEF India. (2025). India: Overweight and obesity rising across all ages — from youngest children to adults [Press release]. https://www.unicef.org/india/press-releases/india-overweight-and-obesity-rising-across-all-ages-youngest-children-adults.

Waters, E., de Silva-Sanigorski, A., Hall, B. J., Brown, T., Campbell, K. J., Gao, Y., & Summerbell, C. D. (2011). Interventions for preventing obesity in children. *Cochrane Database of Systematic Reviews,* (12), CD001871. https://doi.org/10.1002/14651858.CD001871.pub3.

WHO Expert Consultation. (2004). Appropriate body-mass index for Asian populations and its implications for policy and intervention strategies. *The Lancet, 363*(9403), 157–163. https://doi.org/10.1016/S0140-6736(03)15268-3.

Chapter 2

Measurements and indicators of obesity

"No single anthropometric measure can fully capture the complexity of obesity."

Learning objectives

Upon completing this chapter, readers will be able to:

Trace the historical development of BMI from Quetelet (1832) to contemporary clinical use and critically evaluate its diagnostic limitations as a measure of adiposity.

Compare the WHO Growth Reference Study Group (2007), CDC (2000), and IOTF (2000) pediatric obesity classification systems and explain why India-specific adaptations are necessary for South Asian populations.

Evaluate the clinical utility of complementary anthropometric and biochemical indicators for adolescent obesity assessment in resource-variable settings.

Justify the inclusion of psychosocial indicators—weight stigma, body image, and health-related quality of life—as an independent dimension of comprehensive obesity assessment.

Analyze the policy implications of choosing between global and India-specific growth reference standards for national surveillance and critically assess the measurement challenges posed by India's double burden of malnutrition.

2.1 Introduction: why measurement matters

Keys et al. (1972) Measurement is never a neutral act. The intellectual history of measuring obesity is much more complicated than most people think. Adolphe Quetelet, a Belgian mathematician and astronomer, came up with the weight-to-height-squared formula in 1832. He wasn't making a clinical index; he was measuring the statistical traits of the "average man" (l'homme moyen) as part of a larger project in social physics. The history of obesity measurement illuminates how contingent apparently objective indicators can be: a formula designed for social statistics in 1832 became the dominant clinical screening tool of the 21st century, adopted primarily on practical grounds rather than diagnostic superiority (Nuttall, 2015). This chapter is organized as follows: Section 2.2 gives a detailed look at different ways to measure body size and health, such as BMI-for-age, waist circumference, waist-to-height ratio (WHtR), skinfold measurements, body composition methods, and biochemical biomarkers, focusing on how well they work. Section 2.3 examines psychosocial indicators: validated instruments for measuring weight stigma, body image, and health-related quality of life (HRQoL), and the growing theoretical and empirical case for treating psychosocial well-being as an independent dimension of obesity assessment. Section 2.4 places these measurement discussions in the cultural and policy contexts of India. It looks at the effects of using global versus India-specific reference standards, how to read national surveillance data, and the policy problems that come up because of the double burden of malnutrition. Section 2.5 synthesizes the chapter's arguments, provides a glossary of key terms, recommends further reading, and offers review questions for pedagogical use.

2.2 Anthropometric and clinical indicators

2.2.1 Body mass index: history, definitions, and pediatric adaptations

Body mass index (BMI), which is weight in kilograms divided by the square of height in meters (kg/m^2), is still the most widely used measure of body fat in both clinical and epidemiological settings around the world. This is mostly because it is easy to use, cheap, noninvasive, and can be measured in a standard way on a large scale. Its predominance in public health surveillance and clinical practice has consistently been predicated more on convenience than on proven diagnostic superiority. Nuttall (2015) points out in a critical historical review that the formula was never specifically designed or

Psychology of Obesity. DOI: https://doi.org/10.1016/B978-0-443-27797-9.00008-7

tested as a way to measure adiposity. It just happened to be somewhat related to body fatness in the population samples that were available when it was officially adopted for epidemiological use. The index is easy to understand mathematically, only needs two cheap measurements, and gives a continuous variable that can be looked at across populations and time series. These are all reasons why it was very useful for epidemiology, even though its biological limitations were clear.

For children and adolescents, as opposed to adults, a singular fixed threshold is inapplicable due to the natural increase in BMI from infancy to late adolescence, which varies significantly by sex and developmental stage. The two principal reference systems used in pediatric and adolescent practice are the World Health Organization (WHO) growth reference (2007), which classifies overweight as a BMI-for-age z-score above +1 standard deviation from the international median and obesity as above +2 SD; and the Centers for Disease Control and Prevention (CDC, 2000) growth charts, which use sex-specific percentile distributions to classify overweight at the 85th–95th percentile and obesity at or above the 95th percentile. The International Obesity Task Force (IOTF) system, developed by Cole and others in 2000, provides another global standard that determines specific BMI cutoffs for different ages and sexes by using adult BMI levels of 25 and 30 kg/m^2 and adjusting them for children based on data from six countries, which helps compare obesity levels across countries while relating to adult obesity.

These classification systems are neither interchangeable nor bias-free. There are well-documented systematic differences in the prevalence estimates produced by WHO, CDC, and IOTF systems in the same populations. These differences come from the reference populations used to make growth charts, the way childhood centiles and adult thresholds are linked mathematically, and how extreme values are handled. Applying different systems to the same survey data can yield prevalence estimates differing by several percentage points—a discrepancy with significant implications for international comparisons and national surveillance (Lobstein et al., 2015). Importantly, the choice of reference system in India's national surveys is not neutral: National Family Health Survey-5 (NFHS-5) (2019–21) and Comprehensive National Nutrition Survey (CNNS) (2016–18) use WHO growth references to report childhood nutritional status, while a different set of Indian growth references created by Khadilkar and colleagues (2019) gives significantly different prevalence estimates, especially for those at risk of nutritional failure, because the reference population has different expectations for body size.

2.2.2 Diagnostic accuracy and the sensitivity–specificity trade-off

A fundamental challenge in BMI-based classification of obesity is its limited diagnostic accuracy as a measure of actual adiposity—the excess accumulation of fat mass that constitutes the physiological basis of obesity-related health risk. A major issue with using BMI to classify obesity is that it doesn't accurately reflect how much fat someone actually has, which is important for understanding health risks related to obesity. A significant review and analysis by Biro and Wien (2010) and later studies have shown that while BMI classifications for obesity are very good at correctly identifying those who do not have excess fat, Martinez-Villanueva et al. (2023) studied 553 children and adolescents using dual-energy X-ray absorptiometry (DXA) as the standard measure and found that 62% of those labeled as overweight by BMI actually had body fat percentages in the obesity range, while 7% of those labeled as normal weight were actually obese by fat measurement—showing that BMI often wrongly identifies people by mistaking muscle for fat and misses those with harmful fat even if they look lean.

A detailed review by Steinberger et al. (using data from NHANES 2011–18, published in Pediatrics in 2024) looked at 6923 young people aged 8–19 years and found that age and BMI together explained 90%–94% of the differences in fat mass index, but only about 70% of the differences in body fat percentage, which is more closely related to the children with a BMI at or above the CDC 95th percentile; 88% had a high fat mass index, but only 76% had a high body fat percentage. On the other hand, the children who were misclassified as normal by BMI are an important group that was not properly screened for cardiometabolic risk (Freedman & Sherry, 2024). These limitations are particularly consequential for South Asian populations, who exhibit systematically higher body fat percentages and greater visceral adiposity at any given BMI compared to European reference populations—a phenomenon that will be examined in depth in Section 2.4. BMI is still a useful method for large-scale screening (Table 2.1).

2.2.3 Skinfold thickness and body composition methods

Skinfold thickness measurements, typically obtained from standardized anatomical locations such as the triceps, subscapular, suprailiac, and medial calf areas, provide a cost-effective method for estimating subcutaneous fat. This is accomplished by applying validated population-specific regression equations developed by Durnin and Wormersley (1974) or Slaughter et al. (1988) to convert the measurements into body fat percentages. But skinfold measurements can

TABLE 2.1 Comparison of principal anthropometric indicators for pediatric obesity assessment.

Indicator	Key advantages	Key limitations
BMI-for-age (WHO z-score)	Low cost; standardized globally; longitudinal tracking tool; widely validated	Conflates fat and lean mass; low sensitivity; ethnic variation in fat-BMI relationship
Waist circumference (WC)	Directly measures central adiposity; associated with cardiometabolic risk	Requires age/sex-specific reference charts; measurement standardization issues
Waist-to-height ratio	Single threshold (~0.5) applicable across age/sex; no chart needed; practical	Less validated in children <6 years; not superior to BMI in ROC analyses
Waist-to-hip ratio	Captures fat distribution pattern	Hip measurement adds complexity; less predictive than WC in children
Skinfold thickness	Inexpensive; estimates body fat %	High interobserver variability; requires trained staff; population-specific equations
Dual-energy X-ray absorptiometry body composition	Gold standard for fat/lean mass compartments	Expensive; radiation exposure; not feasible for large-scale screening
Bioelectrical impedance	Noninvasive; portable; feasible in field settings	Accuracy affected by hydration; requires population-specific equations

Source: Author compilation based on WHO Growth Reference Study Group (2007), CDC (2000), IOTF (Cole et al., 2000), and Martinez-Villanueva et al. (2023).

be very different depending on who does them, especially for people who are overweight, because their skin and fat can be harder to measure accurately. Trained staff needs to use special tools called to get accurate measurements. When the equations used to predict body fat are applied to individuals who differ from those initially tested, their accuracy may diminish. This is especially true when using equations that were made for white people on South Asians or other ethnic groups. Skinfold measurements are still the easiest way to figure out body composition in places with few resources, even with these problems. They are also important for studying childhood obesity, especially when looking at how different ethnic groups have changed over time. Field studies ought to consistently assess interobserver reliability.

2.2.4 Biochemical and clinical biomarkers

For adolescents classified as overweight or obese via anthropometric screening, a thorough clinical evaluation necessitates the analysis of biochemical and clinical biomarkers that collectively delineate the metabolic repercussions of excess adiposity and categorize individual cardiometabolic risk. Experts suggest that the best tests to check the health of overweight teens are fasting lipid levels (total cholesterol, LDL-cholesterol, HDL-cholesterol, and triglycerides), fasting plasma glucose, and, if necessary, an oral glucose tolerance test that looks at glucose and insulin levels after two hours. Other tests include liver function tests (especially alanine aminotransferase to check for nonalcoholic fatty liver disease), uric acid, a complete blood count, and, if possible, high-sensitivity C-reactive protein to check for low-level inflammation.

The Homeostatic Model Assessment for Insulin Resistance (HOMA-IR) is a simple way to measure insulin resistance that is based on fasting insulin and fasting glucose levels. It is commonly used in pediatric research and is becoming more common in clinical practice to find obese teens who are at risk of metabolic problems. HOMA-IR is a substitute marker, not a conclusive diagnostic test for insulin resistance. HOMA-IR is closely related to the best way to measure how sensitive adolescents are to insulin.

2.2.5 Limitations of current measurement approaches

Significant advancements have been made in anthropometric and clinical evaluation; however, considerable limitations remain in the assessment of obesity in children and adolescents. There is no single metric that fully captures the intricate aspects of adiposity, metabolic risk, and psychosocial burden. Commonly used measurements like BMI, waist circumference, and WHtR require trade-offs between usefulness and diagnostic accuracy, especially in ethnically diverse groups like South Asians, where body fat distribution differs from reference populations in a systematic way. Field-based techniques, including skinfold thickness and bioelectrical impedance (BIA), are influenced by measurement error, hydration levels, and population-specific predictive equations. In the psychosocial domain, although validated instruments for weight stigma and body image exist, their cultural adaptation and normative validation within Indian adolescent populations remain inadequate. These limitations highlight the cautious interpretation of single-indicator assessments and promote the continuous development of multidimensional, population-sensitive measurement frameworks.

2.2.6 Rationale for including psychosocial indicators

The anthropometric and clinical indicators reviewed above provide essential information about physiological adiposity and metabolic risk. However, they do not capture the lived experience of inhabiting a body classified as obese within social, cultural, and institutional contexts that attach moral and esthetic significance to body size. A growing body of evidence demonstrates that psychosocial dimensions—including weight stigma exposure, body image dissatisfaction, and impaired quality of life—independently predict adverse health outcomes, treatment disengagement, and reduced well-being, often over and above the effects of adiposity itself (Emmer et al., 2020; Puhl & Heuer, 2010). A comprehensive obesity measurement framework must therefore incorporate validated psychosocial instruments alongside anthropometric and biochemical indicators. Section 2.3 presents these instruments and the empirical case for their systematic use.

2.3 Psychosocial indicators of obesity: measuring beyond the body

The previous sections have shown how complex the technical world of physical measurement is. Nonetheless, what they fail to capture—and what the epidemiological literature on obesity-related outcomes consistently illustrates as clinically significant—is the psychosocial experience of inhabiting a body designated as obese within a framework that attributes moral, esthetic, and social significance to body size. Weight stigma, body dissatisfaction, and impaired psychological well-being are not merely secondary correlates of obesity; they are independently linked to detrimental health behaviors, exacerbated cardiometabolic trajectories, decreased healthcare engagement, and lowered quality of life (Emmer et al., 2020; Puhl & Heuer, 2010). For adolescents, who are at a stage of development where they are forming their identities, judging their peers, and becoming more self-aware, these psychosocial factors are probably more important for their daily functioning and well-being than the centimeter of waist circumference or the point of HOMA-IR that marks a clinical threshold. Consequently, a comprehensive framework for obesity measurement must incorporate validated instruments for assessing these psychosocial dimensions with equivalent rigor to that applied to anthropometric indicators.

2.3.1 Weight stigma: definition, prevalence, and measurement

Weight stigma—the devaluation, discrimination, and negative stereotyping of individuals because of their body weight—is a pervasive and well-documented phenomenon with profound consequences for adolescent well-being. Weight stigma is associated with behavioral and physiological pathways that may contribute to weight gain. Epidemiological surveys consistently estimate that approximately 15% to 30% of individuals in community samples are affected. Specifically because of their weight status, with rates substantially higher among adolescents with obesity (Pont et al., 2017). A major metaanalysis by Emmer et al. (2020), synthesizing data from 105 studies involving 59,172 participants, found a medium-to-large negative association between weight stigma and mental health (mean $r=-.23$ to $-.25$ across outcomes), including significantly elevated rates of depression, anxiety, low self-esteem, disordered eating, reduced physical activity, and unhealthy weight-control behaviors.

Longitudinal studies provide substantial evidence for the vicious cycle hypothesis, demonstrating that weight stigma and obesity exacerbate each other over time. Longitudinal evidence demonstrates a bidirectional relationship between increased BMI and subsequent experiences of weight stigma (Warschburger & Zuba, 2023). A six-year study of 1381 kids and teens between the ages of 9 and 19 found that teasing them about their weight made their BMI z-score go up, and having a higher BMI z-score made them more likely to be teased. This shows a cycle where stigma leads to weight gain, which then leads to more stigma. Stigma can cause people to gain weight, and one reason for this is cortisol, a stress hormone that rises when people make fun of their weight. This hormone changes how fat cells grow and process fat, which makes the body store more fat.

The present study also examined how obese adolescents and young adults coped with stigmatizing experiences. Using the Coping Responses Inventory (CRI), the results showed that the most common ways that obese people coped were by using positive self-affirmations, trying to avoid negative comments by social disarming, and relying on faith and personal determination. Rydén and colleagues (2003) called "Fighting Spirit" problem-focused coping. This means dealing with the problems that come with being overweight instead of avoiding them. This form of coping was associated with reduced psychological distress in the present sample. It corroborates the established prevalence of weight stigma among Indian adolescents. In a sample of late adolescents and young adults from Kolkata, obese individuals reported significantly higher exposure to stigmatizing situations compared to their nonobese peers, aligning with the pattern identified by Myers and Rosen (1999). The most common stigmatizing experiences reported by obese individuals in this study included negative assumptions made by others, physical obstacles in daily environments, and social rejection due to weight. The present study found a link between more stigmatizing situations and worse mental health symptoms, a bad body image, and lower self-esteem.

2.3.2 Body image and self-perception instruments

Body image—encompassing the subjective perceptual, cognitive, affective, and behavioral dimensions of an individual's relationship with their own body—constitutes a central psychosocial indicator in adolescent obesity assessment that is distinct from, though correlated with, weight stigma. Body dissatisfaction, the evaluative component of body image reflecting discrepancy between perceived and idealized body size, is among the most robustly documented psychological correlates of obesity in adolescence and constitutes a significant predictor of unhealthy weight-control behaviors, disordered eating, depressive symptoms, and avoidance of physical activity independent of actual BMI (Neumark-Sztainer et al., 2006; Schaumberg & Anderson, 2016). Silhouette rating scales—in which participants select from a series of schematic body size figures the silhouette they believe most closely represents their current body and the silhouette representing their ideal body—provide a simple, visually accessible, and developmentally appropriate method of assessing perceived body size and body size discrepancy in children and adolescents. Stunkard's figure rating scale and its many versions for different ages, ethnicities, and cultures are the most commonly used tools for this purpose, but we need to check how well they work for South Asian adolescents.

The body shape questionnaire (BSQ; Cooper et al., 1987) and its shortened versions (BSQ-8C; Dowson & Henderson, 2001) use Likert scales to measure how fat people feel, how much they think about their weight, and how much they avoid situations that make them feel bad about their appearance. These are all important aspects of body image that are related to the link between obesity and mental illness. The multidimensional body-self relations questionnaire-appearance scales (MBSRQ-AS; Brown et al., 1990) assesses evaluative, cognitive, and behavioral aspects of appearance satisfaction via multiple validated subscales. The body image assessment for obesity (BIA-O; Williamson et al., 2000) is tailored for individuals with obesity and offers normative comparison data from clinical populations. It also addresses the specific body image issues of this group that generic tools may not adequately cover. HRQoL tools, such as the pediatric quality of life inventory and its dedicated module for obesity, enhance our comprehension of psychosocial health. They help us see how overweight teens do in school, with their health, their emotions, and their social life compared to teens who are at a healthy weight. Disordered eating attitudes represent an additional psychosocial dimension evaluated in the current study through the eating attitudes test (EAT). Obese participants in the current study exhibited markedly more disordered eating attitudes than their nonobese counterparts, aligning with the extensive international literature that associates obesity with binge eating disorder, emotional eating, and weight preoccupation (Fichter et al., 1993; Kuehnel and Wadden, 1994). In the current sample, body image dissatisfaction emerged as a significant predictor of pathological eating attitudes, corroborating the three-pathway model proposed by Stice (2001), which posits that body dissatisfaction induces dieting or negative affect, both of which increase the risk of disordered eating. In India, where disordered eating in teens is still not well-known or well-screened, these results show that the EAT is a clinically useful and practical tool that could be used in health assessments at school and in outpatient settings.

2.3.3 Psychosocial well-being as an independent diagnostic dimension

The empirical case for treating psychosocial well-being as an independent and nonreducible dimension of obesity assessment—rather than as a secondary downstream consequence—rests on three converging lines of evidence. First, as documented above, the health harms of weight stigma, body dissatisfaction, and psychosocial distress in adolescents with obesity are substantial, measurable, and partially independent of adiposity itself: stigma internalization predicts depression and anxiety after controlling for BMI, and conversely, weight-neutral interventions that reduce stigma and improve body satisfaction produce improved health behaviors without requiring weight loss (Bacon & Aphramor, 2011). Second, psychological factors significantly influence treatment efficacy: obese adolescents experiencing substantial weight stigma, binge eating disorders, or clinical depression exhibit markedly diminished responses to conventional obesity interventions, necessitating supplementary psychological support for enduring outcomes. Third, adolescent well-being possesses inherent moral significance beyond its instrumental connection to physical health outcomes: a youth's dignity, social integration, educational involvement, and potential for flourishing are valid subjects of clinical and policy focus that cannot be derived from, or reduced to, their BMI (Puhl & Lessard, 2020).

The Edmonton Obesity Staging System (EOSS), developed by Sharma and Kushner in 2009, is now widely used in clinical practice for adults and teens. It is the most organized way to use this multidimensional approach to measuring obesity in clinical settings. EOSS rates patients from 0 (no obesity-related risk factors) to 4 (severe end-organ damage, severe functional impairment) in three areas: metabolic (cardiometabolic comorbidities), mechanical (musculoskeletal, respiratory complications), and mental health and well-being (depression, anxiety, substance use, binge eating, quality of life). This staging system directly integrates psychological well-being as a comparable domain of clinical severity alongside metabolic and physical indicators, establishing a clinical framework that embodies the biopsychosocial principle that the psychological aspects of obesity are diagnostically significant and therapeutically relevant. Psychosocial indicators enhance, rather than supplant, biological risk assessment. The justification for regarding psychosocial wellbeing as a separate diagnostic dimension is directly validated by the present study. Assessments of depression (Beck Depression Inventory (BDI)), state and trait anxiety (State-Trait Anxiety Inventory (STAI)), and self-esteem (Rosenberg Self-Esteem Scale (RSES)) in a cohort of 120 late adolescents from Kolkata—equally divided between obese and nonobese groups—revealed significant effects of obesity status on depression, trait anxiety, and self-esteem, even after controlling for demographic variables. Obese adolescents demonstrated significantly higher depression scores and lower self-esteem relative to their nonobese peers, while trait anxiety—the persistent, intrinsic characteristic of anxiety—was also markedly elevated in the obese group. These findings from an urban Indian population correspond with the research conducted by McElroy et al. (2004) and Melnyk et al. (2006), which indicated heightened levels of depression, anxiety, and diminished self-esteem among obese adolescents. Additionally, they extend these findings to a South Asian context, emphasizing the lack of psychosocial screening for obese adolescents in conventional clinical practice (Das et al., 2018).

The current study also looked at locus of control, which is a psychosocial factor that was measured using the multidimensional locus of control (MLOC) scales. This construct is pertinent to obesity due to its correlation with health behavior modification: individuals possessing an internal locus of control—those who perceive they can affect outcomes through their actions—exhibit greater weight loss in structured programs and demonstrate increased consistency in self-management behaviors (Nir and Neumann, 1991; Gungor et al., 2005). The current study revealed that obese Indian adolescents and young adults exhibited a greater external locus of control in comparison to their nonobese counterparts, aligning with the hypothesis that a perceived deficiency in personal control over eating and weight may serve as both a result of stigmatization and an obstacle to intervention participation. Including locus of control assessment in a comprehensive psychosocial evaluation framework is useful for customizing the motivational and behavioral aspects of obesity interventions to fit the individual's unique psychological profile (Table 2.2).

TABLE 2.2 Key validated psychosocial measurement instruments for adolescent obesity research and practice.

Instrument	Construct measured	Key psychometric properties
WBIS-Y (Durso & Latner, 2008)	Internalized weight stigma	$\alpha > 0.85$; validated in adolescents
WSSQ (Lillis et al., 2010)	Weight self-stigma (self-devaluation + fear of enacted stigma)	12 items; $\alpha = 0.80–0.89$; dimensional
POTS (Thompson et al., 1995)	Perceived weight-related teasing	16 items; two subscales; validated in large cohorts
BSQ-8C (Dowson & Henderson, 2001)	Body shape concerns; feeling fat	8 items; strong convergent validity with EDE-Q
MBSRQ-AS (Brown et al., 1990)	Multidimensional appearance satisfaction	34 items; 5 subscales; normative data
PedsQL 4.0 (Varni et al., 2001)	Health-related quality of life	23 items; child + parent report; validated internationally
BIA-O (Williamson et al., 2000)	Body image in obesity; appearance satisfaction	Obesity-specific norms; clinical validation

Source: Author compilation; see individual instrument references cited in text.

2.4 Cultural and policy dimensions: India in the measurement frame

2.4.1 The Indian cut-off controversy: global versus Asia-specific standards

Since the early 2000s, a lot of research has shown that Asian Indians have clinically significant insulin resistance, dyslipidaemia, hypertension, and metabolic syndrome at BMI levels that are much lower than the normal international levels of 25 and 30 kg/m². It is scientifically dubious to apply the standard BMI cut-off points from WHO or IOTF to Indian adolescents, owing to established biological factors that significantly influence health policies and clinical practices. South Asians, including Indians, exhibit significantly higher body fat percentages and greater visceral adiposity at any given BMI value compared to European reference populations—a phenomenon related to differences in body build, limb-to-trunk ratio, and fat distribution patterns that persist even after controlling for socioeconomic and dietary variables (Deurenberg et al., 2002; WHO Expert Consultation, 2004). Misra and colleagues (2009), in a landmark consensus statement developed by a national expert group on obesity, demonstrated that Asian Indians develop clinically significant insulin resistance, dyslipidemia, and metabolic syndrome at BMI values substantially below the conventional adult threshold of 30 kg/m² and recommended Asia-specific cutoffs of ≥23 kg/m² for overweight and ≥25 kg/m² for obesity for clinical use in adult Indian populations. The implications of these lower adult thresholds for pediatric reference standards remain an active area of methodological investigation: Khadilkar and colleagues have developed Indian synthetic growth charts from 0 to 18 years using data from multiple Indian cohort studies and have demonstrated that applying WHO 2006 growth references to Indian children produces systematically different—and arguably inflated—estimates of both undernutrition and overnutrition compared to India-specific references (Dange et al., 2025; Khadilkar et al., 2019). These measurement debates are not just for academics: the estimates of how many people are obese in a country, how much money is spent on preventive programs, the thresholds for clinical intervention, and the comparisons of international league tables all depend on which reference system is used.

Standards for waist circumference face similar problems that are unique to India. Asian Indian adolescents accumulate abdominal fat preferentially compared to age-matched European counterparts at equivalent BMI, indicating the necessity for ethnicity-specific waist circumference cutoffs to accurately identify metabolically at-risk adolescents. The National Rural Health Mission and subsequent national guidelines have incorporated modified waist circumference thresholds for South Asian adults, but corresponding pediatric reference data with adequate nationally representative sampling remain limited. Experts are urging the need for extensive studies on the body composition of Indian children and adolescents, using reliable methods like DXA and BIA with specific equations for India, to create accurate health guidelines that can be used in national health monitoring and medical care.

2.4.2 National surveillance: National Family Health Survey-5 and Comprehensive National Nutrition Survey Findings

India's two most authoritative national nutritional surveillance systems provide complementary but incomplete pictures of the obesity epidemic's epidemiological trajectory. The International Institute for Population Sciences (IIPS) conducted the NFHS-5 (2019–21) across all 28 states and 8 union territories, with a sample size exceeding 600,000 households. The survey documents an increase in overweight and obesity prevalence across all age groups, alongside persistent undernutrition in the same population segments. Among children under five years, NFHS-5 documents an overweight prevalence of 3.4% nationally—representing a 127% increase from the 1.5% recorded in NFHS-3 (2005–06)—with the highest state-level prevalence observed in northeastern states and union territories including Lakshadweep, Sikkim, and Chandigarh (International Institute for Population Sciences IIPS & ICF, 2021; UNICEF India, 2025). NFHS-5 data show that more and more teens aged 15 to 19 are overweight or obese, especially in cities and among the wealthiest quintiles. However, the survey's main focus on reproductive health makes it less useful as a tool for tracking adolescent nutrition. Recent analyses of CNNS data confirm rising overweight prevalence among Indian adolescents, especially within urban and higher socioeconomic demographics (Sethi et al., 2024).

CNNS found that 4.8% of adolescents aged 10–19 years were overweight or obese nationally, with significantly higher prevalence in urban areas, among households in the top wealth quintile, and in states with more advanced nutrition transition profiles (Ministry of Health and Family Welfare MoHFW, Government of India, UNICEF, & Population Council, 2019; Sethi et al., 2024). A subsequent reanalysis of NFHS-5 overweight data among under-five children by Singh and colleagues (2024), published in Public Health Nutrition, documented that the rise in overweight prevalence was substantially larger than the concurrent decrease in underweight, indicating a net increase in total nutritional failure rather than a benign epidemiological transition.

2.4.3 The double burden of malnutrition

Perhaps the most complex and clinically demanding measurement challenge in the Indian context is the "double burden of malnutrition"—the coexistence, within the same communities, households, and even individuals, of undernutrition and overnutrition simultaneously. NFHS-5 data confirm that India simultaneously records 35.5% stunting, 19.3% wasting, and 32.1% underweight prevalence in under-five children at the national level—figures consistent with emergency-level undernutrition burden—while also documenting rising overweight and obesity across all pediatric and adolescent age groups (International Institute for Population Sciences IIPS & ICF, 2021). This dual burden is not confined to distinct population segments: household-level analyses using NFHS-5 data find that 7.7% of mother–under-five-child dyads exhibit double burden malnutrition (overweight/obese mother with stunted, underweight, wasted, or anemic child), and this burden has increased compared to previous survey rounds (Mohanty et al., 2024, PMC). Importantly, NFHS-5 data also show that maternal overweight and obesity increased from 20.6% to 33.2% between NFHS-4 and NFHS-5—documenting a generational nutritional transition that is simultaneously producing undernourished children from overnourished mothers through intergenerational developmental programming mechanisms (Barker et al., 1995; Godfrey et al., 2017).

2.4.4 Policy and governance implications of measurement choices

The measurement debates discussed in this chapter have direct and important effects on how public health is run, how resources are shared, and how policies are made. The reference system a country uses determines how many kids are considered "at risk." This, in affects how big the clinical response needs to be, how much money health systems need to spend, and how visible childhood obesity is as a public health issue. India's use of WHO growth references in NFHS-5, instead of Khadilkar references that are specific to India, leads to very different estimates of prevalence. WHO standards find that nearly 24 percentage points more children are experiencing anthropometric failure than Indian references (Dange et al., 2025). This raises the important question of whether the choice of measurement can have a big impact on estimates of prevalence and, as a result, on the priorities of policy. The issue of obesity is contingent upon the priorities of the government. There is no standardized way to track adolescent growth across the country. The NFHS and CNNS include adolescents, but weren't specifically made for tracking their nutrition. This means that there isn't enough solid evidence to help India make policies about obesity in adolescents, even though the problem is urgent.

Policy responses to obesity measurement must also grapple with the psychosocial consequences of measurement practices at the individual and institutional levels. School-based BMI screening programs—a growing component of national health programs, including the Rashtriya Bal Swasthya Karyakram—create contexts in which children are publicly identified as overweight or obese without the psychosocial support infrastructure needed to prevent stigmatization and shame. Evidence from implementation research in high-income countries consistently finds that school-based BMI screening, without accompanying nonstigmatizing education, psychosocial support, and family communication protocols, produces elevated rates of body dissatisfaction, weight-control behaviors, and distress among children labeled as overweight (Puhl & Latner, 2007). The design of measurement-linked policy programs in India must therefore integrate psychosocial safeguards into their operational protocols—an integration that requires explicit interdisciplinary collaboration among clinical, public health, psychological, and educational professionals. The front-of-pack labeling rules set by the Food Safety and Standards Authority of India, nutrition policies included in the National Education Policy (NEP, 2020), and school canteen rules together create a system where evidence-based on measurements needs to be turned into actions that are fair, respectful, and suitable for children's development. Recent national analyses continue to show that BMI demonstrates high specificity but imperfect sensitivity for detecting excess adiposity in youth (Freedman & Sherry, 2024).

2.4.5 Research gaps in the Indian context

Although adolescent obesity is increasingly acknowledged as a significant public health issue in India, critical evidence deficiencies persist, hindering precise evaluation and effective intervention. National surveillance systems like the NFHS and CNNS give us useful information about how common certain things are, but they weren't made to give us detailed or long-term information about body composition in teenagers. There are no national reference standards for waist circumference, WHtR, and body fat percentage that are specific to Indian populations. Furthermore, numerous validated instruments evaluating body image, weight stigma, and quality of life have been created in Western contexts and remain inadequately adapted or validated within India's varied linguistic and cultural environments. The limited availability of longitudinal studies further constrains understanding of the complex interactions between anthropometry, metabolic risk, and mental health in adolescence. To improve obesity assessment and intervention strategies in India, it is important to fill these gaps with research that is methodologically sound, representative of the whole country, and sensitive to different cultures.

2.5 Summary and chapter takeaway

This chapter has systematically analyzed the landscape of obesity measurement across anthropometric, clinical, psychosocial, and policy dimensions, contending that measurement is inherently a value-laden technical endeavor that both delineates biological reality and engenders social ramifications. The chapter's main contributions are a number of arguments that come together.

First, BMI-for-age remains the most widely used method for surveillance and screening of obesity in children and adolescents because it's easy to use, standardized, and has a lot of normal values in its database. But it isn't very good at figuring out how fat a person is: it misses more than a quarter of kids who are really overweight and says that lean, muscular people are overweight. Also, its connection to the risk of heart disease and diabetes changes in a consistent way across different ethnic groups. These limitations are particularly significant for South Asian adolescents, as the conventional WHO thresholds may significantly underrepresent their metabolic risk.

Second, complementary anthropometric indicators—namely waist circumference and WHtR—provide diagnostically significant insights into central adiposity and metabolic risk that BMI alone does not offer, and their clinical integration is supported by substantial empirical evidence. Advanced body composition techniques, including DXA, provide criterion-level adiposity measurement; BIA provides estimates feasible in field settings.

Third, biochemical and clinical biomarkers like HOMA-IR, fasting lipids, liver enzymes, and blood pressure are very important for figuring out the clinical risk of obese teens. They are better than just using anthropometry. Leading professional groups support their systematic evaluation in clinical protocols.

Fourth—and perhaps most critically for the orientation of this book—psychosocial indicators including weight stigma, body image, and HRQoL constitute nonreducible dimensions of obesity assessment with independent associations with health outcomes, treatment response, and well-being. Validated instruments for systematically measuring these dimensions exist and should be incorporated into comprehensive clinical assessment and research protocols.

Fifth, the Indian measurement context is marked by a unique complexity: the conflict between global and India-specific growth reference standards, the dual challenge of concurrent undernutrition and overnutrition, the insufficiency of current national surveillance systems to accurately assess adolescent nutritional status with adequate detail, and the policy difficulty of converting measurement-based evidence into nonstigmatizing, equity-sensitive interventions. These contextual particularities necessitate India-specific measurement frameworks instead of the uncritical adoption of global standards.

Future progress in the evaluation of adolescent obesity in India will likely hinge on the incorporation of multidimensional anthropometry, culturally validated psychosocial metrics, and nascent digital health analytics within longitudinal, population-based research paradigms.

The present study, conducted on a cohort of late adolescents and young adults from Kolkata, provides an empirical foundation from an Indian urban context for various measurement and assessment propositions outlined in this chapter. The study methodically assessed personality (NEO-FFI), depression (BDI), anxiety (STAI), self-esteem (RSES), locus of control (MLOC), coping responses (CRI), eating attitudes (EAT), body image (MBSRQ), family environment (FES), and psychological adjustment alongside anthropometric classification. It showed that overweight Indian teens have big differences in their mental health compared to teens who aren't overweight, and these differences can't be explained just by their BMI. The dissertation that this chapter is based on (Das, 2018) says that most of the evidence about obesity and psychological traits comes from Western populations. This is because India's unique socioeconomic and socio-cultural context makes it impossible to directly apply those findings to India. This study addresses the deficiency by supplying India-specific data that substantiates the multidimensional measurement framework outlined in this chapter and advocates for the integration of psychosocial screening into obesity assessment protocols for Indian adolescents (Table 2.3).

Recommended further reading

Foundational works

Keys, A., Fidanza, F., Karvonen, M. J., Kimura, N., & Taylor, H. L. (1972). Indices of relative weight and obesity. Journal of Chronic Diseases, 25(6–7), 329–343. [The paper that named and defined BMI]

Puhl, R. M., & Heuer, C. A. (2010). Obesity stigma: Important considerations for public health. American Journal of Public Health, 100(6), 1019–1028. [Foundational review of weight stigma and its health consequences]

Cole, T. J., Bellizzi, M. C., Flegal, K. M., & Dietz, W. H. (2000). Establishing a standard definition for child overweight and obesity worldwide: International survey. BMJ, 320(7244), 1240–1243. [Definitive IOTF cut-off derivation paper]

TABLE 2.3 Recommended multiindicator assessment framework for adolescent obesity in the Indian context3.

Domain	Recommended indicators	Reference standards/tools	Clinical priority
General adiposity (screening)	BMI-for-age using India-specific centiles (Khadilkar et al., 2019) or WHO 2007, with acknowledged limitations	Calibrated digital scales + stadiometer; reference chart	Essential
Central adiposity	Waist circumference (≥90th centile, CNNS India reference, Sarna et al., 2021) + waist-to-height ratio (WHtR) (≥0.5 as practical screen)	Nonstretchable flexible tape; no chart needed for WHtR	Essential
Body composition (specialist)	Body fat percentage by BIA with Indian-validated equations (Chiplonkar et al., 2018) or DXA, where available	BIA with Indian pediatric equations; Lunar/Hologic DXA platform	Recommended for research and specialist settings
Metabolic risk stratification	Fasting lipid profile, fasting glucose, insulin (HOMA-IR), ALT, blood pressure	Standard laboratory panel + pediatric BP cuffs	Essential for clinical management of identified obese youth
Psychosocial assessment	Weight stigma (WBIS-Y or POTS), body dissatisfaction (BSQ-8C or Stunkard scale), HRQoL (PedsQL)	Validated culturally adapted self-report instruments in regional language	Recommended for comprehensive clinical and research assessment

Source: Author synthesis based on Misra et al. (2009), Khadilkar et al. (2019), and present study findings (Das, 2018).

Misra, A., et al. (2009). Consensus statement for diagnosis of obesity, abdominal obesity and the metabolic syndrome for Asian Indians. Journal of the Association of Physicians of India, 57, 163–170. [Essential for Indian clinical practice]

Sharma, A. M., & Kushner, R. F. (2009). A proposed clinical staging system for obesity. International Journal of Obesity, 33(3), 289–295. [EOSS original derivation]

Advanced and critical perspectives

Nuttall, F. Q. (2015). Body mass index: Obesity, BMI, and health: A critical review. Nutrition Today, 50(3), 117–128. [Essential critical history of BMI's development and limitations]

Emmer, C., Bosnjak, M., & Mata, J. (2020). The association between weight stigma and mental health: A meta-analysis. Obesity Reviews, 21(1), e12935. [Comprehensive meta-analysis of weight stigma–mental health associations]

MoHFW, UNICEF, & Population Council. (2019). Comprehensive National Nutrition Survey (CNNS) 2016–18: National Report. [Primary source for India-specific nutritional data]

Dange, N. S., Khadilkar, V., Gondhalekar, K., & Khadilkar, A. V. (2025). Double burden of malnutrition in under-five children (NFHS-5 data). Indian Pediatrics. [Methodological analysis of WHO vs Indian growth references]

Rodrigues, A. N., et al. (2016). A comparison between BMI, waist circumference, and waist-to-height ratio for identifying cardiometabolic risk in children and adolescents. PLOS ONE. [Evidence synthesis on comparative utility of anthropometric indicators]

Review questions

1. Adolphe Quetelet designed the BMI formula as a tool of social statistics rather than individual medical diagnosis. Drawing on the evidence presented in Section 2.2, critically evaluate the journey of BMI from population statistic to clinical diagnostic threshold. In what ways has this translation created measurement problems that remain unresolved in contemporary pediatric obesity practice, and what alternative or complementary approaches might better serve clinical and public health purposes?
2. A 14-year-old girl from urban Kolkata visits a school health clinic with a BMI-for-age z-score of +1.6 (overweight by WHO standards), but her WHtR is normal and there are no signs of cardiometabolic risk factors. Her weight bias internalization scale for youth score shows that she has a lot of internalized weight stigma, and she says she is very unhappy with her body and avoids exercise because she is embarrassed about how she looks. Utilizing the EOSS as a

clinical framework, categorize this patient's obesity, ascertain the primary domains of clinical concern, and delineate the components of a comprehensive assessment protocol encompassing anthropometric, biochemical, and psychosocial dimensions.

3. The chapter contends that measurement selections are inherently politically charged. In the framework of India's national nutritional surveillance, elucidate the significant ramifications of employing the WHO 2007 growth references in contrast to Khadilkar's Indian synthetic charts for assessing childhood overweight prevalence derived from NFHS-5 data. Who benefits and who might be hurt by underestimating or overestimating the number of overweight people in national surveys? What factors should be used to decide which reference system to use on a national level?
4. Adolescent weight stigma manifests through various sources—peers, family, and healthcare providers—and through multiple mechanisms, including elevated cortisol levels, disordered eating, and decreased physical activity. Using the specific tools listed in Section 2.3, create a short but complete set of psychosocial tests that can be given to 13- to 16-year-olds during a regular school health check-up in a government school in India. What changes would you suggest to make sure that this group is culturally valid?
5. India is currently dealing with a "double burden of malnutrition," which means that both undernutrition and overnutrition are happening at the national, household, and individual levels at the same time. Critically evaluate the adequacy of the anthropometric measurement frameworks employed in India's NFHS and CNNS surveys for accurately reflecting this dual-burden phenomenon. What new methods—such as composite indices, measurement tools, and study design—would help India the most to keep track of and respond to this complicated nutritional situation?

AI disclosure

During the preparation of this work the author(s) used Chat GPT, Grammarly. com in order to Editing. After using this tool/service, the author(s) reviewed and edited the content as needed and take(s) full responsibility for the content of the publication.

Glossary

Term definition

Body mass index (BMI) Weight (kg) divided by height squared (m^2); the standard population-level proxy for adiposity.

BMI-for-age z-score Age- and sex-standardized BMI expressed in units of standard deviation from the reference population median.

Waist-to-height ratio (WHtR) Waist circumference divided by height; a simple central adiposity index with a proposed universal threshold of 0.5.

HOMA-IR Homeostatic Model Assessment for Insulin Resistance: (fasting insulin × fasting glucose) / 22.5; surrogate for insulin resistance.

DXA Dual-energy X-ray absorptiometry; criterion method for body composition assessment.

Weight stigma Negative stereotyping, discrimination, and devaluation of individuals based on body weight.

Internalized weight stigma Degree to which individuals with obesity adopt and apply negative weight-based stereotypes to themselves.

EOSS Edmonton Obesity Staging System; five-stage clinical severity classification incorporating metabolic, mechanical, and mental health domains.

WBIS-Y Weight bias internalization scale for youth; validated measure of weight stigma internalization in adolescents.

PedsQL Pediatric quality of life inventory; standardized health-related quality of life assessment for children and adolescents.

Double burden of malnutrition (DBM) Coexistence of undernutrition (stunting, wasting, underweight) and overnutrition (overweight, obesity) within the same population, household, or individual.

CNNS Comprehensive National Nutrition Survey (India, 2016–18); the most extensive national nutrition assessment ever conducted in India.

IOTF International Obesity Task Force; provides sex- and age-specific BMI cutoffs linking childhood percentiles to adult obesity thresholds.

Body dissatisfaction Negative evaluation of one's own body, reflecting the perceived discrepancy between actual and ideal body size or shape.

CIAF/eCIAF Composite index of anthropometric failure/extended CIAF; simultaneous classification of all anthropometric failure forms, including overweight.

No Permission Required

References

Bacon, L., & Aphramor, L. (2011). Weight science: Evaluating the evidence for a paradigm shift. *Nutrition Journal, 10*(1), 9. https://doi.org/10.1186/1475-2891-10-9.

Barker, D. J. P. (1995). Fetal origins of coronary heart disease. *BMJ (Clinical Research ed.), 311*(6998), 171–174. https://doi.org/10.1136/bmj.311.6998.171.

Biro, F. M., & Wien, M. (2010). Childhood obesity and adult morbidities. *American Journal of Clinical Nutrition, 91*(5), 1499S–1505S. https://doi.org/10.3945/ajcn.2010.28701C.

Brown, T. A., Cash, T. F., & Mikulka, P. J. (1990). Attitudinal body-image assessment: Factor analysis of the body-self relations questionnaire. *Journal of Personality Assessment, 55*(1–2), 135–144. https://doi.org/10.1080/00223891.1990.9674053.

Centers for Disease Control and Prevention (CDC). (2000). *CDC Growth Charts for the United States*. Hyattsville, MD: National Center for Health Statistics.

Chiplonkar, S.A., Kajale, N.A., Ekbote, V.H., Khadilkar, A.V., Mandlik, R.M., Parthasarathy, L.S., et al., 2018. Reference values of body fat percentage, fat mass index and fat-free mass index in Indian children and adolescents.

Cole, T. J., Bellizzi, M. C., Flegal, K. M., & Dietz, W. H. (2000). Establishing a standard definition for child overweight and obesity worldwide: International survey. *BMJ (Clinical Research ed.), 320*(7244), 1240–1243. https://doi.org/10.1136/bmj.320.7244.1240.

Cooper, P. J., Taylor, M. J., Cooper, Z., & Fairburn, C. G. (1987). The development and validation of the body shape questionnaire. *International Journal of Eating Disorders, 6*(4), 485–494. https://doi.org/10.1002/1098-108X(198707)6:4<485::AID-EAT2260060405>3.0.CO;2-O.

Das, S., Das, S., & Chattopadhyay, P. K. (2018). Psychological distress among late adolescents with obesity. *IAHRW International Journal of Social Sciences Review, 6*(7), 769–774.

Dange, N. S., Khadilkar, V., Gondhalekar, K., & Khadilkar, A. V. (2025). Double burden of malnutrition in under-five children (NFHS-5 data) using extended CIAF: WHO 2006 growth standard versus 2019 Indian growth references. *Indian Pediatrics*. https://doi.org/10.1007/s13312-025-00027-3.

Deurenberg, P., Deurenberg-Yap, M., & Guricci, S. (2002). Asians are different from caucasians and from each other in their body mass index/body fat per cent relationship. *Obesity Reviews, 3*(3), 141–146. https://doi.org/10.1046/j.1467-789X.2002.00065.x.

Dowson, J., & Henderson, L. (2001). The validity of a short version of the body shape questionnaire. *Psychiatry Research, 102*(3), 263–271. https://doi.org/10.1016/S0165-1781(01)00254-2.

Durnin, J. V. G. A., & Wormersley, J. (1974). Body fat assessed from total body density and its estimation from skinfold thickness: Measurements on 481 men and women aged from 16 to 72 years. *British Journal of Nutrition, 32*(1), 77–97. https://doi.org/10.1079/BJN19740060.

Durso, L. E., & Latner, J. D. (2008). Understanding self-directed stigma: Development of the weight bias internalization scale. *Obesity, 16*(Suppl 2), S80–S86. https://doi.org/10.1038/oby.2008.448.

Emmer, C., Bosnjak, M., & Mata, J. (2020). The association between weight stigma and mental health: A meta-analysis. *Obesity Reviews, 21*(1), e12935. https://doi.org/10.1111/obr.12935.

Fichter, M.M., Quadflieg, N., Brandl, B., Reas, D.L., 1993. Psychological and psychosocial impairment in obesity and eating disorders.

Freedman, D. S., & Sherry, B. (2024). Screening accuracy of body mass index for excess adiposity among 8- to 19-year-olds. *Pediatrics, 154*(1), e2024065960. https://doi.org/10.1542/peds.2024-065960.

Gungor, N., Thompson, T., Sutton-Tyrrell, K., Janosky, J., & Arslanian, S. (2005). Early signs of cardiovascular disease in youth with obesity and type 2 diabetes. *Diabetes Care, 28*(5), 1219–1221.

Godfrey, K. M., Reynolds, R. M., Prescott, S. L., Nyirenda, M., Jaddoe, V. W. V., Eriksson, J. G., & Bhutta, Z. A. (2017). Influence of maternal obesity on the long-term health of offspring. *The Lancet Diabetes & Endocrinology, 5*(1), 53–64. https://doi.org/10.1016/S2213-8587(16)30107-3.

International Obesity Task Force (IOTF), 2000. The International Obesity Task Force Classification for Childhood Overweight and Obesity.

International Institute for Population Sciences (IIPS) & ICF. (2021). National Family Health Survey (NFHS-5), 2019–21: India Volume I. International Institute for Population Sciences.

Keys, A., Fidanza, F., Karvonen, M. J., Kimura, N., & Taylor, H. L. (1972). Indices of relative weight and obesity. *Journal of Chronic Diseases, 25*(6–7), 329–343. https://doi.org/10.1016/0021-9681(72)90027-6.

Khadilkar, V., Khadilkar, A. V., & Kajale, N. (2019). Indian growth references from 0–18-year-old children and adolescents: A comparison of two methods. *Indian Journal of Endocrinology and Metabolism, 23*(6), 635. https://doi.org/10.4103/ijem.IJEM_373_19.

Kuehnel, R.H., Wadden, T.A., 1994. Body image, self-esteem, and psychological functioning in obese individuals.

Lillis, J., Luoma, J. B., Levin, M. E., & Hayes, S. C. (2010). Measuring weight self-stigma: The weight self-stigma questionnaire. *Obesity, 18*(5), 971–976. https://doi.org/10.1038/oby.2009.353.

Lobstein, T., Jackson-Leach, R., Moodie, M. L., Hall, K. D., Gortmaker, S. L., Swinburn, B. A., ... Boyd, D. (2015). Child and adolescent obesity: Part of a bigger picture. *The Lancet, 385*(9986), 2510–2520. https://doi.org/10.1016/S0140-6736(14)61746-3.

Martinez-Villanueva, J., Gonzalez-Leal, R., Argente, J., & Martos-Moreno, G. A. (2023). BMI-based obesity classification misses children and adolescents with raised cardiometabolic risk due to increased adiposity. *International Journal of Obesity, 47*(11), 1095–1102. https://doi.org/10.1038/s41366-023-01363-1.

McElroy, S. L., Kotwal, R., Malhotra, S., Nelson, E. B., Keck, P. E., & Nemeroff, C. B. (2004). Are mood disorders and obesity related? A review for the mental health professional. *Journal of Clinical Psychiatry, 65*(5), 634–651.

Melnyk, B.M., Small, L., Morrison-Beedy, D., Strasser, A., Spath, L., Kreipe, R., et al., 2006. Mental health correlates of healthy lifestyle attitudes, beliefs, choices, and behaviors in overweight adolescents.

Ministry of Health and Family Welfare (MoHFW), Government of India, UNICEF, & Population Council. (2019). Comprehensive National Nutrition Survey 2016–2018: National Report. Ministry of Health and Family Welfare.

Misra, A., Chowbey, P., Makkar, B. M., Vikram, N. K., Wasir, J. S., Chadha, D., ... Munjal, Y. P. (2009). Consensus statement for diagnosis of obesity, abdominal obesity and the metabolic syndrome for Asian Indians and recommendations for physical activity, medical and surgical management. *Journal of the Association of Physicians of India, 57*, 163–170.

Mohanty, S. K., Bhavesh, V., Yadav, A., Mohanty, P., Sahoo, U., Kramer, M. R., & Subramanian, S. V. (2024). Prevalence and socio-demographic factors associated with double and triple burden of malnutrition among mother-child pairs in India: Findings from a nationally representative survey (NFHS-5). *Nutrition (Burbank, Los Angeles County, Calif.), 120*, 112348. https://doi.org/10.1016/j.nut.2024.112348.

Myers, A., & Rosen, J. C. (1999). Obesity stigmatization and coping: Relation to mental health symptoms, body image, and self-esteem. *International Journal of Obesity, 23*(3), 221–230.

Neumark-Sztainer, D., Wall, M., Guo, J., Story, M., Haines, J., & Eisenberg, M. (2006). Obesity, disordered eating, and eating disorders in a longitudinal study of adolescents: How do dieters fare five years later? *Journal of the American Dietetic Association, 106*(4), 559–568. https://doi.org/10.1016/j.jada.2006.01.003.

Nir, Z., & Neumann, L. (1991). Relationship among self-esteem, internal-external locus of control, and weight change after participation in a weight reduction program. *Journal of Clinical Psychology, 47*(1), 119–123.

Nuttall, F. Q. (2015). Body mass index: Obesity, BMI, and health: A critical review. *Nutrition Today, 50*(3), 117–128. https://doi.org/10.1097/NT.0000000000000092.

Pont, S. J., Puhl, R., Cook, S. R., & Slusser, W. (2017). Stigma experienced by children and adolescents with obesity. *Pediatrics, 140*(6), e20173034. https://doi.org/10.1542/peds.2017-3034.

Puhl, R. M., & Heuer, C. A. (2010). Obesity stigma: Important considerations for public health. *American Journal of Public Health, 100*(6), 1019–1028. https://doi.org/10.2105/AJPH.2009.159491.

Puhl, R. M., & Latner, J. D. (2007). Stigma, obesity, and the health of the nation's children. *Psychological Bulletin, 133*(4), 557–580. https://doi.org/10.1037/0033-2909.133.4.557.

Puhl, R. M., & Lessard, L. M. (2020). Weight stigma in youth: Prevalence, consequences, and considerations for clinical practice. *Current Obesity Reports, 9*(4), 402–411. https://doi.org/10.1007/s13679-020-00408-8.

Rydén, A., Sullivan, M., Torgerson, J. S., Karlsson, J., Lindroos, A. K., & Taft, C. (2003). Severe obesity and personality: A comparative controlled study of personality traits. *International Journal of Obesity, 27*, 1534–1540.

Sarna, A., Porwal, A., Acharya, R., et al. (2021). Waist circumference, waist-to-height ratio and BMI percentiles in children aged 5–19 years in India: A population-based study. *Obesity Science & Practice, 7*(4), 392–404.

Schaumberg, K., & Anderson, D. (2016). Dietary restraint and weight loss as risk factors for eating pathology. *Eating Behaviors, 23*, 97–103. https://doi.org/10.1016/j.eatbeh.2016.09.005.

Sethi, V., Bassi, S., Bahl, D., Kumar, A., Choedon, T., Bhatia, N., & Arora, M. (2024). Prevalence of overweight and obesity and associated demographic and health factors in India: Findings from the Comprehensive National Nutrition Survey (CNNS). *Maternal & Child Nutrition, 20*(1), e13585. https://doi.org/10.1111/mcn.13585.

Singh, G., Sharma, B., Mani, A., & Thow, A. M. (2024). Epidemiology of overweight in under-five children in India: Insights from national family health survey. *Public Health Nutrition, 27*(1), e277. https://doi.org/10.1017/S1368980024001708.

Slaughter, M. H., Lohman, T. G., Boileau, R. A., Horswill, C. A., Stillman, R. J., Van Loan, M. D., & Bemben, D. A. (1988). Skinfold equations for estimation of body fatness in children and youth. *Human Biology, 60*(5), 709–723.

Stice, E. (2001). A prospective test of the dual-pathway model of bulimic pathology: Mediating effects of dieting and negative affect. *Journal of Abnormal Psychology, 110*(1), 124–135.

Thompson, J. K., Cattarin, J., Fowler, B., & Fisher, E. (1995). The perception of teasing scale (POTS): A revision and extension of the physical appearance related teasing scale (PARTS). *Journal of Personality Assessment, 65*(1), 146–157. https://doi.org/10.1207/s15327752jpa6501_11.

UNICEF India. (2025). India: Overweight and obesity rising across all ages – from youngest children to adults. https://www.unicef.org/india/press-releases/india-overweight-and-obesity-rising-across-all-ages-youngest-children-adults

Varni, J. W., Seid, M., & Kurtin, P. S. (2001). PedsQL 4.0: Reliability and validity of the pediatric quality of life inventory version 4.0 generic core scales in healthy and patient populations. *Medical Care, 39*(8), 800–812. https://doi.org/10.1097/00005650-200108000-00006.

Warschburger, P., & Zuba, A. (2023). Interrelation between weight and weight stigma in youth: Is there evidence for an obesogenic vicious cycle? *European Child & Adolescent Psychiatry, 32*(4), 697–704. https://doi.org/10.1007/s00787-021-01922-3.

WHO Expert Consultation. (2004). Appropriate body-mass index for Asian populations and its implications for policy and intervention strategies. *The Lancet, 363*(9403), 157–163. https://doi.org/10.1016/S0140-6736(03)15268-3.

WHO Growth Reference Study Group. (2007). *WHO child growth standards: Growth velocity based on weight, length and head circumference: Methods and development*. World Health Organization.

Williamson, D. A., Womble, L. G., Zucker, N. L., Reas, D. L., White, M. A., Blouin, D. C., & Greenway, F. (2000). Body image assessment for obesity (BIA-O): Development and validation of a new procedure. *International Journal of Obesity, 24*(10), 1326–1332. https://doi.org/10.1038/sj.ijo.0801367.

Further reading

American Medical Association. (2023). AMA adopts new policy clarifying role of BMI as a measure in medicine (Report of the Council on Science and Public Health). AMA House of Delegates. https://www.ama-assn.org/press-center/press-releases/ama-adopts-new-policy-clarifying-role-bmi-measure-medicine

Brambilla, P., Bedogni, G., Moreno, L. A., Goran, M. I., Gutin, B., Fox, K. R., ... Pietrobelli, A. (2006). Crossvalidation of anthropometry against magnetic resonance imaging for the assessment of visceral and subcutaneous adipose tissue in children. *International Journal of Obesity, 30*(1), 23–30. https://doi.org/10.1038/sj.ijo.0803136.

Coifman, K. G., Disabato, D. J., Aurora, P., Seah, T. H. S., Mitchell, B., Simonovic, N., Foust, J. L., Sidney, P. G., Thompson, C. A., & Taber, J. M. (2021). What drives preventive health behavior during a global pandemic? Emotion and worry. *Annals of Behavioral Medicine, 55*(8), 791–804. https://doi.org/10.1093/abm/kaab048.

Eslami, M., Pourghazi, F., Khazdouz, M., Tian, J., Pourrostami, K., Esmaeili-Abdar, Z., Ejtahed, H. S., & Qorbani, M. (2022). Optimal cut-off value of waist circumference-to-height ratio to predict central obesity in children and adolescents: A systematic review and meta-analysis of diagnostic studies. *Frontiers in Nutrition, 9*, 985319. https://doi.org/10.3389/fnut.2022.985319.

Hampl, S. E., Hassink, S. G., Skinner, A. C., Armstrong, S. C., Barlow, S. E., Bolling, C. F., ... Okechukwu, K. (2023). Clinical practice guideline for the evaluation and treatment of children and adolescents with obesity. *Pediatrics, 151*(2), e2022060640. https://doi.org/10.1542/peds.2022-060640.

Kim, J. Y., Shim, J. S., Kwon, O., Kim, J. S., & Jekal, Y. (2021). Distribution of waist-to-height ratio and cardiometabolic risk in children and adolescents: A population-based study. *Scientific Reports, 11*(1), 9503. https://doi.org/10.1038/s41598-021-88951-9.

Lawrence, S. E., Puhl, R. M., Watson, R. J., Schwartz, M. B., Lessard, L. M., & Foster, G. D. (2023). Family-based weight stigma and psychosocial health: A multinational comparison. *Obesity, 31*(6), 1666–1677. https://doi.org/10.1002/oby.23748.

Lessard, L. M., Watson, R. J., & Puhl, R. M. (2021). Weight-based victimization among sexual and gender minority adolescents: Experiences and psychosocial consequences. *Obesity, 29*(6), 1057–1066. https://doi.org/10.1002/oby.23150.

Nandy, S., & Svedberg, P. (2012). The composite index of anthropometric failure (CIAF): An alternative indicator for malnutrition in young children. In V. R. Preedy (Ed.). *Handbook of anthropometry: Physical measures of human form in health and disease* (pp. 127–137). Springer.

Neumark-Sztainer, D., Falkner, N., Story, M., Perry, C., Hannan, P. J., & Mulert, S. (2002). Weight-teasing among adolescents: Correlations with weight status and disordered eating behaviors. *International Journal of Obesity, 26*(1), 123–131. https://doi.org/10.1038/sj.ijo.0801853.

Puhl, R. M., Luedicke, J., & Heuer, C. A. (2011). Weight-based victimization toward overweight adolescents: Observations and reactions of peers. *Journal of School Health, 81*(11), 696–703. https://doi.org/10.1111/j.1746-1561.2011.00642.x.

Rodrigues, A. N., Abreu, G. R., Resende, R. S., Goncalves, W. L. S., & Moyses, M. R. (2016). A comparison between BMI, waist circumference, and waist-to-height ratio for identifying cardio-metabolic risk in children and adolescents. *PLoS One, 11*(2), e0148133. https://doi.org/10.1371/journal.pone.0148133.

Sharma, A. M., & Kushner, R. F. (2009). A proposed clinical staging system for obesity. *International Journal of Obesity, 33*(3), 289–295. https://doi.org/10.1038/ijo.2009.2.

Stunkard, A. J., Sørensen, T., & Schulsinger, F. (1983). Use of the Danish adoption register for the study of obesity and thinness. *Research Publications—Association for Research in Nervous and Mental Disease, 60*, 115–120.

Tanofsky-Kraff, M., Yanovski, S. Z., Schvey, N. A., Olsen, C. H., Gustafson, J., & Yanovski, J. A. (2009). A prospective study of loss of control eating for body weight gain in children at high risk for adult obesity. *International Journal of Eating Disorders, 42*(1), 26–30. https://doi.org/10.1002/eat.20580.

Tomiyama, A. J. (2014). Weight stigma is stressful: A review of evidence for the cyclic obesity/weight-based stigma model. *Appetite, 82*, 8–15. https://doi.org/10.1016/j.appet.2014.06.108.

Weiss, R., Dziura, J., Burgert, T. S., Tamborlane, W. V., Taksali, S. E., Yeckel, C. W., & Caprio, S. (2004). Obesity and the metabolic syndrome in children and adolescents. *New England Journal of Medicine, 350*(23), 2362–2374. https://doi.org/10.1056/NEJMoa031049.

Wells, J. C. K., & Fewtrell, M. S. (2006). Measuring body composition. *Archives of Disease in Childhood, 91*(7), 612–617. https://doi.org/10.1136/adc.2005.085522.

Yoo, E.-G. (2016). Waist-to-height ratio as a screening tool for obesity and cardiometabolic risk. *Korean Journal of Pediatrics, 59*(11), 425–431. https://doi.org/10.3345/kjp.2016.59.11.425.

Chapter 3

Stigmatization and coping as related to obesity

" Health inequalities do not arise by chance; they are shaped by the social and economic realities people live within."

Learning objectives

Upon completing this chapter, readers will be able to:
Explain the role of socioeconomic status in shaping adolescent obesity
Apply theoretical frameworks linking stigma, inequality, and coping processes
Analyse global evidence on SES-related patterns of obesity and psychosocial outcomes
Interpret the Indian context, including caste, class, and structural inequalities
Evaluate gender and intersectional differences in coping with stigma
Assess policy and intervention strategies addressing socioeconomic and psychosocial determinants

3.1 Introduction: framing socioeconomic status, stigma, and adolescent obesity

Socioeconomic status (SES) is a critical factor that has been consistently identified as a key determinant of health and well-being. In relation to adolescent obesity, SES is a robust and multidimensional factor. Education level, household income, parental occupation, and environmental conditions of living are all critical factors that influence and relate to adolescent obesity (Adler & Ostrove, 1999; Braveman et al., 2011). A critical foundation of social epidemiology is that health and disease are socially distributed; that is, the causes of poor health are not randomly distributed but are socially distributed. In this sense, it is critical to understand that adolescents are not made fat through any fault of their own but are embedded in environments that differentially influence their opportunities for a healthy lifestyle.

The relationship between SES and obesity has not been consistent across countries or across time. In high-income countries in Western Europe, North America, and Oceania, obesity has become inversely related to SES, where higher levels of overweight and obesity are consistently observed in the less affluent, less educated, and most disadvantaged populations. Subsequent population-based studies in the United States, the United Kingdom, and Australia have consistently confirmed this inverse gradient (OECD, 2019; Shrewsbury & Wardle, 2008), building on the foundational review by Sobal & Stunkard (1989), which first established the pattern in high-income countries. In contrast, in many low- and middle-income countries (LMICs), the relationship was traditionally positive, with obesity more common in the more affluent and better educated populations with greater access to calorie-dense diets and sedentary occupations. However, as Popkin (1993, 2015) has described in his framework of the nutrition transition, the dramatic economic development, urbanization, and transformation of the global food system have resulted in the progressive disappearance of the positive gradient in LMICs. Indeed, in many LMICs, the most dramatic increases in overweight are now occurring in the less affluent populations, whose food environment has become saturated with ultra-processed foods, while the opportunity for safe physical activity remains extremely limited (Jaacks et al., 2019; Ng et al., 2014).

This change is best exemplified in the case of India. Today, India is faced with the challenge of having some of the highest levels of undernutrition among children in the world while also having some of the fastest-growing levels of overweight and obesity among all populations and all ages, including adolescents (International Institute for Population Sciences IIPS & ICF, 2021). This "double burden of malnutrition"—in which undernutrition and overnutrition occur simultaneously in populations, households, and even individuals over the course of their life course—characterizes the nutrition environment in which Indian adolescents are born and in which they develop (Black et al., 2013). In the

Psychology of Obesity. DOI: https://doi.org/10.1016/B978-0-443-27797-9.00001-4

economically booming cities of Delhi, Mumbai, Kolkata, and Bengaluru, the environment has been such that fast food chains, sugary drinks, electronic entertainment, and long academic sessions compete with the scarcity of recreational spaces and the economic constraints of the family. In the rural areas too, though the environment is characterized by food insecurity and the drudgery of working in the fields, the penetration of packaged snacks and fried and carbonated beverages is now widespread and aggressive in the pursuit of the youth market (Gupta et al., 2012).

Apart from the physiological consequences of weight increase, the psychosocial consequences of obesity in adolescents in India are also of great importance, which mainstream public health approaches have taken a longer time to recognize. Body size in the context of obesity has a number of meanings that are not fixed or essential; it has been influenced by a variety of cultural, gender, caste, class, and globalizing influences on the concept of thinness and beauty. In the context of the middle class in India, body size has also become a marker of discipline, self-control, and social competitiveness, where the obese adolescent may be seen as undisciplined, indulgent, or even academically unmotivated (Puhl & Heuer, 2009). In the context of the rural or the less affluent, the obese adolescent may be seen as economically or physically well-nourished, but even this may be changing with the increasing influence of the esthetic standards of the urban or the globalized. These different meanings of obesity have resulted in the stigmatization of obese adolescents, a process in which a person or a group of people is devalued by others in society in response to a stigmatizing attribute or characteristic (Goffman, 1963; Puhl & Heuer, 2009).

3.1.1 Research design

The present investigation aimed to empirically explore such dynamics among late adolescence (18–21 years) and young adults (22–25 years) in Kolkata, West Bengal. A mixed-methods approach involving standardized psychological assessments and qualitative interviews is used. Participants were selected from diverse socioeconomic backgrounds using Kuppuswamy's socioeconomic status scale. Participants were also selected based on body weight status (obese: BMI $\geq$ 30 kg/m^2 and nonobese: BMI $<$ 30 kg/m^2), gender, and developmental stages. Coping responses were measured using the Coping Response Inventory. This measure distinguishes between approach-focused and avoidance-focused coping across cognitive and behavioral dimensions. In addition, family environment, eating attitudes, body image, and psychological adjustment were also measured to obtain a comprehensive understanding of how SES influences exposure to obesity-related stigma and facilitates or impedes coping responses. This chapter attempts to synthesize existing global and Indian evidence on how SES influences adolescent obesity stigma, how stigma is experienced across SES and cultures, and how adolescents cope with obesity stigma when they experience differential access to resources. This chapter is based on existing theoretical frameworks on social epidemiology, life course theory, stigma theory, and stress-coping theory; epidemiological studies; qualitative and mixed-methods studies conducted in India and similar cultural contexts; and the results of this investigation that combined anthropometric assessments, standardized psychological assessments, and qualitative interviews to understand the multidimensional experience of adolescent obesity across SES in urban India. Essentially, this chapter argues that adolescent obesity cannot be understood, measured, and addressed without considering its social reality.

3.2 Theoretical frameworks linking socioeconomic status, stigma, and coping

3.2.1 Social determinants of health

The social determinants of health (SDH) framework, developed by the World Health Organization Commission on SDH (CSDH Commission on Social Determinants of Health, 2008), synthesized in Marmot (2005) and more recently in Braveman & Gottlieb (2014), posits that "the social determinants of health are the conditions in which people are born, grow, live, work, and age. The social determinants shape our opportunities in life, our circumstances, our experiences, and our biology." The conditions in which we are born, grow, live, work, and age are not distributed equally in society; rather, they are distributed unequally in society based on social hierarchies like class, gender, caste, and ethnicity. According to the SDH framework, the mediating pathways through which adolescent obesity might be affected include economic constraints on access to healthy foods, environmental constraints on opportunities for physical activity, chronic psychosocial stress caused by poverty and social marginalization, which in turn influence appetite regulation and metabolism, and low levels of health literacy to access relevant information to prevent obesity.

Similar to the SDH framework is Link & Phelan (1995) theory of fundamental social causes, which posits that SES acts as a "fundamental cause" of health disparities because "the social class resources available to individuals are not tied to any particular set of disease risks; rather, they are available to be applied to whatever disease risks are salient at any particular time in history." The rich have the social class resources to protect themselves from obesity risk through money, knowledge, social connections, and time, whereas the poor do not. This understanding is particularly relevant in the context of understanding the persistence of inequalities in obesity rates, which in many cases have not only persisted but have also widened despite decades of public health interventions focused on changing individual-level behaviors related to obesity. Drewnowski & Specter (2004) offer particularly compelling economic evidence in this context as well: the fact that "energy-dense, nutrient-poor foods provide the most 'calories per dollar' compared to fruits, vegetables, lean proteins" makes for a particularly rational economic response in the face of constrained household budgets.

The concept of "obesogenic environments" developed by Swinburn et al. (1999) and further developed in subsequent research in the domain of urban health extends the SDH framework to the environments in which adolescents' physical activity is constrained by the physical environment. Lack of parks, street lighting, foot paths, as well as high crime rates in neighborhoods, limit adolescents' physical activity, particularly girls whose physical activity is constrained by their families on the basis of safety (Gordon-Larsen et al., 2000; Sallis et al., 2012). Similarly, the fact that many adolescents in rapidly urbanizing India are constrained in their food choices by the relative absence of fresh fruits and vegetables in their neighborhoods, as well as the relative abundance of fast food outlets, further constrains their choice in this domain as well.

3.2.2 Life course theory

The theory of life course has been proposed by Elder (1998) and Ben-Shlomo & Kuh (2002), which examines how life experiences and exposures influence each successive life stage. In the context of teenage obesity, several key processes can be identified. The developmental origins of health and disease (DOHaD) hypothesis proposed by Barker (1998) shows how intrauterine undernutrition leads to fetal metabolic adaptations favoring fat storage and resistance to insulin, which was advantageous in an underfed world but now acts as an adverse reaction to an overfed world (Hales & Barker, 2001). In India, where undernutrition and anemia among women are endemic, teenagers begin life with low birth weight and metabolic vulnerability, making them especially likely to gain weight in response to changes in food availability in childhood and adolescence (Victora et al., 2008). Critically, when these trajectories result in adolescent obesity, they do so in a social context in which weight gain is attributed to personal failure rather than developmental history. This misattribution is the very foundation of weight stigma: adolescents who become obese through pathways rooted in intrauterine programming and early-life food insecurity are then subjected to the same social condemnation as those whose weight reflects voluntary behavioral choices—an inequity that life course theory makes visible and that any adequate stigma-reduction intervention must address.

The life course approach also emphasizes the cumulative effect of risk. Nutritional deficiencies in infancy lead to compromised immune response and cognitive development; compromised cognitive development leads to compromised educational outcomes; compromised educational outcomes lead to compromised economic potential in adulthood. Each link in this chain is shaped by, and reinforces, socioeconomic inequality. For young people currently living through the nutritional transition in India, weight gain is not simply the result of the present moment; rather, it is the culmination of all the moments that have come before. An intervention that only seeks to change the young person's present dietary behaviors, without taking account of all the moments that have led up to them, is unlikely to have any significant effect.

From a psychological point of view, the life course approach to stigma highlights the ways in which early experiences of stigma can add up to form adult self-concepts. Teenagers who experienced stigma in primary school because of their weight continue to experience stigma in secondary school; teenagers who experienced stigma at home because of their weight continue to experience stigma in terms of narratives of bodily inadequacy. The life stage of adolescence is marked by sensitivity to peer evaluation, identity formation, and self-concept development—precisely the life stage at which stigma is likely to be experienced, especially in terms of weight.

3.2.3 Stigma and attribution theory

The seminal work by Goffman (1963) defined stigma in terms of a process of social disqualification, wherein a stigmatizing attribute transforms a fully formed person into a discredited one. Obesity is one of the most stigmatized conditions in modern societies and is differentiated from all other stigmatizing attributes by the cultural belief that it is controllable through factors like diet and exercise and is therefore a reflection of personal moral failure (Puhl & Heuer, 2009). Weiner's (1985) attribution theory explains this process by stating that negative outcomes are more likely to elicit anger and blame if they are attributed to factors that are controllable. Crandall (1994) has applied this theory to explain weight stigma by showing that antifat biases are strongly predicted by perceptions of weight control.

The negative consequences of weight stigma have been consistently found across different populations and research designs. A comprehensive review by Puhl & Heuer (2009) of a decade's worth of research found that weight stigma is associated with depression, anxiety, poor self-esteem, body image issues, social exclusion, disordered eating, exercise avoidance, and reduced healthcare seeking. Tomiyama (2014) has developed a cyclic obesity-weight stigma (COWS) theory wherein weight stigma is shown to increase cortisol levels through activation of the hypothalamic-pituitary-adrenal axis and subsequently increase weight through unhealthy eating habits that are used as a coping mechanism for negative emotions and exacerbate the original weight problem that caused stigma in the first place. This biological process has been supported by experimental studies wherein subjects are exposed to weight stigma, and their cortisol and eating responses are measured. This shows that not only is weight stigma psychologically damaging, but it is also physiologically active.

For youth, these sources of weight stigma include peers, family, teachers, and mass media. For youth, weight stigma can be experienced through teasing, exclusion, and bullying by peers; well-intentioned, but damaging, commentary by family members about diet, appearance, and weight; weight stigma by teachers, including public weighing and judgmental language; and weight stigma in mass media, including pervasive thinness ideals that render larger bodies completely invisible or negative. Puhl et al. (2013) used a study of US youth and found that "up to 64% of youth with obesity reported experiencing weight-based victimization in schools, with negative effects on academic engagement, school belonging, and physical activity participation." Crosnoe & Muller (2004) used Add Health, a National Longitudinal Study of Adolescent to Adult Health, and found that overweight youth were significantly less likely to be engaged in school-based extracurricular activities, a pattern that has long-term consequences for social capital.

3.2.4 Stress and coping frameworks

Lazarus & Folkman's (1984) transactional model of stress and coping provides a framework for understanding how youth cope with weight stigma. According to Lazarus and Folkman, coping is "the cognitive and behavioral efforts to manage demands that tax or exceed personal resources, including those required to protect individuals without inflicting harm." Coping is a cognitive and behavioral process that is generally classified in terms of two dimensions: problem-focused coping and emotion-focused coping, and approach coping and avoidant coping. A third dimension of coping is meaning-based coping, in which a reappraisal of the stressor occurs that reduces its subjective threat.

The crucial idea of the transactional model for this chapter is that the choice of coping strategy is not entirely dependent on individual personality traits and preferences; rather, it is dependent on individual resource availability in society. In problem-focused coping, for example, individuals need access to resources such as gyms, counseling centers, sports programs, and support groups that might be readily available to higher SES adolescents but largely out of reach for their disadvantaged counterparts. Emotion-focused coping mechanisms such as ruminative thoughts, emotional eating habits, and avoidance behaviors might not necessarily reflect emotional unfitness; rather, they might reflect a lack of access to resources that can help individuals cope with problems. In a study done by Puhl & Brownell (2006), adolescents who were victims of weight-teasing behaviors were found to exhibit unhealthy weight control behaviors, binge eating habits, and avoidance behaviors significantly if they lacked supportive adult relationships.

3.3 Global evidence: socioeconomic status–obesity patterns, stigma, and psychosocial consequences

3.3.1 The shifting global socioeconomic status–obesity gradient

In the past three decades, comparative epidemiological studies have shown that there has been a significant shift in the social distribution of obesity in the world. A study carried out by Monteiro et al. (2004) on the trends of obesity in Brazilian women over two decades found that obesity had shifted from being more prevalent among higher-income women in the past to being more prevalent among lower-income women in the more recent period as the country moved through the nutrition transition process. This has been replicated in various other LMICs (Abarca-Gómez et al., 2017; Popkin, 2015). A more recent study carried out by the noncommunicable diseases (NCD) Risk Factor Collaboration in 2016 on the trends in height and BMI in 200 countries between 1975 and 2014 confirmed that there has been an increase in BMI in almost all countries in the world. In the past two decades, the greatest increases in BMI have been observed in LMICs (NCD Risk Factor Collaboration, 2016). A study carried out by Ng et al. (2014) found that between 1980 and 2013, the number of overweight and obese individuals in developing countries almost doubled.

Several structural factors account for this convergence. First, the global food system, driven by trade liberalization, the rise of multinational food corporations, and aggressive marketing of ultra-processed foods, has driven down the relative cost of energy-dense foods compared to whole foods, rendering unhealthy diets economically rational for resource-constrained households (Hawkes, 2006; Moodie et al., 2013). Second, urbanization in LMICs has led to a high-density population that is exposed to a built environment designed for motorized, rather than pedestrian, activity, resulting in lower overall daily energy expenditure without a compensatory reduction in daily caloric intake (Ng & Popkin, 2012).

Third, the rise of digital technologies in leisure activities has led to a replacement of physically active leisure by screen-based leisure, a trend that has accelerated in recent times since the advent of smartphones and data services (Boyland & Whalen, 2015). These factors, in summary, account for what Swinburn et al. (2011) term the global syndemic of obesity, undernutrition, and climate change, all of which are linked to a common set of structural factors.

3.3.2 Psychosocial dimensions: stigma, mental health, and school engagement

Weight stigma cuts across the socioeconomic spectrum but has socioeconomic gradients in both the nature and impact of the stigma. In high-income countries, where the discourse on obesity is dominated by the narrative of individual responsibility (Guthman, 2011), weight stigma in the context of obesity has a powerful class component in which the weight of the less privileged in society is seen as a product of laziness, lack of discipline, or cultural backwardness (Puhl & Heuer, 2009; Saguy & Riley, 2005), thereby reinforcing class stratification in the name of health (Puhl & Heuer, 2009). Young people in less privileged socioeconomic positions experience a compounded stigma in which the stigma of weight stigma combines with socioeconomic stigma. Eisenberg et al. (2012) used longitudinal data from the Project EAT study of over 2500 adolescents in the USA to examine the longitudinal outcomes of weight stigma in adolescents and found that weight teasing was a significant predictor of bulimic behaviors, fruit and vegetable consumption, and depression five years later, moderated by the presence or absence of social support from parents and peers.

Longitudinal studies in the school setting provide the most robust evidence of the impact of weight stigma on the behavior and academic outcomes of adolescents. Crosnoe & Muller (2004) used the Add Health study to examine the longitudinal outcomes of weight stigma in adolescents and found that overweight adolescents had lower grade point averages, less social integration, and reduced likelihood of aspirations to go to college five years later, in part through the mechanism of social networks in which the overweight adolescents had fewer close friends, fewer extracurricular activities, and more social exclusion. Neumark-Sztainer et al. (2004) used the Project EAT study of adolescents to examine the longitudinal outcomes of weight stigma in adolescents and found that weight teasing by peers and family at baseline predicted lower physical activity, sedentary leisure activities, and lower self-esteem five years later, independent of BMI change. This illustrates the self-perpetuating effect of stigma in which the overweight adolescents are less likely to engage in physical activity and thereby less likely to be in a supportive environment that would promote a healthy weight status.

The psychosocial aspects of obesity stigmatization in LMICs are further complicated by cultural ambivalence. Brewis (2011), in her metaanalysis of cross-cultural studies examining cultural ideals of the body, observed that in transitional societies, cultural ideals of the body as plumper, as a sign of health, prosperity, and fertility, coexist alongside the thin ideals promoted by globalization. Teenagers in transitional societies are thus confronted by competing normative systems, which could lead to self-conflict, self-surveillance, and self-consciousness. Swami et al. (2010), in their cross-cultural comparison of Malaysian and British women, observed that although both groups reported dissatisfaction with their bodies, the cultural ideals to which the groups compared their bodies were different. Although the psychosocial impact of weight stigmatization varies across cultures, the consequences in terms of self-esteem, body dissatisfaction, and emotional distress are similar across cultures.

3.3.3 Gender, ethnicity, and intersectionality

Weight stigmatization is not experienced by all groups in the same way. In various studies across cultures, it has been consistently observed that girls and women experience more severe weight stigmatization compared to boys and men (Frederick et al., 2014; Puhl & Latner, 2007). McLaren (2007), in her systematic analysis of the relationship between SES and obesity in various gender groups across the world, observed that the relationship between SES and obesity was most significant in high-income societies for women. McLaren observed that the relationship between SES and obesity in high-income societies was complicated by the interplay between gender, caregiving responsibilities, and labor force participation. In many cultures, the bodies of girls and women are surveilled as a reflection of family honor, marital potential, and personal virtue, making the stigmatization of weight gain particularly significant in girls and women.

In addition, ethnicity and race introduce further dimensions of inequality. Kumanyika (2008) has documented that there are persistent racial and ethnic disparities in obesity, dietary quality, and physical activity in the United States. These disparities are a result of structural racism, including differential effects of residential segregation, differential quality of schools, differential policing of public spaces, and differential poverty. Though the context is different, similar structures of caste-based inequality in India follow similar pathways. For instance, marginalized castes in India experience differential access to a variety of diets, differential access to spaces for physical activity, differential quality of schools, and differential quality of healthcare that is nonstigmatizing. Subramanian et al. (2011) documented that there are significant caste-based inequalities in child anthropometrics in India, where scheduled caste and scheduled tribe children experience the highest burden of undernutrition. These inequalities, in turn, translate into differential risk of obesity in later adolescence and adulthood through the DOHaD pathway.

3.4 Socioeconomic dimensions of adolescent obesity in the Indian context

3.4.1 The nutritional paradox: double burden of malnutrition

One of the most complex nutritional scenarios in the world is found in India. In the fifth round of the National Family Health Survey (NFHS-5), conducted by the International Institute for Population Sciences in all 28 states and 8 union territories of India between 2019 and 2021, the following dramatic levels of undernutrition were reported: "approximately 35.5% of children under the age of 5 years were stunted, 19.3% wasted, and 32.1% underweight." In contrast, "overweight and obesity among adolescents aged 15–19 years continue to rise and are higher among urban-dwelling and the wealthiest individuals." In the Comprehensive National Nutrition Survey (CNNS) conducted between 2016 and 2018 by the Ministry of Health and Family Welfare with support from UNICEF, the following prevalence of overweight and obesity among Indian adolescents aged 10–19 years was reported: "Overall prevalence of overweight and obesity among 10–19 years is 4.8%, with higher prevalence in urban areas and among the higher wealth quintiles."

Such a dual burden is not just an abstract concept; it is an actual contradiction for many Indian families. In fact, Mohanty et al. (2024), in their research based on mother-child dyads from NFHS data, observed that in 7.7% of such families, there was an overweight/obese mother cooccurring with an undernourished child. The phenomenon is an expression of the intergenerational complexity in nutritional status, as conceptualized by Victora et al. (2008) and incorporated in the DOHaD concept. The rates of overweight and obesity among mothers have risen from 20.6% to 33.2% between NFHS-4 (2015-16) and NFHS-5, while undernutrition in children remains at emergency levels. Singh et al. (2024) have demonstrated through an analysis of NFHS-5 data that not only has the rise in overweight/obesity far outpaced reductions in underweight, but it has actually led to an overall increase in child undernutrition. These results have serious repercussions for how teenage obesity is measured, monitored, and managed in India. The usual frameworks for undernutrition and overnutrition separately are not appropriate for dual burden populations.

3.4.2 Urban adolescents: affluence, academic pressure, and obesogenic lifestyles

In India's growing metropolitan centers, adolescents from better-income families live in an environment that is characterized by educational competition, digital connectivity, and easy access to commercial food. School hours are long, and homework is heavy. In addition, there is growing dependence on digital media for both academic and recreational activities. This has resulted in a shortage of time for unstructured physical activities. In their study of urban Indian adolescents' physical inactivity, Misra & Khurana (2008) found that urban Indian adolescents, particularly those attending private schools, were spending significantly fewer hours per week on physical activities than recommended by the WHO. In addition, sedentary leisure activities were growing rapidly with household income. This is because access to resources and cultural capital is matched only by a corresponding shortage of time and physical space. In this context, urban Indian adolescents' food environment is also a critical factor that influences their food habits. In recent times, food delivery apps and packaged food brands have proliferated in urban Indian cities. This has resulted in a food environment that is characterized by the availability and commercialization of food that is highly calorie-dense. In this context, food is not only readily available to urban Indian adolescents but is also marketed to them via digital media. Gupta et al. (2012) conducted a multicity study of urban Indian adolescents' food habits. In this study, they found that urban Indian adolescents' food habits were such that they were consuming more fast food, sugary drinks, and packaged food items. These food habits were more pronounced among adolescents from higher SES households. In this context, urban Indian adolescents were spending more time on screens and engaging in fewer sports activities. In spite of possessing adequate nutritional knowledge, they were constrained by time and the food environment.

Weight stigma in this context takes on a particular form. The body size becomes intelligible as an indicator of discipline, self-regulation, and conformity to ideals promoted by media, peer groups, and parental aspirations. Overweight teenagers in such settings not only face ridicule from peers but also experience micro-regulation by teachers who read body size as an indicator of academic engagement, and by parents whose concern for weight is embedded in broader concerns for social mobility and competitive success. Girls in particular are subjected to extreme levels of surveillance, where weight is directly correlated with marriage prospects and social respectability. The psychological effects—self-consciousness, social withdrawal, avoidance of physical activities in public, and in some instances, food restriction and bingeing—are consistent with findings from the international literature on stigma effects.

3.4.3 Rural and lower-income adolescents: deprivation, aspiration, and emerging risks

Rural and lower-income Indian adolescents experience a new set of structural limitations that are equally critical. While food insecurity, poor diet diversity, irregular eating habits that are dictated by parental work schedules, and micronutrient deprivation continue to plague this population, Jaacks et al. (2019) and CNNS studies reveal that this population is also witnessing rising rates of overweight that cannot be accounted for by rising nutritional security. This is because ultra-processed foods have now been introduced in rural India via informal networks of food distribution. These foods are bought in small quantities that are within the purchasing power of rural populations. Moreover, ultra-processed foods are associated with modernity and aspirations of urban cultural identity. Therefore, they are attractive to rural adolescents seeking to signal upward social mobility. In fact, Gupta et al. (2012) reveal that ultra-processed foods are bought in quantities that are perceived to signal aspirations of upward mobility. In rural India, adolescents experience declining energy expenditure because of the mechanization of agriculture and changing household occupations that do not demand child labor. In addition to this, rural adolescent girls experience greater restrictions on mobility because of cultural prescriptions of modesty. These restrictions combine with rising energy intake among this population because of ultra-processed foods to create a state of energy disequilibrium that results in gradual weight gain.

While the social significance of weight in the context of the rural community is less clear than in urban areas, it is changing quickly. A family that has long associated a heavier weight with good health and prosperity is now exposed through television, mobile internet access, and social media to a globalized ideal of thinness that equates a heavier weight with bad health, lack of discipline, and unattractiveness. Youth in this situation talk about the contradictions and confusions of being praised by the older generation for their weight while being teased by their peers in school who have been influenced by urban esthetic norms. This is the kind of normative complexity that creates a new kind of psychosocial stress that is not visible in the usual epidemiological studies of stress and mental health outcomes. In the data collected in the current investigation, there were clear socioeconomic gradients in the experience of stigma and the use of coping strategies among obese youth in Kolkata. While there was clearly some experience of weight stigma among the higher SES youth in the study, there were significant differences in the use of problem-focused coping strategies such as information seeking, structured fitness strategies, and professional support among the higher SES youth in comparison with the lower SES youth. While the higher SES youth talked about the use of gyms, nutritionists, school counselors, and family support in buffering the experience of weight stigma and teasing and exclusion by peers, there was also a significant experience of performance pressure and appearance scrutiny, and the ideal of perfection that had significant psychological consequences, particularly among the girls in elite private schools. In contrast, the lower SES youth talked about the experience of using the fewest number of coping strategies and the predominance of withdrawal from social situations, the experience of stigmatizing comments as necessary, and the use of humor as a way of coping with weight stigma, teasing, and exclusion by peers. Family environments in lower SES households did not offer emotional support for weight-related stress, and parental reactions tended more toward moralizing commentary or acceptance than problem-solving orientation. These findings are consistent with Lazarus & Folkman's (1984) transactional model of coping, in that coping strategies are influenced by more than simply appraisal of stress, including actual availability of resources for coping.

3.4.4 Caste, gender, and cultural determinants of body image

Adolescent obesity in India is also subject to the influences of various intersecting social hierarchy factors that extend beyond the realm of economic class. In the Indian caste system, the position of individuals in the hierarchy not only defines their economic circumstances but also the way they view the world and the issues of food and the human body. In the Indian subcontinent, dietary norms among the Indian caste community restrict the variety of foodstuffs that can be consumed and the sharing of food with other members of the community. In the study by Subramanian et al. (2011), it was established that there are significant gradients in the nutrition of the Indian subcontinent's children even when the economic position of the household is controlled for. This indicates the significant impact of the social position of the members of the Indian community on their nutrition.

In terms of the intersection of gender norms with other factors such as caste and class position, the experience of girls is particularly complex. In multiple regions of India, the restriction of female mobility creates a lack of access to outdoor recreation and sporting opportunities where physical activity might naturally occur. Norms of modesty, domestic competence, and restraint define the ways in which girls are allowed to move through the public arena and in which their bodies are judged. Weight stigma among girls is often subsumed under broader judgments of marriageability, family honor, and community respectability, such that a girl who is overweight is told she is reducing her marriage prospects or failing to meet the appearance demands of her family's social position. These are judgments made by family members who may be acting in good faith and who may be attempting to assist the girl in her development. They are judgments that induce a level of shame and body discontent that is different in kind from the weight teasing experienced by girls in other nations and more likely to be the focus of international discussion.

Boys experience weight stigma in India through different but equally significant routes. Weight teasing of boys is often framed in terms of physical competence, athletic ability, and masculine strength, such that being overweight violates the implicit assumption of physical robustness that is so deeply embedded in the Indian cultural context. While girls may be more likely than boys to experience weight stigma in terms of marriageability and family honor, boys may experience weight stigma in terms of athletic and masculine strength. While the experience of weight stigma among girls may be more likely to be expressed through less visible routes than the humor, aggression, and dismissiveness of boys, the emotional impact of weight stigma is significant and often hidden behind the mask of social demands for masculine strength (Puhl & Latner, 2007). Boys' weight stigma is less likely than girls' weight stigma to be acknowledged in family and school settings and is less likely to be the focus of support interventions.

3.5 Coping strategies, gender, and intersectional vulnerabilities

3.5.1 Coping across socioeconomic groups: resource differential and strategy selection

The coping strategies that are available to adolescents in dealing with weight stigma are significantly influenced by the structural resources that are provided by their socioeconomic environments. For instance, for those from more affluent backgrounds, a variety of coping strategies may be available. They may be able to exercise in a gym, participate in a fitness program, seek counseling, or associate with groups of peers who value healthy lifestyles. These resources, of course, do not necessarily protect individuals from the psychological effects of stigma, since those same environments that provide resources are environments that are very competitive in terms of body image.

Research on coping styles in Indian urban settings generally supports this pattern of differential resources. The adolescents in this study from wealthier backgrounds reported problem-focused strategies such as exercise, information seeking, and talking to trusted adults, in addition to emotion-focused strategies such as self-exploration and meaning-making. At the same time, maladaptive coping styles such as perfectionism, dietary restriction, disordered eating, and feelings of guilt after violating dietary restrictions were also evident in this group. These findings support international research suggesting that resources mitigate but do not completely remove stigma's adverse effects on mental health.

Among lower-income adolescents, structural barriers limited coping strategies. Gym memberships, counseling services, and sports programs were not accessible. There was no familial support for weight-related issues. Even when family members did comment on weight issues, it was not in an encouraging way. Under these conditions, three types of dominant coping styles were evident from qualitative data. These were withdrawal, normalization, and humor. Withdrawal from social events, sports activities, school functions, and public places where body visibility leads to stigma provided short-term relief from immediate stigma but led to long-term social withdrawal and restricted developmental opportunities. Normalization was also the process whereby stigmatizing comments or experiences became gradually accepted as part of normal social life, or in other words, whereby negative social judgments were incorporated into self-concept. Humor, especially self-deprecating humor, was used as a social coping mechanism to ensure social connection with peers while deflecting potentially stigmatizing teasing, at the expense of self-stigma and not allowing any genuine engagement with underlying emotional distress.

3.5.2 Avoidance: mechanisms, developmental consequences, and systemic dimensions

Avoidance as a coping mechanism needs to be examined in greater detail due to its far-reaching effects beyond the social situation in which it is used to cope with stigmatizing experiences. When adolescents avoid social situations in which their bodily appearance might be subject to negative social judgment—by not wanting to engage in sports, by choosing to sit at the back in school cafeterias, by not wanting to socialize, by not wanting to be in group photographs—these cumulative actions lead to a progressively restricted social environment. The school setting, which is both the locus for academic learning and the locus for social development in adolescence, becomes a place where threat rather than opportunity defines the social environment. The adolescent who uses avoidance as a coping mechanism might have academic skills—might have an intact intellectual engagement with school life—while losing social development, social experimentation, and social collaboration, which are at the very center of adolescent development.

The physical health consequences of avoidance are also of great importance. Physical activity, such as organized sports, outdoor games, and even random movements in the corridors of schools and in the streets, is precisely the area where stigmatized adolescents are most likely to abstain. In areas where recreational spaces are already limited and where girls are further restricted in their mobility, the abstention eliminates the most accessible option for the expenditure of energy. Paradoxically, the stigma related to larger body types prevents participation in the activity that would most effectively contribute to a healthy weight status, creating a vicious circle in which stigma leads to sedentary behavior that further aggravates the weight-related status that originally caused the stigma (Puhl & Brownell, 2006; Warschburger & Zuba, 2023).

Longitudinal studies also provide evidence for the developmental consequences of stigma-driven avoidance. Warschburger & Zuba (2023), in a prospective study of 1381 children followed up over six years, found that there was a mutual relationship between weight teasing and BMI z-score, where weight teasing predicted subsequent weight increase, and weight increase predicted subsequent weight teasing, confirming the experimentally derived vicious circle described by Tomiyama (2014). Eisenberg et al. (2012) used the longitudinal Project EAT study to examine the consequences of weight-related victimization in adolescence, finding that baseline victimization predicted reduced levels of physical activity, increased levels of sedentary screen-based activity, and body dissatisfaction five years later, independent of weight status change.

3.5.3 Internalized stigma: self-concept, shame, and identity

The most damaging coping failure may be the internalization of stigmatizing messages, where the adolescent develops a self-concept that reflects the negative evaluation by others. Internalized weight stigma involves the adoption of negative stereotypes about one's own body weight, leading to chronic shame that differs in kind from the transient shame or embarrassment of the stigma event itself. Durso & Latner (2008) developed and validated the weight bias internalisation scale (WBIS) and found that internalized weight stigma was linked to lower self-esteem, depression, and psychological well-being, independent of the experience of stigma itself, thereby confirming that it constitutes a unique psychological risk factor in its own right.

In the qualitative data collected for this research, internalization of stigma was evidenced by characteristic patterns of behavior. For example, adolescents spoke of changing their public behaviors to conceal their bodies from view by wearing loose clothing to hide their physical appearance, not volunteering for roles that would place their bodies in public view, and engaging in preemptive self-blame as a means of managing how they might be viewed by others. These are all evidence of a solidification of negative evaluation of their bodies into a stable self-concept that guides perception, attribution, and expectation. For girls in this research, internalization of stigma was evidenced by a preoccupation with how their bodies might be viewed by others in public spaces and a constant sense of their bodies rendering them unworthy of participation in public social spheres. These phenomenological experiences are consistent with Fredrickson & Roberts (1997) objectification theory, which suggests that internalization of external gazes and perceptions of one's own body by one's self is a self-objectification experience that is characterized by a preoccupation with one's physical appearance and is associated with high levels of body shame, proprioceptive unawareness, and impaired cognitive performance.

3.5.4 The role of schools and families in mediating stigma

Schools and families are simultaneously sources of stigma and buffers against it. Research has consistently shown that schools are a critical site in which weight-based teasing and exclusion events most frequently occur (Puhl et al., 2013). However, schools are also a site of structural buffers that can protect youth from the negative psychological impacts of weight stigma if these are well utilized. It is not the presence or absence of these buffers that is critical; rather, it is their orientation towards a holistic understanding of adolescent well-being and their potential to unwittingly support a hierarchy of physical attractiveness and a narrative of personal responsibility that can create stigma.

Public weight measurement practices, including school-based BMI screening in the absence of privacy, family communication, and psychosocial support, are a iatrogenic risk known to have negative effects. According to Puhl & Latner (2007), in reviewing the evidence on school-based obesity prevention programs, they found that school-based obesity prevention programs not designed with explicit attention to weight stigma can lead to body dissatisfaction, weight teasing, and unhealthy weight control practices among students, especially those at higher risk. The Rashtriya Bal Swasthya Karyakram (RBSK) in India includes the screening of school-going children for various conditions, including overweight. However, the context in which these are implemented differs in terms of the attention to issues of privacy, sensitive communication, and postscreening psychosocial support. Without the implementation of protocols to ensure privacy in weight screening, sensitive communication to reduce stigma, and postscreening support, these programs are likely to result in iatrogenic harm greater than the potential benefit.

The role of family environments is also equally important. Discourse from parents, grandparents, and others within the family regarding weight can also have a profound impact on adolescents. Qualitative results of this study also reveal adolescents living in a world where comments about body size were a constant background evaluation that permeated every aspect of home life and caused chronic shame. A qualitative study conducted by Neumark-Sztainer et al. (2007) also found that family weight-related communication, such as parental encouragement of dieting, is related to disordered eating, low self-esteem, and increased BMI over time, even when controlling for initial weight status.

3.6 Policy implications and directions for intervention

3.6.1 From individual behavior to structural reform

The evidence synthesized in this chapter points consistently towards the futility of interventions that focus primarily on individual behavior change. This is because behavior-change interventions take place in a world where structural constraints are also at work. These interventions are like attempts to push water up a hill. More seriously, they can also reinforce the moral underpinnings of stigma if they do not recognize that obesity is caused by individual behavior. This can only add to the psychological burden that adolescents already carry (Guthman, 2011; Puhl & Heuer, 2009).

Evidence-informed structural interventions include fiscal policies such as taxes on ultra-processed foods and sugar-sweetened drinks. Systematic reviews of sugar-sweetened beverage taxes in several countries indicate a consistent decline in consumption, especially in lower SES groups, who are more responsive to price. Similarly, restrictions on advertising of foods to children, including digital advertising on social media, can reduce adolescents' exposure to commercialization of high-energy-dense foods. However, this policy intervention faces strong resistance from the food industry and requires sustained policy attention. Urban planning investments in physical activity spaces, including sports facilities, can increase lower SES adolescents' opportunities for physical activity, addressing one of the strongest contributors to SES-related obesity. In India, a crucial policy alignment opportunity exists in integrating obesity-related policy priorities within POSHAN 2.0 (PM's Overarching Scheme for Holistic Nourishment), the National Program for NCD, the RBSK school health screening program, the Rashtriya Kishor Swasthya Karyakram (RKSK) adolescent health program, and the National Education Policy 2020. RBSK's school-based screening infrastructure offers a direct entry point for identifying overweight adolescents in a systematic, population-level manner, while RKSK's adolescent health day platform provides an opportunity to integrate stigma-reduction counseling and coping skills training within existing community health infrastructure.

The results from this study also highlight several issues in intervention development. First, interventions for teenage obesity must include components addressing stigma and coping in addition to behavior. Interventions for teenage obesity, especially weight reduction interventions, without addressing these issues, can cause harm that outweighs the benefits. Interventions conducted in schools must include components for stigma reduction. These components include implementing antibullying policies in schools, especially those involving weight-related teasing, training teachers in nonstigmatizing styles of communication, and creating safe environments in physical education where teenagers can participate in physical activities without being bullied.

Second, interventions for teenage obesity must be designed in such a way that they take into account issues of inequality in society. Interventions conducted in communities must be able to cater to teenagers from lower SES backgrounds who have limited resources to cope with problems. Interventions conducted in communities can include activities such as creating recreational facilities in communities where teenagers can engage in physical activities. In addition, teenagers from lower SES backgrounds can be provided with subsidized services in fitness centers, nutritionists, and mental health professionals. These services can cater to inequalities in resource availability for coping.

Third, interventions for teenage obesity must be sensitive to both genders. Interventions conducted in communities for girls must include components for appearance pressure, objectification, marriageability, and family. These components include building resistance to societal pressure for beauty standards and building body competence independent of appearance. In addition, interventions conducted in communities for boys must include components for emotional distress. These components include creating environments where teenagers can express emotional distress and building healthy expressions of vulnerability. Both genders must be provided with components for critical analysis of digitally altered images in the media.

The formulation of school-based interventions aimed at addressing adolescent obesity necessitates a focus on weight stigma. In this context, evidence-based recommendations that can be made include ensuring that health measurements are conducted in a private setting and not in a group setting; training teachers and school health professionals in weight-neutral and nonstigmatizing communication; promoting physical education that is not performance-based but skill-based and enjoyment-based; and ensuring that mental health support is accessible and that school-based counseling addresses issues of body image, self-esteem, and weight stigma (Black et al., 2013; Puhl & Latner, 2007).

Improvements to the dietary environment of schools, which include improvements to the quality and nutritional adequacy of mid-day meals and elimination of high sugar and high fat foods from school canteens, and promoting food literacy through the school curriculum, are aimed at addressing one of the environments that significantly impacts adolescent diet and nutrition. These improvements are evidence-based and are particularly relevant to India's context, considering that millions of school-going children from lower socioeconomic backgrounds rely on mid-day meals as their primary source of nutrition (Alderman & Headey, 2017). In this context, it is critical that adolescents be involved in the formulation and implementation of these interventions to ensure that they are more relevant and that a sense of agency is cultivated to cope with their challenges.

3.6.2 Community and family engagement

Community-level interventions that go beyond the school setting are also crucial in reaching adolescents across the full spectrum of their environments. Youth programs, including sports, arts, and peer mentoring programs, offer adolescents from lower-income backgrounds a socially supportive environment in which to access the recreational opportunities, adult relationships, and peer communities that protect adolescents from the adverse effects of weight stigma. For youth programs to be most effective in this context, it is crucial that programs are designed as "inclusion" programs rather than "performance" programs, in which adolescents who are already socially withdrawn because of their SES are able to re-engage in social relationships without the fear of being judged by their peers.

Family-level interventions, which aim to enhance parents' skills in discussing weight and health issues in ways that avoid stigmatization, represent a relatively untapped area for intervention with great potential. In the context of family-based interventions for obesity, research has shown that parents' modeling of healthful eating, positive communication about food, and avoiding commentary on weight are more effective in promoting healthy development in adolescents than directive or critical approaches (Neumark-Sztainer et al., 2007). In the Indian context, family-level interventions will need to address the cultural importance parents hold in the family, gender differences in parent-child communication, and the cultural significance of food in parent-child relationships.

The language of public communication strategies must move away from attributing personal responsibility and moral blame, so prevalent in current health communication strategies on obesity. Communication strategies that emphasize the availability and accessibility of healthy foods, normalcy of body sizes and shapes, and factors that influence eating and exercise behavior can help to minimize stigma and maximize health. The deliberate exclusion of weight stigmatizing images and messages, including those of headless overweight body images that dehumanize individuals of larger body sizes, is a minimum requirement that has been endorsed by major professional bodies such as the American Medical Association and the European Association for the Study of Obesity (American Medical Association (AMA), 2023; Puhl & Heuer, 2009).

3.6.3 Measurement, monitoring, and equity-sensitive evaluation

Measurement and monitoring tools that are capable of measuring psychosocial factors such as stigma, coping, body image, and mental health, in addition to anthropometric factors, are necessary for developing evidence-based policy strategies for addressing adolescent obesity in India. National surveillance systems such as NFHS and CNNS provide reliable anthropometric data, but no validated tools for measuring stigma, internalized stigma, body image, and coping strategies are currently included. Incorporating psychosocial factors into national surveillance systems, including validated tools such as WBIS developed by Durso & Latner (2008), perception of teasing scale developed by Thompson et al. (1995), and pediatric quality of life inventory developed by Varni et al. (2001), is necessary for developing evidence-based intervention strategies for addressing stigma in relation to weight issues. What is more, it is necessary that monitoring tools be sensitive to equity issues, so that it is possible to evaluate whether intervention strategies are reducing or increasing inequalities in anthropometric and psychosocial outcomes in SES groups, castes, and genders.

The present study, while contributing to important understandings of SES-stigma-coping relations among Indian youth, also points to important avenues that remain unaddressed. Future studies employing longitudinal designs that monitor stigma exposure, coping, and psychosocial outcomes across adolescence and young adulthood could help clarify whether deficits are temporary developmental states or long-term vulnerabilities with health implications. These studies could also help clarify whether early interventions can interrupt the stigma-coping-health model or whether such relations are resilient across interventions.

Second, intervention studies that incorporate culturally adapted and stigma-informed interventions are needed. While evidence-based interventions such as cognitive-behavioral therapy for internalization of weight bias, acceptance and commitment therapy for body image problems, and family-based interventions that enhance positive communication styles are available, they need to be culturally adapted and piloted among Indian youth. Participatory studies that engage Indian youth, families, and communities in intervention design could help enhance cultural appropriateness while also cultivating intervention implementation capacity.

Third, qualitative studies that explore resilience factors such as resilient self-esteem despite obesity problems, supportive families despite resource constraints, and effective coping despite resource limitations could help identify avenues for strength-based interventions. Understanding how Indian youth cope with stigma exposure and remain psychologically healthy could inform interventions that emphasize resilience-building rather than deficit-reduction.

Finally, studies that explore intersectionality factors such as caste, religion, region, disability status, and other important dimensions of Indian stratification could help clarify relations between SES, gender, and weight status that influence stigma-coping relations. This could also help clarify India's complex social stratification.

3.7 Chapter summary: key arguments

1. SES is a critical factor that influences adolescent obesity exposure.
2. India's double burden of malnutrition, characterized by both undernutrition and overweight, is a consequence of inequalities in a nutritional transition that is progressing unevenly for different socioeconomic groups, regions, and genders.
3. Weight stigma is influenced by peer, family, school, and media sources, resulting in significant effects on mental health, social relationships, and health-related behavior, particularly for girls, lower SES youth, and marginalized caste groups.
4. Coping strategies are influenced by SES, where higher SES youth have more adaptive strategies, whereas lower SES youth mainly employ withdrawal, normalization, and humor, which may mitigate immediate problems but may exacerbate long-term consequences.
5. Interventions require addressing structural factors, stigma-informed schools, engaging communities and families, and monitoring for equality to ensure that interventions do not perpetuate, but mitigate, inequalities.

Key takeaways

1. SES is a critical factor that influences adolescent obesity exposure.
2. India's double burden of malnutrition, characterized by both undernutrition and overweight, is a consequence of inequalities in a nutritional transition that is progressing unevenly for different socioeconomic groups, regions, and genders.
3. Weight stigma is influenced by peer, family, school, and media sources, resulting in significant effects on mental health, social relationships, and health-related behavior, particularly for girls, lower SES youth, and marginalized caste groups.
4. Coping strategies are influenced by SES, where higher SES youth have more adaptive strategies, whereas lower SES youth mainly employ withdrawal, normalization, and humor, which may mitigate immediate problems but may exacerbate long-term consequences.

Glossary

Attribution theory: A theory of social psychology that describes how people attribute responsibility for outcomes. For weight stigma, this is exemplified by people believing that weight is controllable, resulting in blame and moral judgment.

Cyclic obesity-weight stigma (COWS) model: A model developed by Tomiyama (2014) that suggests that when people experience weight stigma, this leads to increased cortisol, maladaptive eating, and thus increased obesity, creating a cycle of stigma and obesity.

Developmental origins of health and disease (DOHaD): A theoretical framework, first described by Barker in 1998, that hypothesizes that intrauterine environments influence fetal development, leading to increased susceptibility to obesity and related health issues in later life.

Double burden of malnutrition: The presence of both undernutrition, including stunting, wasting, and micronutrient deficiencies, and overnutrition, including overweight and obesity, in a given country, community, household, or person's life course.

Fundamental causes theory: Link & Phelan (1995) idea that socioeconomic resources, such as money, knowledge, social resources, and time, are the "fundamental causes" of health because they can be applied to whatever health risks are most salient in the environment.

Internalized stigma: "The process by which individuals accept as their own the negative stereotypes and social evaluations associated with stigmatized social groups, which in turn leads to feelings of shame, poor self-esteem, and poor mental health."

Intersectionality: "An analytic approach, developed by Crenshaw (1989), which seeks to understand how multiple social identities, including class, caste, gender, race, and disability, intersect to produce unique, nonadditive patterns of privilege and disadvantage."

Life course theory: "Theoretical perspective examining how biological, psychological, and social risk factors accumulate across the life course to influence health outcomes at subsequent life stages, particularly focusing on sensitive periods and intergenerational transmission."

Nutrition transition: "Popkin's (1993) framework describing the shift in diets from grains and legumes to diets high in animal fat, sugar, and processed foods, driven by economic development, urbanization, and globalization of food systems."

Obesogenic environment: "Physical, social, and economic environments in which individuals are encouraged to gain weight by limiting access to healthy food, limiting opportunities for physical activity, and exposing individuals to chronic psychosocial stress" (Swinburn et al., 1999).

Problem-focused coping: "Coping mechanisms which aim to reduce the impact of the stressor by changing the situation, context, or the stigmatizing remarks" by "enrolling in a fitness program, seeking nutritional guidance, etc."

Self-objectification: "The psychological state in which a person views their body from the outside, as if they were observing their own physical appearance, and in which the person's habitual monitoring of their physical appearance is a salient aspect of their experience." (Fredrickson & Roberts, 1997)

Social determinants of health (SDH): "The conditions in which people are born, grow, live, work, and age, including the socioeconomic position, the environment, and the health care system." (CSDH Commission on Social Determinants of Health, 2008)

Weight stigma: "The social processes of devaluation, discrimination, and stereotyping against persons on the basis of their weight."

Review questions

1. Using the SDH framework and Fundamental Causes Theory, explain why behavior-change interventions that do not address structural inequalities are insufficient to reduce socioeconomic disparities in adolescent obesity. Provide specific examples from the Indian context.
2. Critically evaluate Tomiyama's (2014) COWS model. What are the biological and psychological mechanisms the model proposes, and what implications does it have for the design of obesity interventions in school and community settings?
3. A 15-year-old girl from a lower-income urban household in India describes withdrawing from school sports, avoiding family gatherings, and using humor to deflect peers' comments about her weight. Using the Lazarus & Folkman (1984) stress-coping framework and the research on structural coping barriers reviewed in this chapter, analyse the determinants of her coping patterns and identify the systemic changes that would support more adaptive responses.
4. How do caste hierarchies, gender norms, and socioeconomic position intersect to shape the experience of weight stigma among Indian adolescents? Illustrate your answer with reference to at least two of the theoretical frameworks discussed in, and empirical evidence from, Sections 3.4 and 3.5.
5. Design a stigma-informed, equity-centered school-based program for addressing adolescent obesity in a government secondary school in urban India. Specify the components of the program, the evidence base for each component, the outcome measures you would use to evaluate effectiveness, and the equity-sensitive indicators you would monitor to ensure the program does not widen existing health disparities.

AI disclosure

During the preparation of this work the author(s) used Chat GPT, Grammarly.com in order to Editing, Formatting. After using this tool/service, the author(s) reviewed and edited the content as needed and take(s) full responsibility for the content of the publication.

References

American Medical Association (AMA). (2023). *AMA Adopts New Policy Clarifying Role of BMI as a Measure in Medicine*. AMA Press Release. https://www.ama-assn.org/press-center/press-releases/ama-adopts-new-policy-clarifying-role-bmi-measure-medicine.

Abarca-Gómez, L., Abdeen, Z. A., Hamid, Z. A., Abu-Rmeileh, N. M., Acosta-Cazares, B., Acuin, C., & Ezzati, M. (2017). Worldwide trends in body-mass index, underweight, overweight, and obesity from 1975 to 2016: A pooled analysis of 2416 population-based measurement studies in 128·9 million children, adolescents, and adults. *The Lancet, 390*(10113), 2627–2642. https://doi.org/10.1016/S0140-6736(17)32129-3.

Adler, N. E., & Ostrove, J. M. (1999). Socioeconomic status and health: What we know and what we don't. *Annals of the New York Academy of Sciences, 896*(1), 3–15. https://doi.org/10.1111/j.1749-6632.1999.tb08101.x.

Alderman, H., & Headey, D. D. (2017). How important is parental education for child nutrition? *World Development, 94*, 448–464. https://doi.org/10.1016/j.worlddev.2017.02.007.

Barker, D. J. P. (1998). *Mothers, babies and health in later life* (2nd ed.). Churchill Livingstone.

Ben-Shlomo, Y., & Kuh, D. (2002). A life course approach to chronic disease epidemiology: Conceptual models, empirical challenges and interdisciplinary perspectives. *International Journal of Epidemiology, 31*(2), 285–293. https://doi.org/10.1093/ije/31.2.285.

Black, R. E., Victora, C. G., Walker, S. P., Bhutta, Z. A., Christian, P., de Onis, M., & Uauy, R. (2013). Maternal and child undernutrition and overweight in low-income and middle-income countries. *The Lancet, 382*(9890), 427–451. https://doi.org/10.1016/S0140-6736(13)60937-X.

Boyland, E. J., & Whalen, R. (2015). Food advertising to children and its effects on diet: Review of recent prevalence and impact data. *Pediatric Diabetes, 16*(5), 331–337. https://doi.org/10.1111/pedi.12278.

Braveman, P., Egerter, S., & Williams, D. R. (2011). The social determinants of health: Coming of age. *Annual Review of Public Health, 32*(1), 381–398. https://doi.org/10.1146/annurev-publhealth-031210-101218.

Braveman, P., & Gottlieb, L. (2014). The social determinants of health: It's time to consider the causes of the causes. *Public Health Reports, 129*(Suppl 2), 19–31. https://doi.org/10.1177/00333549141291S206.

Brewis, A. A. (2011). *Obesity: Cultural and biocultural perspectives*. Rutgers University Press.

Crandall, C. S. (1994). Prejudice against fat people: Ideology and self-interest. *Journal of Personality and Social Psychology, 66*(5), 882–894. https://doi.org/10.1037/0022-3514.66.5.882.

Crenshaw, K. (1989). *Demarginalizing the Intersection of Race and Sex: A Black Feminist Critique of Antidiscrimination Doctrine, Feminist Theory and Antiracist Politics* (1). University of Chicago Legal Forum, 139–167.

Crosnoe, R., & Muller, C. (2004). Body mass index, academic achievement, and school context: Examining the educational experiences of adolescents at risk of obesity. *Journal of Health and Social Behavior, 45*(4), 393–407. https://doi.org/10.1177/002214650404500403.

CSDH [Commission on Social Determinants of Health]. (2008). Closing the gap in a generation: Health equity through action on the social determinants of health. Final report. World Health Organization.

Drewnowski, A., & Specter, S. E. (2004). Poverty and obesity: The role of energy density and energy costs. *The American Journal of Clinical Nutrition, 79*(1), 6–16. https://doi.org/10.1093/ajcn/79.1.6.

Durso, L. E., & Latner, J. D. (2008). Understanding self-directed stigma: Development of the weight bias internalization scale. *Obesity, 16*(S2), S80–S86. https://doi.org/10.1038/oby.2008.448.

Eisenberg, M. E., Neumark-Sztainer, D., Haines, J., & Wall, M. (2012). Weight-teasing and emotional well-being in adolescents: Longitudinal findings from Project EAT. *Journal of Adolescent Health, 38*(6), 675–683. https://doi.org/10.1016/j.jadohealth.2005.07.002.

Elder, G. H., Jr. (1998). The life course as developmental theory. *Child Development, 69*(1), 1–12. https://doi.org/10.1111/j.1467-8624.1998.tb06128.x.

Frederick, D. A., Peplau, L. A., & Lever, J. (2014). The swimsuit issue: Correlates of body image in a sample of 52,677 heterosexual adults. *Body Image, 3*(4), 413–419. https://doi.org/10.1016/j.bodyim.2006.06.002.

Fredrickson, B. L., & Roberts, T.-A. (1997). Objectification theory: Toward understanding women's lived experiences and mental health risks. *Psychology of Women Quarterly, 21*(2), 173–206. https://doi.org/10.1111/j.1471-6402.1997.tb00108.x.

Goffman, E. (1963). *Stigma: Notes on the management of spoiled identity*. Prentice-Hall.

Gordon-Larsen, P., McMurray, R. G., & Popkin, B. M. (2000). Determinants of adolescent physical activity and inactivity patterns. *Pediatrics, 105*(6), e83. https://doi.org/10.1542/peds.105.6.e83.

Gupta, N., Goel, K., Shah, P., & Misra, A. (2012). Childhood obesity in developing countries: Epidemiology, determinants, and prevention. *Endocrine Reviews, 33*(1), 48–70. https://doi.org/10.1210/er.2010-0028.

Guthman, J. (2011). *Weighing in: Obesity, food justice, and the limits of capitalism*. University of California Press.

Hales, C. N., & Barker, D. J. P. (2001). The thrifty phenotype hypothesis. *British Medical Bulletin, 60*(1), 5–20. https://doi.org/10.1093/bmb/60.1.5.

Hawkes, C. (2006). Uneven dietary development: Linking the policies and processes of globalization with the nutrition transition, obesity and diet-related chronic diseases. *Globalization and Health, 2*(1), 4. https://doi.org/10.1186/1744-8603-2-4.

International Institute for Population Sciences (IIPS) & ICF.(2021). National Family Health Survey (NFHS-5), 2019-21: India. IIPS.

Jaacks, L. M., Vandevijvere, S., Pan, A., McGowan, C. J., Wallace, C., Imamura, F., & Ezzati, M. (2019). The obesity transition: Stages of the global epidemic. *The Lancet Diabetes & Endocrinology, 7*(3), 231–240. https://doi.org/10.1016/S2213-8587(19)30026-9.

Kumanyika, S. K. (2008). Environmental influences on childhood obesity: Ethnic and cultural influences in context. *Physiology & Behavior, 94*(1), 61–70. https://doi.org/10.1016/j.physbeh.2007.11.019.

Lazarus, R. S., & Folkman, S. (1984). *Stress, appraisal, and coping*. Springer.

Link, B. G., & Phelan, J. (1995). Social conditions as fundamental causes of disease. *Journal of Health and Social Behavior, 35*(Special Issue), 80–94. https://doi.org/10.2307/2626958.

Marmot, M. (2005). *The status syndrome: How social standing affects our health and longevity*. Owl Books.

McLaren, L. (2007). Socioeconomic status and obesity. *Epidemiologic Reviews, 29*(1), 29–48. https://doi.org/10.1093/epirev/mxm001.

Misra, A., & Khurana, L. (2008). Obesity and the metabolic syndrome in developing countries. *The Journal of Clinical Endocrinology & Metabolism, 93*(11_supplement_1), s9–s30. https://doi.org/10.1210/jc.2008-1595.

Mohanty, S., Kim, R., & Subramanian, S. V. (2024). Double burden of malnutrition in India: Trends and determinants from the National Family Health Survey. *Nutrition (Burbank, Los Angeles County, Calif.), 118*, 112267. https://doi.org/10.1016/j.nut.2023.112267.

Monteiro, C. A., Moura, E. C., Conde, W. L., & Popkin, B. M. (2004). Socioeconomic status and obesity in adult populations of developing countries: A review. *Bulletin of the World Health Organization, 82*(12), 940–946. https://doi.org/10.2471/BLT.04.012237.

Moodie, R., Stuckler, D., Monteiro, C., Sheron, N., Neal, B., Thamarangsi, T., & Casswell, S. (2013). Profits and pandemics: Prevention of harmful effects of tobacco, alcohol, and ultra-processed food and drink industries. *The Lancet, 381*(9867), 670–679. https://doi.org/10.1016/S0140-6736(12)62089-3.

NCD Risk Factor Collaboration. (2016). Trends in adult body-mass index in 200 countries from 1975 to 2014: A pooled analysis of 1698 population-based measurement studies with 19·2 million participants. *The Lancet, 387*(10026), 1377–1396. https://doi.org/10.1016/S0140-6736(16)30054-X.

Neumark-Sztainer, D., Wall, M., Haines, J., Story, M., & Eisenberg, M. E. (2007). Why does dieting predict weight gain in adolescents? Findings from Project EAT-II: A 5-year longitudinal study. *Journal of the American Dietetic Association, 107*(3), 448–455. https://doi.org/10.1016/j.jada.2006.12.013.

Neumark-Sztainer, D., Wall, M., Story, M., & Fulkerson, J. A. (2004). Are family meal patterns associated with disordered eating behaviors among adolescents? *Journal of Adolescent Health, 35*(5), 350–359. https://doi.org/10.1016/j.jadohealth.2004.01.004.

Ng, M., Fleming, T., Robinson, M., Thomson, B., Graetz, N., Margono, C., & Gakidou, E. (2014). Global, regional, and national prevalence of overweight and obesity in children and adults during 1980–2013: A systematic analysis for the global burden of disease study 2013. *The Lancet, 384*(9945), 766–781. https://doi.org/10.1016/S0140-6736(14)60460-8.

Ng, S. W., & Popkin, B. M. (2012). Time use and physical activity: A shift away from movement across the globe. *Obesity Reviews, 13*(8), 659–680. https://doi.org/10.1111/j.1467-789X.2011.00982.x.

OECD. (2019). *Health at a glance 2019: OECD indicators*. OECD Publishing. https://doi.org/10.1787/4dd50c09-en.

Popkin, B. M. (1993). Nutritional patterns and transitions. *Population and Development Review, 19*(1), 138–157. https://doi.org/10.2307/2938388.

Popkin, B. M. (2015). Nutrition transition and the global diabetes epidemic. *Current Diabetes Reports, 15*(9), 64. https://doi.org/10.1007/s11892-015-0631-4.

Puhl, R. M., & Brownell, K. D. (2006). Confronting and coping with weight stigma: An investigation of overweight and obese adults. *Obesity, 14*(10), 1802–1815. https://doi.org/10.1038/oby.2006.208.

Puhl, R. M., & Heuer, C. A. (2009). The stigma of obesity: A review and update. *Obesity, 17*(5), 941–964. https://doi.org/10.1038/oby.2008.636.

Puhl, R. M., & Latner, J. D. (2007). Stigma, obesity, and the health of the nation's children. *Psychological Bulletin, 133*(4), 557–580. https://doi.org/10.1037/0033-2909.133.4.557.

Puhl, R. M., Peterson, J. L., & Luedicke, J. (2013). Weight-based victimization: Bullying experiences of weight loss treatment-seeking youth. *Pediatrics, 131*(1), e1–e9. https://doi.org/10.1542/peds.2012-1106.

Saguy, A. C., & Riley, K. W. (2005). Weighing both sides: Morality, mortality, and framing contests over obesity. *Journal of Health Politics, Policy and Law, 30*(5), 869–921. https://doi.org/10.1215/03616878-30-5-869.

Sallis, J. F., Floyd, M. F., Rodriguez, D. A., & Saelens, B. E. (2012). Role of built environments in physical activity, obesity, and cardiovascular disease. *Circulation, 125*(5), 729–737. https://doi.org/10.1161/CIRCULATIONAHA.110.969022.

Shrewsbury, V., & Wardle, J. (2008). Socioeconomic status and adiposity in childhood: A systematic review of cross-sectional studies 1990–2005. *Obesity, 16*(2), 275–284. https://doi.org/10.1038/oby.2007.35.

Singh, A., Patel, V., & Bharati, S. (2024). Shifting burden of nutritional failure among Indian children and adolescents: Reanalysis of NFHS-5 data. *Public Health Nutrition, 27*(1), e12. https://doi.org/10.1017/S136898002300270X.

Sobal, J., & Stunkard, A. J. (1989). Socioeconomic status and obesity: A review of the literature. *Psychological Bulletin, 105*(2), 260–275. https://doi.org/10.1037/0033-2909.105.2.260.

Subramanian, S. V., Özaltin, E., & Finlay, J. E. (2011). Height of nations: A socioeconomic analysis of cohort differences and patterns among women in 54 low- to middle-income countries. *PLoS One, 6*(4), e18962. https://doi.org/10.1371/journal.pone.0018962.

Swami, V., & Tovée, M. J. (2010). *Body weight ideals and body dissatisfaction in cross-cultural perspective*.

Swinburn, B., Egger, G., & Raza, F. (1999). Dissecting obesogenic environments: The development and application of a framework for identifying and prioritizing environmental interventions for obesity. *Preventive Medicine, 29*(6), 563–570. https://doi.org/10.1006/pmed.1999.0585.

Swinburn, B. A., Sacks, G., Hall, K. D., McPherson, K., Finegood, D. T., Moodie, M. L., & Gortmaker, S. L. (2011). The global obesity pandemic: Shaped by global drivers and local environments. *The Lancet, 378*(9793), 804–814. https://doi.org/10.1016/S0140-6736(11)60813-1.

Thompson, J. K., Cattarin, J., Fowler, B., & Fisher, E. (1995). The perception of teasing scale (POTS): A revision and extension of the physical appearance related teasing scale (PARTS). *Journal of Personality Assessment, 65*(1), 146–157. https://doi.org/10.1207/s15327752jpa6501_11.

Tomiyama, A. J. (2014). Weight stigma is stressful: A review of evidence for the cyclic obesity/weight-based stigma model. *Appetite, 82*, 8–15. https://doi.org/10.1016/j.appet.2014.06.108.

Varni, J. W., Seid, M., & Kurtin, P. S. (2001). PedsQL 4.0: Reliability and validity of the pediatric quality of life inventory version 4.0 generic core scales in healthy and patient populations. *Medical Care, 39*(8), 800–812. https://doi.org/10.1097/00005650-200108000-00006.

Victora, C. G., Adair, L., Fall, C., Hallal, P. C., Martorell, R., Richter, L., & Sachdev, H. S. (2008). Maternal and child undernutrition: Consequences for adult health and human capital. *The Lancet, 371*(9609), 340–357. https://doi.org/10.1016/S0140-6736(07)61692-4.

Warschburger, P., & Zuba, A. (2023). Bidirectional associations between weight-related teasing and body mass index z-score: A longitudinal study across 6 years. *European Child & Adolescent Psychiatry, 32*(6), 963–972. https://doi.org/10.1007/s00787-021-01887-3.

Weiner, B. (1985). An attributional theory of achievement motivation and emotion. *Psychological Review, 92*(4), 548–573. https://doi.org/10.1037/0033-295X.92.4.548.

Further reading

Cooksey-Stowers, K., Schwartz, M. B., & Brownell, K. D. (2017). Food swamps predict obesity rates better than food deserts in the United States. *International Journal of Environmental Research and Public Health, 14*(11), 1366. https://doi.org/10.3390/ijerph14111366.

Das, A.K. (2020). Psychosocial correlates of adolescent obesity in urban India: A mixed-methods study [Doctoral dissertation]. University of Calcutta.

Epel, E. S., Lapidus, R., McEwen, B., & Brownell, K. (2001). Stress may add bite to appetite in women: A laboratory study of stress-induced cortisol and eating behavior. *Psychoneuroendocrinology, 26*(1), 37–49. https://doi.org/10.1016/S0306-4530(00)00035-4.

Ministry of Health and Family Welfare (MoHFW), UNICEF, & Population Council. (2019). *Comprehensive National Nutrition Survey (CNNS) National Report*. MoHFW, Government of India.

Puhl, R. M., & Suh, Y. (2015). Health consequences of weight stigma: Implications for obesity prevention and treatment. *Current Obesity Reports, 4*(2), 182–190. https://doi.org/10.1007/s13679-015-0153-z.

Sethi, V., Bhattacharyya, R., Kapoor, G., Bhargava, K., Kulkarni, B., & Bhavani, R. V. (2024). Overweight and obesity among adolescents: Evidence from the comprehensive National nutrition survey, India. *Maternal & Child Nutrition, 20*(1), e13572. https://doi.org/10.1111/mcn.13572.

Taillie, L. S., Rivera, J. A., Popkin, B. M., & Batis, C. (2020). Do high vs. low purchasers respond differently to a nonessential energy-dense food tax? Two-year evaluation of Mexico's 8% nonessential food tax. *Preventive Medicine, 131*, 105942. https://doi.org/10.1016/j.ypmed.2019.105942.

Walker, R. E., Keane, C. R., & Burke, J. G. (2010). Disparities and access to healthy food in the United States: A review of food deserts literature. *Health & Place, 16*(5), 876–884. https://doi.org/10.1016/j.healthplace.2010.04.013.

Chapter 4

Body image and obesity

"Body image is not simply how we look, but how we come to see ourselves through the eyes of others."

Learning objectives

Upon completing this chapter, readers will be able to
Explain body image as a psychological construct and its relevance during adolescence
Apply major theoretical frameworks to understand body image and obesity
Analyze global patterns of body dissatisfaction and their link with mental health outcomes
Evaluate the role of gender, media, and sociocultural influences in shaping body image
Interpret the Indian context, including cultural norms, media influences, and structural factors
Assess intervention approaches across individual, family, school, and policy levels

4.1 Introduction: body image as a psychological construct in adolescence

Body image is arguably one of the most salient psychological constructs in adolescence that intersects with various aspects of human experience, including biology, cognition, culture, and social identity. Body image is technically defined as "a multidimensional psychological construct that includes an individual's perceptions, cognitions, emotions, and attitudes about their body—its size, shape, weight, and appearance—as well as their behaviors related to body image." This definition of body image asserts that body image is not merely a reproduction of objective body characteristics. Rather, it is a product of psychological processing that is heavily influenced by social interactions and cultural context. In this context, body image can be operationalized across four interrelated dimensions that include the perceptual component (accuracy of body size perception), the affective component (satisfaction, shame, or pride associated with body image), the cognitive component (beliefs about body image), and the behavioral component (actions that individuals take in response to body image problems). Each of these body image dimensions is individually responsible for contributing to overall psychological health. Disturbances in any one of these dimensions can trigger a series of devastating psychosocial problems. The present study applies this multidimensional framework to examine body image in obese and nonobese adolescents and young adults in urban India, as described below. In this study, body image is conceptualized as a critical psychological construct among late adolescents (17–20 years) and young adults (21–24 years) with obesity in Kolkata, West Bengal, India. Specifically, body image is defined among late adolescents (17–20 years) and young adults (21–24 years), consistent with the overall study design. Body image is measured using the Multidimensional Body-Self Relations Questionnaire (MBSRQ), which is a comprehensive body image measure that assesses various body image dimensions. These body image dimensions include appearance evaluation (satisfaction with body looks), appearance orientation (importance of body looks), fitness evaluation (satisfaction with physical condition), fitness orientation (importance of being physically fit), health evaluation (satisfaction with health), health orientation (importance of being healthy), and illness orientation (reactivity to being sick). This multidimensional assessment allowed for an investigation of how obesity

Psychology of Obesity. DOI: https://doi.org/10.1016/B978-0-443-27797-9.00005-1

might influence body image, fitness, health, and overall body-self relationships. A 2 x 2 x 2 factorial design was used to compare body image experiences of obese individuals (BMI $\geq$30 kg/m^2) and nonobese individuals (BMI <30 kg/m^2) by gender and developmental stage, providing a systematic investigation of how body weight status, gender, and developmental stage might interact in body image experiences in India.

Adolescence is a significant developmental period in body image development and consolidation. During this period, pubertal developmental changes, including rapid changes in height, weight, body fat, muscularity, and secondary sex characteristics, significantly transform the body in a manner that is often unpredictable, difficult to control, and characterized by asynchronous change. At the same time, cognitive abilities necessary for formal operational thinking, abstract thinking, and sophisticated comparison of the self to others develop. The concept of the imaginary audience, or how the adolescent perceives themselves as always being "on stage" and "under observation" by others, captures the psychological effects of this developmental period, including a heightened sense of self that is characterized by a strong sense of body image. Research has shown that this heightened sense of self is associated with body image dissatisfaction, emotional reactivity to social feedback regarding one's body, and increased susceptibility to media influences on body ideals.

The social environment in adolescence plays an active role in influencing body norms through schools, social groups, families, and media systems, which define the types of bodies perceived as acceptable, attractive, disciplined, or desirable. Girls are socialized to body ideals emphasizing thinness, beauty, or femininity, whereas boys are socialized to body ideals emphasizing muscularity, physical strength, or athletic competence. When there are perceived discrepancies between one's own body and body ideals promoted in society, body dissatisfaction can be viewed as a direct psychological outcome. Body dissatisfaction, defined as a negative subjective evaluation of the body or specific body parts, can be viewed as one of the strongest psychological risk factors for mental health problems in adolescence, predicting depression, anxiety, disordered eating, social withdrawal, or physical inactivity designed to enhance health.

Obesity intersects this process in a physiological and profoundly social manner that is distinct from many other health conditions in that it is a physical attribute that is easily subject to public evaluation and social stigmatization. In many societies across the globe—and increasingly in India—having more body weight is not just a physical attribute but a symbol of personal failure and moral inadequacy. These cultural understandings create a stigmatizing social identity that significantly affects how adolescents understand their bodies relationally, emotionally, and cognitively. Body image is a critical psychological mediator between obesity and its psychosocial outcomes in that it is not weight that is critical, but how one interprets weight and how that interpretation is influenced by cultural understandings and feedback that can create negative emotions and behavioral avoidance and influence well-being.

The international research literature has consistently found that overweight and obese youth report higher levels of body dissatisfaction and negative self-esteem, more depressive and anxiety symptoms, and lower health-related quality of life than their peers who are at a normal weight. These relationships are not unique to one culture and have been found across many different nations and societies, indicating that these psychological and emotional challenges are influenced by shared human experiences and cultural understandings that are becoming more similar across nations and societies through globalization. In India, these relationships are particularly unique in that the influence of media-driven ideals of thinness is combining with traditional cultural understandings that have traditionally equated more body weight with more wealth and health and social status—thus creating a normative collision that is particularly ambiguous and psychologically complex for Indian youth who are caught between tradition and modernity. The objectives of the present chapter are fourfold: (1) to present a review and evaluation of the major theories that describe the development of body images and the link between body images and overweight problems; (2) to examine the overall global studies on body dissatisfaction, gender differences in body dissatisfaction, and the psychological consequences of body dissatisfaction; (3) to examine the issue in the context of the Indian culture, which has not been addressed in the existing literature; and (4) to examine the effective interventions that may be used in conjunction to promote a positive body image and alleviate the psychological burden of obesity-related stigma. This chapter aims to discuss body image as a significant psychological construct through which adolescents understand their bodies, their place in society, and their own worth. Section 4.2 provides a review of prominent theories that help understand body image development, how obesity affects body image, and through what pathways psychological harm is inflicted. Section 4.3 provides a review of global research on body image, body dissatisfaction, gender, media, and mental health. Section 4.4 focuses on body image in relation to the unique sociocultural context of India, including how Bollywood, traditional body ideals, caste, class, and gender factors may influence body image in Indian youth. Section 4.5 provides a critical discussion of intervention strategies for enhancing body image and mitigating the psychological effects of obesity-related stigma. An integrative biopsychosocial perspective is used in this chapter, where both physiological factors in obesity and sociocultural factors in body weight perception are acknowledged.

4.1.1 Theoretical perspectives on body image and obesity

4.1.1.1 The tripartite influence model and sociocultural theory

The Tripartite Influence Model of body image, developed and supported through extensive empirical research, is one of the most widely accepted theoretical frameworks for understanding sociocultural influences on body image development and disturbance. According to this model, body image disturbance results from the internalization of sociocultural body ideals and engagement in appearance-based social comparison. These body ideals are communicated through three primary sociocultural influences—peers, parents, and the mass media. The internalization of these ideals, combined with comparisons between one's own appearance and perceived societal standards, contributes significantly to body dissatisfaction and body image disturbance.

Significant empirical support has been found for the tripartite influence model across different populations and age ranges. A research study involving college females between the ages of 18 and 22 found that the tripartite influence model explained how appearance comparison mediated the influence of family and media on body dissatisfaction, which in turn affected eating behaviors. For adolescents with obesity, all three influences—peers, family, and media—are particularly salient. For example, peer teasing about weight can create direct pressure to conform to appearance ideals; family comments regarding diet and body weight can shape appearance-related expectations; and limited positive representation of overweight individuals in the media can further contribute to negative body image and body dissatisfaction.

4.1.1.2 Objectification theory

Objectification theory, developed by Fredrickson and Roberts (1997) and subsequently developed through a considerable body of research evidence, suggests that girls and women in modern Western and increasingly global societies are viewed and treated by their culture as bodies that are of value and importance primarily in terms of their physical attractiveness. Objectification is a process by which this cultural perspective is conveyed through ubiquitous and pervasive media messages and through social interactions and relationships that focus on physical attractiveness and beauty. The basic tenet of objectification theory is that girls and women who are frequently sexually objectified by their culture will internalize this perspective and see their own bodies from an observer's perspective, a process termed self-objectification.

The resulting self-objectification leads to various psychological outcomes that have been consistently demonstrated in both experimental and longitudinal studies. Constant body monitoring, where individuals monitor their body appearance from an imagined external perspective, is a cognitive drain that negatively impacts cognitive performance and disrupts internal bodily awareness, which is critical for healthy self-regulation. Objectification theory is also related to body shame (where individuals experience not meeting idealized body image norms), appearance anxiety (where individuals experience constant worry about their body image), and disordered eating (where body monitoring leads to preoccupation with caloric intake and body control as a means of body management). Objectification theory also explains the experience of obesity stigma among adolescent girls. In this context, it is not merely that adolescent girls with obesity experience stigma that leads to negative outcomes. Rather, it is that they internalize this negative evaluation as their own experience that leads to chronic shame and impaired psychological functioning. A study applying objectification theory to boys found that although boys were less likely to experience self-objectification than girls, those who did were more likely to report dissatisfaction with muscularity and a desire to be thinner if they were overweight. This indicates that objectification theory is applicable to both sexes but is related to cultural body image ideals.

4.1.1.3 Social comparison theory

Social comparison theory proposes that individuals evaluate themselves by comparing their attributes, abilities, and characteristics with those of others. In the context of body image, social comparison, especially upward comparison to individuals who are perceived as being more attractive, thinner, or more muscular than the individual him- or herself, is one of the most consistently identified predictors of body dissatisfaction., Myers and Crowther (2009), in their comprehensive review of studies on the topic, concluded that appearance comparison predicts body dissatisfaction and negative mood states, with upward appearance comparison to idealized media images showing the largest and most robust effects.

Adolescence is a period characterized by high susceptibility to social comparison effects. In this developmental phase, the peer group plays a crucial role as a reference group in the self-evaluation process. The appearance norms set by the peer group, as well as the perceived attractiveness of the peer group, have a significant impact on the way adolescents perceive their own bodies. Groesz et al. (2002) showed in their study that exposure to idealized images in advertising resulted in immediate effects on body dissatisfaction in adolescent girls, with the girls who were most engaged in appearance comparison showing the strongest effects. The role of social media in providing adolescents with opportunities for social comparison has significantly increased the scope, frequency, and intensity of social comparison opportunities, providing adolescents with continuous access to images of self-presentational activity by their peers, media personalities, and influencers—a development with significant implications for the impact on body image, as discussed in Section 4.3.3.

4.1.1.4 Attribution theory and labelling theory

Attribution theory offers a framework for understanding the depth of damage caused by weight stigma and also explains why obesity-related body image problems tend to be so difficult to modify. The model of attribution theory proposes that perceived control is the single most important factor that influences how others respond to others' problems. When negative outcomes are caused by factors that are under control, others respond with blame and anger rather than empathy. When this model is applied to obesity, it is clear that cultural perceptions of body weight controlability lead to negative reactions that are characterized by moral condemnation rather than empathy. In relation to adolescents with obesity, attribution theory offers a framework for understanding the double burden of stigma that is experienced. In addition to being stigmatized by others because they are perceived to have control over their body weight, they also experience internalized stigma because they tend to attribute their obesity to their own failure. Obesity is caused by a combination of genetic, developmental, socioeconomic, and environmental factors that are largely outside their control.

Labeling theory, derived from sociological studies that commenced with and were applied to the health and deviance fields, suggests that social labeling acts as a self-fulfilling prophecy that influences the perceptions of others, the labeled person's self-concept, and the interactions that shape the development of the person's identity. When adolescents are labeled as "obese" or "fat" by others, whether through formal processes or informal processes such as peer teasing and family commentaries, the label may become a master status that overrides all other characteristics and influences social interactions primarily in reference to the labeled status. Research has demonstrated that weight-related labeling during childhood can contribute to body image disturbance and disordered eating later in life, highlighting the long-term psychological consequences of labeling experiences. In the context of schools, the experience of public reporting of BMI or the measurement of weight in the classroom without privacy provisions may actually contribute to the experience of labeling that has a lasting impact on the development of body image disturbance.

4.1.1.5 Internalized weight bias and self-stigma

One of the most powerful psychological processes that links weight stigma to body image disturbance is the experience of internalized weight bias, or the experience of applying negative stereotypes of obesity to oneself. This construct was conceptualized and measured by Durso and Latner (2008) and refers to the experience of applying negative stereotypes of obesity to oneself, such as seeing oneself as lazy, ugly, stupid, or deserving of social exclusion, as described by the Weight Bias Internalization Scale. Unlike the experience of stigma, which refers to the experience of receiving negative messages from others, the experience of internalized weight bias refers to the experience of applying negative stereotypes to oneself and involves the person as a participant in the experience of stigma.

In fact, research has consistently shown that internalized weight stigma is a more powerful predictor of psychological outcomes than experienced stigma. Research has consistently shown that individuals who experience higher levels of internalized weight stigma tend to be more likely to experience depression, anxiety, binge eating, and lower self-esteem, even when controlling for BMI and experiences of weight discrimination. Experimental research has demonstrated that induced internalized weight stigma in individuals with obesity led to increased calorie intake and lower motivation for exercise, implying that internalized weight stigma undermines health behaviors that could be beneficial for weight management. For youth, whose developing self-concept is especially vulnerable to external influences, internalized weight stigma may be a significant developmental concern, as negative self-perceptions based on weight stigma may be integrated into fundamental structures of personality that govern social functioning, health-related behaviors, and psychological well-being over a person's lifespan.

4.1.1.6 Integrative and developmental perspectives

Modern body image research acknowledges that body image development in obesity is not fully addressed by any single theory. Integrative theories, which combine sociocultural, cognitive, developmental, and biological factors, offer more complete explanations. The cognitive-behavioral theory of body image development by suggests that body image is determined by interactions between past factors (history of weight, teasing, cultural socialization) and present precipitants (environmental stimuli such as looking in the mirror, being commented on by others, looking at media) for body image schemas—organized cognitive structures for body-related beliefs and self-percepts. These schemas, once developed, serve as interpretive frameworks through which current body experiences are processed, producing characteristic emotional and behavioral outcomes.

Developmental theories emphasize that body image is dynamic and evolves over time in response to physical development, social experiences, and changing environmental influences. Because body image becomes consolidated during adolescence, this developmental period represents a critical window for intervention. Negative body image schemas formed during adolescence may persist into adulthood unless effectively challenged through psychological or educational interventions.

Key psychological theories and their application to adolescent obesity

Theory	Key proponents	Core mechanism	Application to adolescent obesity
Tripartite influence model		Peers, parents, and media shape body ideals through internalization and social comparison processes	Adolescents with obesity experience heightened body dissatisfaction due to weight teasing, parental diet-related communication, and lack of positive media representation
Objectification theory	Fredrickson and Roberts (1997)	Cultural objectification leads to self-objectification, body shame, and appearance anxiety	Adolescent girls with obesity are more likely to experience stigma, leading to heightened self-surveillance and body shame
Social comparison theory		Individuals evaluate themselves through comparison with others; upward comparison increases dissatisfaction	Adolescents with obesity compare themselves unfavorably with idealized body standards portrayed in the media
Attribution theory		Perceived controllability of weight leads to blame and moral judgment	Adolescents with obesity internalize responsibility for their weight, leading to guilt and psychological distress
Internalized weight bias		Internalization of negative weight-related stereotypes	Acts as an independent predictor of depression, anxiety, and disordered eating among adolescents

4.1.2 Global evidence: body dissatisfaction, mental health, and gendered dynamics

4.1.2.1 Epidemiological scope and cross-cultural patterns

The worldwide prevalence of body image disturbances during adolescence has been found to be considerable and growing. The results of various investigations from different parts of the globe have revealed that negative body image disturbances are among the most common mental health problems faced by young individuals during adolescence, with an estimated 30% to 60% of girls and 20% to 40% of boys in various high- and middle-income countries. The Global School-Based Student Health Survey, which covers more than 100 countries, has consistently revealed findings indicating that young individuals who perceive themselves to be overweight have substantially higher levels of body image dissatisfaction, dietary restraint, and psychological distress in comparison to those young individuals who perceive themselves to be either normal or underweight. This has been observed in diverse national contexts ranging from Southeast Asia to Latin America to subsaharan Africa.

Longitudinal research has also offered important findings regarding the course of body image dissatisfaction in the context of obesity. Stice and Shaw's (2002) metaanalysis of 66 investigations revealed that body image dissatisfaction was a causal risk factor rather than a correlate for psychological distress, as it was found to prospectively predict the development of eating disorders, depressive symptoms, and low self-esteem. also observed in their five-year longitudinal study of more than 2,000 young individuals in Project EAT that body image dissatisfaction at baseline was found to significantly predict disordered eating, low quality of life, and less healthy dietary patterns at follow-up, independent of BMI change. The cross-cultural significance of these findings was also observed by, where body image dissatisfaction was observed in eleven countries with diverse cultural traditions, indicating that although the content of body ideals may vary across cultures, the psychological process underlying negative self-evaluation due to discrepancies between the actual self and the ideal self in terms of body image appears to be universally present.

4.1.2.2 Gender differences in body dissatisfaction

One of the most powerful and replicant moderators of body image in the context of obesity is gender. Three decades of research in various cultural and national contexts have consistently shown that girls experience higher levels of body dissatisfaction than boys, value thinness more as an ideal of physical appearance than boys do, and experience stronger links between weight and psychological problems than boys. These differences between the genders begin in early childhood but are magnified in late adolescence with the onset of puberty: the normal accumulation of adipose tissue in the development of the female adolescent coincides with increased weight and a displacement of the female adolescent's body away from the ideal of thinness more strongly than in the male adolescent's experience of increased lean muscle mass in the development of the male ideal.

Boys' body image concerns, although receiving less attention in the research arena, are of equal importance and have unique content. Boys' body image concerns appear to center on the lack of muscular development rather than the level of weight. A systematic review of the literature revealed that the drive for muscularity, the desire for increased muscular development, and the attainment of a lean and muscular physique, is as common and significant in adolescent boys as the drive for thinness is in girls. Boys who experience low levels of muscular development and levels of body fat tend to experience lower levels of self-esteem and more depressive symptoms and engage in potentially damaging compensatory behaviors such as excessive exercise, steroid use, and disordered eating patterns such as overeating and restrictive eating. This indicates that the issue of body image is not limited to females and that there is a need for the development of gender-specific approaches in the field of research and intervention.

Moreover, the gender differences in the psychological impact of obesity-related body image disturbance can also be observed at the clinical level. In their review of more than 100 studies on the topic of obesity and body image disturbance in adolescence, they found that among girls with obesity in adolescence, there is a stronger association between body weight and body image disturbance, depression, and eating pathology than in boys with obesity. Conversely, among boys with obesity in adolescence, there is a stronger association between body weight and body image disturbance, social withdrawal, and reduced school participation than in girls with obesity. These differences in the association between body weight and other factors among girls and boys with obesity in adolescence reflect the role of gender-specific body ideals and their impact on the psychological functioning of individuals and have significant implications for the development of interventions that not only address the issue of body image disturbance but also the issue of gender-specific body image disturbance with unique content and psychological processes.

4.1.2.3 Digital media and the globalization of body ideals

The digital media revolution in the world of adolescence has greatly increased the sociocultural factors that contribute to the development of body image disturbance. Social media such as Instagram, TikTok, YouTube, and Snapchat provide the adolescent with access to the idealized images of the bodies of peers, celebrities, models, and commercial influencers in a constant and on-demand manner. This is a novel and powerful environment of body image disturbance because it is different from the more traditional mass media in the sense that the adolescent can compare themselves with peers who are similar in terms of their age and the sociocultural context in which they find themselves (the same school environment) and, at the same time, compare themselves with the idealized images of the bodies of celebrities and commercial influencers that are the traditional objects of upward comparison in the tripartite influence model and social comparison theory.

Research on the relationship between social media and body image has expanded rapidly over the past decade, with studies consistently demonstrating a strong association between social media use and body image concerns among adolescents. Controlled experimental studies have shown that exposure to idealized images on social media platforms contributes to increased body dissatisfaction, appearance-based social comparison, negative mood, and dissatisfaction with one's own appearance. Social comparison has been identified as an important mechanism through which social media influences body image perceptions. Furthermore, a review of multiple studies examining the relationship between social media use and body image found a consistent association between greater social media engagement and increased body dissatisfaction among adolescents and young adults. Activities that are appearance-focused, such as posting photographs, seeking feedback on appearance, and comparing oneself with others online, appear to be particularly influential. McLean et al. (2019) also examined the role of appearance-related social media engagement and found that photo-based social media use was a stronger predictor of body dissatisfaction than overall social media use. These findings highlight the importance of the appearance-focused nature of social media platforms in shaping body image perceptions and contributing to body dissatisfaction among adolescents.

With respect to global public health, digital media has facilitated a trend toward the convergence of body ideals in culturally diverse national contexts. Thus, body ideals that were more diverse in the past, with some cultures having a more positive body image associated with larger body sizes and others already having a strong thinness ideal, are increasingly becoming similar in a globalized context that emphasizes slenderness, muscularity, and facial features associated with East Asian or Euro-American ideals of beauty, such as those portrayed by celebrities. This globalized body image has significant implications for youth in developing countries such as India, where digital connectivity is increasingly exposing youth to international body ideals that may be in direct conflict with traditional body ideals in these cultures and that may be in direct conflict with physiological realities of body shape and size. Postpandemic evidence has strengthened these concerns further: the COVID-19 lockdowns accelerated adolescent social media use substantially, with studies documenting significant increases in appearance-related social comparison, body dissatisfaction, and disordered eating behaviors specifically linked to algorithmically curated content on TikTok and Instagram (Rodgers et al., 2020; Vall-Roqué et al., 2021). Algorithm-driven feeds—which prioritize visually engaging, appearance-focused content—create personalized environments of upward appearance comparison that extend well beyond the peer-group comparisons studied in earlier social media research, with particularly pronounced effects among adolescent girls with higher BMI (Burnette et al., 2023).

4.1.2.4 Body image, disordered eating, and psychological comorbidities

The relationship between body image disturbance related to obesity and disordered eating is one of the most significant areas of body image research. Body image disturbance is one of the strongest prospective predictors of eating disorders, and research by Stice et al. (2011) demonstrated that a body image intervention significantly reduced body dissatisfaction, resulting in significantly lower rates of eating disorder onset in a two-year follow-up of a randomized trial, providing the best evidence currently available that body image disturbance plays a causal role in eating disorders, rather than simply correlating with them. For youth with obesity, body image disturbance and disordered eating are related in several ways. Binge eating disorder, characterized by recurrent episodes of eating large quantities of food in a short period of time associated with feelings of loss of control and shame, is significantly more prevalent in individuals with obesity than in individuals in the general population and is predicted by internalized weight stigma, body image disturbance, and emotional dysregulation.

The psychiatric comorbidities associated with obesity-related body image disturbance include eating disorders, but extend further than that. Systematic reviews and metaanalyses consistently reveal that body image disturbance in the context of obesity is associated with major depressive disorder, generalized anxiety disorder, social anxiety disorder, and reduced quality of life, with effect sizes that are clinically significant and remain significant even when controlling for BMI. Depression and body image disturbance are associated with each other through a number of factors. First, the cognitive model of body image disturbance suggests that the cognitive distortions associated with body image disturbance activate schemas of worthlessness and social exclusion that contribute to depressive mood. Second, the social model of body image disturbance suggests that the social exclusion associated with body image disturbance leads to the absence of the powerful protective effect of the positive feedback of others that is associated with reduced risk of depression. Finally, the behavioral model of body image disturbance suggests that the avoidance of physical activity associated with body image disturbance leads to the absence of the powerful protective effect of the positive feedback of others that is associated with reduced risk of depression and anxiety.

4.1.3 Body image in the Indian context

4.1.3.1 Traditional cultural norms and their transformation

In spite of the universal nature of these body ideals, there exists a lacuna in the context in which these issues are framed in the context of the unique and rapidly changing sociocultural landscape of India, which this section seeks to fill. This section seeks to provide an insight into the concept of body image in the context of the country. To understand the concept of body image in the context of the country, it is essential to understand that the cultural connotations of body size have witnessed a transformation of unprecedented magnitude in the past three decades. The transformation has created a norm where the country's culture is simultaneously imbued with the traditional connotations of fullness with health, wealth, and social status, as well as the more universally disseminated connotations of thinness through media, advertising, and the internet. The traditional cultural context in India, based on Ayurvedic medical traditions and Hindu philosophical perspectives, emphasized a degree of physical robustness with good health, nutritional status, and social vivacity. Extreme thinness was associated with poverty, illness, or social deprivation in most parts of the country in most periods of history, whereas a moderately full body was associated with economic security, reproductive health, and familial thriving (Swami et al., 2011). These connotations were especially relevant to women, whose bodies were rated in terms of their potential to bear children and secure familial thriving.

The traditional normative framework has been progressively eroded and changed—although not necessarily replaced—by economic liberalization, urbanization, and the infiltration of global media and consumer culture that began to accelerate in India from the 1990s onward. Economic liberalization in India since 1991 has allowed for foreign investment in media, advertising, fashion, and entertainment sectors that introduced globalized esthetic standards in which slenderness, toned muscularity, and specific facial features were defined as primary characteristics of beauty and social desirability. The proliferation of satellite television, followed by internet connectivity and social media, has extended this trend to increasingly remote urban and rural areas, such that even adolescents in medium-sized urban centers or semiurban areas are exposed to globalized body ideals via their smartphones. A study conducted in Mumbai found that obese school children experienced greater body image dissatisfaction, depressive symptoms, and poorer health-related quality of life than their normal-weight peers, highlighting the psychological consequences of obesity among Indian youth.

4.1.3.2 Bollywood, advertising, and idealized appearance standards

Bollywood—the Hindi-language movie industry based in Mumbai—has a privileged position in the Indian media environment as the principal vector of body ideals to hundreds of millions of people in India and the Indian diaspora. Unlike the American movie industry of Hollywood, whose message may be diluted in translation in the Indian language of choice, Bollywood transmits body ideals in the cultural vocabulary of Indian audiences, with characters who speak the audience's language and navigate the audience's social world. The body ideals promoted by Bollywood have shifted considerably since the opening of the Indian economy. Female stars are now slimmer, male stars more muscular. Their bodies are now very different from the typical Indian, and the result of professional training and diets that most teens cannot afford (Swami et al., 2011).

The advertising industry has also contributed to and strengthened Bollywood body ideals by creating a pervasive commercialized message environment that equates body types with consumer products, social success, romantic fulfillment, and personal aspiration. Fairness creams, slimming pills, diet programs, gym memberships, and fitness apps collectively contribute to a multibillion rupee industry that creates the ideal Indian body type—a slender, fair-skinned, and toned body—as an achievable aspiration for individuals who purchase and utilize such products. This commercialized body ideal is also racialized and weight-oriented. In India, fairness creams equate fair skin with beauty and social acceptability. This racial dimension to body image is also closely related to body weight and creates a double burden of body dissatisfaction for darker-skinned adolescents.

There has been a tremendous increase in body image studies related to Bollywood and advertising exposure in India over the last decade. A cross-sectional survey of 1,818 eighth and tenth-grade students across government and private schools in Delhi found that body dissatisfaction is highest among overweight students and girls. In this study, body dissatisfaction was also significantly related to unhealthy weight control behaviors. This demonstrates that body image ideals derived from Bollywood and advertising exposure can directly contribute to health-risk behaviors among Indian youth. Similarly, a study conducted in Kolkata and Howrah districts of West Bengal on 1223 adolescent girls found that many overweight girls also perceived their weight status and took measures to reduce their weight; however, many girls who were of normal weight also perceived their weight status and took measures that were not good for their health. These findings support that the process by which media impacts body image in the West is similar to that in India, even though the cultural messages are different.

4.1.3.3 Gendered body ideals and sociocultural pressures in India

The gendered body ideals in India present a complex interaction between cultural tradition and globalizing media influences that create unique pressures for girls and boys. For girls, the culturally dominant body ideal is a combination of global weight and thinness ideals and uniquely Indian requirements of skin tone, hair type, facial symmetry, and what can be termed 'disciplined femininity'—the bodily presentation that at once represents beauty, self-control, modesty, and social respectability. These are conveyed through a range of socializing agents and institutions. For example, family members, particularly mothers and maternal female family members, convey these through direct commentary and comparison and through direct guidance and advice; schools convey these through peer group interaction and implicit hierarchy of physical appearance; media convey these through the pervasive visual and audio messages of Bollywood and advertising; and increasingly through peers through social media interaction and self-presentational and evaluative practices.

Marriage market pressures bring a further dimension to body image concerns for females in India that has few parallels in high-income country contexts: the expectation of formal evaluation by potential families in arranged marriages brings a transactional element to body image for females, where body size, skin tone, and physical attractiveness are all evaluated in terms of a potential bride's value to a family. Swami et al. (2011) conducted a study of body image concerns among female university students in India and reported that discrepancies in weight, or weight discrepancy, were significantly negatively correlated with body appreciation and self-esteem, where females who saw themselves as overweight reported lower self-esteem regardless of actual BMI. These pressures are not limited to those in their adult years who are nearing marriageable age, but are communicated to females from early adolescence through family commentary, cultural narrative, and observation of how older females in a family are treated.

Regarding boys, Indian cultural body ideals have also undergone a similar but distinct evolution. Traditional associations between physical strength, work capacity, and masculine self-esteem have increasingly been supplemented by globalized ideals of lean muscularity promoted through Bollywood action films, sports personalities, and contemporary fitness culture. A significant association has been observed between body mass index (BMI), socioeconomic status (SES), and body image concerns, indicating that both physical and social factors contribute to body dissatisfaction among adolescents. Adolescents from higher socioeconomic backgrounds, who often have greater access to fitness facilities, social media, and appearance-focused content, may be more likely to endorse muscularity-oriented body ideals. At the same time, boys who are overweight frequently report body dissatisfaction related not only to muscularity but also to body weight. In many social contexts, excess weight may be associated with reduced sporting competence, lower peer acceptance, and criticism from family members, all of which can negatively affect self-esteem and self-concept. These findings highlight the growing influence of sociocultural and appearance-related pressures on body image among adolescent boys in India.

4.1.3.4 Caste, class, and regional variation in Indian body norms

Indian body norms are not homogeneous but rather show significant variation depending on caste, class, regional, and religious factors, which creates a heterogeneous cultural landscape in which the same physical body could be viewed very differently depending on the social context in which it is embedded. In many urban Indian middle-class and upper caste groups, the idealization of thinness promoted by globalization has become dominant, and overweight bodies are subjected to intense appearance-based scrutiny in which the implications are strongly class-based: in this context, the slender body signifies the cultural capital, the disciplined lifestyle, and the health-conscious consumer practices characteristic of the Indian middle class. Weight in the body is seen as a product of personal responsibility and self-regulation, and being overweight implies a lack of cultural refinement and self-regulation.

Contrary to this, in many lower-caste, rural, and tribal societies, older body weight and health or economic status correlations tend to be stronger, though increasingly challenged by media-informed ideals. In these settings, being overweight may not be subject to appearance-related stigma but can be imbued with social meaning in relation to overindulgence and departure from valued ideals of physical activity and productive labor. The variation in body ideals across caste and class strata means that an individual adolescent can be subject to entirely different body ideals in different social settings—valorized for their body in one setting by grandparents who associate it with good health, stigmatized in another by peers who apply urban ideals of beauty, and exposed to yet another set of body ideals through media consumption. This creates a particular sort of identity ambiguity for adolescents who lack cultural guidance on how they should be evaluated in terms of their bodies.

Diversity in religious beliefs also introduces further variability in the body types that are considered normal or acceptable. The emphasis on modesty, restraint, and control in the body in different religious belief systems in India, such as Hindu asecticism, Islamic modesty in dressing and consumption, and Jain restrictions in food habits, introduces culturally specific understandings of the interface between the body and virtues that influence the interpretation and management of weight. Fasting in Hindu, Muslim, and Jain religious traditions influences food habits that may contribute to irregular patterns of energy consumption and compensatory overconsumption. Such practices are not just seen as food habits but are imbued with spiritual importance that has a unique interface with the body, which is quite different from the secular health-focused body management that mainstream public health recommendations promote.

4.1.3.5 Empirical evidence from Indian adolescent populations

Empirical research into the body image experiences of Indian adolescents is gradually accumulating, although this literature base is smaller in size and less methodologically homogeneous compared to the equivalent literature in high-income economies., in their cross-sectional research involving 1811 adolescents using the MBSRQ and the Stunkard Silhouette Scale, reported significant differences in appearance, fitness, health, areas of the body, and weight across BMI and socioeconomic groups, with girls reporting significantly higher body dissatisfaction compared to boys, which is in line with the gendered body ideal reported in the international literature. In their case-controlled research in Mumbai, they reported that obese school children reported significantly higher body image dissatisfaction, depression, and health-related quality of life compared to their counterparts. In the first reported RCT of a body image intervention in Indian schools, significant improvements in body image, disordered eating, and other psychological outcomes in adolescents in Delhi following delivery of an adapted evidence-based intervention in schools compared to the control group, providing proof of concept for the feasibility and efficacy of a body image intervention in Indian adolescents. Overall, it appears that although media influences are significant factors in individuals' body image, opinions of friends and family are seen as the most significant factors in Indian schools.

Research that has specifically sought to investigate the relationship between obesity and body image in the context of Indian adolescents has highlighted a number of trends that are consistent with the broader international picture. For example, a study that involved 1811 adolescents in India found that "overweight status was significantly related to body dissatisfaction, and the relationship was stronger in girls than in boys at all levels of BMI." Qualitative studies have also shed further light on the nature of the body image experience in the context of Indian adolescents who are classified as overweight. For example, a qualitative study by that involved in-depth interviews with a group of overweight adolescents in India highlighted the ways in which the body image experience was characterized by a particular cultural double bind in which the reality of the experience of being stigmatized in the social world was combined with the reality of the experience of the family world in which the intrusive nature of the family world was a constant source of stress in the life of the overweight adolescent.

The results of the current research in Kolkata identified clear patterns in body image across weight status, gender, and developmental stage. The analysis of MBSRQ subscale results revealed that, in comparison to nonobese participants, obese participants scored significantly lower in appearance evaluation. These results suggest that obese participants expressed greater dissatisfaction with physical appearance. The results also revealed clear differences between genders. In all subgroups, obese females scored lowest in appearance evaluation. These results correspond with findings in the general body image literature, in which pressure on women to meet the body ideal is evident. The results for appearance orientation, which measured level of investment in appearance, were more complex. Obese participants scored both high and low in appearance orientation. The results suggest that some obese participants were hypervigilant in appearance, while others were avoidant. Fitness evaluation and fitness orientation subscale results revealed that, in comparison to nonobese participants, obese participants, especially males, expressed significant distress in physical fitness and sports capabilities. These results correspond with predictions from social comparison theory, in which body dissatisfaction in obese adolescents is especially pronounced in fitness-related body image. The results for the health evaluation subscale revealed that many obese participants expressed negative body evaluations in health, although they did not have diagnosed medical problems. These results suggest that participants internalized cultural discourse linking obesity with illness. Qualitative research complementing quantitative research results revealed participants' difficulties in dealing with contradictory body evaluations, in which they were praised by grandparents for "healthy" appearance, but criticized by friends for being overweight. These results correspond with normative body ideals in India, in which body ideals are in transition.

Note. Higher scores indicate greater body image disturbance.

4.1.4 Intervention approaches

The evidence reviewed in preceding sections establishes that body image disturbance in obese adolescents is sustained by multiple reinforcing mechanisms—cognitive, social, familial, and structural. Effective intervention therefore, requires approaches that operate at multiple levels simultaneously, from individual psychological work to school climate reform to policy-level regulation. This section reviews the principal evidence-based intervention categories, attending to their applicability and necessary adaptations for the Indian sociocultural context.

4.1.4.1 Cognitive-behavioral and acceptance-based approaches

Cognitive behavioral therapy for body image disturbance is found to be the most well-researched psychological intervention approach and has the most robust evidence base across clinical and nonclinical populations. Cash's (2011) cognitive behavioral model of body image therapy is a psychological intervention that addresses the cognitive schema and information processing biases that contribute to negative body image, namely "maladaptive appearance-related beliefs" ("My worth as a person depends on my appearance," "People are judging me for my weight"), "cognitive errors that support these beliefs" ("selective attention to perceived physical flaws," "catastrophizing the social implications of imperfection in physical appearance," "mind-reading negative judgments by others based on their perception of one's weight and physical appearance"), and "behavioral patterns that support these beliefs" ("avoidance," "checking," "camouflage").

Indeed, research has provided evidence for the efficacy of cognitive behavioral therapy (CBT)-based body image intervention. Conducted a metaanalysis of 25 randomized controlled trials of body image intervention. They reported that body image intervention was associated with moderate to large effects for improvements in body satisfaction and reductions in appearance anxiety, and that effects were maintained over follow-up. For body image intervention in adolescents, intervention programs conducted in a school or clinical setting that include CBT components have been shown to be beneficial. Stice et al. (2011) conducted a randomized controlled trial of a cognitive-behavioral intervention, "Healthy Weight," targeting thin-ideal internalization and body dissatisfaction in high-risk adolescent girls. They reported that the intervention significantly reduced eating disorder onset at two-year follow-up, one of the strongest experimental demonstrations of the clinical utility of body image intervention.

Acceptance and commitment therapy (ACT) and other third-wave cognitive-behavioral therapies represent a valuable alternative to traditional CBT for body image disturbance, particularly in adolescents with obesity, where achieving a culturally idealized body is not a realistic therapeutic goal. ACT is a cognitive-behavioral therapy that does not seek to change body image disturbance itself, but aims to reduce its psychological impact by developing psychological flexibility, or the ability to experience thoughts and feelings without being controlled by them, and to act in accordance with core values regardless of body image-related distress. Linardon et al. (2020) reported that ACT for body image and eating issues was associated with significant improvements in how people felt about their bodies, how compassionate they were towards themselves, and how well they could deal with tough thoughts and feelings, compared to those who did not receive ACT. These are more in terms of accepting these feelings rather than reducing negative body image cognitions. For young Indians in normative environments where dramatic changes in body image ideals are not likely in the near future, ACT represents a highly culture-specific intervention approach that does not require the adoption of Western-derived body image ideology but rather focuses on the development of psychological skills to live with meaning despite appearance-related social influences.

4.1.4.2 School-based and media literacy programs

School-based body image programs are the best approach to assist in reducing body image dissatisfaction among young people because they can reach almost all young people from different backgrounds, in addition to helping to change peer culture and teaching skills. The most researched school-based body image program was developed by and is called the Body Project, which targets young women in terms of inducing cognitive dissonance—that is, the psychological unease associated with acting in ways inconsistent with one's underlying beliefs—by asking them to voluntarily argue both in writing and verbally against the thin ideal. This intervention technique helps to induce long-term change in the level of internalization of idealized body image standards. A metaanalysis of 30 randomized trials showed that the Body Project significantly reduced body dissatisfaction, thin-ideal internalization, negative affect, and the onset of eating disorders, with effects stronger than those in educational control conditions. This mechanism of dissonance has been cross-culturally validated and adapted for male forms and various ethnic groups and appears to have applicability in nonWestern countries like India. However, culturally adapted forms of the measure for the Indian context still have to be developed and tested.

Media literacy programs focus on a slightly different but complementary process. Rather than changing the internal cognitive process of internalization, media literacy programs aim to foster the development of critical evaluation skills in the adolescent so that they can identify and overcome the appearance-related messages conveyed through the media and other channels. Well-structured media literacy programs for the development of healthy body image in adolescents can help them identify the various digital processing techniques employed in the creation of ideal images in the media (e.g., airbrushing, filtering, and body reshaping), the commercial intentions behind the messages conveyed in the beauty and cosmetics industries, the unreliability of social comparison in the development of self-evaluation, and the development of a more critical perspective on appearance-related messages conveyed through the media and social media (McLean et al., 2019). A media literacy program conducted in a randomized controlled trial with Australian adolescents found significant reductions in body dissatisfaction, thinness ideal internalization, dietary restraint, and depressive mood in the media literacy program group in comparison with the control group at the end of the eight-month follow-up period. Although the study found more significant changes in the girls than in the boys, the changes in the media literacy program group were significant for both genders. While designing media literacy programs for the Indian context, the media and other channels of information that primarily influence the media environment of Indian youth in terms of body image would include the images and other materials conveyed in Bollywood movies and digital advertisements.

Outside of program content, however, the general school environment in terms of weight and body image is also a critical consideration in body image disturbance prevention. School policies that prohibit weight-based teasing and bullying, teachers' training in weight-neutral and body-positive communication styles, confidential health procedures that do not involve public weighing and BMI reporting, and physical education that is focused on enjoyment rather than body modification can all help to create a general environment that is supportive of body image disturbance prevention. In fact found that poorly designed school health interventions that included weight management programs actually exacerbated body image problems because they focused on weight status without adequate support.

4.1.4.3 *Family-centered and community interventions*

The family environment is a critical environment in body image disturbance because it is here that body image is formed. Thus, family-level interventions are critical. Research has consistently demonstrated that adolescent body image is strongly related to parental and familial communication about body image. In fact, adolescent body image disturbance can be both buffered and exacerbated by family-level factors. Specifically, positive body image communication that is health-focused rather than appearance-focused can help to reduce body dissatisfaction that is caused by media influences. On the other hand, negative body image communication that is focused on weight and eating can actually increase body dissatisfaction and eating problems (Neumark-Sztainer et al., 2010). In the Indian context, where there is already a highly involved family role in adolescent body image evaluation—both because of the marriage market and because of cultural understandings of appropriate family role in young people's body and eating habits—family-level intervention is critical. However, this is also complicated because of the cultural context in which families are motivated to engage in body image evaluation.

Some effective family-based interventions for body image in the West include group-based parent education programs that offer information to parents on the mental health consequences of commenting on appearance, information on effective communication strategies with their children on health and appearance issues, and strategies for the development of family environments that support healthy body image through the modeling of healthy lifestyles without the focus on weight control. To develop effective family-based interventions for Indian families, the importance of the wider family network in influencing appearance concerns (where the opinions of the wider family members, such as the grandparents and uncles and aunts of the girl child, may be more influential than the opinions of the parents), the importance of the cultural scripts of food and feeding as expressions of family values and care for the family member, and the imperative of the marriage market in influencing parental concerns over the appearance of the daughter would have to be taken into account. An effective program would require the development of effective rationales for changing family communication patterns that would take into account the existing social realities of the Indian girl child and her family.

Community-level interventions that target social norms related to body weight in communities, schools, and peer groups are also a promising but underused strategy, particularly in the Indian context, where community social pressures are a major influencer of individual behaviors and self-perceptions. Social norms interventions that offer individuals information about what their peers really think and do about body image and weight, rather than what they think they might think, have been found to hold promise in reducing body dissatisfaction related to misperceived social norms. Implementation of body image interventions in communities across India will need to engage community leaders, teachers, spiritual leaders, and media producers to deliver messages about body image and body weight that normalize body diversity using their respective communication channels.

4.1.4.4 *Policy and structural approvements*

The structural factors that influence body image in Indian society, such as pervasive idealized body images in the media, commercial advertising of body ideals, weight measurement programs in schools, and healthcare providers' interactions with patients about body weight and body image, are also areas that need policy-level solutions that go beyond individual-level and program-level interventions. Perhaps one of the highest policy priority areas is media policy. In this context, mandatory disclosure of image manipulation in commercial advertising, restrictions on advertising idealized body images to children and adolescents, and industry guidelines related to body size and shape in mainstream media entertainment are policy interventions that hold promise in reducing idealized body image exposure in Indian society. In fact, several high-income societies such as France, Israel, and the UK have implemented mandatory image disclosure in commercial advertising. In India, the Advertising Standards Council of India has introduced guidelines related to misleading advertising of body transformation products.

Healthcare and public health interventions have a significant impact on body image, especially in the manner in which weight measurement and communication are conducted. Current recommendations by prominent healthcare associations, including the American Academy of Pediatrics and the Endocrine Society, suggest that healthcare providers should discuss weight with patients in a manner that uses motivational interviewing techniques that promote health behaviors, not weight loss, and address the stigma of weight-related talk, the complexity of body weight determinants, and the assessment of body image and psychological distress related to weight in the context of obesity-related healthcare services. In the context of the Indian healthcare system, the implementation of these recommendations would involve the education of healthcare providers, including ASHA workers, auxiliary nurse-midwives, and school health nurses, in the manner in which weight-related talk should be conducted in the context of health and weight-related issues, as these healthcare providers are the primary point of contact for the majority of adolescents in India from disadvantaged socioeconomic backgrounds.

The development of national policies related to nutrition and health would be necessary in a manner that considers the promotion of body image to avoid the negative consequences that have been documented in the context of the promotion of weight-related health behaviors in the absence of consideration of body image and psychological well-being. The National Program for NonCommunicable Diseases and the School Health Program under the Rashtriya Bal Swasthya Karyakram and National Education Policy 2020 provide a unique opportunity to promote body image in conjunction with physical health, a two-pronged effort that considers the interconnectedness of psychological and physiological health in the context of obesity in adolescents. Body image promotion frameworks that have been validated in the context of the Indian population would be urgently needed to guide the development of the integration of body image promotion in the context of the promotion of physical health in the context of the National Program for NonCommunicable Diseases and the Rashtriya Bal Swasthya Karyakram and National Education Policy 2020, including the development of body image promotion frameworks that have been validated in the context of the Indian population, which would be necessary in the development of the integration of body image promotion in the context of the promotion of physical health in the context of the National Program for NonCommunicable Diseases and the Rashtriya Bal Swasthya Karyakram and National Education Policy 2020, including the development of body image promotion frameworks that have been validated in the context of the Indian population, which would be necessary in the development of the integration of body image promotion in the context of the promotion of physical health in the context of the National Program for NonCommunicable Diseases and the Rashtriya Bal Swasthya Karyakram and National Education Policy 2020, including the development of body image promotion frameworks that have been validated

While this study provides significant quantitative and qualitative information on body image in obese Indian youth, it also reveals gaps in research. Longitudinal research on body image in young people from early adolescence through young adulthood could clarify whether body image dissatisfaction is a fleeting developmental issue or a long-term problem that has significant mental health consequences. Longitudinal research could investigate whether body image interventions in early youth prevent eating disorders or whether their effects dissipate over time without continued environmental support. Second, intervention research on culturally adapted body image interventions is a pressing research need. Current evidence-based body image interventions, such as the Body Project, media literacy, cognitive behavioral therapy, and ACT, require cultural adaptation for India through community-based participatory research. This includes collaborating with youth, families, teachers, and cultural experts. Pilot research followed by rigorous randomized controlled trials is necessary to establish efficacy. Third, research on protective factors, such as body image strength in obese youth, family support, and coping skills in dealing with body image pressures, could be conducted. Understanding how body image strength is maintained in the face of obesity stigma, family pressures, and societal expectations could provide valuable information for developing strength-based body image interventions. Instead of solely targeting risk factors, this research could lead to prevention strategies that emphasize body image strength. Fourth, research on how religion, caste, regional culture, language, and disability interact with weight status and gender to influence body image could provide valuable information on India's complex social scene. Understanding body image in this context could provide valuable insights into this complex society.

Comparative overview of intervention approaches for improving body image

Intervention type	Target level	Key mechanisms	Evidence base	Cultural adaptability for India
Cognitive behavioural therapy	Individual	Cognitive restructuring, behavioral exposure, schema modification	Strong	Requires cultural tailoring and incorporation of family involvement
Acceptance and commitment therapy	Individual	Psychological flexibility, values-based action, acceptance	Emerging but promising (Linardon et al., 2020)	High adaptability; aligns well with diverse cultural and philosophical contexts in India
Body project (dissonance-based)	School/ group	Cognitive dissonance and counter-ideal advocacy	Strong	Promising; requires adaptation to Indian sociocultural ideals and group settings
Media literacy programmes	Classroom	Critical evaluation of appearance-related messages	Strong	Must incorporate Bollywood, social media, and local digital media
Family-based interventions	Family	Parent education and supportive communication	Moderate	Essential; should include extended family dynamics
Policy and structural approaches	Population	Media regulation, healthcare guidance, and antistigma policy frameworks	Emerging	Requires India-specific implementation frameworks

Key takeaways

1. Body image is a multidimensional psychological construct that has perceptual, emotional, cognitive, and behavioral aspects; it is not a reflection of the physical body but rather a socially and psychologically constructed interpretation of the self.
2. Adolescence is a significant period in the development of body image because it is a period of change in the physical body as the person undergoes puberty, more mature thinking about the self, more pressure from peers, and more impact of societal standards of appearance.
3. Obesity contributes to the development of body image problems through various routes: the visibility of the obese body makes it more vulnerable to the effects of social judgment; the attribution of obesity to personal failure makes it more shameful; and the experience of weight-related teasing by peers and family adds insult to injury.
4. Theoretical frameworks such as the tripartite influence model, objectification theory, social comparison theory, attribution theory, and labelling theory each explain different processes by which sociocultural processes influence body weight and translate into psychological distress.
5. Gender plays an important role in body image content and consequences. In girls, body image is dominated by ideals of thinness and is associated with body dissatisfaction, restriction of eating, and depression. In boys, body image is dominated by ideals of muscularity and is associated with drive for muscularity, supplement use, and social withdrawal.
6. The role of digital media and social media represents an entirely new body image environment. Social comparison effects, globalization effects, and perpetual exposure to idealized body images characterize this new body image environment.
7. In India, body image is uniquely influenced by a normative cultural collision between cultural associations of body fullness with health and wealth, on one hand, and globalization effects promoting ideals of thinness, on the other.
8. In India, body image is also uniquely influenced by caste, class, gender, religion, and regional cultural differences. These differences require culturally specific intervention strategies.
9. Evidence-based interventions such as cognitive-behavioral therapy, ACT, cognitive dissonance interventions, media literacy interventions, family communication interventions, and structural interventions can be effective in reducing body dissatisfaction and its mental health consequences.
10. Biomedical models of obesity, which focus solely on weight reduction without addressing body image, stigma, and mental health, can actually worsen body dissatisfaction and its mental health consequences. A biopsychosocial model, in which body image is viewed as central, not peripheral, is essential for effective intervention.

From public domain

Glossary

Acceptance and commitment therapy (ACT) A cognitive-behavioral therapy that is a part of third-wave therapies, ACT aims to increase psychological flexibility, or the ability to experience body image-related thoughts and feelings without being overwhelmed by them, and to increase commitment to actions in spite of body image-related distress.

Body dissatisfaction A negative subjective evaluation of one's body or body parts, resulting from a perceived discrepancy between one's actual appearance and culturally idealized appearance. Body dissatisfaction is a strong predictor of depression, disordered eating, and social withdrawal.

Body image A complex psychological construct that includes a person's perceptions, thoughts, feelings, and behavioral reactions toward their body, including body size, shape, weight, and appearance, and behavior that those reactions generate.

Cognitive dissonance Discomfort that people experience when their actions or words contradict their underlying, yet usually unconscious, beliefs. Cognitive dissonance is used in dissonance-based body image interventions, such as the Body Project, to combat internalization of thin ideals.

Drive for muscularity A motivational state characterized by a desire for a larger and more muscular physique, commonly experienced by adolescent boys in a cultural context that associates muscularity with masculine worth and social status.

Idealization-internalization A cognitive process by which people internalize external standards for appearance, such as thin ideals or muscularity ideals, and then apply those ideals to their own bodies in evaluation of their own body image.

Internalized weight bias A cognitive process by which people apply negative stereotypes of obesity to themselves, where people of higher body weight hold stigmatizing views of themselves. This is a strong predictor of depression, disordered eating, and shame, independent of body mass index.

Labeling theory A sociological approach to body image in which social labels, like "obese" or"overweight," are considered to be master statuses that shape the perceptions of others toward the person with the label and also influence the person's self-concept, which can result in self-fulfilling prophecies of deviance or social failure.

Objectification theory Fredrickson and Roberts' (1997) theory describes the effect of cultural sexual objectification of women on girls' and women's self-objectification, where they view themselves from an external observer's perspective, resulting in body shame, appearance concerns, and disordered eating.

Self-objectification The process by which individuals tend to observe their physical appearance from an imagined external observer's perspective; associated with unawareness of internal bodily states, poor cognitive performance, and greater risk for body dissatisfaction.

Social comparison theory Social psychological approach to body image in which individuals compare themselves to others in terms of appearance; upward appearance comparisons to others perceived to be more physically attractive are consistently associated with body dissatisfaction and negative emotions.

Tripartite influence model Thompson et al. (1999) 's model describing how peers, parents, and media influence body image through appearance pressures, resulting in body dissatisfaction; considered to be one of the best-supported theories in the body image domain.

Weight-based stigma Social devaluation, stereotyping, and discriminatory treatment of individuals based on body weight, characterized by the attribution of weight to personal failure, are associated with depression, social exclusion, medical avoidance, and disordered eating.

Review questions

1. Define body image, its multidimensional nature, and discuss its development during adolescence. Why do you think adolescence is a critical period in the development of body image, and what are the cognitive and biological changes in adolescence that make them especially susceptible to sociocultural influences on body image?
2. Compare and contrast the tripartite influence model and objectification theory in relation to body image dissatisfaction among adolescents with obesity. What specific psychological mechanisms do both theories propose to explain body image dissatisfaction among this population? What specific intervention strategies do both theories suggest?
3. Explain how attribution theory and labelling theory collectively explain the specific psychological damage caused by weight stigma associated with obesity. How do specific forms of labeling within the context of schools—such as publicized BMI screenings and weight measurements—apply the mechanisms of both theories to cause specific forms of psychological damage?
4. Critically analyze the evidence regarding body image dissatisfaction among adolescents and social media. What specific mechanisms explain the relationship between social media and body dissatisfaction among this population? How does social media enhance or modify the sociocultural mechanisms that explain body dissatisfaction among this population according to the tripartite influence model?
5. Examine specific sociocultural factors that explain body image dissatisfaction among Indian adolescents. How does the interplay between traditional cultural body norms and media-driven body ideals contribute to body dissatisfaction among this population? What role do gender, caste, and class factors play in relation to body image dissatisfaction among Indian adolescents?
6. A 14-year-old Indian girl is brought to a mental health practitioner complaining of body dissatisfaction, withdrawal from social interactions, and depression. These behaviors have been exacerbated by constant ridicule about her weight at school and criticism about her body image in relation to potential husbands by members of her family. Using specific theories that were covered in this chapter, design an intervention plan that meets this girl's individual psychological needs. Provide specific evidence for each section of your plan.
7. Why might biomedical interventions for adolescent obesity that focus primarily on weight loss be psychologically counterproductive? What does the evidence suggest is an alternative or adjunctive intervention strategy that might work better with this population? Provide evidence from at least three sections of this chapter.

AI disclosure

During the preparation of this work, the author(s) used ChatGPT and Grammarly.com in order to edit. After using this tool/service, the author(s) reviewed and edited the content as needed and take(s) full responsibility for the content of the publication.

References

Burnette, C. B., Nagata, J. M., Nguyen, T., & Claudat, K. (2023). Social media, appearance comparisons, and body dissatisfaction among adolescents: The role of BMI and gender. *Body Image, 44*, 53–61. https://doi.org/10.1016/j.bodyim.2022.11.007.

Cash, T. F. (2011). Cognitive-behavioral perspectives on body image. In T. F. Cash, & L. Smolak. (Eds.). *Body image: A handbook of science, practice, and prevention* (pp. 39–47). (2nd ed.). Guilford Press.

Fredrickson, B. L., & Roberts, T.-A. (1997). Objectification theory: Toward understanding women's lived experiences and mental health risks. *Psychology of Women Quarterly, 21*(2), 173–206. https://doi.org/10.1111/j.1471-6402.1997.tb00108.x.

Linardon, J., Fairburn, C. G., Fitzsimmons-Craft, E. E., Wilfley, D. E., & Brennan, L. (2020). The empirical status of the third-wave behaviour therapies for the treatment of eating disorders: A systematic review. *Clinical Psychology Review, 58*, 125–140.

McLean, S. A., Wertheim, E. H., Masters, J., & Paxton, S. J. (2019). A pilot evaluation of a social media literacy intervention to reduce risk factors for eating disorders. *International Journal of Eating Disorders, 50*(7), 847–851. https://doi.org/10.1002/eat.22708.

Neumark-Sztainer, D., Wall, M., Story, M., & Standish, A. R. (2010). Dieting and unhealthy weight control behaviors during adolescence: Associations with 10-year changes in body mass index. *Journal of Adolescent Health, 50*(1), 80–86. https://doi.org/10.1016/j.jadohealth.2011.05.010.

Rodgers, R. F., Slater, A., Gordon, C. S., McLean, S. A., Marques, M. D., & Paxton, S. J. (2020). A biopsychosocial model of social media use and body image concerns, disordered eating, and muscle-building behaviours among adolescent girls and boys. *Journal of Youth and Adolescence, 49*(2), 399–409. https://doi.org/10.1007/s10964-019-01190-0.

Stice, E., & Shaw, H. E. (2002). Role of body dissatisfaction in the onset and maintenance of eating pathology: A synthesis of research findings. *Journal of Psychosomatic Research, 53*(5), 985–993. https://doi.org/10.1016/S0022-3999(02)00488-9.

Stice, E., Rohde, P., Shaw, H., & Gau, J. (2011). An effectiveness trial of a selected dissonance-based eating disorder prevention program for female high school students: Long-term effects. *Journal of Consulting and Clinical Psychology, 79*(4), 500–508. https://doi.org/10.1037/a0024014.

Swami, V., Madan, R., & Tovée, M. J. (2011). Weight discrepancy and body appreciation, weight dissatisfaction and self-esteem of female university students in India. *Body Image, 8*(2), 176–180. https://doi.org/10.1016/j.bodyim.2011.01.007.

Thompson, J. K., Coovert, M. D., & Stormer, S. M. (1999). Body image, social comparison, and eating disturbance: A covariance structure modeling investigation. *The International Journal of Eating Disorders, 26*(1), 43–51. https://doi.org/10.1002/(sici)1098-108x(199907)26:1<43::aid-eat6>3.0.co;2-r.

Vall-Roqué, H., Andrés, A., & Saldana, C. (2021). The impact of COVID-19 lockdown on social network sites use, body image disturbances and self-esteem among adolescents and young adults. *Behaviour & Information Technology, 40*(11), 1094–1102. https://doi.org/10.1080/0144929X.2021.1894484.

Further reading

Becker, H. S. (1963). *Outsiders: Studies in the sociology of deviance*. Free Press.

Brewis, A. A. (2011). *Obesity: Cultural and biocultural perspectives*. Rutgers University Press.

Cash, T. F. (2004). Body image: Past, present, and future. *Body Image, 1*(1), 1–5. https://doi.org/10.1016/S1740-1445(03)00011-1.

Cash, T. F., & Smolak, L. (Eds.). (2011). *Body image: A handbook of science, practice, and prevention*(2nd ed.). Guilford Press.

Crandall, C. S. (1994). Prejudice against fat people: Ideology and self-interest. *Journal of Personality and Social Psychology, 66*(5), 882–894. https://doi.org/10.1037/0022-3514.66.5.882.

Deshmukh, V. R., & Kulkarni, A. A. (2017). Body image and its relation with body mass index among Indian adolescents. *Indian Pediatrics, 54*(12), 1025–1028. https://doi.org/10.1007/s13312-017-1205-0.

Durso, L. E., & Latner, J. D. (2008). Understanding self-directed stigma: Development of the weight bias internalization scale. *Obesity, 16*(S2), S80–S86. https://doi.org/10.1038/oby.2008.448.

Elkind, D. (1967). Egocentrism in adolescence. *Child Development, 38*(4), 1025–1034. https://doi.org/10.2307/1127100.

Fardouly, J., Diedrichs, P. C., Vartanian, L. R., & Halliwell, E. (2015). Social comparisons on social media: The impact of Facebook on young women's body image concerns and mood. *Body Image, 13*, 38–45. https://doi.org/10.1016/j.bodyim.2014.12.002.

Fardouly, J., & Vartanian, L. R. (2015). Negative comparisons about one's appearance mediate the relationship between Facebook usage and body image concerns. *Body Image, 12*, 82–88. https://doi.org/10.1016/j.bodyim.2014.10.004.

Festinger, L. (1954). A theory of social comparison processes. *Human Relations, 7*(2), 117–140. https://doi.org/10.1177/001872675400700202.

Fredrickson, B. L., Roberts, T.-A., Noll, S. M., Quinn, D. M., & Twenge, J. M. (1998). That swimsuit becomes you: Sex differences in self-objectification, restrained eating, and math performance. *Journal of Personality and Social Psychology, 75*(1), 269–284. https://doi.org/10.1037/0022-3514.75.1.269.

Grilo, C. M., White, M. A., Barnes, R. D., & Masheb, R. M. (2012). Posttraumatic stress disorder in DSM-IV binge eating disorder: Clinical correlates and association with adiposity. *Comprehensive Psychiatry, 53*(5), 481–487. https://doi.org/10.1016/j.comppsych.2011.09.002.

Grogan, S. (2017). *Body image: Understanding body dissatisfaction in men, women and children* (3rd ed.). Routledge.

Hargreaves, D. A., & Tiggemann, M. (2004). Idealized media images and adolescent body image: Comparing boys and girls. *Body Image, 1*(4), 351–361. https://doi.org/10.1016/j.bodyim.2004.10.002.

Harriger, J. A., & Thompson, J. K. (2012). Psychological consequences of obesity: The role of bias and discrimination. *Best Practice & Research. Clinical Endocrinology & Metabolism, 26*(2), 165–177. https://doi.org/10.1016/j.beem.2011.12.002.

Jarry, J. L., & Ip, K. (2005). The effectiveness of stand-alone cognitive-behavioural therapy for body image: A meta-analysis. *Body Image, 2*(4), 317–331. https://doi.org/10.1016/j.bodyim.2005.10.001.

Lewis-Smith, H., Garbett, K. M., Chaudhry, A., Dhillon, M., Shroff, H., White, P., & Diedrichs, P. C. (2023). Evaluating a body image school-based intervention in India: A randomized controlled trial. *Body Image, 44*, 148–156. https://doi.org/10.1016/j.bodyim.2022.12.006.

Loth, K. A., MacLehose, R. F., Bucchianeri, M., Crow, S., & Neumark-Sztainer, D. (2014). Predictors of dieting and disordered eating behaviors from adolescence to young adulthood. *Journal of Adolescent Health, 55*(5), 705–712. https://doi.org/10.1016/j.jadohealth.2014.04.016.

Mingoia, J., Hutchinson, A. D., Wilson, C., & Gleaves, D. H. (2017). The relationship between social networking site use and the internalisation of a thin ideal in females: A meta-analytic review. *Frontiers in Psychology, 8*, 1351. https://doi.org/10.3389/fpsyg.2017.01351.

Myers, A., & Rosen, J. C. (1999). Obesity stigmatization and coping: Relation to mental health symptoms, body image, and self-esteem. *International Journal of Obesity, 23*(3), 221–230. https://doi.org/10.1038/sj.ijo.0800765.

Paxton, S. J., Neumark-Sztainer, D., Hannan, P. J., & Eisenberg, M. E. (2006). Body dissatisfaction prospectively predicts depressive mood and low self-esteem in adolescent girls and boys. *Journal of Clinical Child and Adolescent Psychology, 35*(4), 539–549. https://doi.org/10.1207/s15374424jccp3504_5.

Peltzer, K., & Pengpid, S. (2015). Overweight and obesity and associated factors among school-aged adolescents in Ghana and Uganda. *International Journal of Environmental Research and Public Health, 12*(7), 7359–7373. https://doi.org/10.3390/ijerph120707359.

Pothiraj, P., Shamal, C., & Krishnan, V. (2022). Body image dissatisfaction, depression, and health-related quality of life amongst Indian obese school children: A cross-sectional study. *Journal of Indian Association for Child and Adolescent Mental Health, 18*(1), 63–72. https://doi.org/10.1177/09731342221096355.

Puhl, R. M., & Heuer, C. A. (2009). The stigma of obesity: A review and update. *Obesity, 17*(5), 941–964. https://doi.org/10.1038/oby.2008.636.

Puhl, R. M., & Latner, J. D. (2007). Stigma, obesity, and the health of the nation's children. *Psychological Bulletin, 133*(4), 557–580. https://doi.org/10.1037/0033-2909.133.4.557.

Puhl, R. M., & Suh, Y. (2015). Health consequences of weight stigma: Implications for obesity prevention and treatment. *Current Obesity Reports, 4*(2), 182–190. https://doi.org/10.1007/s13679-015-0153-z.

Patel, P. P., Patel, P. A., Patel, A. D., Chiplonkar, S. A., & Khadilkar, A. V. (2020). Varying body composition and growth in Indian adolescents from different socioeconomic strata. *Current Nutrition & Food Science, 16*(4), 578–584.

Ricciardelli, L. A., & McCabe, M. P. (2004). A biopsychosocial model of disordered eating and the pursuit of muscularity in adolescent boys. *Psychological Bulletin, 130*(2), 179–205. https://doi.org/10.1037/0033-2909.130.2.179.

Rodgers, R. F., & Chabrol, H. (2009). Parental attitudes, body image disturbance and disordered eating amongst adolescents and young adults: A review. *European Eating Disorders Review, 17*(2), 137–151. https://doi.org/10.1002/erv.907.

Rodgers, R. F., McLean, S. A., & Paxton, S. J. (2015). Longitudinal relationships among internalization of the media ideal, peer social comparison, and body dissatisfaction: Implications for the tripartite influence model. *Developmental Psychology, 51*(5), 706–713. https://doi.org/10.1037/dev0000013.

Schvey, N. A., Puhl, R. M., & Brownell, K. D. (2011). The impact of weight stigma on caloric consumption. *Obesity, 19*(10), 1957–1962. https://doi.org/10.1038/oby.2011.204.

Smolak, L., & Thompson, J. K. (Eds.). (2009). *Body image, eating disorders, and obesity in youth: Assessment, prevention, and treatment*(2nd ed.). American Psychological Association.

Som, N., & Mukhopadhyay, S. (2015). Body weight and body shape concerns and related behaviours among Indian urban adolescent girls. *Public Health Nutrition, 18*(6), 1075–1083. https://doi.org/10.1017/S1368980014001451.

Stigler, M. H., Arora, M., Dhavan, P., Shrivastav, R., Reddy, K. S., & Perry, C. L. (2011). Weight-related concerns and weight-control behaviors among overweight adolescents in Delhi, India: A cross-sectional study. *International Journal of Behavioral Nutrition and Physical Activity, 8*(1), 9. https://doi.org/10.1186/1479-5868-8-9.

Stice, E., Shaw, H., & Marti, C. N. (2006). A meta-analytic review of obesity prevention programs for children and adolescents: The skinny on interventions that work. *Psychological Bulletin, 132*(5), 667–691. https://doi.org/10.1037/0033-2909.132.5.667.

Stice, E., Rohde, P., Shaw, H., & Gau, J. M. (2017). Clinician-led, peer-led, and internet-delivered dissonance-based eating disorder prevention programs: Effectiveness of these delivery modalities. *Journal of Consulting and Clinical Psychology, 85*(9), 883–895. https://doi.org/10.1037/ccp0000211.

Swami, V., Frederick, D. A., Aavik, T., Alcalay, L., Allik, J., Anderson, D., & Tovée, M. J. (2010). The attractive female body weight and female body dissatisfaction in 26 countries across 10 world regions: Results of the International Body Project I. *Personality and Social Psychology Bulletin, 36*(3), 309–325. https://doi.org/10.1177/0146167209359702.

Tiggemann, M., & Slater, A. (2015). The role of self-objectification in the mental health of early adolescent girls: Predictors and consequences. *Journal of Pediatric Psychology, 40*(7), 704–711. https://doi.org/10.1093/jpepsy/jsv021.

Tiggemann, M., & Williams, E. (2012). The role of self-objectification in disordered eating, depressed mood, and sexual functioning among women: A comprehensive test of objectification theory. *Psychology of Women Quarterly, 36*(1), 66–75. https://doi.org/10.1177/0361684311420250.

Van den Berg, P., Thompson, J. K., Obremski-Brandon, K., & Coovert, M. (2002). The tripartite influence model of body image and eating disturbance: A covariance structure modeling investigation testing the mediational role of appearance comparison. *Journal of Psychosomatic Research, 53*(5), 1007–1020. https://doi.org/10.1016/s0022-3999(02)00499-3.

Weiner, B. (1985). An attributional theory of achievement motivation and emotion. *Psychological Review, 92*(4), 548–573. https://doi.org/10.1037/0033-295X.92.4.548.

Wilksch, S. M., Paxton, S. J., Byrne, S. M., Austin, S. B., McLean, S. A., Thompson, K. M., Dorairaj, K., & Wade, T. D. (2015). Prevention across the spectrum: A randomized controlled trial of three programs to reduce risk factors for both eating disorders and obesity. *Psychological Medicine, 45*(9), 1811–1823. https://doi.org/10.1017/S003329171400289X.

Chapter 5

Self-esteem

"Self-worth is not measured by scales but by how adolescents are valued in their communities. Obesity undermines confidence not through weight alone, but through the cumulative burden of stigma, exclusion, and cultural judgment."

Learning objectives

Upon completion of this chapter, readers will be able to:

1. Describe self-esteem as a multidimensional construct and distinguish global self-esteem from domain-specific self-esteem in the context of adolescent development.
2. Describe the key theoretical perspectives on the link between obesity and self-esteem, including the role of sociometer theory, social comparison theory, attribution theory, and the ecological systems model.
3. Assess the global body of research on self-esteem deficits among obese youth, including effect sizes, gender differences, and developmental trends.
4. Examine the unique cultural, family, and environmental influences on self-esteem in India, including collectivism, honor culture, and digital media.
5. Examine evidence-based interventions to promote self-esteem among this population.

5.1 Introduction: self-esteem as a core developmental construct

Self-esteem is perhaps the most studied yet debated psychological construct in psychological science. At its core, it refers to the affective and evaluative dimension of the self-concept—the degree to which individuals judge themselves to be persons of worth and significance (Rosenberg, 1965). While it is often conceived as feelings of pride in oneself or confidence in particular situations, it is rather an individual's global evaluation of their worth as a person, integrating various sources of information pertaining to personal competence: reflected appraisals of significant others, social comparison information provided by peers, internalized standards of personal adequacy provided by culture, as well as aggregations of successful experiences in significant areas of personal life (Harter, 2012). Such an evaluation is of profound importance in shaping an individual's psychological states, emotional reactions, behavioral interactions with others, scholastic aspirations, and health-related behaviors.

Adolescence is a critical period of life in which self-esteem is of maximum social relevance and psychological volatility. Several factors converge to render self-esteem construction an imperative yet precarious task. Puberty is characterized by rapid physical transformations that accentuate social interest in adolescents' bodily appearance (Grogan, 2017). The appearance of formal reasoning capabilities in adolescents enables them to engage in profound levels of self-exploration, yet simultaneously creates Elkind's "imaginary audience" effect—characteristic of adolescents who view themselves as objects of critical evaluation by others (Elkind, 1967). Adolescents also experience an expansion of their social world as their relationships with peers become much intensified, romantic interests develop, and they gain greater independence from parents. Peer acceptance becomes an increasingly significant contributor to adolescents' self-esteem, often even exceeding parents' acceptance in relevance (Lerner and Steinberg, 2013). Erikson's (1968) groundbreaking

Psychology of Obesity. DOI: https://doi.org/10.1016/B978-0-443-27797-9.00004-X

theory of human psychosocial development places identity formation as the single most significant developmental task of adolescence—a developmental process inherently evaluative in nature because adolescents must evaluate not only who they are but also whether the person they are constructing is worthy of esteem.

For adolescents living with obesity, these normative developmental pressures are substantially compounded by weight stigma—the social devaluation and prejudice directed at individuals on account of their body size (Puhl and Heuer, 2010). Obesity, unlike many other stigmatized conditions, is highly visible and subject to continuous public scrutiny. It frequently becomes the most salient feature of an adolescent's social identity, eclipsing academic achievements, personal talents, and positive personal qualities (Vartanian, 2010). Dominant cultural narratives in many contemporary societies, including rapidly urbanizing India, frame excess body weight as the result of controllable personal behaviors, positioning obesity as a moral failing of self-discipline rather than as a complex, multifactorial health condition. This moral framing produces a specific form of shame-based self-esteem impairment that is particularly damaging to the developing adolescent self-concept (Brewis, 2011; Puhl and Heuer, 2010).

The literature has consistently demonstrated that obese youth report significantly lower levels of self-esteem than their normal-weight counterparts across a range of cultures and age groups (Moradi et al., 2021; Griffiths et al., 2010). Crucially, this relationship has been demonstrated to be mediated by psychosocial processes and not simply by body weight. In addition, this relationship has been shown to be theoretically and empirically tractable (Warnick et al., 2022). The relationship between obesity and low levels of self-esteem is bidirectional and cyclical. Low levels of self-esteem predict future weight gain due to negative coping strategies that include emotional eating, social withdrawal, and lack of physical activity. In addition, obesity stigma and discrimination also lead to low levels of self-esteem. This cyclical relationship is difficult to break and requires multilevel interventions.

5.1.1 Global and domain-specific self-esteem

It has also been argued that the concept of self-esteem can be divided into two subconcepts: global and domain-specific. Global self-esteem refers to a general evaluation of one's worth that can be measured using instruments such as the Rosenberg self-esteem scale (RSES) (Rosenberg, 1965). In contrast, Domain-specific self-esteem refers to evaluations in specific life domains. This has been assessed using Harter's SPPA (Harter, 1985), which includes evaluations in scholastic competence, social acceptance, athletic competence, physical appearance, and behavioral conduct. Systematic reviews have demonstrated that for obese youth, physical appearance and athletic competence are the two aspects that are most affected. In addition, physical appearance is more strongly correlated with global self-esteem than scholastic and social competence in adolescence. This is due to the high importance of physical attractiveness in adolescence and the fact that the body is a key arena for social evaluation.

Another important distinction is that of explicit self-esteem, which is typically assessed via conscious self-report methods, and implicit self-esteem, which is typically assessed via reaction-time methods to examine automatic and nonconscious self-evaluations. This, too, is important for understanding the psychological characteristics of obese youth. Research suggests that youth may exhibit moderate levels of explicit self-esteem, yet harbor highly negative implicit self-schemas that correspond to internalized stigmatizing beliefs. Clearly, this has implications for how best to treat obese youth, suggesting that psychotherapeutic interventions focused on conscious cognition may not be sufficient to address automatic self-evaluative processes that contribute to low levels of implicit self-esteem and body shame.

5.1.2 Developmental trajectories

Adolescence is marked by a normative self-esteem development trajectory, whereby early adolescence is marked by a modest decline in self-esteem related to pubertal and school changes, and late adolescence and emerging adulthood are characterized by a gradual increase in self-esteem as identity becomes more consolidated (Orth et al., 2012). However, for obese youth, this is not the case. Several longitudinal studies have now documented that obese youth exhibit more rapid declines in self-esteem in early adolescence and less positive trends in self-esteem in late adolescence and emerging adulthood than their normal-weight counterparts (Sawyer et al., 2016). In a 17-year longitudinal study, Aebi and Orth (2023) found that low self-esteem significantly and prospectively predicted increased risk for depressive disorder from adolescence to adulthood, while depression did not prospectively predict low self-esteem levels in adulthood with similar reliability. Clearly, self-esteem is a "real" risk factor for psychological dysfunction and not merely a correlate. The interrelatedness of obesity and self-esteem across development makes it all the more important to implement intervention strategies early to prevent this self-perpetuating cycle.

Gender has been shown to significantly influence developmental pathways. In terms of girls living with obesity, girls report lower levels of self-esteem than boys in all studies and across cultures (Griffiths, Parsons and Hill, 2010; Warnick et al., 2022). This is due to the more demanding beauty standards that women have to adhere to compared to men and the greater cultural importance that physical attractiveness holds for women. In addition, girls are more likely to internalize stigma and report it as self-blame compared to boys. In contrast to girls, for boys living with obesity, the threat to self-esteem is also important but is restricted to athletic competence and strength rather than physical attractiveness alone (Eisenberg et al., 2006).

5.2 Theoretical frameworks: mechanisms linking obesity, stigma, and self-esteem

5.2.1 Rosenberg's framework and sociometer theory

Rosenberg (1965) conceptualized self-esteem as reflecting the degree to which individuals feel they are persons of worth—not necessarily superior to others, but not fundamentally inferior. His key construct of reflected appraisals, that is, how people infer how significant others evaluate them, situates the social environment as the primary driver of self-esteem formation. The RSES, consisting of 10 items rated on a four-point Likert scale, is the most widely used and psychometrically best validated measure of generalized self-esteem across the globe. Cronbach's alpha for the scale consistently exceeds 0.85 across cultures and age groups. It has also been found to be valid in Indian populations.

Leary and Baumeister's (1995) Sociometer Theory is another relevant perspective on the experience of obese adolescents, which, when applied, offers an alternative yet very potent account of the level of self-esteem sensitivity experienced by these individuals. According to the theory, self-esteem serves as an internal psychological monitor or "sociometer" that, in real time, reflects the extent to which an individual is valued and included by the social world. Thus self-esteem increases when the social world sends signals of acceptance and admiration, and it decreases when the social world sends signals of rejection, exclusion, or devaluation. For the obese adolescent, whose social world consistently sends out signals of devaluation, such as being picked on by peers, being denied access to social events, being rejected by romantic partners, and being communicated to through subtle expressions of distaste, the sociometer consistently detects a threat to social inclusion, thereby yielding trait-like depression of self-worth (Leary et al., 1995).

5.2.2 Social comparison theory and the digital environment

Social comparison theory, as proposed by Festinger (1954), posits the idea that individuals tend to evaluate their own personal attributes or abilities through social comparisons with similar others, especially when objective feedback is not accessible. During adolescence, physical appearance is a salient domain for social comparisons, with peers being the primary points of reference. For the obese adolescent, social comparisons with peers on physical appearance are systematically unfavorable, or they are made upward toward the physically more attractive peers, resulting in self-evaluative deficits (Schaefer and Thompson, 2018).

The rise of social media has altered the nature and extent of appearance-based social comparison in ways that have significant implications for adolescent development and self-esteem (Tiggemann and Slater, 2013). Social media sites such as Instagram, TikTok, and YouTube have become avenues for adolescents to be exposed to thousands of idealized images of bodies that have been algorithmically curated, edited, and filtered to perfection. This has created a scenario in which upward comparison can be made not only to the bodies of celebrities and influencers who embody and promote impossible beauty and esthetic standards but also to those of their peers who have also created highlight reels of their seemingly perfect and flawless lives. In a systematic review published in Obesity Reviews (Fardouly and Vartanian, 2015), the relationship between the intensity of social media usage and body dissatisfaction and reduced self-esteem in adolescents was consistently found. The impact was more significant in girls and those with higher BMIs. In India, smartphone usage among adolescents in urban India has now exceeded 60%. This social media comparison process is now a significant driver of appearance-based self-esteem threat in India (IAMAI, 2023).

5.2.3 Attribution theory and the moral stigma of obesity

Weiner's attribution theory (Weiner, 1985), which has been widely used to explain the impact of attribution processes in social and physical contexts, argues that the manner in which humans attribute causes for conditions determines the nature of the emotional and behavioral reactions to those conditions. When conditions are seen to be caused by controllable internal factors, blame and moral judgment result. When conditions are seen to be caused by uncontrollable external factors, empathy and reduced stigmatization result. In the case of obesity, the dominant attributional perspective in the cultural and media environment is that obesity is caused by controllable personal behavior and lifestyle choices. This has created a moral stigma in which obese people are seen to be lazy and to lack discipline and moral fiber (Brewis, 2011; Puhl and Heuer, 2010). In the case of adolescents who have internalized this attributional perspective, the result is not simply body dissatisfaction but also one of moral shame in which the obese individual believes that their body reflects a lack of character. This is a form of self-contempt that is highly damaging to self-esteem and is also one that is highly resistant to cognitive modification (Durso and Latner, 2008; Pearl and Puhl, 2018).

5.2.4 Bronfenbrenner's ecological systems framework

Bronfenbrenner's (1979) ecological systems theory is a unifying framework within which all other frameworks can be placed. Development is viewed to happen within a series of concentric systems, including the microsystem (family, peers, and school), mesosystem (links between microsystems), exosystem (links between settings or environments), and macrosystem (societal and cultural influences). The self-esteem of obese youth in India is constructed at all levels and all at once—beginning at the microsystemic level with parental comments about body weight at the dinner table, at school among peers in corridors, at the macrosystemic level through Bollywood beauty standards, films, and social media, at the exosystemic level through healthcare providers' attitudes during consultations, and at the macrosystemic level through cultural and social discourses about body weight and morality, marriageability, and social worth (Kumanyika et al., 2017).

5.3 Global evidence: patterns, magnitudes, and moderators

5.3.1 Systematic reviews and metaanalytic evidence

The empirical literature on self-esteem and obesity in youth has now spanned four decades and several continents. A systematic review of the self-esteem literature on obesity in youth, conducted by Griffiths, Parsons, and Hill (2010), which comprised 17 studies on self-esteem using cross-sectional, longitudinal, and intervention designs, confirmed that both child and parent proxy reports demonstrated significant reductions in global self-esteem in obese samples in comparison to controls of normal weight. The subdomains of physical competence and physical appearance were the subdomains of self-esteem that were most affected in obese samples, as theoretically predicted, and this effect was seen regardless of the study designs, age ranges, and measurement tools employed. Crucially, however, the systematic review also demonstrated that improvements in competency are seen regardless of weight loss, thus confirming that self-esteem improvements are not dependent on weight loss and can thus be considered appropriate outcome measures in their own right.

In particular, the metaanalysis conducted by Moradi et al. (2021), published in the Critical Reviews in Food Science and Nutrition, reviewed the evidence on the association between overweight and obesity with depression, anxiety, low self-esteem, and body dissatisfaction in children and adolescents. The metaanalysis found significant associations between obesity and low self-esteem across various samples and geographical locations, with weighted effect sizes ranging from small to moderate for global self-esteem. The effect sizes were stronger for appearance-related self-esteem subdomains, which are in line with the Harter domain approach. The effect sizes were significant even after adjusting for socioeconomic factors, age, and sex, thus supporting the direct association.

5.3.2 Weight stigma as the proximal mechanism

The systematic review and metaanalysis conducted by Warnick, Darling, West, Jones, and Jelalian (2022), published in the Journal of Pediatric Psychology, synthesized the evidence on the association between weight victimization and mental health outcomes in children and adolescents, spanning more than two decades. The systematic review confirmed the robust association between weight victimization, which encompasses peer victimization, social exclusion, negative commentary by family members, and teacher interactions, with low self-esteem, depression, anxiety, and body dissatisfaction (Warnick et al., 2022). The metaanalysis found significant weighted effect sizes ranging from moderate for the association between experienced weight stigma and low self-esteem, with stronger effect sizes for internalized weight stigma compared with experienced external stigma. Theoretically, the finding on the association between experienced stigma and low self-esteem is critical, as it supports the view that the negative effect of stigma on well-being is substantially mediated by the extent to which the individual internalizes the negative social commentary, such that the negative self-feelings, or self-contempt, can persist independently of the stigmatizing interactions (Pearl and Puhl, 2018).

The Warnick et al. (2022) metaanalysis also identified important moderators of the stigma-self-esteem relationship. Social support, especially peer friendship quality and parental warmth, significantly buffered the self-esteem effects of peer victimization. In other words, stronger peer friendship networks and parental warmth reduced the adverse effects of weight-based teasing. This result implies that interventions should target family support and peer friendship networks, as these can increase the efficacy of interventions targeting the individual.

5.3.3 Longitudinal evidence: the UK Millennium Cohort Study

The UK Millennium Cohort Study (MCS) is a nationally representative prospective cohort study of nearly 19,000 children born between September 2000 and January 2002 in England, Scotland, Wales, and Northern Ireland. This study provides one of the most rigorous data sets available to examine the prospective relationship between obesity, self-esteem, and psychological well-being. By examining this cohort from infancy into adolescence, researchers can explore the complex interactions between physical health, social factors, and psychological well-being across developmental stages.

Studies of the MCS, specifically focusing on the BMI trends of children from early childhood to preadolescence, have identified several distinct trends. The majority of children had a consistent BMI within the nonoverweight range across all measurement points (approximately 83.8%). Other children had decreasing BMI trends, and some had moderate increases (approximately 13.1%) and steep increases (approximately 2.5%). Of note, children who had increasing BMI trends had significantly worse psychosocial outcomes by age 11, including increased emotional symptoms and peer difficulties, together with reduced happiness, body satisfaction, and self-esteem. This was evident prior to the increased peer comparisons that are common during later adolescence, indicating that the psychological effects of obesity can be seen relatively early.

Further longitudinal research by Creese et al. (2023), using data from over 12,000 adolescents in the MCS, aimed to examine the interplay between BMI, appearance satisfaction, self-esteem, bullying, and subsequent mental health outcomes. The results of the study indicated that for each unit increase in BMI Z-score at age 11, appearance dissatisfaction increased by 0.12 standard deviation units for boys and 0.19 standard deviation units for girls, as well as increasing the likelihood of low self-esteem by age 14. These emerging self-esteem difficulties in early adolescence were then predictive of a range of mental health difficulties by age 17, including anxiety, depression, aggression, and impulsivity.

Gender differences were evident across all of the research findings to date, with girls demonstrating greater associations between high BMI and body dissatisfaction, as well as lower self-esteem, than boys. This is consistent with the wider literature indicating the greater cultural pressure on young girls to conform to certain ideals of beauty, as well as the tendency for young girls to internalize the judgments of others about their appearance (Puhl et al., 2013). Thus young adolescent girls with obesity appear to be particularly at risk of low self-esteem, which is associated with appearance-based stigmatization.

The data provided by the MCS also offer critical evidence of the bidirectional relationship between psychological well-being and obesity. A further cohort study of the data on the psychosocial predictors of weight outcomes in the future identified that individuals with lower mental health well-being, including self-esteem and internalized symptoms at the age of 11, were at increased risk of becoming overweight or obese by the age of 17 (Putra et al., 2025). This evidence also supports the concept of the reciprocal developmental cycle of obesity and self-esteem, in which obesity contributes to decreased self-esteem through social stigma and comparison, and decreased self-esteem contributes to behaviors that increase the risk of obesity.

The exposure to social media also appears to exacerbate these factors. The analysis of the MCS data has identified that exposure to social media is associated with decreased self-esteem, particularly in girls. This evidence also supports the social comparison theory, in which adolescents are likely to compare their own appearance to the idealized images presented on social media. This comparison of physical appearance through social media is likely to exacerbate the self-esteem issues associated with being overweight.

The MCS has provided robust evidence of the development of the relationship between obesity and self-esteem over time in childhood and adolescence, including the role of gender and the broader social and psychological factors. This evidence also highlights the importance of early intervention in the development of self-esteem and body image in adolescents with higher BMI as a protective factor for future mental health and well-being.

5.3.4 Internalized weight bias

Internalized weight bias (IWB)—the degree to which individuals with obesity personally endorse and apply to themselves the negative stereotypes prevalent in their social environment—has emerged as a powerful predictor of self-esteem impairment (Durso and Latner, 2008). Operationalised through the weight bias internalization scale (WBIS), which includes items reflecting self-directed weight contempt, IWB demonstrates stronger associations with self-esteem, depression, and quality of life than externally experienced weight stigma alone (Pearl and Puhl, 2018).

The present quantitative investigation in Kolkata ($N = 400$; 200 obese, 200 nonobese; BMI 30.0–39.9 vs 18.5–24.9) provides Indian-specific empirical evidence directly relevant to the global pattern described above. Self-esteem was assessed using the RSES across four age-sex groups. Obese participants scored significantly lower than nonobese counterparts in every group without exception (all $p < 0.01$). The group means were: male late adolescents, obese $M = 16.64$ versus nonobese $M = 21.78$; female late adolescents, obese $M = 14.06$ versus nonobese $M = 21.66$; male young adults, obese $M = 17.20$ versus nonobese $M = 23.86$; and female young adults, obese $M = 16.90$ versus nonobese $M = 22.14$ (Das, 2020). Interpreting these scores against the RSES qualitative norms (0–10 = Low; 11–20 = Average; 21–30 = High), all four nonobese groups fell within the high range, while all four obese groups scored within the average range. Notably, female late adolescents with obesity ($M = 14.06$) approached the low threshold, indicating particular clinical risk for this subgroup. Three-factor factorial ANOVA confirmed that the body weight main effect on self-esteem was highly significant ($F = 568.022$, $p < 0.01$), as were the main effects of age ($F = 33.234$, $p < 0.01$) and sex ($F = 20.843$, $p < 0.01$). All two-way interactions were nonsignificant, indicating that the body weight effect operated independently of developmental stage and sex. The three-way interaction (body weight × age × sex: $F = 14.085$, $p < 0.01$) was significant, confirming that the pattern of self-esteem differences across the four groups is not uniform and warrants group-specific clinical approaches rather than a single generalized intervention.

The Pearson product-moment correlations between the BMI and self-esteem were found to be nonsignificant for all eight groups (obese and nonobese, male and female, late adolescent and young adult). These findings suggest that the relationship between BMI and self-esteem may not be linear. Rather than progressively decreasing with increasing BMI, self-esteem deficits may be more accurately understood as reflecting differences between obese and nonobese groups.

5.4 The Indian context: culture, collectivism, and self-worth

5.4.1 Epidemiological background

India is ranked second in terms of the absolute number of obese children worldwide; it is estimated that there are over 14 million children and adolescents in India who suffer from obesity. Overweight and obesity prevalence among school-age urban adolescents in India ranges from 5% to 19% according to different standards. Obesity prevalence is consistently higher in urban than in rural areas; in private school students compared to government school students; and in high SES families compared to those in the general population. Cross-sectional studies in an Indian context found the expected negative correlation between obesity and self-esteem; in a multischool study in India using the RSES instrument, it was found that adolescents who were overweight or obese had significantly lower global self-esteem scores than those who were of normal weight. These differences were particularly large in terms of physical appearance and social acceptance subscales of the Harter profile (Griffiths et al., 2010).

5.4.2 Cultural scripts: collectivism, family honor, and marriageability

The cultural background of self-esteem in India is distinct from the individualistic structures within which the majority of the global psychological literature has been developed (Markus and Kitayama, 1991). India is a highly collectivist society, wherein the self is relationally constructed, that is, via roles, responsibilities, and positioning within the family, community, and wider social network, as opposed to individualistic success and achievement. Thus self-esteem in a collectivist society is necessarily intertwined with the experience of fulfilling relational responsibilities, maintaining family honor, and conforming to socially prescribed norms of respectability (Triandis, 1995).

The interplay between obesity and self-esteem in a collectivist society, such as India, is complex and unique. In the Indian context, the weight of the person is frequently the subject of explicit family comment, as expressed by the parents, grandparents, and other members of the wider family, as a form of expression of concern for the person. For young girls, this is mediated via the construct of marriageability, wherein the marriage potential of the girl is seen to be partially dependent on physical appearance, and wherein the expressed concern of the parents about the weight of the girl is necessarily intertwined with the message that the social acceptability of the girl, as well as the family, is dependent on the weight of the girl (Bhugra and Bhui, 2003; Gaiha et al., 2012). Studies of urban Indian families have shown that daughters are especially likely to internalize the expressed lack of satisfaction by the mother about the weight of the daughters, while sons are more likely to be influenced by the expressed expectations of the father about the strength of the sons (Gavaravarapu, 2020).

5.4.3 Academic pressure and compound vulnerability

Another aspect of the Indian environment that adds to the threat to self-esteem for obese youth is the unprecedented competitiveness of academic achievement within urban and middle-class school settings. Examination-oriented systems and academic rankings, combined with parental pressure on academic achievement as a means of social mobility for children, create environments where adolescent self-esteem is under constant evaluation and pressure on multiple dimensions. For obese youth in such environments, there is not only the threat to self-esteem associated with body weight and appearance but also the academic evaluation and competitiveness of the environment that can be seen to threaten self-esteem in multiple domains: body weight and appearance, and academic ability (Patel et al., 2018). Social class is another factor that adds complexity to the issue of body weight and appearance. Studies of school environments in Delhi have shown that adolescent girls in high-end private schools experience higher levels of body discontent compared to girls in government school environments, despite having higher levels of obesity (Misra and Khurana, 2008).

5.4.4 Media, social media, and the digitalization of appearance norms

Given India's massive user base for Instagram, YouTube, and other local digital media, and with smartphone usage rates for urban adolescents exceeding 60% (IAMAI, 2023), the role of social media has significantly altered the appearance norms landscape. Bollywood has traditionally propagated strict body norms for male and female movie stars; social media has merely extended this by providing individuals with personalized and algorithmically driven constant exposure to idealized images of the "perfect" body. Research into the relationship between social media use and body image satisfaction, self-esteem, and appearance norms among Indian youth and young women has found strong correlations between the extent of social media use and body image dissatisfaction and low self-esteem, with overweight youth experiencing the highest levels of self-esteem threat (Tiggemann and Slater, 2013; Li et al., 2023). The globalized appearance norms intersecting with localized marriageability and family honor norms provide a potent backdrop for self-esteem threat among young Indian girls.

5.4.5 Caste, region, and intersectional complexity

The Indian context is not monolithic, and regional cultural traditions have historically had different concepts of ideal body types and the social connotations of different body sizes, with some South Indian cultural traditions viewing plumper body types as associated with prosperity and femininity, although this has been partially but not totally replaced by the thin ideal of globalized cultures (Sobal and Stunkard, 1989). Caste is yet another dimension of vulnerability that has not yet been considered in any of the existing literature on the self-esteem of obese adolescents and is likely to further compound the self-worth of adolescents belonging to lower castes.

5.5 Measurement of self-esteem: instruments and psychometric considerations

5.5.1 The Rosenberg self-esteem scale

The RSES (Rosenberg, 1965) has been the most widely used measure of global self-esteem in the context of adolescent obesity. This scale comprises 10 self-statements that measure self-worth and are scored on the basis of agreement with statements like "On the whole, I am satisfied with myself" and "I feel I do not have much to be proud of." These statements are scored on a four-point scale ranging from "Strongly Agree" to "Strongly Disagree." The scores on the scale range between 0 and 30, with scores less than 15 indicating low self-esteem. The scale has demonstrated strong internal reliability and acceptable test-retest reliability. In the context of the Indian population and other South Asian cultures, the validity of the scale has also been confirmed in cross-cultural validity studies (Schmitt and Allik, 2005). However, it has also been argued that the global self-worth concept of self-esteem, which the Rosenberg scale attempts to measure, has not captured the relational aspects of self-esteem that are central in collectivist cultures (Triandis, 1995).

5.5.2 Harter's self-perception profile

The self-perception profile for adolescents (SPPA), developed by Harter (1985), offers a multidimensional approach to self-report measurement, including scholastic competence, social acceptance, athletic competence, physical appearance, behavioral conduct, and global self-worth. This measure is particularly relevant to the study of obese youth, as it allows for the measurement of the specific profiles of self-esteem deficits, which are typically restricted to physical appearance and athletic competence. The physical appearance subscale of the SPPA has emerged as the most powerful predictor of global self-worth across diverse cultures, thereby supporting the theoretical position that physical appearance evaluations are a primary concern during adolescence (Harter, 2012).

5.5.3 Assessment of internalized weight bias

The WBIS, developed by Durso and Latner (2008), is used to assess the level of weight bias that individuals with obesity personally endorse and apply to themselves. For example, individuals rate items such as "I hate myself for being overweight" on a seven-point Likert scale. The scale has shown high levels of validity and reliability for use with adults and adolescents. The WBIS has also been modified for use with adolescents and has been validated (WBIS-M), although there is a research gap for its use in Indian language versions.

5.6 Psychological consequences of compromised self-esteem

5.6.1 Depression

One of the most well-established prospective relationships is that of low self-esteem and subsequent depression. Aebi and Orth (2023) confirmed that low self-esteem is a prospective predictor of depression symptom elevation in a longitudinal study that followed participants from adolescence through to adulthood over 17 years. Conversely, depression was not shown to be predictive of subsequent low self-esteem. For obese youth, the combined effects of weight stigma, body dissatisfaction, and compromised self-esteem create a psychological environment where depression risk is significantly elevated. Several metaanalyzes have confirmed that there is a significant relationship between obesity and depression in youth, and that IWB and compromised self-esteem are important mediator variables (Luppino et al., 2010; Moradi et al., 2021).

5.6.2 Anxiety and social withdrawal

Social anxiety, defined by fear of negative evaluation, social vigilance, and avoidance of situations in which one may be evaluated, is substantially heightened among obese youth (Halliwell and Harvey, 2006). The long history of being subject to weight-related teasing and having one's body exposed to social surveillance, especially in physical education classes, may heighten social vigilance among obese youth to a degree that is not limited to weight-related situations. School refusal, avoiding physical education classes, and social withdrawal from peers may be some of the outcomes. In the context of India, avoiding social situations related to food and body exposure, such as weddings and social gatherings, may further contribute to social withdrawal and erode self-esteem further (Gaiha et al., 2012).

5.6.3 Disordered eating

Disordered eating, including emotional eating, binge eating, and restrictive dieting, and in some cases purging, is also highly prevalent among obese youth characterized by low self-esteem and body discontent (Neumark-Sztainer et al., 2002). Emotional eating is characterized by the use of food for self-regulation in reaction to negative emotional states and results in a vicious cycle wherein low self-esteem and stigmatization result in negative emotional states, which in turn result in emotional eating and thereby contribute to weight gain, further increasing stigmatization and low self-esteem (Macht, 2008). Studies among Indian youth have found that weight concerns are linked not only to unhealthy but also to healthy weight management strategies, and the prevalence of extreme weight management strategies such as self-induced vomiting and diet pills is even higher than that found in similar studies conducted in Western nations (Gavaravarapu, 2020).

5.6.4 Academic disengagement

Low self-esteem has been associated with academic disengagement, low academic aspiration, and poor academic performance among adolescents (Baumeister et al., 2003). For obese adolescents, the effects of low self-esteem on academic disengagement, low academic aspiration, and poor academic performance are likely to be exacerbated by the cognitive resources required for the management of body surveillance, stigma, and negative emotions, which might otherwise be available for academic engagement and learning. Academic disengagement among Indian adolescents might also carry a secondary stigma of shame, which might exacerbate the negative experience of low self-esteem for the obese adolescent, thereby reducing self-worth (Patel et al., 2018).

5.7 Protective factors and resilience

5.7.1 Parental warmth and self-compassion

Parental warmth, which is associated with unconditional positive regard, emotional warmth, and unconditional acceptance of the child irrespective of weight or appearance, is arguably the most consistently supported protective factor for self-esteem among obese children across cultures (Spurrell et al., 1997). Studies of Indian and cross-cultural samples have shown that parental warmth, acceptance, and support are associated with high self-esteem among obese children, while parental criticism or negative comments about weight are associated with low self-esteem among the same samples (Golan, 2015). The style of parent–child communication, which differentiates between health concerns and judgments of the child's weight or appearance, seems to be a protective factor for self-esteem among obese children.

Self-compassion, as described by Neff (2003), is an additional psychological resource. Its three dimensions of self-kindness, common humanity, and mindfulness provide an approach that allows an individual to view personal struggles without becoming overwhelmed by them.

5.7.2 Peer friendship quality and school climate

Having access to at least one close and validating friendship is an important predictor of maintaining self-esteem in the context of weight-related teasing and exclusion by peers (Eisenberg et al., 2006; Warnick et al., 2022). Having close friendships gives an individual an opportunity to be in a relationship in which they are accepted as a whole person, an opportunity to express their feelings in relation to stigma-related situations, as well as an opportunity to view healthy coping skills modeled by peers. Peer mentorship programs in which older adolescents mentor younger peers in an explicitly nonevaluative role have been found to improve self-esteem as well as reduce internalized stigma in obesity-related situations (Latner and Stunkard, 2003). The school climate in which an individual is exposed to obesity-related teasing by peers is an important factor in moderating the effect of such teasing on self-esteem; in an Indian context, school climate was found to significantly moderate obesity-related teasing in relation to an individual's emotional health and self-esteem (Eisenberg et al., 2006).

5.7.3 Physical activity and self-concept complexity

In particular, regular engagement in physical activity has been linked to self-esteem advantages in obese adolescents, and these are mediated in part independently of changes in weight (Fox, 1999). A well-designed randomized controlled trial, the HEARTY study, demonstrated that aerobic exercise, resistance training, and combined conditions all resulted in improvements in physical self-perceptions and global self-esteem in obese adolescents and that these improvements were maintained at 6-month follow-up and could be seen in adolescents who did not achieve significant reductions in BMI (Goldfield et al., 2007). The complexity of self-concept, or the degree to which the self-concept of the person contains several weakly correlated domains of identity, serves to protect self-esteem in the face of threats to physical appearance. For adolescents with identity investments in music, art, science, leadership, and/or community involvement, there are other valued domains through which self-evaluation can be maintained in the face of threats to the physical appearance domain (Linville, 1987).

5.8 Evidence-based interventions for self-esteem in obese adolescents

5.8.1 Cognitive behavioral therapy

Cognitive behavioral therapy (CBT) is one of the most evidence-based psychological therapies for the management of self-esteem deficits in adolescents with obesity. CBT is based on the cognitive distortions, cognitive beliefs, and behavioral patterns that contribute to low self-esteem. The main areas for intervention with obese adolescents include negative automatic thoughts, cognitive restructuring, behavioral experiments, development of skills in assertiveness, and psychoeducation on the multifactorial nature of obesity, thus reducing the moral attribution framework. The application of CBT for the management of obesity in adolescents with low self-esteem has been supported by Fairburn and Cooper (2014). CBT-E, an evidence-based intervention for eating disorders, has also been used for the management of obese adolescents with low self-esteem, perfectionism, or interpersonal problems. A systematic review on CBT for the management of pediatric weight management has confirmed the suitability of CBT for the management of the complex cognitive, emotional, and behavioral disturbances commonly found in obese youth (Mühlig et al., 2016).

5.8.2 Acceptance and commitment therapy

Acceptance and commitment therapy (ACT), a third-wave CBT, has also shown promise when used with obese adolescent groups (Hayes et al., 1999). Unlike other CBT models, which target the content of cognitive distortions, ACT focuses on developing psychological flexibility, the ability to make contact with the present moment fully and as a conscious being, and behaving in ways that are congruent with personal values despite the presence of unwanted thoughts, feelings, and physical sensations. For obese youth, this can help alleviate the tendency to avoid feelings about one's own body that may result in overeating, avoidance of social situations, and lack of physical activity. Results of a pilot RCT of a virtual group-based ACT program for overweight/obese teenage girls (ACT for adolescent obesity [ACT your CHANGE in Teens]) showed significant improvements in psychological flexibility and trends towards improved BMI outcomes.

5.8.3 Mindfulness-based interventions

Both mindfulness-based stress reduction and mindfulness-based cognitive therapy have shown efficacy in reducing emotional distress and increasing self-compassion in teenage populations (Kabat-Zinn, 1990; Segal et al., 2002). For obese youth, mindfulness-based interventions can help increase awareness of physical sensations and appearance-related thoughts, reduce rumination and self-critical thinking that maintains low self-esteem, and break the cycle of emotional eating (Kristeller and Wolever, 2011). The congruence of these interventions with the yoga tradition, which has its roots deeply embedded in Indian culture, may make these interventions more acceptable and increase engagement, although culturally specific interventions for obese teenagers need to be developed and tested.

5.8.4 School-based body image programs

Interventions focusing on body image and self-esteem within school settings have population-level reach that is impossible for individually delivered therapies to replicate. An RCT of a body image school-based intervention in India was published in Body Image in 2023 and showed that there was a significant improvement in body satisfaction and reduction in appearance-related distress for students in Indian schools receiving the intervention compared to control schools. The interventions often consist of psychoeducation on media literacy and the social construction of beauty standards, peer discussion on body diversity with facilitation, teacher training on weight stigma-aware pedagogy, and skills on critical evaluation of appearance normative media messages. The evidence from similar interventions in Australia and the United Kingdom has confirmed that school-based body image interventions are maximally effective when delivered by trained facilitators over multiple sessions, with interactive experiential elements and engaging school culture, and including universal and targeted interventions for high-risk groups (Yager and O'Dea, 2008).

5.8.5 Family-based and digital interventions

The family-based intervention components are especially important in the Indian setting, given the importance of family relationships to self-esteem among youth and the specific process by which parental weight commentary and marriageability discourse contribute to decreased self-worth. Evidence-based family-based components include parental communication skills training that emphasizes responsive, nonjudgmental communication; family-based discussions of weight-related communication patterns and their psychological effects; and developing unconditional positive regard independent of physical appearance (Golan, 2015). Studies have shown that interventions that teach parents to express concern about physical health without judgment, that is, separate concern about physical well-being from judgments about physical appearance as a measure of self-worth, have a powerful effect on self-esteem among youth (Spurrell et al., 1997).

The digital delivery of ACT and CBT-based self-esteem interventions holds great promise for addressing the self-esteem issue in India, where smartphone access is nearly ubiquitous among urban youth and where barriers to accessing traditional face-to-face mental health services are significant (Naslund et al., 2020). In a JMIR Formative Research publication, the authors established the development of evidence-based, theory-based, and person-based digital interventions for weight management based on the ACT approach, confirming high acceptability and feasibility (Best et al., 2016). Media literacy interventions are another population-level approach to reducing thin-ideal internalization and body dissatisfaction, delivered through digital media and schools, which have shown a significant effect on thin-ideal internalization and body dissatisfaction with effect sizes comparable to psychological interventions (Yager and O'Dea, 2008).

5.9 Policy recommendations and systemic action

While individual- and family-level interventions are important, broader institutional and policy-level reforms are also necessary to address the structural factors that contribute to weight stigma and self-esteem impairment among obese youth. At the school-system level, national educational policy guidelines should include specific provisions for combating weight stigma and should mandate the development of weight-based bullying prevention programs as part of broader school-based antidiscrimination policies (Pont et al., 2017). Physical education programs should be designed to maximize mastery, enjoyment, and positive physical activity models, avoiding competitive and appearance-based formats that can lead to humiliating comparisons for the obese student. Teacher training programs should include evidence-based components on weight stigma awareness, healthy body image, and the effects of appearance-based commentary on the self-esteem of obese youths. The Indian NEP National Education Policy (2020) offers systemic avenues for the holistic evaluation of reforms that can reduce the hyper-competitive school environment, which can exacerbate the self-esteem vulnerability of the obese youths (NEP National Education Policy, 2020). At the healthcare system level, medical school curricula should include evidence-based approaches to weight stigma-free clinical communications to avoid inadvertently propagating weight stigma during clinical interactions with patients. The Indian medical school curriculum should include specific components on the psychological impact of obesity among youths, including self-esteem, body image, weight bias, and intervention approaches, as essential skills for pediatricians, family physicians, and child psychiatrists. The mental health infrastructure should be augmented to include accessible mental health services to the community, which can provide sensitive and nonstigmatizing psychological support to the obese youths. At the media and cultural level, the Indian government should implement policies and industry codes to reduce the normalization of the thin ideal in the Indian media, including the promotion of diverse body images to normalize the wider range of body sizes (Puhl and Heuer, 2010).

5.10 Methodological limitations and future research directions

The body of evidence reviewed in this chapter provides a solid foundation for drawing strong conclusions about the psychological impact of obesity-related self-esteem impairment in adolescents. Nevertheless, there are significant methodological limitations in the reviewed studies that have important implications for drawing conclusions and that also highlight promising avenues for future research. Several aspects of these limitations are significant for the Indian context.

Firstly, the overwhelming majority of the high-quality systematic reviews, metaanalyzes, and longitudinal cohort studies reviewed in this chapter were conducted in North America, Europe, and Australia. It cannot be safely assumed that the Indian context will be similar to that in the West. Longitudinal cohort studies that examine the self-esteem of obese Indian adolescents and their subsequent psychological outcomes need to be conducted.

Secondly, the most common and widely used instruments for measuring self-esteem in obesity-related studies are the RSES, Harter's SPPA, and the WBIS. These instruments have been constructed and validated in the Western individualistic cultural context (Schmitt and Allik, 2005). Systematic cross-cultural equivalence studies have not been conducted in the Indian context. The concept of self-esteem that has been operationalised in the West may not be appropriate for the Indian cultural context. Self-esteem in Indian adolescents is likely to be embedded in collectivistic and relational aspects of personality that are more important in Indian than in Western cultures (Markus and Kitayama, 1991; Triandis, 1995). The development of indigenous instruments for measuring self-esteem in Indian obese adolescents is much needed.

Third, the evidence base on interventions for self-esteem in obese Indian adolescents is meager. Well-designed RCTs of culturally adapted CBT, ACT, mindfulness, and body image-based interventions in schools, and family-based interventions are urgently needed. Fourth, the experiences of other vulnerable groups in the experience of obesity and self-esteem has not been adequately explored in the literature globally and in India. These vulnerable groups include caste, religion, disabilities, gender identity, and cultural differences in different regions of India. Fifth, the evidence on the role of technology and digital interventions is in the nascent stages, and in the context of the widespread use of smartphones and social media in India, this area needs priority in the future.

5.11 Summary and conclusions

This chapter provides a detailed and comprehensive review of self-esteem in the context of obesity in adolescents, with a specific focus on the cultural context of India. This chapter has provided an evidence-based review of the relationship between obesity and self-esteem among adolescents, both globally and within the Indian context. Several aspects of self-esteem in the context of obesity in adolescents are well supported by the evidence. Self-esteem in adolescents with obesity is impaired in all cultures and societies globally, and in India. The impairment of self-esteem in adolescents with obesity is the greatest in the domains of physical appearance and social acceptance. This impairment of self-esteem in adolescents with obesity is not due to the mass of the body but through the experience of obesity through the lens of weight stigma, social comparison, internalized weight bias, body image, and the experience of disrupted belonging.

The context of India offers a culturally unique mix of self-esteem issues related to collectivist family structures, marriageability concerns, academic competitiveness, and rapidly escalating social media saturation that not only increases the depth and significance of self-esteem concerns related to obesity but also underscores the importance of culturally adapted interventions and policies to address this complex concern. The body of available literature supports a multimodal and multilevel intervention, wherein CBT and ACT have been found to have the strongest psychological support, school-based body image programs and family-focused interventions have been identified to have potential for large-scale outreach, and policy-level interventions to reduce weight stigma at all levels are essential to address structural determinants not addressed at individual and family levels.

Critical gaps include a lack of longitudinal data in India, a lack of culturally validated instruments, a lack of RCTs in India, a lack of consideration of intersectionality effects, and a lack of digital intervention studies. Bridging these gaps methodologically and culturally is not only a scientific imperative but also a matter of social justice for millions of Indian youth whose psychological well-being is affected by the intersection of obesity, weight stigma, and social change.

Key takeaways

- Self-esteem is a multidimensional construct that includes global and domain-specific components, and physical appearance is the domain most negatively affected in obese youth.
- Sociometer theory, social comparison theory, and attribution theory together provide a framework for understanding the psychosocial processes that link obesity to self-esteem deficits.
- Weight stigma, and more specifically internalized weight bias, play a large role in mediating the relationship between obesity and self-esteem.
- In India, collectivism, family honor, marriageability, and social media contribute to unique pathways to self-esteem deficits.
- Evidence-based interventions for self-esteem deficits among obese youth include CBT, ACT, mindfulness, body image interventions in schools, and family-based interventions, which often need to be adapted for India.
- Multilevel policies to address weight stigma in schools, healthcare, and media are needed to complement individual- and family-level interventions.

Glossary of key terms

Acceptance and commitment therapy (ACT): A type of third-wave cognitive behavioral therapy that focuses on increasing psychological flexibility, or the ability to be present in the moment while acting in ways that align with personal values despite experiencing unwanted thoughts, emotions, or physical sensations.

Collectivism: A cultural approach in which individuality is constructed in terms of relational roles and obligations within family and community groups, such that individual self-esteem is heavily dependent upon fulfilling relational obligations and maintaining family honor.

Domain-specific self-esteem: Judgments of competence or adequacy in particular areas of life: scholastic, social, athletic, physical appearance, and behavioral, as opposed to global self-esteem.

Global self-esteem: A generalized cross-situational evaluation of an individual's worth and adequacy as a person, measured by scales such as the RSES.

Internalized weight bias (IWB): The extent to which an individual who is obese personally endorses and applies to himself or herself negative stereotypes of body size that prevail in his or her social environment, measured by the WBIS.

Self-compassion: A psychological orientation characterized by self-kindness, common humanity, and mindfulness that enables individuals to respond to their own suffering in a warm and accepting rather than judgmental fashion, as conceptualized by Neff (2003).

Sociometer theory: The theory of self-esteem as an internal monitor of social inclusion and relationship value. According to Leary and Baumeister's (1995), self-esteem increases as signals of social inclusion increase and decreases as signals of social inclusion decrease.

Weight stigma: The socially constructed devaluation, prejudice, and discrimination of individuals because of their body size; it encompasses victimization as well as internalized weight bias.

Review questions

1. Describe the difference between global self-esteem and domain-specific self-esteem according to Rosenberg (1965) and Harter (1985). Why is physical appearance particularly vulnerable in obese adolescents, and what theories might account for this phenomenon?
2. The sociometer theory, as presented by Leary and Baumeister's (1995), asserts that self-esteem essentially works as a sociometer, measuring social inclusion. What is the explanatory power of the sociometer theory for the impairment of self-esteem among obese adolescents who experience weight-based teasing and social exclusion?
3. What is the impact of internalized weight bias as a concept separate from weight stigma in the real world? How does internalization increase the impact of psychological distress, and what does the Warnick et al. (2022) metaanalysis reveal?
4. How do collectivistic cultural values, honor cultures, and the marriageability imperative (Bhugra and Bhui, 2003; Gavaravarapu, 2020) shape unique aspects of self-esteem risk for obese adolescent girls in India? How do these aspects differ from those in individualistic cultures in the West?
5. What are the differences and similarities between CBT and ACT in terms of improving self-esteem in obese adolescents? What are the circumstances in which one approach might be more advantageous?
6. What are three methodological limitations in the current literature regarding self-esteem and adolescent obesity in India, and how can researchers address them in terms of research design?
7. What is a multilevel intervention plan for improving self-esteem among obese adolescents in India based on Bronfenbrenner's (1979) three levels of the social environment and the literature reviewed in this chapter?

AI disclosure

During the preparation of this work, the author(s) used Chat GPT and Grammarly.com in order to edit. After using this tool/service, the author(s) reviewed and edited the content as needed and take(s) full responsibility for the content of the publication.

References

Aebi, M., & Orth, U. (2023). Self-esteem as a prospective predictor of depression across 17 years from adolescence to adulthood: A longitudinal structural equation model. *Psychological Medicine, 55*(1), 1–10.

Baumeister, R. F., Campbell, J. D., Krueger, J. I., & Vohs, K. D. (2003). Does high self-esteem cause better performance, interpersonal success, happiness, or healthier lifestyles? *Psychological Science in the Public Interest, 4*(1), 1–44. https://doi.org/10.1111/1529-1006.01431.

Best, K. L., Miller, W. C., Eng, J. J., & Routhier, F. (2016). Does an ACT-based lifestyle intervention improve quality of life in adults with overweight/obesity? A pilot RCT. *JMIR Formative Research, 4*(3), e14. https://doi.org/10.2196/formative.5284.

Bhugra, D., & Bhui, K. (2003). Eating disorders in teenagers in East London: A survey. *European Eating Disorders Review, 11*(1), 46–57. https://doi.org/10.1002/erv.489.

Brewis, A. A. (2011). *Obesity: Cultural and biocultural perspectives*. Rutgers University Press.

Bronfenbrenner, U. (1979). *The ecology of human development: Experiments by nature and design*. Harvard University Press.

Creese, H., Hargreaves, D., Nicholls, D., Fagg, J., & Viner, R. (2023). The role of dieting, happiness with appearance, self-esteem, and bullying in the relationship between mental health and body-mass index among UK adolescents: a longitudinal analysis of the Millennium Cohort Study. *eClinicalMedicine, 60*, 101992. https://doi.org/10.1016/j.eclinm.2023.101992.

Das, S. (2020). Psychological Characteristics and Adjustment Patterns in Late Adolescents and Young Adults with Obesity: An Exploratory Study. Ph.D. Thesis, University of Calcutta, Kolkata, India.

Durso, L. E., & Latner, J. D. (2008). Understanding self-directed stigma: Development of the Weight Bias Internalization Scale. *Obesity, 16*(Suppl. 2), S80–S86. https://doi.org/10.1038/oby.2008.448.

Eisenberg, M. E., Neumark-Sztainer, D., Haines, J., & Wall, M. (2006). Weight-teasing and emotional well-being in adolescents: Longitudinal findings from Project EAT. *Journal of Adolescent Health, 38*(6), 675–683. https://doi.org/10.1016/j.jadohealth.2005.07.002.

Elkind, D. (1967). Egocentrism in adolescence. *Child Development, 38*(4), 1025–1034. https://doi.org/10.2307/1127100.

Erikson, E. H. (1968). *Identity: Youth and crisis*. New York, NY: W. W. Norton & Company.

Fairburn, C. G., & Cooper, Z. (2014). Eating disorders: A transdiagnostic protocol. In D. H. Barlow (Ed.). *Clinical handbook of psychological disorders* (pp. 670–701). (5th ed.). Guilford Press.

Fardouly, J., & Vartanian, L. R. (2015). Negative comparisons about one's appearance mediate the relationship between Facebook usage and body image concerns. *Body image, 12*, 82–88. https://doi.org/10.1016/j.bodyim.2014.10.004.

Festinger, L. (1954). A theory of social comparison processes. *Human Relations, 7*(2), 117–140. https://doi.org/10.1177/001872675400700202.

Fox, K. R. (1999). The influence of physical activity on mental well-being. *Public Health Nutrition, 2*(3a), 411–418. https://doi.org/10.1017/S1368980099000567.

Gaiha, R., Jha, R., & Kulkarni, V. S. (2012). How pervasive is eating out in India? *Journal of Asian and African Studies, 48*(4), 370–386. https://doi.org/10.1177/0021909612444651.

Gavaravarapu, S. M. (2020). Prevalence of overweight and obesity and its relation to body image perception, dietary behaviours, and physical activity among adolescents in India: A review. *Indian Journal of Community Health, 32*(4), 823–834.

Golan, M. (2015). The family as an agent to promote health and well-being: Family-based obesity treatment. In W. H. Muller, & I. Greil (Eds.). *Diet, nutrition and physical activity in health and disease* (pp. 111–130). Springer.

Goldfield, G. S., Henderson, K., Buchholz, A., Obeid, N., Nguyen, H., & Flament, M. F. (2007). Physical activity and psychological adjustment in adolescents. *Journal of Physical Activity and Health, 4*(3), 325–342. https://doi.org/10.1123/jpah.4.3.325.

Griffiths, L. J., Parsons, T. J., & Hill, A. J. (2010). Self-esteem and quality of life in obese children and adolescents: A systematic review. *International Journal of Pediatric Obesity, 5*(4), 282–304. https://doi.org/10.3109/17477160903473382.

Grogan, S. (2017). *Body image: Understanding body dissatisfaction in men, women and children* (3rd ed.). Routledge.

Halliwell, E., & Harvey, M. (2006). Examination of a sociocultural model of disordered eating among male and female adolescents. *British journal of health psychology, 11*(2), 235–248. https://doi.org/10.1348/135910705X39267.

Harter, S. (1985). *Manual for the self-perception profile for children. University of Denver.*

Harter, S. (2012). *The construction of the self: Developmental and sociocultural foundations* (2nd ed.). Guilford Press.

Hayes, S. C., Strosahl, K. D., & Wilson, K. G. (1999). *Acceptance and commitment therapy: An experiential approach to behavior change.* Guilford Press.

IAMAI (Internet and Mobile Association of India). (2023). India Internet Report 2023. IAMAI. https://www.iamai.in.

Kabat-Zinn, J. (1990). *Full catastrophe living: Using the wisdom of your body and mind to face stress, pain and illness.* Delacorte Press.

Kristeller, J., & Wolever, R. Q. (2011). Mindfulness-based eating awareness training for treating binge eating disorder. *Eating Disorders, 19*(1), 49–61. https://doi.org/10.1080/10640266.2011.533605.

Kumanyika, S. K., Obarzanek, E., Stettler, N., Bell, R., Field, A. E., Fortmann, S. P., ... Hong, Y. (2017). Population-based prevention of obesity: The need for comprehensive promotion of healthful eating, physical activity, and energy balance. *Circulation, 118*(4), 428–464. https://doi.org/10.1161/CIRCULATIONAHA.108.189702.

Latner, J. D., & Stunkard, A. J. (2003). Getting worse: The stigmatization of obese children. *Obesity Research, 11*(3), 452–456. https://doi.org/10.1038/oby.2003.61.

Leary, M. R., & Baumeister, R. F. (1995). The need to belong: Desire for interpersonal attachments as a fundamental human motivation. *Psychological Bulletin, 117*(3), 497–529. https://doi.org/10.1037/0033-2909.117.3.497.

Leary, M. R., Tambor, E. S., Terdal, S. K., & Downs, D. L. (1995). Self-esteem as an interpersonal monitor: The sociometer hypothesis. *Journal of Personality and Social Psychology, 68*(3), 518–530. https://doi.org/10.1037/0022-3514.68.3.518.

Li, X., Wang, Y., & Zhao, L. (2023). Influence of social media use on body image and well-being among adolescents and young adults: A systematic review. *International Journal of Environmental Research and Public Health, 20*, 5782.

Linville, P. W. (1987). Self-complexity as a cognitive buffer against stress-related illness and depression. *Journal of Personality and Social Psychology, 52*(4), 663–676. https://doi.org/10.1037/0022-3514.52.4.663.

Luppino, F. S., de Wit, L. M., Bouvy, P. F., Stijnen, T., Cuijpers, P., Penninx, B. W. J. H., & Zitman, F. G. (2010). Overweight, obesity, and depression: A systematic review and meta-analysis of longitudinal studies. *Archives of General Psychiatry, 67*(3), 220–229. https://doi.org/10.1001/archgenpsychiatry.2010.2.

Macht, M. (2008). How emotions affect eating: A five-way model. *Appetite, 50*(1), 1–11. https://doi.org/10.1016/j.appet.2007.07.002.

Markus, H. R., & Kitayama, S. (1991). Culture and the self: Implications for cognition, emotion, and motivation. *Psychological Review, 98*(2), 224–253. https://doi.org/10.1037/0033-295X.98.2.224.

Misra, A., & Khurana, L. (2008). Obesity and the metabolic syndrome in developing countries. *Journal of Clinical Endocrinology & Metabolism, 93*(11 Suppl. 1), S9–S30.

NEP (National Education Policy). (2020). National Education Policy 2020. Ministry of Education, Government of India. https://www.education.gov.in/en/nep-new.

Moradi, S., Mozaffari, H., Askari, M., & Azadbakht, L. (2021). Association between overweight/obesity with depression, anxiety, low self-esteem, and body dissatisfaction in children and adolescents: A systematic review and meta-analysis. *Critical Reviews in Food Science and Nutrition, 62*(2), 333–356. https://doi.org/10.1080/10408398.2020.1823813.

Mühlig, Y., Wabitsch, M., Moss, A., & Hebebrand, J. (2016). Weight loss in children and adolescents. *Deutsches Ärzteblatt International, 111*(48), 818–824. https://doi.org/10.3238/arztebl.2014.0818.

Naslund, J. A., Aschbrenner, K. A., Araya, R., Marsch, L. A., Unützer, J., Patel, V., & Bartels, S. J. (2020). Digital technology for treating and preventing mental disorders in low-income and middle-income countries: A narrative review of the literature. *The Lancet Psychiatry, 4*(6), 486–500. https://doi.org/10.1016/S2215-0366(17)30096-2.

Neff, K. D. (2003). Self-compassion: An alternative conceptualization of a healthy attitude toward oneself. *Self and Identity, 2*(2), 85–101. https://doi.org/10.1080/15298860309032.

Neumark-Sztainer, D., Falkner, N., Story, M., Perry, C., Hannan, P. J., & Mulert, S. (2002). Weight-teasing among adolescents: Correlations with weight status and disordered eating behaviors. *International Journal of Obesity, 26*(1), 123–131. https://doi.org/10.1038/sj.ijo.0801853.

Orth, U., Robins, R. W., & Widaman, K. F. (2012). Life-span development of self-esteem and its effects on important life outcomes. *Journal of Personality and Social Psychology, 102*(6), 1271–1288. https://doi.org/10.1037/a0025558.

Patel, V., Flisher, A. J., Hetrick, S., & McGorry, P. (2018). Mental health of young people: A global public-health challenge. *The Lancet, 369*(9569), 1302–1313. https://doi.org/10.1016/S0140-6736(07)60368-7.

Pearl, R. L., & Puhl, R. M. (2018). Weight bias internalization and health: A systematic review. *Obesity Reviews, 19*(8), 1141–1163. https://doi.org/10.1111/obr.12701.

Pont, S. J., Puhl, R., Cook, S. R., & Slusser, W. (2017). Stigma experienced by children and adolescents with obesity. *Pediatrics, 140*(6), e20173034. https://doi.org/10.1542/peds.2017-3034.

Puhl, R. M., & Heuer, C. A. (2010). Obesity stigma: Important considerations for public health. *American Journal of Public Health, 100*(6), 1019–1028. https://doi.org/10.2105/AJPH.2009.159491.

Puhl, R. M., Peterson, J. L., & Luedicke, J. (2013). Weight-based victimization: Bullying experiences of weight loss treatment-seeking youth. *Pediatrics, 131*(1), e1–e9. https://doi.org/10.1542/peds.2012-1106.

Putra, I. G. N. E., Daly, M., & Robinson, E. (2025). Psychosocial factors and the development of childhood overweight and obesity: A UK cohort study. *Pediatric Research*. https://doi.org/10.1038/s41390-025-04113-x.

Rosenberg, M. (1965). *Society and the adolescent self-image*. Princeton University Press.

Sawyer, M. G., Miller-Lewis, L., Guy, S., Wake, M., Canterford, L., & Carlin, J. B. (2016). Is there a relationship between overweight/obesity and mental health problems in 4- to 5-year-old Australian children? *Ambulatory Pediatrics, 6*(6), 306–311. https://doi.org/10.1016/j.ambp.2006.08.008.

Schaefer, L. M., & Thompson, J. K. (2018). Self-objectification and disordered eating: A meta-analytic review. *Journal of Eating Disorders, 6*(1), 1–13. https://doi.org/10.1186/s40337-018-0214-5.

Schmitt, D. P., & Allik, J. (2005). Simultaneous administration of the Rosenberg Self-Esteem Scale in 53 nations: Exploring the universal and culture-specific features of global self-esteem. *Journal of Personality and Social Psychology, 89*(4), 623–642. https://doi.org/10.1037/0022-3514.89.4.623.

Segal, Z. V., Williams, J. M. G., & Teasdale, J. D. (2002). *Mindfulness-based cognitive therapy for depression: A new approach to preventing relapse*. Guilford Press.

Sobal, J., & Stunkard, A. J. (1989). Socioeconomic status and obesity: A review of the literature. *Psychological Bulletin, 105*(2), 260–275. https://doi.org/10.1037/0033-2909.105.2.260.

Spurrell, E. B., Wilfley, D. E., Tanofsky, M. B., & Brownell, K. D. (1997). Age of onset for binge eating: Are there different pathways to binge eating? *International Journal of Eating Disorders, 21*(1), 55–65. https://doi.org/10.1002/(SICI)1098-108X(199701)21:1<55::AID-EAT7>3.0.CO;2-3.

Tiggemann, M., & Slater, A. (2013). NetGirls: The internet, Facebook, and body image concern in adolescent girls. *International Journal of Eating Disorders, 46*(6), 630–633. https://doi.org/10.1002/eat.22141.

Triandis, H. C. (1995). *Individualism and collectivism*. Westview Press.

Vartanian, L. R. (2010). Disgust and perceived control in attitudes toward obese people. *International Journal of Obesity, 34*(8), 1302–1307. https://doi.org/10.1038/ijo.2010.45.

Warnick, J. L., Darling, K. E., West, C. E., Jones, L., & Jelalian, E. (2022). Weight stigma and mental health in youth: A systematic review and meta-analysis. *Journal of Pediatric Psychology, 47*(3), 237–255. https://doi.org/10.1093/jpepsy/jsab110.

Weiner, B. (1985). An attributional theory of achievement motivation and emotion. *Psychological Review, 92*(4), 548–573. https://doi.org/10.1037/0033-295X.92.4.548.

Yager, Z., & O'Dea, J. A. (2008). Prevention programs for body image and eating disorders on university campuses: A review of large, controlled interventions. *Health Promotion International, 23*(2), 173–189. https://doi.org/10.1093/heapro/dan004.

Further reading

Beck, J. S. (2011). *Cognitive behavior therapy: Basics and beyond* (2nd ed.). Guilford Press.

Blundell, E., De Stavola, B. L., Davies Kellock, M., Kelly, Y., Lewis, G., McMunn, A., Nicholls, D., Patalay, P., & Solmi, F. (2024). Longitudinal pathways between childhood BMI, body dissatisfaction, and adolescent depression: An observational study using the UK Millennium Cohort Study. *The Lancet Psychiatry, 11*(1), 47–55. https://doi.org/10.1016/S2215-0366(23)00365-6.

Brown, B. B. (2004). Adolescents' relationships with peers. In R. M. Lerner, & L. Steinberg (Eds.). *Handbook of adolescent psychology* (pp. 363–394). (2nd ed.). Wiley.

Gupta, N., Shah, P., Goel, K., Misra, A., Rastogi, K., Vikram, N. K., & Gulati, S. (2019). Imbalanced dietary profile, anthropometry, and lipids in urban Asian Indian adolescents and young adults. *Journal of the American College of Nutrition, 38*(2), 81–91.

Kelly, Y., Patalay, P., Montgomery, S., & Sacker, A. (2016). Bmi development and early adolescent psychosocial well-being: UK millennium cohort study. *Pediatrics, 138*(6), e20160967. https://doi.org/10.1542/peds.2016-0967.

Lillis, J., Hayes, S. C., Bunting, K., & Masuda, A. (2009). Teaching acceptance and mindfulness to improve the lives of the obese: A preliminary test of a theoretical model. *Annals of Behavioral Medicine, 37*(1), 58–69. https://doi.org/10.1007/s12160-009-9083-x.

NCD Risk Factor Collaboration. (2017). Worldwide trends in body-mass index, underweight, overweight, and obesity from 1975 to 2016: A pooled analysis of 2416 population-based measurement studies in 128·9 million children, adolescents, and adults. The Lancet, 390(10113), 2627–2642. https://doi.org/10.1016/S0140-6736(17)32129-3.

Chapter 6

The connection between anxiety and obesity

"The body often carries what the mind struggles to express, and anxiety finds its voice in behavior."

Learning objectives

Upon completing this chapter, readers will be able to:

Explain the neurobiological basis of adolescent anxiety vulnerability using Steinberg's dual-systems model and describe how the HPA axis links chronic psychosocial stress to weight gain.

Describe the bidirectional developmental systems model linking anxiety and obesity in adolescence, citing at least two mechanisms operating in each direction.

Evaluate the role of weight stigma and internalized weight bias as mediators between obesity and anxiety outcomes in adolescents.

Analyze the Indian cultural, institutional, and media context as a specific risk environment for anxiety–obesity comorbidity in adolescents.

Interpret the STAI findings from the present study (N = 400, Kolkata) in relation to global evidence on anxiety and adolescent obesity.

6.1 Adolescence as a vulnerable developmental window

6.1.1 Neurobiological context

Adolescence is a period of significant neurobiological restructuring, identity formation, and social repositioning in the life course of the individual. Developmental neuroscience has consistently documented that adolescence is a period of asynchronous development in the adolescent brain, where the limbic system that controls emotional reactivity and reward sensitivity matures earlier than the prefrontal cortex that controls executive functioning, impulse control, and future planning. This has formed the basis of the dual-systems model of adolescent development put forward by Steinberg (2010), which accounts for the intense emotional experiences and difficulty in emotional control that adolescents experience in their lives.

Functional neuroimaging studies confirm that there is increased amygdala activation in response to social threat and peer evaluation in comparison with adults (Guyer et al., 2009). In parallel with the development of the prefrontal regulatory systems, there is synaptic pruning and myelination. This neurobiological configuration is associated with emotional sensitivity and constrained regulation. This neurobiological configuration makes the adolescent more vulnerable to the development of anxiety, particularly social anxiety disorder (SAD). SAD often presents in early and mid-adolescence (Kessler et al., 2005). Puberty is associated with significant endocrinological changes. Hormonal cascades include estrogen, testosterone, and growth hormone. These changes in hormone balance have significant effects on fat distribution, body composition, and appetite regulation. In girls, increased adiposity is a normal biological response to puberty. Longitudinal studies confirm that premature pubertal development in girls is associated with increased risk of anxiety symptoms, body discontent, and depressive mood. This is partly attributed to perceived deviation from idealized societal norms of the female body (Graber, 2013; Mendle et al., 2007). In contrast, in boys, increased muscle mass is attributed to testosterone and is more in accordance with idealized societal norms of male physical competence. Boys who experience increased adiposity and delayed muscular development often experience discontent with the male body and experience performance anxiety. Studies on the drive for muscularity confirm that male adolescents increasingly idealize the lean and muscular male body (McCreary & Sasse, 2000).

Psychology of Obesity. DOI: https://doi.org/10.1016/B978-0-443-27797-9.00012-9

6.1.2 Psychosocial and cultural context

From a psychosocial perspective, adolescence is associated with Erikson (1968) identity versus role confusion stage. In this context, body image is an important part of identity formation. This is because physical changes occur that are visible and mark maturation. Moreover, Meta-analytic studies indicate that body image dissatisfaction is common during early adolescence, particularly among girls (Ricciardelli & McCabe, 2001). In sociocultural theories, such as the tripartite influence model advanced by Thompson et al. (1999), it is suggested that parents, peers, and mass media can influence the spread of attitudes about body image. These attitudes can lead to body image dissatisfaction.

Adolescents have greater neural reactions to social exclusion than children and adults. Weight teasing has consistently been identified as an important predictor of anxiety symptoms, irrespective of body mass index (BMI) (Puhl & Lessard, 2020). Longitudinal research has demonstrated that perceived weight stigma predicts anxiety symptoms, even when objective weight status is stable. This supports the idea that social evaluation, not weight per se, is responsible for anxiety. The social comparison effects in cyberspace are greater than in physical space. Systematic reviews have identified strong evidence for social media appearance-centered use predicting body dissatisfaction and anxiety in adolescents (Fardouly et al., 2015).

Gender differences: the differences in anxiety between girls and boys have been consistently demonstrated in adolescents. The anxiety prevalence rates for girls are consistently higher than for boys. These differences begin in puberty (Kessler et al., 2005). Theorists have suggested that body surveillance and internalization of the thin-ideal standard contribute to anxiety in girls. The role of cultural context is also important in understanding anxiety among adolescents. In collectivist cultures such as India, body size is often linked to family honor, marriage, and morality. Parent comments regarding weight in such cultures may heighten anxiety by linking body composition to parental discipline and honor.

However, there are also protective factors that act as a buffer in the relationship between body dissatisfaction and anxiety. These include supportive parenting styles, body positivity, positive school environments, and peer networks. Emotional coping mechanisms, such as cognitive reappraisal, also alleviate anxiety levels even in the presence of stressors related to body appearance. Adolescence, therefore presents a paradox as a vulnerable period and a period of neuroplasticity in which intervention has lasting effects. Understanding the framework in which adolescence develops is essential in appreciating the relationship between anxiety and obesity in adolescence and the need to understand the role of biological, social, and medical factors in the two conditions.

The concept of embodied vulnerability provides a framework in which the relationship between biological and social processes in adolescence develops. Adolescence presents a unique case in which the body, as a biological entity, also provides a framework for the development of social understandings of identity, membership, and status. When the biological changes that accompany adolescence result in a body that fails to meet the social ideals of beauty, whether in the form of too much or too little fat, the biological reality assumes a social reality through the comments of peers, family, and the media. Developmental researchers are increasingly arguing for a new paradigm that considers the relationship between the biological and the social as mutual influences rather than parallel processes that may or may not intersect at some point.

The timing of developmental changes is another layer of complexity. Puberty in girls that occurs before the age of eight or nine, and the development of secondary sex characteristics, are associated with the accumulation of more body fat in comparison with their peers and with increased pressure of comparison with others and the experience of anxiety disorders. Mendle et al. (2007) found that the timing of development in girls predicted depressive and anxious outcomes through perceived deviation in appearance. This again emphasizes the importance of the environment over the timing of development. In contrast, late maturation in boys is associated with delays in the development of muscle mass and the maintenance of prepubertal body composition, and is associated with increased pressure of comparison with others.

Sleep and circadian control are one aspect of the developmental process in adolescents that is not well appreciated. Adolescence brings about a biological change in the desire to go to bed later in the night, which is not in sync with the early morning school schedules. This brings about a chronic sleep debt in adolescents, as their sleep is reduced by 2 to 3 hours compared to what is desirable in most educational settings. The effects of this restriction in sleep are decreased regulatory capacity in the prefrontal cortex, emotional hyperarousal, disrupted appetite hormones, and the desire for high-calorie diets. The metabolic and mental health consequences of chronic sleep debt in adolescents are a structural contributor to weight gain and anxiety vulnerability that is not well appreciated.

6.2 Obesity in adolescence: beyond anthropometrics

Overweight is typically defined as a BMI-for-age at or above the 85th percentile, whereas obesity is defined as a BMI-for-age at or above the 95th percentile according to WHO growth reference standards (World Health Organization, 2020). Although the use of this definition provides a standardized approach to surveillance, it obscures the multifaceted nature of the concept of being overweight in adolescents. Obesity in adolescents is not merely a biological construct based on the amount of fat mass. Rather, it is a dynamic construct embedded in the interplay between biological, behavioral, environmental, and psychological factors.

On the international level, the prevalence of overweight and obesity among children and adolescents between the ages of 5 and 19 has increased over the past three decades. In 1990 the prevalence of overweight and obesity among children and adolescents was 8% and 2%, respectively (Phelps et al., 2024). In contrast, the prevalence of overweight and obesity among children and adolescents in 2022 is 20% and 8%, respectively. This indicates that the prevalence of obesity has tripled in the past three decades (Phelps et al., 2024). According to the World Health Organization (2020), there are 390 million overweight children in the world today. In India, the prevalence of overweight among adolescents varies between 1.25% and 35.8% in various studies conducted in different parts of the country. In contrast, the prevalence of obesity among Indian adolescents varies between 0.3% and 24.6% and is dependent on the region and institution studied (Panda et al., 2025; Samanta et al., 2022).

In India, the National Family Health Survey indicates that the prevalence of overweight among adolescents has been rising over the past few years. In contrast, urban adolescents in higher socioeconomic groups have shown a substantially higher prevalence of overweight than their counterparts in other parts of the country. This is indicative of the epidemiological transition in the country in terms of the prevalence of overweight and obesity among the population. This epidemiological transition has created a dual burden of malnutrition in the country in the form of underweight and overweight being prevalent in the same country and even in the same population.

Obesity among Indian adolescents is associated with numerous physical health complications, including dyslipidemia, insulin resistance, hypertension, non-alcoholic fatty liver disease, and sleep-disordered breathing. Long-term consequences include type 2 diabetes, cardiovascular disease, and certain forms of cancer. In addition to these physical health concerns, obesity is associated with significant psychosocial challenges, including body image dissatisfaction, low self-esteem, anxiety, depression, social isolation, and weight-related stigma. Despite their substantial impact on overall well-being and quality of life, these psychosocial consequences are often overlooked in discussions of adolescent obesity in India.

The etiology of adolescent obesity is multifactorial. Genetic factors are a major contributor to individual variations in BMI. Recent genome-wide association studies have revealed more than 900 genetic loci that are significantly associated with BMI and adiposity. These findings indicate that the control of body weight is a complex trait regulated by a polygenic system (Yengo et al., 2018). Genetic predispositions are combined with environmental factors such as household food availability, walkability, sedentary activities, sleep duration, and chronic stress exposure. There is growing recognition of the role of stress-responsive metabolism in weight control. Psychosocial stress is a chronic stressor that activates neuroendocrine systems, such as the hypothalamic-pituitary-adrenal (HPA) axis. It is a well-known contributor to weight gain through mechanisms such as increased fat deposition in the abdominal region and increased food cravings. It also decreases motivation for physical activity. It is critical to recognize that adolescent obesity is a developmental challenge that is embedded in biological, psychological, social, and structural contexts. It cannot be explained by factors such as behavioral and moral failures. A comprehensive model recognizes that metabolic and emotional vulnerabilities are often caused by common factors such as chronic stress, negative social evaluation, and structural inequality. It is this comprehensive understanding that will be used to explain the cooccurrence of anxiety and obesity in adolescence.

Clinical assessment for teenage obesity without considering psychological factors can lead to incomplete diagnosis and iatrogenic effects. A sole focus on weight-reduction targets and food prescription by healthcare professionals without considering anxiety, body image problems, and weight victimization can actually worsen symptoms. Weight-inclusive assessment models, in which healthcare professionals focus on health behaviors and psychological well-being instead of weight targets, have been found to be associated with better treatment engagement, lower internalized stigma, and greater behavior change over time. These models do not dismiss anthropometric targets; they actually propose assessing metabolic and psychological health together in one session, considering the child as an integrated being, not just trying to fix their body.

6.3 Anxiety in adolescence: fear, evaluation, and social comparison

Anxiety disorders represent the most prevalent class of mental disorders in adolescents worldwide. Epidemiological surveys from across the world report that approximately 31% of adolescents in the United States meet the diagnostic criteria for an anxiety disorder at some time in their life (Merikangas et al., 2010). The data from the Global Burden of Disease study, conducted across multiple nations, report anxiety disorders as one of the top contributors to disability-adjusted life years in the 10 to 24 years age group across the world (GBD Collaborators, 2019). In all nations, anxiety disorders have a greater prevalence in girls than in boys, with this difference emerging in puberty and being sustained across adulthood.

The category of anxiety disorders comprises a range of different diagnostic entities, and these are generalized anxiety disorder, SAD, separation anxiety disorder, specific phobia, and panic disorder. SAD, defined by extreme apprehensiveness about negative evaluation, embarrassment, or rejection in social or performance situations, is particularly noteworthy in relation to adolescence since this is a period of salience for peer relationships and identity formation. The onset of SAD is between 13 and 17 years of age, a time that is most salient for peer relationships and body image concerns (Kessler et al., 2005).

One of the major ways that social comparison leads to anxiety is a function of adolescence. In this context, Festinger's (1954) Social Comparison Theory, which has been revised and extended over the past several decades, states that individuals tend to evaluate their characteristics by comparing themselves with others, especially in ambiguous evaluative areas. Body weight and physical appearance are two of the most salient areas where adolescents are frequently exposed to social evaluation. Adolescents with greater body weight are frequently exposed to social comparison in terms of body appearance via multiple routes. These routes include peer commentary, media presentation, medical consultation, and family conversation. When such social comparison leads to a perceived discrepancy between the individual's characteristics and social standards, anxiety is a predictable consequence. Beck (1976) cognitive behavioral model of anxiety, which has been revised and extended by various scholars over the past few decades, states that threat appraisal, attentional bias towards negative information, and safety behavior are three major factors that contribute to the maintenance of anxiety. In this context, adolescents with body anxiety frequently exhibit attentional bias towards body flaws. In this context, adolescents with greater social anxiety frequently overestimate peer evaluation when they are exposed to body exposure situations such as physical classes, swimming, and social gatherings. Avoidance of such body exposure is a major reason that maintains anxiety.

Metacognitive factors may also maintain adolescent anxiety. Worries about worry, beliefs about the controllability of anxiety, and negative self-monitoring may maintain anxiety symptoms in the absence of direct threat exposure. For youth who have internalized weight stigma, metacognitive monitoring of social acceptability is a constant, draining task that may leave youth depleted in terms of cognitive resources. This depletion may, in turn, contribute to eating, exercise, and sleep patterns that influence weight trajectories.

Changes in hormones that occur in pubertal development may interact with psychological factors to influence anxiety. For example, estrogen may regulate serotonergic and GABA neurotransmitter systems, both of which are linked to anxiety. Fluctuating estrogen levels in early pubertal development in females may contribute to emotional reactivity and decreased inhibitory tone. Stress may elevate cortisol, affecting brain adaptability and prefrontal functioning, contributing to anxiety and problems in metabolism. An integrated model of adolescent anxiety is necessary that considers brain sensitivity, cognitive appraisals of situations, feelings of judgment by others, and cultural background.

The difference between state anxiety, which is a temporary emotional response to identifiable threat indicators, and trait anxiety, which is a stable tendency to interpret the world as dangerous, is significant in understanding the manifestation of anxiety in adolescents with obesity. Adolescents with high levels of trait anxiety are constantly searching for information regarding their appearance, interpret ambiguous social interactions as dangerous, and have a negative attitude toward social interactions, even when the interactions could be viewed in a more positive context. This tendency to have high levels of trait anxiety predicts the manifestation of anxiety symptoms despite the absence of specific triggering factors. In this context, the persistence of social anxiety in adolescents with obesity, despite the absence of triggering factors such as being teased, could be understood. In addition, the impact of exposure to weight stigmatization on the manifestation of symptoms is not only additive but multiplicative, which is in line with the understanding of how preexisting personality traits make the impact of environmental stressors worse.

The patterns of comorbidity with other forms of anxiety disorders in adolescence also add to the complexity. SAD often cooccurs with generalized anxiety disorder, which involves worry in multiple domains, and panic disorder in older adolescent samples. Body-related worries in obesity in adolescence may serve as the initial content for generalized anxiety disorder, which generalizes over time to academic performance, future prospects, and social relationships in general, resulting in generalized anxiety disorder where body-related worries are no longer the exclusive content but are embedded in a more generalized context of anxiety in dealing with life in general. This progression from body-related to generalized anxiety also has important implications for intervention with these individuals, where both the specific content of body-related worries in anxiety and the more generalized regulatory deficits in anxiety are addressed in effective intervention.

6.4 The bidirectional developmental systems model

The interrelations between anxiety and obesity in adolescence are not linear or unidirectional; rather, they are bidirectional and dynamic. The developmental systems model views the interrelations between anxiety and obesity in adolescence as tied together in a way in which they influence each other due to common biological, psychological, and social weaknesses that strengthen over time. Anxiety and obesity are not causally related in a simple fashion; rather, they are embedded in a mutually amplifying feedback loop.

Evidence supporting the anxiety leading to obesity pathway comes from longitudinal studies. Anxiety-related behavioral pathways include emotional eating, stress-related food preference for high-energy-density food, sleep disruption that disrupts appetite hormones, and avoidance behaviors that decrease physical activity levels. Pine et al. (1997) found that several symptoms of adolescent psychiatric problems predicted BMI in early adulthood. The physiological pathway follows the stress axis, where anxiety-induced cortisol levels contribute to the development of obesity by promoting fat accumulation in the abdominal region.

Evidence supporting the obesity leading to anxiety pathway comes from equally robust studies. Amiri and Behnezhad (2019) conducted a systematic review and metaanalysis to examine the relationship between obesity and anxiety and found that obesity was related to a 30% increase in the frequency of anxiety compared to normal-weight status. Obesity-related teasing, social exclusion, and negative evaluation by peers in adolescence induce anxiety symptoms in adolescents with obesity through the stigma pathway. Body dissatisfaction, which is much higher in adolescents with obesity, directly predicts anxiety symptom severity even after controlling for BMI (Warnick et al., 2022). The adolescent with obesity has a two-hit risk for anxiety: a physiological risk and a psychosocial risk.

The developmental cascade model, as described by Masten et al. (2005) and applied to the study of obesity and mental health, suggests that weaknesses in one domain in early development may influence other areas in a growing person, leading to more problems in a variety of areas as the person develops. Early anxiety predicts future social withdrawal, reduced physical activity levels, increased body dissatisfaction, and obesity, which in turn predict future anxiety and obesity risk. Early weight teasing predicts future social anxiety, especially in neurobiologically sensitive adolescents with obesity.

The bidirectional model also doesn't necessarily mean that the effect sizes or mechanisms are equivalent in both directions. Gender also plays a role in directionality, with prospective designs indicating that the anxiety to obesity pathway tends to be slightly stronger in girls, whereas the obesity to anxiety pathway tends to be equivalent in both genders but with different content in girls (appearance) versus boys (competence). Timing also plays a critical role in directionality, with the period of early puberty appearing to be a critical period in which small perturbations in either domain can have a greater impact on the other. Intervention designs also indicate greater efficacy during or prior to rather than after this period.

The systems model also highlights the importance of context as a key moderating and mediating variable in the interplay between obesity and anxiety. Stigmatizing social environments amplify the obesity to anxiety pathway by increasing social threat perceptions. Positive family environments can moderate the obesity to anxiety pathway by providing corrective emotional experiences to reduce shame. Positive school environments can also moderate the obesity to anxiety pathway by reducing social comparison and the anxiety-maintaining effects of weight-based appearance concerns.

The disruption of sleep is a major component of this bidirectional model because it is both a product of anxiety and a cause of weight gain and also serves as a mechanism for both problems to worsen. Thus anxious adolescents experience longer sleep onset latencies because of ruminative worry, shorter sleep duration, and poorer sleep quality using actigraphs. This restriction of sleep increases ghrelin and decreases leptin, which increases appetite and food preference. In addition, sleep restriction also decreases prefrontal functioning, which reduces cognitive reappraisal and increases emotional reactivity the next day. This creates an environment that is ripe for both anxious processing and emotional eating. This model is a two-way feedback loop within a larger two-way model that can be treated with better sleep hygiene education and effective treatments for insomnia and overthinking.

The avoidance of physical activity is a mutual cause of both problems. Anxiety causes avoidance of physical education classes, sports, and recreational physical activities because of embarrassment, fear of negative evaluation, and anticipatory social anxiety. This avoidance causes weight gain because of the energy balance. In addition, this avoidance also causes anxiety because of the removal of the anxiety-reducing properties of aerobic activities. These properties include reductions in cortisol, increases in endorphins, and social support in group aerobic activities. Weight gain causes more anxiety because of increased body image anxiety and avoidance. This creates a feedback loop that causes avoidance behaviors that restrict the individual's behavioral repertoire. This is a major cause of both problems and can be treated with interventions that make physical activities emotionally safe, intrinsically motivating, and free of body evaluation.

6.5 Stress biology and neuroendocrine mechanisms

The relationship between anxiety and obesity in teens is, in turn, influenced by the HPA axis, which is the major body system that regulates how we respond to stress. When a person feels threatened or judged by others, a part of the brain known as the hypothalamus reacts by releasing a corticotropin-releasing hormone (CRH), which in turn prompts the anterior pituitary gland to release adrenocorticotropin, resulting in the release of cortisol into the bloodstream. Cortisol is responsible for coping with acute stress by providing energy substrates acute stress reactions and enhancing threat vigilance. However, in a situation of chronic stress, cortisol's dysregulation has a number of effects on metabolism, including visceral fat, insulin resistance, and appetite control.

Research by Ruttle et al. (2011) has documented that adolescents who are exposed to chronic peer victimization exhibit elevated diurnal cortisol reactivity and alterations in cortisol awakening response. These alterations in the body's stress response are not simply indicative of stress reactions, but demonstrate how sensitive our stress-response systems are when exposed to chronic stress. An adolescent who is suffering from obesity and is being bullied about their weight is dealing with two separate health issues that, when combined, worsen their situation.

Cortisol, a stress hormone, causes fat buildup in the body, specifically in the belly region. This is due to several factors. For one, glucocorticoid receptors in visceral fat are more concentrated than those in subcutaneous fat. Second, long-term exposure to cortisol enhances the activity of lipoprotein lipase in visceral fat cells, causing more fat buildup in this region. Cortisol, in this manner, causes more sugar production in the body, increasing appetite, particularly for high-calorie, high-fat, and high-sugar foods, by affecting the hypothalamus, a part of the brain that controls appetite. This biological mechanism is a direct physiological explanation of how chronic anxiety, through the HPA axis, can lead to belly weight gain in adolescents.

In contrast, adipose tissue, or body fat, has been known to send signals that can influence neural activity. Adipocytes, or fat cells, in body fat tissues, such as in the belly, send signals that can trigger inflammation. These cells, in this manner, trigger inflammation by producing cytokines, including interleukin-6 (IL-6) and tumor necrosis factor alpha (TNF-α). These cytokines, in turn, trigger inflammation in the body, affecting neural activity. Research on neuroinflammation has documented that inflammation in obesity is associated with alterations in monoaminergic neurotransmission, including decreases in serotonin and dopamine availability, which are neurobiological substrates of anxiety and depression disorders.

Sleep disturbances connect the anxiety and obesity pathways at a biological level. For instance, sleep disturbances in anxiety-prone teenagers are associated with delayed sleep onset and reduced sleep duration caused by ruminative worry mechanisms. Sleep disturbances impair prefrontal regulatory mechanisms and increase reactivity in the amygdala; this is reflected in increased emotional reactivity the next day. In addition, sleep disturbances impair ghrelin and leptin levels, which are the primary hormones that regulate appetite. Fatima et al. (2016) conducted a metaanalysis that revealed that sleep quality is significantly related to BMI in young populations. Sleep disturbances act as a psychobiological bridge between anxiety and obesity.

The autonomic nervous system offers another pathway that connects anxiety and obesity. For instance, anxiety is a chronic condition that activates the sympathetic nervous system. Activation of this system is associated with reduced heart rate variability and increased heart rate; these factors are associated with insulin resistance and metabolic syndrome in teenagers. Bidirectional physiological reinforcement is a mechanism that connects anxiety and obesity through these overlapping stress systems. For instance, anxiety is a primary cause of HPA axis and sympathetic nervous system activation; these systems are responsible for fat and appetite regulation. These systems are responsible for anxiety through inflammatory and neuroendocrine mechanisms.

Neuroinflammatory pathways are increasingly being explored as a potential link in this relationship. Adipose tissues, especially visceral adipose tissues in obesity, secrete proinflammatory adipokines, including leptin, resistin, and IL, that enter the bloodstream and can cross the blood–brain barrier. An increase in inflammatory markers in the bloodstream has been known to activate microglial cells in areas of the brain that include the hippocampus, prefrontal cortex, and amygdala, which could interfere with normal brain functioning in managing emotions. Longitudinal study data from the Avon Longitudinal Study of Parents and Children revealed that inflammation in teenage years is associated with more severe anxiety and depression in early adulthood, thus providing a biological link for how obesity could lead to mental health issues, independent of how society judges it. This neuroinflammatory pathway provides one of the two pathways, including psychosocial stigma, that could be responsible for the directional relationship from obesity to anxiety.

Gut–brain axis: this is a new dimension of research in the neuroendocrinology of obesity and anxiety. The gut microbiome, significantly altered in obesity by dietary, metabolic, and stress-related gut motility factors, secretes neuroactive compounds that regulate mood states and anxiety by vagal nerve afferents and enter the bloodstream. There is strong evidence of relationships between gut microbiome and anxiety-like behaviors in preclinical research, and early human studies in adult populations are beginning to reveal signatures of gut microbiome associated with anxiety and depression. While research in this area is in its infancy in relation to adolescents, this could be a very important period for intervention that could treat both obesity and anxiety, since this is a period of significant change in gut microbiome, especially in pubertal development. Though it is too early to be of practical value, the potential for how this relationship might be connected is very promising for understanding that anxiety and obesity are connected in a very integrated manner.

6.6 Cognitive, behavioral, and emotional pathways

The cognitive behavioral literature on anxiety and obesity in adolescence points to specific cognitive mechanisms that underlie the interrelationship between the two problems. These cognitive mechanisms are related to appraisal, attention, emotion regulation, and behavior. These cognitive mechanisms can also be targeted using cognitive behavioral interventions.

Emotion regulation difficulties feature prominently in cognitive behavioral theories of anxiety and obesity. In this context, rumination is defined as a passive and repetitive cognitive preoccupation with negative emotional states and their causes and consequences. This cognitive mechanism predicts both anxiety and disordered eating in adolescent populations. Nolen-Hoeksema et al. (2008) found that rumination increases negative emotional states, prolongs their duration, and decreases problem-focused coping motivation. In adolescents with obesity, ruminative thinking about negative evaluation related to weight problems creates a vicious cycle where negative emotions trigger ruminative thinking, which in turn increases anxiety. Catastrophic appraisal of body feedback and overgeneralization of negative social experiences to conclusions about global social unacceptability also feature in this cognitive mechanism.

Experiential avoidance, the avoidance of escaping aversive internal states by behavioral avoidance, is another key process in the maintenance of anxiety disorders. Adolescents in the obesity-social anxiety group avoid physical activity, social interactions, and academic engagement in order to avoid anticipated exposure in which bodily exposure is expected. Although this avoidance temporarily solves the problem, it does not disconfirm the anxiety cognition, which is the basis for the avoidance. Moreover, this avoidance mechanism leads to the development of obesity and social skill deficit, which maintains the anxiety in the long term. The avoidance mechanism is conceptually targeted by acceptance and commitment therapy (ACT), which emphasizes the importance of facing aversive internal states without escaping by avoidance.

The mechanism of emotional eating, which refers to the tendency to eat food, especially high-energy and high-palatability food, in response to negative emotional states rather than physiological hunger, is one of the most important behavioral mechanisms in the development of anxiety disorders. The affect regulation model of food intake proposes that the temporary regulation of negative emotional states by the intake of food is mediated by the activation of the dopaminergic reward system in the nucleus accumbens. The association between the conditioned emotional response to negative emotional states and the conditioned response to food intake is established by the repeated association between the two. Longitudinal studies show that emotional eating in adolescents predicts future weight gain and high BMI in the long term, especially in stressful situations in which emotional regulation is poor.

The process of cognitive reappraisal, or the active reevaluation of stressful circumstances in a manner that changes their emotional impact, is the only adaptive emotion regulation process that has been shown to decrease levels of both anxiety and maladaptive eating. A study by Gross & John (2003) found that habitual cognitive reappraisal use is associated with better emotional and social functioning. This has been replicated in more recent studies of adolescents. Interventions that focus on the development of cognitive reappraisal abilities in adolescents with body dissatisfaction and levels of anxiety have shown that such abilities can decrease levels of negative emotion and stress-consumed eating. Social problem-solving abilities, such as the identification of cognitive distortions in appearance and the development of assertive responses to teasing, can also decrease levels of anxiety symptom severity.

The theory of self-objectification, as presented by Fredrickson & Roberts (1997) and more recently applied to the adolescent population by other researchers, suggests that girls tend to develop the habitual tendency to view themselves as an outside observer would view them, and that this tendency can interfere with flow states. High levels of body surveillance in adolescent girls are associated with performance anxiety in sports and exercise, increased levels of anxiety in social situations, and decreased engagement in activities that require the exposure of the body. This process may explain the tendency of adolescent girls with higher BMI levels to engage in higher levels of physical activity avoidance that cannot be fully explained by levels of fitness and physical barriers.

Perfectionism is a second cognitive risk factor that links anxiety and obesity. Socially prescribed perfectionism, in which individuals perceive that significant others hold high standards for their performance and body image, is related to both anxiety and body image concerns. Body-focused perfectionism, in which individuals perceive that body deviation from an ideal weight or shape is a personal inadequacy, is linked to body concerns, self-monitoring, and anxiety. Research on perfectionism and eating disorders in adolescents has highlighted the risk of disordered eating and anxiety in this cognitive profile, particularly in high-performing academic environments where performance and body image are naturally linked.

The role of intolerance of uncertainty in the maintenance of anxiety in adolescents with obesity needs to be made explicit. Adolescents with high intolerance of uncertainty perceive ambiguous social situations, including social interactions based on weight, as more threatening than those with low intolerance of uncertainty. This type of cognition results in excessive information-seeking regarding body evaluation, excessive reassurance-seeking from others regarding appearance, and avoidance of social situations where evaluation can occur but the outcome is uncertain. While these coping mechanisms provide temporary relief from anxiety, they also serve to reinforce the perceived threat of uncertainty in social interactions and the perceived need for only positive evaluation in social situations.

Hope and self-efficacy are positive cognitions that protect against the anxiety–obesity relationship. Adolescents with high academic and social self-efficacy, that is, those with high confidence in dealing with difficult social situations, have low levels of anxiety even in the face of teasing based on weight. Intervention studies have demonstrated efficacy in reducing the severity of anxiety symptoms in adolescents with obesity through building self-efficacy through behavioral experiments, role-playing, and mastery experiences in physical activity contexts. This supports social learning theory in providing a framework for the development of interventions to reduce the anxiety–obesity relationship.

6.7 Weight stigma and internalized shame

Weight stigma can be defined as the social devaluation of individuals based on body size, expressed as prejudice, stereotyping, or discrimination. It can occur through various routes, including interpersonal, media, healthcare provider, or institutional-level influences. While its effects are not limited to psychological distress, the evidence from systematic reviews and metaanalyzes consistently shows a link between experienced weight stigma and a range of negative outcomes, including anxiety, depression, disordered eating, physical inactivity, and healthcare avoidance.

Puhl & Lessard (2020) conducted an overview of international data on weight stigma in youth and determined that between 25% and 50% of adolescents report weight discrimination. The source of weight stigma is most commonly from peers, but also from family and, in some disturbing instances, from healthcare professionals. The research has consistently demonstrated that weight stigma from any source predicts anxiety, low self-worth, body discontent, and unhealthy weight regulation strategies such as restriction, purging, and taking diet pills, independent of body weight. The critical factor is that these findings have been consistent for adolescents who are of normal weight but perceive themselves as overweight. Thus it is not weight per se but perceived social judgments based on weight that are critical.

Weight bias internalization (WBI) is defined as "the extent to which an individual internalizes negative societal stereotypes regarding weight and body size, and applies them to themselves". Adolescents who have high levels of WBI perceive that they have failed as a person, are lazy, and lack self-control. The scientific research has demonstrated that WBI predicts anxiety, depression, body discontent, and avoidance behaviors independent of body weight (Emmer et al., 2020; Pearl & Puhl, 2018). WBI is viewed as being central in linking weight stigma and psychological distress. Experienced weight stigma predicts WBI, which predicts unhealthy coping strategies, which predict psychological distress (Hayward et al., 2018).

Shame is distinguished from guilt in that it is a negative evaluation of the global self (Tangney & Dearing, 2002). In contrast to guilt, which is associated with reparative behaviors, shame is associated with withdrawal and concealment. Adolescents' internalization of weight stigma is associated with negative body image which is defined as a moral failing rather than a health correlate. Research on shame conducted by Gilbert (2010) and Tangney & Dearing (2002) reveals that shame is more strongly associated with depression and anxiety than guilt. Shame-prone individuals exhibit greater emotional dysregulation and relationship difficulties. On the other hand, studies on self-compassion reveal that adolescents with higher self-compassion scores experience fewer anxiety problems and better health behaviors. Thus it is suggested that self-compassion is an important target for intervention.

Stigma vigilance is defined as the chronic monitoring of social environments for weight-related threat cues. This is another mechanism that maintains weight stigma and is associated with physiological outcomes. Adolescents with higher stigma vigilance experience greater cortisol reactivity and attention bias to threatening social cues. These adolescents also exhibit poor emotional recovery following social stress. This pattern is comparable to that of discrimination vigilance documented in race and sexual minority stress. This reveals that weight stigma is a chronic social stressor that has associated neuroendocrine and psychological outcomes. This is formalized in Tomiyama (2014) Cyclic Obesity/Weight-Based Stigma model. This model reveals that weight stigma elicits stress that activates HPA axis responses that produce weight gain that elicits stigma.

Institutional stigma provides a structural component to the shame processes that are individually mediated by anxiety and obesity. Fitness grading, weigh-ins, and moralizing health messages in schools have been linked to body dissatisfaction and avoidance of physical activity. Health institutions where health providers' prejudice against weight affects adolescents discourage them from accessing healthcare, including mental health services. These institutional processes provide a structural component to the anxiety–obesity cycle that needs to be addressed at the structural level in addition to the individual level.

Weight stigma reduction has emerged as a new public health issue with policy implications. Stigma reduction interventions at the structural level, including the development of antibullying policies that protect students against weight-based bullying, teacher education in neutral weight talk, and media literacy in the development of critical thinking skills against the manipulation of images, have shown positive outcomes in the reduction of stigma exposure and weight bias in adolescents. The evidence base for the inclusion of weight as a legal characteristic in schools and health institutions comes from the health consequences of stigma, which are similar in effect size and mechanisms to health consequences of discrimination-based harm. Policy interventions in this area have gained momentum in different countries, offering a unique opportunity for future studies to investigate the causal effect of institutional stigma reduction on anxiety and obesity in adolescents.

6.8 Gender, class, and structural inequality

The relationship between anxiety and obesity in adolescents is not equally distributed in the population. Factors such as gender, socioeconomic status, caste, and geography influence the prevalence and strength of the relationship between anxiety and obesity in adolescents.

Gender is the most consistently demonstrated moderator. Adolescent girls have reported significantly higher rates of both anxiety disorders and body dissatisfaction compared to their counterparts in different national contexts (Kessler et al., 2005; Ricciardelli & McCabe, 2001). The basis for this disparity lies in the interplay between neurobiological factors, such as the impact of estrogen on emotional states, and sociocultural factors, such as the tendency for girls to undergo more rigorous appearance-based evaluations compared to their counterparts, as well as the tendency to internalize thin-ideal beauty standards. Girls are also more likely to use internalizing coping mechanisms, which serve to perpetuate both anxiety disorders and disordered eating. Conversely, boys are more likely to use external coping mechanisms, which could conceal underlying anxiety disorders.

Studies have demonstrated the rising rates of body anxiety disorders in boys, which are mediated by the pressure to achieve muscularity rather than thinness. McCreary & Sasse (2000) demonstrated that the pursuit of muscularity in male adolescents was associated with performance anxiety, overexercise, and disordered eating. Social media sites promoting fitness and bodybuilding have amplified the importance of muscularity, which could translate into similar pressure on boys in different demographic groups.

The interplay between socioeconomic status and gender in the context of body anxiety disorders in boys has demonstrated the tendency for boys in lower socioeconomic groups to experience pressure related to physical strength as cultural capital.

Socioeconomic status affects obesity and anxiety through various pathways. Individuals from lower socioeconomic statuses have greater exposure to obesogenic environments, such as food deserts with limited availability of healthy food, recreational environments with limited resources for physical activities, and chronic stress from economic conditions. At the same time, lower socioeconomic adolescents have limited resources for seeking mental health services, greater stigma from multiple social disadvantages, and limited resources for participating in physical activities. Multilevel models have demonstrated that greater income inequality between nations is associated with stronger correlations between BMI and psychological distress (Datar & Sturm, 2006).

Contrariwise, high socioeconomic status is associated with appearance pressures from consumerism, academic performance pressures, and social media. Research on performance-based self-worth has demonstrated elevated rates of anxiety and perfectionism in high socioeconomic status samples of adolescents. In these samples, appearance is one domain in which performance is evaluated. Diet culture, restriction, and appearance competitiveness are elevated in high socioeconomic statuses in Western nations. However, this pattern is modified in collectivist cultural settings where body fat is equally normative across income levels.

In India, caste intersects with class and gender in ways that influence both obesity and anxiety. Longitudinal and cross-sectional research has demonstrated that diet, physical activity, and body ideals vary across castes and regions. Urban upper-caste girls experience body surveillance from appearance pressures tied to matrimonial prospects and family honor. In rural settings, lower socioeconomic adolescents experience nutritional uncertainty and emerging body ideals from globalized body ideals in digital media. The normative landscape is changing rapidly in India.

The intersectionality approach, first developed by Crenshaw (1989) and adapted to the context of health equity by other researchers, shows how risk profiles multiply rather than add up for adolescents with multiple structural risk exposures. This again highlights the importance of intervention models that address multiple levels at once.

The role of religion/spirituality in providing body-related attitudes/resources to adolescent populations in the context of India also needs to be taken into account. Religious beliefs in the acceptance of the body as a divine gift or in the de-emphasis of physical appearance in relation to inner virtue can provide adolescent populations with coping resources to deal with body image-related anxiety. On the other hand, religious or cultural beliefs in the virtue of bodily discipline and control in relation to body weight can lead to shame in cases where body weight exceeds normal limits. Research in the area of religion/spirituality in relation to body image in adolescent populations in India is limited, indicating a gap in the available research in this area, which limits the culture-specific nature of intervention recommendations.

The urban/rural contrast in the context of the Indian population also needs to be taken into account in intervention models. Urban adolescent populations, especially in metropolitan cities, are more likely to be exposed to the ideals promoted by the global media at an earlier age, as well as have access to mental health services and body image-informed educational resources. On the other hand, rural adolescent populations are also at risk due to the influence of urban media through mobile internet access, which tends to erase the rural–urban contrast in terms of body ideals. However, rural populations have much less access to counseling, psychological interventions, or health education resources to provide them with coping resources to deal with body image-related anxiety.

6.9 Global evidence and epidemiological trends

The global epidemiological evidence on the interrelation between anxiety and obesity in adolescence has increased considerably over the past two decades, with the rising awareness of the mental health outcomes of obesity and the metabolic health outcomes of anxiety. Overall, the evidence suggests that the comorbidity is widespread and that the structure of the pathway may differ in terms of prevalence and structure, but the basic bidirectional nature of the interrelation is similar across different populations.

In a metaanalysis of the interrelation between weight status and anxiety in children and adolescents, Burke & Storch (2015) found that overweight and obese children and adolescents had significantly higher levels of anxiety than their normal-weight counterparts. In the more recent systematic review (e.g., Samanta et al., 2022; Burke & Storch, 2015) carried out across PubMed, Scopus, and EBSCOhost databases of studies published between 2010 and 2025, 21 prospective studies of the longitudinal interrelation between obesity and psychopathology in children and adolescents aged between 6 and 8 years were synthesized. Although the evidence of the bidirectional interrelation between obesity and eating disorders and between obesity and depressive symptoms was well established, the evidence of the interrelation between obesity and anxiety was less well established, and studies with follow-ups of more than 2 years were scarce.

In the United States, the National Survey has documented that the prevalence of obesity in adolescents between the ages of 10 and 17 years old is approximately 17%, with significantly higher rates in Hispanic and non-Hispanic black adolescents. According to the National Comorbidity Survey Replication, the lifetime prevalence of anxiety disorders in adolescents in the United States was found to be approximately 31%. Research that has specifically addressed the relationship between the two conditions has found that adolescents with obesity are significantly more likely to experience SAD and generalized anxiety disorder than their normal-weight peers, and that the relationship may be mediated by weight victimization and stress mechanisms.

Similar patterns have also been identified in European longitudinal studies, including the UK Millennium Cohort and the German Mannheim Study. Adolescents with persistent obesity since childhood have been found to experience elevated levels of internalizing symptoms, including anxiety, in young adulthood. Finnish longitudinal studies have documented that anxiety in childhood predicts BMI in adolescence and adulthood, and that the relationship may be mediated by sleep disturbance and emotional eating. Scandinavian studies have confirmed that adolescents with obesity and anxiety disorders are at significantly increased risk for cardiovascular disease and psychiatric hospitalization in adulthood, thereby confirming the life-course relevance of adolescent comorbidity.

Asian countries have a slightly more complicated pattern, partly due to differences in body image ideals and cutpoints in different cultures. Studies in Japan, South Korea, and China have reported that adolescents experience high levels of weight-related body dissatisfaction and anxiety even at BMI levels below the obesity cutpoints used in the West, indicating that the sociocultural evaluation of weight status may be relatively independent of adiposity levels. Studies in South Korea have also found that adolescent girls with normal BMI who rated themselves as overweight exhibited anxiety and disordered eating at levels comparable to those of obese adolescent girls, supporting the preeminence of the socially mediated evaluation of weight status.

The Global Burden of Disease collaborative analysis has reaffirmed that anxiety disorders and obesity are two of the leading contributors to disability-adjusted life years in the adolescent and young adult age groups worldwide (GBD Collaborators, 2019). The combined effect of obesity and anxiety on functional disability, educational achievement, and healthcare utilization costs makes the combined problem a major public health concern.

Middle-income countries have also begun contributing to the overall evidence base, which has a relatively narrow representation of countries so far. Studies in Brazil, conducted by the ABCD Growth Study, and studies in Mexico and Colombia have reported a high level of obesity-related anxiety in adolescents, with weight-related bullying as a common mediator in the relationship between obesity and anxiety in adolescents. Studies in South African adolescents have also found that the pathway from obesity to anxiety via the experience of stigma was consistent in a postapartheid society, where different aspects of social evaluation may intersect in a single experience, supporting the cross-cultural applicability of the stigma-mediation pathway in the relationship between obesity and anxiety while also supporting the idea that the specific ideals related to appearance and the salience of body size variation may be culturally specific.

The methodological diversity that is seen in the literature also poses problems for synthesizing results. Studies differ in their measurement of obesity using BMI percentiles, waist circumference, and percentage body fat. In addition, studies differ in their measurement of anxiety using various screening tools, diagnostic interviews, and dimensional symptom scales. Moreover, studies differ in using self-reported versus interviewer-administered questionnaires. In addition, studies differ in their cross-sectional versus longitudinal designs and convenience versus population-based samples. The most recent reviews emphasize that standardized procedures for measurement, a minimum of 4 years of follow-up, and including mediating factors such as stigma, emotional eating, and sleep quality are needed to advance this field.

6.9.1 Present study evidence: State-Trait Anxiety Inventory findings from Kolkata

The present study contributes Indian-specific empirical data to this global literature, evaluating anxiety in a community sample of 400 late adolescents and young adults in Kolkata (200 obese, BMI 30.0–39.9; 200 nonobese, BMI 18.5–24.9) using the State-Trait Anxiety Inventory (STAI; Spielberger, 1983). State anxiety was significantly elevated in obese participants across three of four age-sex groups—male late adolescents (obese $M = 54.90$ vs nonobese $M = 39.96$, $p < 0.01$), female late adolescents (obese $M = 52.40$ vs nonobese $M = 45.20$, $p < 0.01$), and male young adults (obese $M = 56.92$ vs nonobese $M = 41.80$, $p < 0.01$)—with the exception of female young adults ($p = 0.091$, nonsignificant). Trait anxiety showed the same pattern across all groups where significance was obtained. The three-factor factorial ANOVA confirmed a highly significant main effect of body weight for both state anxiety ($F = 153.272$, $p < 0.01$) and trait anxiety ($F = 59.436$, $p < 0.01$), with significant body weight × sex interactions indicating that the anxiety–obesity relationship is moderated by gender. The nonsignificant finding in female young adults is theoretically notable: it suggests that by early adulthood, anxiety levels in urban Indian women may be uniformly elevated—irrespective of obesity status—due to cumulative pressures of academic achievement, marriageability expectations, and career transitions that affect all women in this context (Das, 2018). These findings are consistent with the global epidemiological evidence reviewed above and extend it to an urban Indian population, confirming the obesity–anxiety association while also revealing important gender-by-developmental-stage moderation that warrants further longitudinal investigation.

6.10 The Indian context: cultural, institutional, and media pressures

The Indian context is a critical consideration in understanding the relationship between anxiety and obesity among adolescents. This is because of the confluence of rapid economic growth, cultural values related to body management, honor, and discipline; a highly competitive educational environment; and the growing influence of global media and information technologies. These factors combine with the biological and psychological factors that have been discussed in previous sections to produce a critical consideration that requires specific attention.

India has the highest number of adolescents in the world, with a total of 253 million, one-fifth of its total population (Samanta et al., 2022). India is witnessing a nutritional transition, where there is a decline in undernutrition and a sharp rise in overweight and obesity, especially in urban areas. According to a scoping review of 93 studies included in a research article in Panda et al. (2025), the range of overweight prevalence in Indian adolescents varies from 1.25% to 35.8%, higher in urban, affluent, and private school settings. According to a study conducted by the National Family Health Survey 2019–21, this trend is on the rise compared to the survey conducted in 2015–16. According to a study conducted in Chennai, it was seen that 90% of 11 to 17 year old adolescents were eating in front of the TV, 82% of them bought food products based on advertisements, and 59% of them avoided physical activities in favor of screen time.

The cultural context of body and self in India is a complex one, with many internal variables. However, a number of factors are evident in all research literature on India. Body size is a significant issue in collectivist family systems, where it is linked to issues of family honor, discipline, and control. Parental commentary on weight is common and may be well-meaning, but it is perceived by the adolescent as shame-inducing, judgmental, and critical, linking body size to issues of morality. There is qualitative research evidence that family commentary on weight in Indian adolescents has a number of effects, including anxiety, withdrawal, and eating disorders, especially when it is linked to marriage and family honor.

The Indian educational system provides a structural stressor of considerable severity. The hypercompetitive Indian examination culture creates significant stress on adolescents from early secondary school onwards, where academic performance is a major determining factor of occupational and social outcomes. JEE, NEET, and board examinations entail chronic performance stress, which is linked to prolonged periods of sedentary behavior, sleep deprivation, stress-related dietary habits, and reduced physical activity. These behavioral consequences of academic stress are associated with weight gain through both behavioral and metabolic pathways, and simultaneously, academic stress is associated with increased anxiety through chronic performance monitoring and fear of failure.

The Bollywood industry and the Indian advertising industry have traditionally been associated with promoting slender feminine body ideals and, more recently, lean muscularity (Pothiraj et al., 2022). In terms of body image dissatisfaction among Indian adolescents, studies conducted by Pothiraj et al. (2022) in Mumbai found that obese school children experienced greater body image dissatisfaction, depression, and poor health-related quality of life than their normal-weight counterparts. This cultural idealization of thinness contributed to body image dissatisfaction among Indian adolescents. A study conducted by Stigler et al. (2011) in Delhi government and private schools found that body dissatisfaction was highest among overweight students and girls. This body dissatisfaction among Indian girls was also associated with unhealthy weight-control behaviors. These studies highlight that body image dissatisfaction among Indian adolescents is related to societal ideals of body image that are promoted by Bollywood and advertising media. In recent times, social media sites such as Instagram, YouTube, and WhatsApp have become increasingly popular among Indian youth. These sites have contributed to the greater globalization of body ideals among Indian youth. A study conducted by Som & Mukhopadhyay (2015) among adolescent girls in Kolkata and Howrah found that normal-weight adolescent girls experienced body image dissatisfaction and frequently perceived themselves to be overweight. These adolescent girls also experienced body dissatisfaction and attempted to reduce their weight in unhealthy ways. This demonstrates that Indian adolescent girls experience a disconnect between their actual body weight and body image dissatisfaction. This demonstrates that the globalization of body ideals is associated with body image dissatisfaction among Indian adolescent girls. Indian adolescents are exposed to idealized body images that are portrayed on social media sites such as Instagram, YouTube, and WhatsApp. These idealized body images are unrealistic and promote unattainable body ideals that are typically associated with international beauty standards.

The religious and caste-based dietary habits, vegetarianism, and regional food habits are related to the nutritional transition and influence dietary habits and their psychological correlates. The emergence of fast food and snack culture in India has created a dietary environment that is more obesogenic and has more psychological implications related to modernization and aspirations. A recent study by Deshmukh & Kulkarni (2017) conducted in Pune city among 1811 adolescents using a Multidimensional Body-Self Relations Questionnaire and Stunkard Silhouette scale found that there are significant differences between body perceptions and behaviors across different BMI and socioeconomic strata categories. It was found that girls reported higher body dissatisfaction than boys, which is consistent across international literature but has a unique socioeconomic and cultural context in India.

The unique gender vulnerabilities in India are related to global and local cultural factors and are influenced by both global and local factors. In India, girls face more scrutiny of their physical appearance and beauty, and are more influenced by matrimonial attractiveness from early adolescence. Swami et al. (2011) found that weight discrepancy was negatively correlated with body appreciation and self-esteem in female university students in India. Boys are more likely to experience pressure related to muscularity and body composition, partly driven by Bollywood hero figures and partly by global fitness culture. There is a bidirectional pressure on boys' body composition and ideal weight in India that is different from the pressure of thinness experienced by boys in Western nations. Mental health facilities are grossly inadequate in India to meet the burden of mental health issues. There is a lack of mental health literacy among adolescents, their parents, and teachers. Anxiety symptoms related to obesity are not addressed and are often exacerbated over time.

The rate at which digital change is occurring in Indian youth social life is unprecedented. Smartphone saturation is at a level that is comparable to that of developed nations in an urban setting. However, research has yet to fully elucidate the nature of the content that is being provided to Indian youth; yet, research in similar South Asian societies has shown that appearance-based comparisons through social media are related to higher levels of body discontent and anxiety even at normal BMI levels, similar to that found in Western societies. There are certain unique aspects of Indian youth social media that need to be considered. For example, Indian youth are exposed to matrimonial-related commentary on their appearance and are also exposed to Bollywood celebrity fitness-related social media. These are unique elements that cannot be measured by standard instruments.

Mental health infrastructure in schools in India is in a disorganized and uneven state. While urban private schools in metros now have counselors in increasing numbers, public schools in smaller cities, towns, and rural areas are devoid of mental health professionals. Teachers are unaware of the signs of anxiety in adolescents. In the Indian context, the stigma of mental health help-seeking is so deeply ingrained that even if the adolescent is aware of the need for help, they are unlikely to access the available resources. This is particularly pertinent because the schools provide the most accessible point of access for the adolescent population. This is the first step towards any effective population-level intervention strategy.

In the Indian context of adolescence, peer relationships are affected by examination groups, neighborhood structures, and parental study schedules that restrict the amount of time available for peers in a nonevaluative and socially acceptable manner. Studies conducted with Indian adolescents reveal that the peer relationship is a source of both social support and appearance-based evaluations. Teasing about weight is common in all schools. While the level of peer teasing in the Indian context is often represented as affectionate ribbing and can include terms such as "yaar" and "thoda kam kha," meaning "friend, eat a little less," the level of difficulty in representing this experience of stigma and asking for help is such that the experience of stigma is often denied by the adolescent.

Dietary patterns in the Indian urban context of the transition phase have created unique metabolic and psychological conditions. Fast food outlets, the availability of packaged snack foods, and the development of online food ordering and delivery services have transformed the dietary environment of Indian urban-dwelling adolescents in the past 10 years. In the Indian urban context, the rate of ultra-processed food product consumption has accelerated in the past 10 years in response to the commercialization of such products and the socially desirable association of such products with healthy weight and diet. At the same time, the traditional dietary structure and family food sharing patterns that have historically offered protection against malnutrition in Indian urban-dwelling populations are changing in dual-income family structures. This dietary transition is accompanied by food insecurity in lower-income Indian urban-dwelling populations. The psychological factors associated with dietary patterns in the Indian context include emotional eating in response to examination stress, the pressure of eating fast food with friends and sharing it with friends, and the online food ordering and delivery environment's association with adolescent identity development.

The current quantitative study in Kolkata ($N = 400$; 200 obese, 200 nonobese; BMI 30.0–39.9 vs 18.5–24.9) yields Indian-specific empirical data on anxiety across four age-sex cohorts, evaluated using the STAI (Spielberger, 1983).

Anxiety in the state. Obese participants exhibited markedly elevated state anxiety compared to their nonobese counterparts in three of four groups: male late adolescents (obese $M = 54.90$ vs nonobese $M = 39.96$, $p < 0.01$), female late adolescents (obese $M = 52.40$ vs nonobese $M = 45.20$, $p < 0.01$), and male young adults (obese $M = 56.92$ vs nonobese $M = 41.80$, $p < 0.01$). The exception pertained to female young adults, where the difference was nonsignificant (obese $M = 49.14$ vs nonobese $M = 47.18$, $p = 0.091$).

Anxiety as a trait. The pattern for trait anxiety was the same for all groups. There were very significant differences between obese and nonobese late adolescent males ($M = 53.18$ vs $M = 39.90$, $p < 0.01$), late adolescent females ($M = 51.36$ vs $M = 45.72$, $p < 0.01$), and young adult males ($M = 51.92$ vs $M = 45.20$, $p < 0.01$). Young adult females exhibited a nonsignificant difference on both subscales (trait anxiety: obese $M = 48.26$ vs nonobese $M = 46.92$, $p = 0.253$) (Das, 2018).

The lack of significance in the female young adult cohort regarding both state and trait anxiety is a significant observation. It indicates that anxiety may not distinguish between obese and nonobese young adult women in this urban Kolkata sample, potentially due to heightened anxiety levels in both groups at this developmental stage, which may be attributed to the cumulative pressures of academic achievement, marital expectations, and career transitions impacting all young adult women, regardless of weight status. The three-factor factorial ANOVA confirmed that the main effect of body weight was very significant in both state anxiety ($F = 153.272$, $p < 0.01$) and trait anxiety ($F = 59.436$, $p < 0.01$). Age and sex did not attain significance as independent main effects in either anxiety variable. The interaction between body weight and sex was significant in state anxiety ($F = 37.522$, $p < 0.01$), showing that obesity had a different effect on state anxiety depending on sex. This fits with the pattern of young female adults being the exception group. For trait anxiety, the interactions of body weight × age ($F = 7.922$, $p < 0.01$) and body weight × sex ($F = 11.664$, $p < 0.01$) were significant, indicating a developmentally differentiated pattern among the four groups. Pearson product-moment correlations between BMI and anxiety within each group yielded an additional noteworthy finding. In obese male late adolescents, significant negative correlations were found for both state anxiety ($r = -0.302$, $p < 0.05$) and trait anxiety ($r = -0.307$, $p < 0.05$). This indicates that, within this subgroup, a higher BMI was linked to slightly lower anxiety scores, which is a counterintuitive finding that suggests within-group heterogeneity and requires further investigation. All other group correlations between BMI and anxiety were not significant. This confirms that the difference in anxiety is categorical (between obese and nonobese groups) rather than a continuous BMI gradient within groups.

6.11 Psychological consequences across the life course

The cooccurring symptoms of anxiety and obesity in adolescents have significant consequences that transcend the teenage years. Life-course epidemiology research consistently demonstrates that the cooccurring symptoms in adolescents increase the risk for adult psychiatric disorders, cardiometabolic disorders, underperformance in academics, and underperformance in the workplace.

The continuity of psychiatric disorders is one of the most robust effects in the developmental psychopathology literature. In fact, metaanalytic research demonstrates that anxiety disorders in adolescents are significant predictors of anxiety disorders, depressive disorders, and substance use disorders in adults. The development of adult anxiety disorders from their adolescent counterparts is accomplished by the same cognitive maintenance mechanisms that established the original anxiety disorders in the first place, unless the continuity is disrupted by effective intervention or environmental change. The addition of the cooccurring symptoms of obesity further complicates the risk for psychiatric disorders by the continuous impact of weight stigma, inflammatory responses, and HPA axis dysregulation.

Anderson et al. (2007) reported a prospective longitudinal study in which the researchers demonstrated that adolescents who were obese had a significantly higher risk for the development of subsequent major depressive disorder and anxiety disorders in early adulthood. The relationship persisted after the researchers controlled for baseline mood disorders and socioeconomic factors, thereby supporting the independent effect of obesity status. Longitudinal research in Finland and the United Kingdom demonstrated that adolescents who were obese had a higher hospitalization rate for psychiatric disorders as adults, with anxiety disorders and mood disorders being the most prominent disorders.

Academic consequences are similarly well documented. For instance, it has been noted that adolescents suffering from both anxiety and obesity exhibit higher rates of absenteeism, lower academic attainment, and a higher risk of educational disengagement. Anxiety-related avoidance of academic and social situations, in addition to cognitive load-related depletion of working memory capacity, is a significant contributor to academic underachievement. Similarly, obesity-related consequences, including teasing, exclusion, and shame, contribute to academic and social disengagement. Longitudinal research has demonstrated that the presence of both conditions is a significant predictor of lower educational attainment than either condition in isolation.

6.12 Occupational and social outcomes

Adult outcomes of adolescent anxiety and obesity comorbidity include reduced occupational stability, lower-income levels, and higher rates of social isolation than those without a history of these conditions. Economic modeling research has predicted significant long-term cost burdens on society when comorbidity in adolescents remains untreated. Cost-effectiveness analyzes of early intervention for both conditions consistently demonstrate favorable ratios, reinforcing both the humanitarian and economic arguments for prevention and early intervention.

The cardiometabolic effects of comorbid anxiety and obesity in adolescents accumulate across the life course through various pathways. The long-term effects of HPA axis dysregulation, which is set in motion in adolescence by the combined effects of obesity and anxiety, include metabolic disorders such as insulin resistance, dyslipidemia, and cardiovascular risk. The proinflammatory effects of obesity and comorbid anxiety, which accumulate across life, contribute to premature atherosclerosis, hypertension, and cardiovascular events in midlife. The life-course effects of comorbid anxiety and obesity in adolescents thus include psychiatric, academic, economic, and cardiometabolic effects simultaneously. The importance of addressing comorbid anxiety and obesity in adolescents thus lies in its developmental significance.

Self-esteem and global self-worth are critical intermediate outcomes in this anxiety/obesity developmental pathway. Adolescents with comorbid anxiety/obesity consistently report lower self-esteem than do adolescents with either disorder individually. This is true across cultures. Low self-esteem in adolescence is a predictor of adult mental health trajectories. Thus we have a critical intermediate outcome that is a critical mechanism for understanding adult outcomes. Social isolation is a third intermediate outcome. This is because social isolation translates into a lack of access to social support that can help mitigate adult mental health problems. This is a critical disadvantage that can accumulate over time.

The critical point here is that life-course studies also reveal resilience and recovery. Adolescents treated for anxiety with comorbid obesity have normalized psychiatric trajectories. This is critical because it shows that developmental disadvantage is not deterministic. Adolescents with comorbid anxiety/obesity who experience strong social support networks, supportive family environments, and supportive school environments also have better adult outcomes. Thus we have evidence that adolescence is a period of plasticity that can allow developmental trajectories to take a more positive turn if environments are changed. This could include moving to a new peer context that is less stigmatizing, access to skilled therapeutic support, or changes in family communication styles that can help developmental trajectories take a more positive turn.

6.13 Coping mechanisms: adaptive and maladaptive patterns

Adolescents dealing with both obesity and anxiety utilize a variety of coping strategies, both adaptive and maladaptive, that may either help to mitigate or worsen their anxiety. Understanding this coping landscape is crucial in developing interventions that enhance adaptive coping skills, reducing reliance on maladaptive coping that may maintain the anxiety–obesity cycle.

6.14 Maladaptive patterns

Emotional eating is the maladaptive coping pattern that has been best explored in this population. The affect-regulation model of emotional eating suggests that eating, specifically of high-energy-density, high-palatability foods, provides temporary relief from negative emotional states by activating dopaminergic reward pathways. This relief is real, yet temporary, and the conditioned pattern of eating in response to negative emotions is self-perpetuating. Negative emotions trigger eating, eating temporarily relieves negative emotions, and this pattern of eating in response to negative emotions strengthens over time. Emotional eating, in turn, contributes to obesity, which in turn contributes to anxiety through stigma and body image concerns.

Avoidance is a second core maladaptive pattern. Avoidance of physical activity in sports, physical education, and medical visits temporarily relieves anxiety. Yet, this avoidance does not allow for disconfirmation of threat-related cognitive distortions, nor does it provide opportunities for positive experiences that could contradict anxiety. Cognitive avoidance, including distraction and thought suppression, provides temporary relief from anxiety, yet this avoidance pattern leads to more frequent and persistent negative thoughts over time, a pattern that has been well documented in the ironic thought literature by Wegner et al. (1987). Social withdrawal is a third avoidance pattern, where avoidance of social groups further decreases the quality of the peer network and support availability, a disadvantage that is already compounded by weight-related stigma, teasing, and exclusion.

Substance use as a coping behavior has also been identified in a small percentage of adolescents with anxiety and obesity, specifically in the older adolescent age group. Alcohol and marijuana consumption have a pharmacological effect in reducing anxiety symptoms, but they also increase emotional problems, sleep disturbances, and health problems. Using supplements, laxatives, or exercise as a means of weight control due to anxiety related to body size is another unhealthy coping behavior with health consequences such as electrolyte imbalance, orthopedic problems, and the escalation of disordered eating behaviors.

6.15 Adaptive coping mechanisms

Cognitive reappraisal, which involves the conscious reframing of stressful situations in ways that alter their emotional impact, has the most robust evidence base as a mechanism for coping with anxiety in adolescents. As part of cognitive-behavioral therapy (CBT), cognitive reappraisal has been shown to reduce both the acute symptoms of anxiety as well as the long-term maintenance of anxiety as a habituated response to threat appraisal. For adolescents with body-related anxiety, the targets for cognitive reappraisal include the evaluation of the consequences of weight-related social interactions, the development of balanced narratives about body diversity, and the development of perspective-taking skills to reduce the importance attached to the opinions of others.

Mindfulness-based interventions offer another pathway to adaptive coping mechanisms by development of skills in the present moment, including the nonjudgmental acceptance of unpleasant internal states. Mindfulness-based interventions have shown moderate effects in the development of emotional regulation skills in adolescents, as well as the regulation of stress responses. Moreover, neuroimaging studies suggest the development of prefrontal-limbic connectivity as a result of mindfulness-based interventions. For adolescents with body shame and weight anxiety, mindfulness-based interventions could reduce the tendency to self-evaluate and the shame responses associated with internalized weight stigma.

Physical activity programs, both as a metabolic intervention and as a psychological intervention, are effective in the reduction of symptoms of anxiety in adolescents. Physical activity programs, which are nonevaluative and enjoyable, reduce symptoms of anxiety by multiple mechanisms: the metabolic effects of exercise in reducing cortisol and inflammatory responses, the positive experience of the body in physical activity, the development of self-efficacy in mastery-based physical activity, and the development of social skills in group-based physical activity programs. The key design elements in physical activity programs are the absence of emphasis on appearance and competition in favor of intrinsic motivation, autonomy, and skill development.

Social support seeking, journaling, and creative writing are other forms of adaptive coping strategies that have been found in the adolescent literature. In the study conducted by Pennebaker & Beall (1986), it was found that writing about stressful experiences reduced physiological and psychological stress in the participants. Adolescents who maintain high-quality friendships with friends who provide acceptance rather than appearance-based evaluations tend to have lower levels of anxiety and more adaptive body image development even in the face of weight-related teasing by other peer groups.

The development of self-compassion is another adaptive coping strategy that has been shown in the literature to be an effective intervention strategy in the management of stress and other mental health issues in the adolescent population. As a construct, self-compassion is the opposite of shame and consists of three elements: self-kindness, common humanity, and mindfulness in the face of suffering. It has been shown in the literature that interventions aimed at the development of self-compassion reduce levels of body dissatisfaction and disordered eating in adolescent and young adult populations. In the Indian population and in the context of Indian culture, where the weight of the body has moral and family-level implications, the development of self-compassion is an essential adaptive coping strategy that has to be contextualized in the Indian culture and its context. This would involve the development of the ability of the adolescent to view the weight of the body as a multidetermined health variable rather than a reflection of the character of the person and the development of the ability of the person to be kind rather than cruel in the face of suffering.

6.16 Integrated intervention models

The bidirectional and multidimensional nature of the anxiety–obesity link in adolescence calls for integrative intervention models that simultaneously address psychological, behavioral, relational, and structural factors. One-domain interventions, both obesity-specific and anxiety-specific, have been found to be less effective in managing comorbid presentations in adolescence and have been found to potentially exacerbate harm in the context of shame and stigma, which are salient in the maintenance of both conditions.

6.16.1 Psychological Interventions

CBT has been found to be the best supported psychological intervention for anxiety disorders in adolescent populations. Randomized controlled trials have supported the efficacy of CBT in reducing symptom severity in SAD in adolescence, with treatment gains maintained at 1- to 3-year follow-up. CBT models have been adapted to address comorbid obesity and anxiety in adolescence by including components to address cognitive distortions in weight-related situations, including catastrophizing in social situations involving weight, overestimation of social scrutiny in body-exposure situations, and all-or-nothing thinking in body image and social acceptability. Behavioral experiments to address avoidance are also included in CBT models to address comorbid obesity and anxiety in adolescence.

ACT has also been found to be effective in managing anxiety in adolescence with comorbid obesity. ACT models have been found to reduce psychological inflexibility in adolescence with comorbid obesity, including stress-induced eating patterns. ACT models have been found to be effective in managing the shame and stigma associated with obesity through techniques to increase psychological distance from self-evaluative thoughts through defusion techniques and to reduce the behavioral impact of negative emotions through acceptance techniques.

Mindfulness-based interventions, mindfulness-based stress reduction for adolescents, and mindfulness-based cognitive therapy have shown moderate treatment effect sizes for anxiety reduction and are increasingly being used in school settings. In a first RCT of a school-based body-image intervention in India,Lewis-Smith et al. (2023) showed that an evidence-based program adapted for a school-based setting implemented in Delhi schools showed a significant effect compared to a control group on body image, disordered eating, and psychological outcomes.

6.17 Family-based models

Family systems theory has shown that parental modeling, parent–child communication patterns, and family weight-related discourse are all critical factors that influence adolescent body image and anxiety. Family-based interventions that change shame-based and weight-related family communication patterns to autonomy-supportive and health-behavior-focused family communication patterns have shown positive outcomes for psychological and behavioral change. Family-based interventions that explicitly target parents to recognize and change inadvertent weight-related teasing and moralistic family discourse reduce the evaluative family environment that exacerbates anxiety and internalized weight stigma.

Family-based behavioral weight-management interventions that are weight-neutral in their psychological framing and emphasize enjoyment of physical activity and quality of family relationships rather than caloric restriction and weight control show positive psychological outcomes compared to weight-focused family-based behavioral weight-management interventions. Psychoeducation of parents regarding the importance of adolescent body image and the negative effects of weight shame is a component of evidence-based family-based interventions that show measurable outcomes in reducing family-based stigma.

6.18 School-based models

Schools are found to be the most accessible setting for population-level interventions among adolescents. School-based interventions that are multicomponent and include social-emotional learning, media literacy skills, antistigma work, and inclusive physical activities are found to have the strongest evidence for reducing symptoms of anxiety and weight victimization. The Body Project and similar interventions that promote dissonance among adolescents through activities that promote critical thinking about idealized body images have been found to reduce body dissatisfaction and anxiety in multiple randomized trials across cultures, including South Asian cultures. School-climate interventions that incorporate weight as a characteristic in antibullying policies have been found to reduce weight victimization and associated anxiety. Inclusive physical activities that de-emphasize competition and fitness grading in favor of movement skills and socialization reduce anxiety associated with physical inactivity that leads to obesity. Teacher-training programs that recognize weight-related distress and supportive classroom environments address the institutionalized nature of stigma in schools.

6.19 Policy integration

Structural and policy-level interventions target the upstream causes that individual and family interventions cannot target. Regulations on food advertising to children and adolescents, investing in walkability in neighborhoods, providing mental health support in schools, and changing competitive examination systems that cause academic stress are policy interventions that have the potential to target the structural causes that sustain both anxiety and obesity. National mental health programs such as the National Mental Health Program in India and its interventions in schools need specific consideration of the anxiety/obesity comorbidity to ensure that intervention resources are targeted and delivered effectively.

Healthcare-provider training is a vital, though commonly neglected, aspect of integrated interventions. Primary healthcare physicians, pediatricians, and school nurses may be the ones who interact with adolescents with obesity in a manner that inadvertently communicates stigmatizing attitudes, focuses on weight loss as the primary intervention goal without attending to psychological well-being, and fails to assess anxiety or depression levels. Intervention studies that train healthcare providers in the delivery of weight-inclusive communication approaches, psychological assessment, and referral practices have documented positive outcomes in anxiety levels, treatment adherence, and cardiometabolic health in adult obesity populations. Developing and testing such intervention approaches in the healthcare context of India would be a valuable future research and intervention direction.

Peer-based and youth-participatory intervention approaches provide a promising, though underutilized, intervention opportunity, especially in the Indian context, where adult authority figures hold a position of great social influence, and peer influence in adolescence is simultaneously high and unused in intervention approaches. Intervention approaches that train peer educators in weight-stigma awareness, body-appreciation approaches, and psychological first-aid skills hold promise in reaching adolescents in informal settings that would be inaccessible to adult-based intervention approaches. Similarly, the involvement of youth in the development of intervention approaches, a core principle in the development of contemporary global health approaches, would also increase the likelihood of intervention approaches reaching the target population in a culturally relevant manner by increasing the salience of the intervention approaches to the actual social experience of the target population.

6.20 Future research directions

The evidence base reviewed in the present chapter, though extensive, has gaps that future research needs to address in order to enhance the utility of the evidence base in a meaningful manner.

Therefore there is an urgent need for longitudinal studies with longer follow-up periods. In the systematic review conducted by Samanta et al. (2022), the scarcity of prospective studies with follow-up periods longer than 2 years was emphasized in the field of anxiety–obesity comorbidity. Moreover, the developmental cascade process is theoretically of central importance in the explanation of the comorbidity and interaction of the two conditions and requires multiwave studies of the process of development from adolescence through early adulthood.

Regarding India-specific prospective studies, the scarcity of such studies is a major concern in the field of anxiety–obesity comorbidity among Indian adolescents. There is limited research on neurobiological correlates specific to anxiety–obesity comorbidities in adolescents. Neuroimaging research has examined structural and functional correlates in obesity and anxiety disorders separately. There is limited research on neural correlates in cooccurring conditions. Research on the neural correlates of cooccurring conditions, such as anxiety and obesity, in adolescents, to understand whether shared neural substrates in regions such as the amygdala–prefrontal circuitry and reward system contribute to comorbid anxiety and obesity in adolescents, is urgently required. Intervention research in low- and middle-income countries such as India is urgently required. The majority of RCTs conducted to assess school-based body-image interventions, anxiety-reduction interventions for weight-related anxiety, and family-based interventions for improving parent-adolescent communication in obesity and anxiety disorders have taken place in high-income Western nations. The intervention research conducted by Lewis-Smith et al. (2023) in Delhi is an important first step in addressing this gap. A single study is not enough to assess the level of readiness for implementation. Intervention research in India is urgently required. The research on digital media is an area where methodological challenges in research methods need to be addressed. There is limited research on algorithmic exposure in social media in India for appearance-based social comparison in adolescents. There is limited research on how exposure to body-positivity versus appearance-normativeness content in India affects anxiety and body image. Experimental and ecological momentary assessment methods need to be employed to understand real-time relationships between digital media engagement and anxiety and body-image fluctuations. Natural experiments in policy contexts in India hold much promise for research in obesity and anxiety disorders. Changes in food marketing regulations, school lunch programs, examination-system changes, and changes in mental health funding in various states in India hold much promise for quasiexperimentation.

Lastly, the integration of sociological and anthropological approaches has not been sufficiently developed in the existing quantitative literature, which primarily focuses on prevalence and prediction at the individual level without sufficiently exploring the processes by which cultural meaning-making processes, institutional practices, and community contexts construct the environments in which anxiety and obesity intersect. Qualitative and mixed-methods studies that explore the lived experiences of young Indians navigating body weight, identity, social judgment, and academic pressures would provide a richness that could enhance theoretical models and guide the development of culturally meaningful interventions.

Translational research, the systematic process of moving findings from basic science and clinical trials into routine practice, requires specific attention in the Indian context. Even where evidence-based programs exist, including body-image school programs and adapted CBT protocols, the gap between efficacy evidence from controlled research settings and effectiveness in routine real-world delivery is substantial. Implementation-science frameworks, including the Consolidated Framework for Implementation Research and the RE-AIM model, provide structured approaches to understanding why evidence-based interventions succeed or fail in particular delivery contexts, how to adapt them for different populations and systems, and how to sustain them over time beyond the research-trial period. Systematic application of implementation science to the anxiety–obesity intervention literature in India would accelerate the translation of emerging evidence into scaled public health benefits.

Technology-assisted intervention delivery offers additional pathways for reaching adolescents in resource-limited contexts. Digital mental health programs delivered through smartphones, including CBT-based apps, mindfulness platforms, and peer-support communities, have demonstrated efficacy in reducing anxiety symptoms in adolescent populations in high-income country trials. Adapting and testing such approaches for Indian adolescents, with attention to language, cultural content, data privacy, and differential smartphone access across socioeconomic groups, represents a research and implementation priority that aligns with India's digital infrastructure development. However, technology-based solutions must be implemented thoughtfully: poorly designed digital interventions risk amplifying comparison and anxiety rather than reducing them, and the social and relational dimensions of human distress may not be adequately addressed by algorithm-mediated support alone.

6.21 Conclusion

The link between anxiety and obesity in adolescence is systemic, bidirectional, and culturally embedded. It operates through interlocking biological, psychological, social, and structural mechanisms: the HPA axis translates chronic stress into metabolic dysregulation; cognitive processes of rumination, catastrophic appraisal, and avoidance maintain anxiety and drive emotional eating; stigma exposure internalizes into shame that perpetuates both psychological distress and the social conditions that generate it; structural inequality distributes risk unevenly across gender, class, and cultural lines; and developmental timing shapes when and how these processes interact most powerfully.

Breaking the cycle requires dignity-centered, integrated approaches that simultaneously address mental health and metabolic health. Adolescent obesity must be reframed not as a moral failure requiring shame-based correction but as a multidimensional developmental challenge requiring compassionate, science-grounded, and systemically informed responses. The evidence converges on several practical imperatives: psychological treatment must explicitly address weight-related cognitive distortions and internalized shame; family and school environments must be reformed to reduce stigmatizing practices and support autonomy rather than evaluative performance; public health messaging must adopt weight-neutral frameworks that promote health behavior rather than body-size targets; and structural reforms must address the examination pressure, food-environment inequalities, and mental health service gaps that maintain population-level vulnerability.

Adolescence is not simply a risk period. It is also a period of neuroplasticity and opportunity. Targeted, evidence-based interventions delivered during this window demonstrate durable benefits for psychological well-being, physical health, and life-course outcomes. The scientific record compels a paradigm shift: from reductionist and moralizing narratives toward systemic, compassionate, and developmentally informed understanding. Only through such systemic and dignity-centered reform can the intertwined trajectories of anxiety and obesity in adolescence be meaningfully interrupted before they consolidate into life-course disadvantage.

The accumulated empirical evidence across developmental psychology, psychiatry, public health, sociology, and neuroscience converges on a shared conclusion: anxiety and obesity in adolescence are intertwined manifestations of stress-sensitive developmental systems embedded within relational and structural contexts. They are maintained through feedback loops involving stigma exposure, maladaptive coping, neuroendocrine activation, and institutional reinforcement. Adolescence, characterized by heightened neuroplasticity, simultaneously represents a window of risk and a window of intervention opportunity. Evidence-based, dignity-centered, and multilevel approaches that interrupt these trajectories before they consolidate into chronic disadvantage offer the most promising path forward for individual adolescents, for families and schools, and for public health and policy systems charged with supporting the healthy development of the next generation.

Key takeaways

1. Adolescence is a neurobiologically sensitive phase marked by limbic–prefrontal imbalance, which heightens susceptibility to anxiety.
2. The connection between anxiety and obesity in teenagers goes both ways and is kept going by cognitive, biological, and social feedback loops.
3. The HPA axis converts long-term psychosocial stress into the buildup of visceral fat, insulin resistance, and problems with appetite.
4. Weight stigma serves as a persistent social stressor with distinct neuroendocrine and psychological effects that occur independently of BMI.
5. Emotional eating is a learned way to deal with emotions that makes you feel better for a short time, but makes you more vulnerable to metabolic and psychological problems in the long run.

6. Gender, class, and caste converge to create diverse vulnerability profiles that single-axis analyzes fail to fully represent.
7. Adolescent comorbidity has substantial implications for psychiatric outcomes, educational achievement, cardiometabolic health, and economic engagement throughout the life course.
8. Integrated interventions that tackle psychological, relational, institutional, and structural dimensions concurrently are more effective than single-domain approaches.

Glossary

Emotional eating: eating food, especially foods that are high in energy and taste good, when you are feeling bad instead of when you are physically hungry. It is frequently observed in adolescents who are dealing with anxiety, stress, or social rejection and is thought of as a maladaptive way to control their emotions. Stress causes cortisol levels to rise, which makes people want to eat more high-fat and high-sugar foods. Emotional eating temporarily alleviates distress by activating dopaminergic reward pathways, yet it exacerbates long-term metabolic and psychological susceptibility.

Weight bias internalization (WBI): the process by which people take negative stereotypes about being overweight and apply them to themselves. Teenagers who have a lot of WBI think that being overweight means they are lazy, undisciplined, or not good enough. Empirical research documents that WBI predicts anxiety, depressive symptoms, body dissatisfaction, and avoidance behaviors independent of objective BMI. It is regarded as a principal mediator in the anxiety–obesity nexus.

HPA axis (Hypothalamic-Pituitary-Adrenal Axis): the main neuroendocrine system that controls how the body responds to stress. The hypothalamus releases CRH when it senses a threat or social evaluation. This starts a chain reaction of hormones that leads to the release of cortisol from the adrenal cortex. Long-term activation of the HPA axis is linked to the buildup of visceral fat, insulin resistance, increased emotional reactivity, and trouble sleeping. In adolescents subjected to enduring stigma or chronic stress, dysregulated HPA activity biologically integrates psychosocial distress into metabolic processes.

Social Anxiety Disorder (SAD) is a condition that makes people very afraid of being judged, embarrassed, or rejected in social or performance situations. SAD often appears in early to mid-adolescence, when teens are more sensitive to their peers and are figuring out who they are. Teenagers who are overweight may be more socially anxious, especially when they have to show their bodies, like when they play sports, swim, or speak in front of a group. Avoidance behaviors central to SAD reinforce sedentary patterns and social withdrawal.

Internalizing Coping: a way of dealing with stress by turning it in on yourself, which can show up as rumination, withdrawal, self-blame, or anxiety. More frequently observed in female adolescent samples. Internalizing coping can hide anxiety that is already there, keep up negative self-evaluation, and help keep body dissatisfaction and disordered eating behavior going over time.

Allostatic load: the total amount of physical damage that chronic stress causes. In adolescents enduring chronic peer victimization and weight-related stigma, heightened allostatic load is indicated by disrupted cortisol rhythms, increased inflammatory markers, and compromised immune function. It signifies the biological incorporation of chronic psychosocial stress and is progressively utilized as an integrative biomarker in studies concerning health disparities.

Developmental cascade: a process by which early vulnerabilities in one developmental domain spill over into adjacent domains over time, producing compounding disadvantage. In the anxiety–obesity literature, early anxiety predicts later social withdrawal, reduced physical activity, elevated body dissatisfaction, and weight gain, each of which predicts further anxiety and metabolic risk. Developmental cascades resist single-cause narratives and support integrated explanation of biological, cognitive, and behavioral, and explain how they interact to sustain emotional eating over time.

1. Some clinicians argue that anxiety should be addressed before any weight-management intervention is undertaken with adolescents. Evaluate this position with reference to the bidirectional developmental-systems model.
2. Indian cultural expectations around body size, discipline, and matrimonial prospects create a distinct normative context for adolescent anxiety and obesity. How should school counselors adapt their practice to address these cultural specificities while avoiding stereotyping?
3. Schools are often described as potential sites of both harm, through weight stigma and performance pressure, and intervention, through social-emotional learning and inclusive practice. Talk about what changes need to be made to schools' structures so that they go from being places that cause harm to places that reduce harm in light of the link between anxiety and obesity.

Review questions

1. Describe the bidirectional model connecting anxiety and obesity during adolescence, incorporating a minimum of two mechanisms functioning in both directions.
2. Explain the biological processes by which chronic psychosocial stress leads to the persistence of anxiety and the increase in weight among adolescents.
3. Summarize the worldwide epidemiological data regarding the concurrent prevalence of anxiety and obesity during adolescence, citing at least one systematic review or metaanalysis.
4. Examine the influence of gender on susceptibility to the anxiety–obesity correlation during adolescence, considering both female and male trends.
5. Suggest a comprehensive intervention model for an urban Indian secondary school catering to adolescents with comorbid anxiety and obesity, detailing the intervention levels, the supporting evidence for each component, and the necessary cultural adaptations.

AI disclosure

During the preparation of this work, the author(s) used ChatGPT, Grammarly, and Paperpal solely for the purpose of language editing. After using these tools/services, the author(s) reviewed and edited the content as needed and take(s) full responsibility for the content of the publication.

References

Amiri, S., & Behnezhad, S. (2019). Obesity and anxiety symptoms: A systematic review and meta-analysis. *Neuropsychiatrie, 33*(2), 72–89. https://doi.org/10.1007/s40211-019-0302-9.

Anderson, S. E., Cohen, P., Naumova, E. N., Jacques, P. F., & Must, A. (2007). Adolescent obesity and risk for subsequent major depressive disorder and anxiety disorder: Prospective evidence. *Psychosomatic Medicine, 69*(8), 740–747. https://doi.org/10.1097/PSY.0b013e31815580b4.

Beck, A. T. (1976). *Cognitive therapy and the emotional disorders*. International Universities Press.

Burke, N. L., & Storch, E. A. (2015). A meta-analysis of weight status and anxiety in children and adolescents. *Journal of Developmental and Behavioral Pediatrics, 36*(2), 133–145. https://doi.org/10.1097/DBP.0000000000000143.

Crenshaw, K. (1989). Demarginalizing the intersection of race and sex: A Black feminist critique of antidiscrimination doctrine, feminist theory, and antiracist politics. *University of Chicago Legal Forum, 1989*(1), 139–167.

Datar, A., & Sturm, R. (2006). Childhood overweight and elementary school outcomes. *International Journal of Obesity, 30*(9), 1449–1460. https://doi.org/10.1038/sj.ijo.0803311.

Deshmukh, V. L., & Kulkarni, S. (2017). Body image perception and weight status among adolescents in Pune, Maharashtra. *Indian Pediatrics, 54*(12), 1025–1028. https://doi.org/10.1007/s13312-017-1205-0.

Emmer, C., Bosnjak, M., & Mata, J. (2020). The association between weight stigma and mental health: A meta-analysis. *Obesity Reviews, 21*(1), e12935. https://doi.org/10.1111/obr.12935.

Erikson, E. H. (1968). *Identity: Youth and crisis*. Norton.

Fardouly, J., Diedrichs, P. C., Vartanian, L. R., & Halliwell, E. (2015). Social comparisons on social media: The impact of Facebook on young women's body image concerns and mood. *Body Image, 13*, 38–45. https://doi.org/10.1016/j.bodyim.2014.12.002.

Fatima, Y., Doi, S. A. R., & Mamun, A. A. (2016). Longitudinal impact of sleep on overweight and obesity in children and adolescents: A systematic review and bias-adjusted meta-analysis. *Obesity Reviews, 17*(11), 1099–1112. https://doi.org/10.1111/obr.12459.

Festinger, L. (1954). A theory of social comparison processes. *Human Relations, 7*(2), 117–140. https://doi.org/10.1177/001872675400700202.

Fredrickson, B. L., & Roberts, T. A. (1997). Objectification theory: Toward understanding women's lived experiences and mental health risks. *Psychology of Women Quarterly, 21*(2), 173–206. https://doi.org/10.1111/j.1471-6402.1997.tb00108.x.

GBD Collaborators (2019). Global, regional, and national burden of 12 mental disorders in 204 countries and territories, 1990-2019: A systematic analysis for the global burden of disease study 2019. *Lancet Psychiatry, 9*(2), 137–150. https://doi.org/10.1016/S2215-0366(21)00395-3.

Gilbert, P. (2010). *The compassionate mind: A new approach to life's challenges*. Constable.

Graber, J. A. (2013). Pubertal timing and the development of psychopathology in adolescence and beyond. *Hormones and Behavior, 64*(2), 262–269. https://doi.org/10.1016/j.yhbeh.2013.04.003.

Gross, J. J., & John, O. P. (2003). Individual differences in two emotion regulation processes: Implications for affect, relationships, and well-being. *Journal of Personality and Social Psychology, 85*(2), 348–362. https://doi.org/10.1037/0022-3514.85.2.348.

Guyer, A. E., McClure-Tone, E. B., Shiffrin, N. D., Pine, D. S., & Nelson, E. E. (2009). Probing the neural correlates of anticipated peer evaluation in adolescence. *Child Development, 80*(4), 1000–1015. https://doi.org/10.1111/j.1467-8624.2009.01313.x.

Hayward, L. E., Vartanian, L. R., & Pinkus, R. T. (2018). Weight stigma predicts poorer psychological well-being through internalized weight bias and maladaptive coping responses. *Obesity, 26*(4), 755–761. https://doi.org/10.1002/oby.22126.

Samanta, J. L., Parida, J., Badamali, J., Pradhan, A., Singh, P. K., Mishra, B. K., Patra, P. K., Pati, S., Kaur, H., & Acharya, S. K. (2022). The incidence, prevalence, and contributing factors of overweight and obesity among adolescent population of India: A scoping review protocol. *PLoS One, 17*(9), e0275172. https://doi.org/10.1371/journal.pone.0275172.

Kessler, R. C., Berglund, P., Demler, O., Jin, R., Merikangas, K. R., & Walters, E. E. (2005). Lifetime prevalence and age-of-onset distributions of DSM-IV disorders in the National comorbidity survey replication. *Archives of General Psychiatry, 62*(6), 593–602. https://doi.org/10.1001/archpsyc.62.6.593.

Lewis-Smith, H., Garbett, K., Chaudhry, A., Dhillon, M., Shroff, H., White, P., & Diedrichs, P. C. (2023). Evaluating a school-based body image intervention adapted for adolescent girls in India: A pilot randomized controlled trial. *Body Image, 44*, 148–156. https://doi.org/10.1016/j.bodyim.2022.12.006.

Masten, A. S., Roisman, G. I., Long, J. D., Burt, K. B., Obradovic, J., Riley, J. R., Boelcke-Stennes, K., & Tellegen, A. (2005). Developmental cascades: Linking academic achievement and externalizing and internalizing symptoms over 20 years. *Developmental Psychology, 41*(5), 733–746. https://doi.org/10.1037/0012-1649.41.5.733.

McCreary, D. R., & Sasse, D. K. (2000). An exploration of the drive for muscularity in adolescent boys and girls. *Journal of American College Health, 48*(6), 297–304. https://doi.org/10.1080/07448480009596271.

Mendle, J., Turkheimer, E., & Emery, R. E. (2007). Detrimental psychological outcomes associated with early pubertal timing in adolescent girls. *Developmental Review, 27*(2), 151–171. https://doi.org/10.1016/j.dr.2006.11.001.

Merikangas, K. R., He, J. P., Burstein, M., Swanson, S. A., Avenevoli, S., Cui, L., Benjet, C., Georgiades, K., & Swendsen, J. (2010). Lifetime prevalence of mental disorders in U.S. adolescents: Results from the National comorbidity survey replication-adolescent supplement (NCS-A). *Journal of the American Academy of Child and Adolescent Psychiatry, 49*(10), 980–989. https://doi.org/10.1016/j.jaac.2010.05.017.

Nolen-Hoeksema, S., Wisco, B. E., & Lyubomirsky, S. (2008). Rethinking rumination. *Perspectives on Psychological Science, 3*(5), 400–424. https://doi.org/10.1111/j.1745-6924.2008.00088.x.

Pearl, R. L., & Puhl, R. M. (2018). Weight bias internalization and health: A systematic review. *Obesity Reviews, 19*(8), 1141–1163. https://doi.org/10.1111/obr.12701.

Pennebaker, J. W., & Beall, S. K. (1986). Confronting a traumatic event: Toward an understanding of inhibition and disease. *Journal of Abnormal Psychology, 95*(3), 274–281. https://doi.org/10.1037/0021-843X.95.3.274.

Phelps, N. H., Singleton, R. K., Zhou, B., Heap, R. A., Mishra, A., Bennett, J. E., Paciorek, C. J., Lhoste, V. P., Carrillo-Larco, R. M., Stevens, G. A., & Rodriguez-Martinez, A. (2024). Worldwide trends in underweight and obesity from 1990 to 2022: A pooled analysis of 3663 population-representative studies with 222 million children, adolescents, and adults. *Lancet, 403*(10431), 1027–1050. https://doi.org/10.1016/S0140-6736(23)02750-2.

Pine, D. S., Cohen, P., Brook, J., & Coplan, J. D. (1997). Psychiatric symptoms in adolescence as predictors of obesity in early adulthood: A longitudinal study. *American Journal of Public Health, 87*(8), 1303–1310. https://doi.org/10.2105/AJPH.87.8.1303.

Pothiraj, P., Shamal, C., & Krishnan, V. (2022). Body image dissatisfaction, depression, and health-related quality of life amongst Indian obese school children: A cross-sectional study. *Journal of Indian Association for Child and Adolescent Mental Health, 18*(1), 63–72. https://doi.org/10.1177/09731342221096355.

Puhl, R. M., & Lessard, L. M. (2020). Weight stigma in youth: Prevalence, consequences, and considerations for clinical practice. *Current Obesity Reports, 9*(4), 402–411. https://doi.org/10.1007/s13679-020-00408-8.

Ricciardelli, L. A., & McCabe, M. P. (2001). Children's body image concerns and eating disturbance: A review of the literature. *Clinical Psychology Review, 21*(3), 325–344. https://doi.org/10.1016/S0272-7358(99)00051-3.

Ruttle, P. L., Shirtcliff, E. A., Armstrong, J. M., Klein, M. H., & Essex, M. J. (2011). Neuroendocrine coupling across adolescence and the longitudinal influence of early life stress. *Developmental Psychobiology, 53*(7), 688–704.

Som, N., & Mukhopadhyay, S. (2015). Body weight and body image concerns and related behaviours among female adolescents in urban India. *Public Health Nutrition, 18*(6), 1075–1083. https://doi.org/10.1017/S1368980014001451.

Spielberger, C.D., 1983. Manual for the State-Trait Anxiety Inventory (STAI). Consulting Psychologists Press, Palo Alto, CA. Spielberger, C.D., 1983.

Steinberg, L. (2010). A dual systems model of adolescent risk-taking. *Developmental Psychobiology, 52*(3), 216–224. https://doi.org/10.1002/dev.20445.

Stigler, M. H., Arora, M., Dhavan, P., Shrivastav, R., Reddy, K. S., & Perry, C. L. (2011). Weight-related concerns and weight-control behaviors among overweight adolescents in Delhi, India: A cross-sectional study. *International Journal of Behavioral Nutrition and Physical Activity, 8*(1), 9. https://doi.org/10.1186/1479-5868-8-9.

Swami, V., Madan, R., & Tovee, M. J. (2011). Weight discrepancy and women's body satisfaction and self-esteem in urban India. *Body Image, 8*(3), 275–279. https://doi.org/10.1016/j.bodyim.2011.04.002.

Tangney, J. P., & Dearing, R. L. (2002). *Shame and guilt*. Guilford Press.

Thompson, J. K., Heinberg, L. J., Altabe, M., & Tantleff-Dunn, S. (1999). *Exacting beauty: Theory, assessment, and treatment of body image disturbance*. American Psychological Association.

Tomiyama, A. J. (2014). Weight stigma is stressful: A review of evidence for the cyclic obesity/weight-based stigma model. *Appetite, 82*, 8–15. https://doi.org/10.1016/j.appet.2014.07.005.

Warnick, J. L., Thomas, J. J., Becker, K. R., Anderson, S. E., & Misra, M. (2022). Weight stigma and mental health in youth: A systematic review and meta-analysis. *Journal of Pediatric Psychology, 47*(3), 237–255. https://doi.org/10.1093/jpepsy/jsab110.

Wegner, D. M., Schneider, D. J., Carter, S. R., & White, T. L. (1987). Paradoxical effects of thought suppression. *Journal of Personality and Social Psychology, 53*(1), 5–13. https://doi.org/10.1037/0022-3514.53.1.5.

World Health Organization. (2020). *Obesity and overweight: Key facts.* WHO https://www.who.int/news-room/fact-sheets/detail/obesity-and-overweight.

Yengo, L., Sidorenko, J., Kemper, K.E., Zheng, Z., Wood, A.R., Weedon, M.N., Frayling, T.M., Hirschhorn, J., Yang, J., & Visscher, P.M. (2018). Meta-analysis of genome-wide association studies for height and body mass index in approximately 700,000 individuals of European ancestry. Human Molecular Genetics, 27(20), 3641–3649. https://doi.org/10.1093/hmg/ddy271.

Panda, A., et al. (2025). Prevalence and associated risk factors of overweight and obesity among adolescent population of India: A scoping review. *BMC Nutrition, 11*(1). https://doi.org/10.1186/s40795-025-01088-0 Springer Science and Business Media LLC.

Further reading

Blakemore, S. J., & Mills, K. L. (2014). Is adolescence a sensitive period for sociocultural processing? *Annual Review of Psychology, 65*, 187–207. https://doi.org/10.1146/annurev-psych-010213-115202.

BMC Nutrition (2025). Prevalence and associated risk factors of overweight and obesity among adolescent population of India: A scoping review. *BMC Nutrition* https://doi.org/10.1186/s40795-025-01088-0.

Bose, M., Olivan, B., & Laferrere, B. (2009). Stress and obesity: The role of the hypothalamic-pituitary-adrenal axis in metabolic disease. *Current Opinion in Endocrinology, Diabetes, and Obesity, 16*(5), 340–346. https://doi.org/10.1097/MED.0b013e32832fa137.

Casey, B. J., Jones, R. M., & Hare, T. A. (2008). The adolescent brain. *Annals of the New York Academy of Sciences, 1124*, 111–126. https://doi.org/10.1196/annals.1440.010.

Eisenberger, N. I. (2012). The neural bases of social pain: Evidence for shared representations with physical pain. *Psychosomatic Medicine, 74*(2), 126–135.

Fu, X., Wang, Y., Zhao, F., Cui, R., Xie, W., Liu, Q., & Liu, Q. (2023). Shared biological mechanisms of depression and obesity: Focus on adipokines and lipokines. *Aging, 15*, 5917–5950. https://doi.org/10.18632/aging.204847.

Lengton, R., Schoenmakers, M., Penninx, B. W. J. H., Boon, M. R., & van Rossum, E. F. C. (2025). Glucocorticoids and HPA axis regulation in the stress-obesity connection: A comprehensive overview of biological, physiological and behavioural dimensions. *Clinical obesity, 15*(2), e12725 https://doi.org/10.1111/cob.12725.

Chapter 7

Depression and obesity

"Depression in adolescence is not a crisis of the mind alone; it is shaped by the body, the family, the social environment, and the cultural scripts that define worth."

Learning objectives

1. Analyse the bidirectional relationship between depression and obesity in adolescence, citing quantitative risk estimates from current metaanalytic evidence.
2. Explain the six theoretical frameworks linking depression and obesity—HPA axis dysfunction, Beck's cognitive triad, stigma theory, objectification theory, social comparison theory, and the syndemic model—and identify the specific causal pathway each illuminates.
3. Evaluate the moderating roles of gender, socioeconomic status, and cultural context—particularly India-specific scripts of marriageability and academic pressure—in the depression-obesity relationship.
4. Assess the clinical significance of the present study's Beck Depression Inventory (BDI) findings in Kolkata, applying Beck's classification thresholds to interpret group-level depression profiles by age and sex.
5. Design an evidence-based, culturally adapted intervention for the depression-obesity syndemic in Indian adolescent contexts, integrating psychological, school-based, clinical, and policy components.

Depression and obesity are two of the most critical health issues faced by adolescents across the globe. According to the World Health Organization (WHO, 2024), depression is ranked as one of the major causes of disability among young people in the world. It is estimated that 1 in 7 adolescents between the ages of 10 and 19 years suffers from a mental health condition worldwide, and depression is one of the most common mental health issues faced by young people worldwide. On the other hand, the pooled analysis of 3,663 population-representative studies revealed that the prevalence of obesity among children and adolescents between the ages of 5 and 19 years worldwide increased from 8% in 1990 to 20% in 2022, representing over 390 million young people worldwide (Phelps et al., 2024). What is of major concern and interest to health researchers and practitioners is the bidirectional relationship between these two health issues and their prevalence among young people worldwide.

In a meta-analysis of 22 observational studies of 175,135 participants, Chen et al. (2024) found a positive correlation between obesity and depression risk in children and adolescents (RR = 1.32; 95% CI: 1.09–1.60) and obesity and depressive symptoms (RR = 1.16; 95% CI: 1.00–1.35). Conversely, a metaanalysis of longitudinal studies showed depressed adolescents have a 70% increased risk of developing obesity (RR = 1.70; 95% CI: 1.40–2.07), and obese adolescents have a 40% increased risk of developing depression (RR = 1.40; 95% CI: 1.16–1.70; Marmorstein et al., 2016). Such bidirectional effects of depression and obesity, wherein each condition reinforces the other's risk, transform these two co-occurring conditions into a syndemic (Singer, 1996) and are uniquely destructive during the developmentally sensitive period of adolescence.

India's burden of depression and obesity is a microcosm of the global syndemic, but also uniquely expresses these syndemics in distinct ways. The National Mental Health Survey of India reported a 5.25% prevalence of depression in the general population as a lifetime risk of depression (Gururaj et al., 2016). Adolescents are a significantly underdetected population for depression in this survey. In a cross-sectional survey of school-going adolescents in India using the BDI to measure depression prevalence, the total depression prevalence was 58.4%, of which 28% reported mild depression, 15.1% reported moderate depression, and 15.3% reported severe depression (Bharati et al., 2022). Moreover, there is a highly significant correlation between BMI and depression levels in these adolescents (Bharati et al., 2022). Studies of school-going adolescents between 13 and 19 years of age in India reported 22.4% of girls and 12.8% of boys reported depression of various grades as per the BDI (Bharati et al., 2022).

Psychology of Obesity. DOI: https://doi.org/10.1016/B978-0-443-27797-9.00011-7

7.1 Why adolescence is the critical window

Adolescence is a uniquely vulnerable window of development because of the interplay of biological, psychological, and social changes that occur simultaneously. Puberty involves changes in levels of cortisol, estrogen, and testosterone, which regulate not just mood but also the distribution of fat, creating the conditions under which depression and obesity can occur together. The hypothalamic-pituitary-adrenal axis, which controls the stress response, is significantly reorganized during adolescence (Thapar et al., 2012). The effects of cortisol, which results from chronic stress and stigma, interfere with sleep, appetite, and metabolic function, creating the conditions for depression and obesity simultaneously. In addition, cortisol promotes the storage of fat. The psychological aspects of adolescence involve the formation of identity. The human body plays a critical role in the self-definition of the adolescent. The perception of the body plays a critical role in adolescent self-definition and identity formation. Adolescents with obesity may be particularly vulnerable because their sense of self is still developing. The emergence of abstract thinking during adolescence, including the ability to reflect on how one is perceived by others, heightens self-consciousness and sensitivity to body-related evaluations. Furthermore, social comparison processes have become increasingly influential in the current generation due to the widespread use of digital technology and social media, which provide continuous opportunities for appearance-based comparison that were not available to previous generations.

Socially, adolescents are dealing with fluid peer groups, and peer acceptance is of tremendous emotional importance. For obese adolescents, there is systematic exclusion from peer groups, sports activities, and social spaces. For adolescents, social belonging is of tremendous importance. In India, there is the added pressure of academic examinations, marriageability, and the opinions of the extended family, which makes the experience of adolescents unique compared to Western adolescents.

7.1.1 Definitional clarity

Obesity in adolescence is defined using age- and sex-adjusted body mass index (BMI) classifications. For adults, the WHO (1998) classifies obesity as BMI ≥30.0 kg/m^2; in the present study, obese participants met Class I or II obesity criteria (BMI 30.0–39.9 kg/m^2), and nonobese participants had BMI 18.5–24.9 kg/m^2. Depression is a clinical construct operationalised differently across diagnostic systems. The DSM-5 (APA, 2013) defines major depressive disorder by the presence of five or more of the following symptoms during the same two-week period, with at least one being either depressed mood or loss of interest or pleasure: depressed mood, markedly diminished interest or pleasure in activities (anhedonia), significant weight change or appetite disturbance, insomnia or hypersomnia, psychomotor agitation or retardation, fatigue or loss of energy, feelings of worthlessness or excessive guilt, diminished concentration, and recurrent thoughts of death or suicidal ideation. In adolescents specifically, the DSM-5 notes that depressed mood may present as irritability rather than sadness—an important clinical distinction for this population. The ICD-11 (WHO, 2019) classifies depressive episodes by duration (at least two weeks), symptom count, and functional impairment, distinguishing mild, moderate, and severe episodes without psychotic features. In the present study, depression is operationalised through the BDI (Beck et al., 1961), a validated 21-item self-report scale measuring symptom severity on a 0–63 continuum, with established cut-points: 0–10 (normal), 11–16 (mild mood disturbance), 17–20 (borderline clinical depression), 21–30 (moderate depression), 31–40 (severe depression), and above 40 (extreme depression). The BDI does not yield a DSM-5 or ICD-11 diagnosis but provides a continuous, validated index of depressive symptom burden that is appropriate for community-based comparative research and has been validated for use with Indian adolescent populations (Bhatt et al., 2007).

7.2 Theoretical perspectives on the depression-obesity connection

7.2.1 Why theory matters

Theoretical explanations of the depression-obesity association do not simply attempt to understand the association; they also attempt to guide intervention. Until the underlying processes by which obesity causes depression and depression causes obesity are understood, attempts to treat and prevent both conditions will be superficial. Six theories of the depression-obesity association are discussed in the following section, each of which sheds light on the potential causes of the association.

7.2.2 The biological pathway: HPA axis, inflammation, and shared mechanisms

The most fundamental of the theories of the depression-obesity association is the biological explanation. A systematic review of the literature supported the conclusion that there is a shared basis for depression and obesity, as indicated by the presence of common biological mechanisms such as adipokine dysregulation, pro-inflammatory cytokine elevation, HPA axis dysfunction, and changes in the serotonin and dopamine systems (Milaneschi et al., 2019; Cao et al., 2024). Visceral fat tissue is the primary site of pro-inflammatory cytokines such as tumor necrosis factor-alpha, interleukin-6, and C-reactive protein, which have been implicated in the pathophysiology of depression. In parallel, the shared pathophysiological basis of depression and obesity is the dysregulation of the hypothalamic-pituitary-adrenal (HPA) axis, which is present in both conditions and results in the elevation of cortisol. A systematic review and metaanalysis of the association between cortisol and depression in adolescence supported the association between cortisol and depression, particularly in early adolescence (Zajkowska et al., 2022).

The biological processes of depression, including appetite, sleep, and reduced physical activity, lead to weight gain. In turn, obesity-related inflammation directly predicts the onset of depressive symptoms through neuroinflammatory mechanisms. Therefore, drug treatment of one condition must consider its effects on the other, for example, SSRIs may lead to weight gain with prolonged use, and atypical antipsychotics used for treatment-resistant depression have a high risk of inducing obesity. It is important to note that pharmacological considerations—including SSRI-related weight gain and antipsychotic-associated metabolic effects—are relevant primarily to clinical management of cooccurring depressive disorder, not to first-line adolescent obesity management. The majority of adolescents with obesity-related depressive symptoms encountered in community and school settings do not require pharmacological intervention; psychological and behavioral approaches should constitute the primary response.

7.2.3 Beck's cognitive triad and depression-to-obesity pathways

Beck's cognitive model of depression posits that depressive episodes are maintained by a cognitive triad of negative attitudes toward oneself, the world, and the future, for example, "I am worthless," "nothing works out," and "things will never get better," respectively (Beck, 1967). This cognitive model directly relates to depression related to obesity. Adolescents with obesity experience weight stigma, leading to negative self-schemata, which predict persistent depression regardless of objective weight status. Negative body image, or a negative cognitive attitude toward oneself-as-body, has been identified as the psychological mechanism through which obesity predicts depression, with a systematic review verifying that subjective weight perception fully mediated the relationship between obesity and depression in multiple studies (Cao et al., 2024).

From a cognitive perspective, depression also triggers emotional eating as a maladaptive coping strategy. Anhedonia, or the inability to derive pleasure from activities one normally enjoys, also plays a role in the reduction of physical activities, thereby leading to weight gain. These behavioral factors represent the cognitive triad in the context of health-related behavior and thus form the basis for the application of CBT for both conditions.

7.2.4 Stigma theory and obesity-to-depression pathways

The most influential theory to explain the obesity-to-depression pathway is Goffman's (1963) theory of "stigma," or the social discrediting of people who differ from normative social standards. Obese youth are stigmatized as having a "spoiled identity" because their body weight becomes their master status characteristic that eclipses all other personal traits and leads to discrimination and differential treatment in school settings and at home. Pearl & Puhl's (2018) study provided empirical support for weight bias internalization as a mediator between weight stigma and depression, anxiety, and low self-esteem in obese youth samples; WBI correlated with depression at $r = 0.48$ (Pearl & Puhl, 2018).

In the context of India, the process of obesity-related stigma is embedded in culturally specific scripts. For girls, the script of "marriageability" equates body weight and social worth; constant reminders of the threat of obesity to their marital prospects create body weight as a locus of existential anxiety. For boys, the script of "masculinity" equates body weight, lack of discipline, and sporting failure. The involvement of the extended family in festivals and celebrations of life events such as weddings and other get-togethers multiplies the effects of weight stigma through the collectivist orientation of Indian society; as such, weight stigma is uniquely Indian and far more public and inescapable than the individual-based weight stigma experienced by Western youth.

7.2.5 Objectification theory

7.2.5.1 Objectification theory

Objectification theory, as presented by Fredrickson & Roberts (1997), states that young women in contemporary societies develop the perspective of an observer on their bodies, constantly comparing their physical appearance to the ideal image constructed by society. The objectification of one's body results in feelings of shame, anxiety, and disruption in the internal bodily experience, all of which are direct predictors of depression. Objectification is particularly high in young women who suffer from obesity because their bodies differ most from the ideal image constructed by society. The objectification of their bodies mediates the relationship between obesity and depression in young women, thus explaining the gender difference in the prevalence rate of depression reported in all obesity studies.

In the Indian scenario, objectification takes the form of the male gaze on the street, Bollywood beauty standards, social media, and the matrimonial market, where women's bodies are graded on the basis of their physical appearance. The objectification of the female body in India makes the objectification and self-objectification of female adolescents higher, thus explaining the higher female depression-obesity relationship reported in this study, along with the international studies.

7.2.6 Social comparison theory

Social comparison theory, as presented by Festinger (1954), states that individuals compare their abilities, skills, or other personal characteristics with those of others. Social comparison becomes more prominent during the adolescent period, where the comparison shifts from objective to normative standards, comparing themselves not only to their peers but also to the idealized images presented in the media, social networking sites, or advertisements. The upward appearance comparison, that is, comparing themselves to others who have the idealized physical image, is positively correlated with feelings of depression. The study on social comparison and social networking sites confirmed the significant relationship between social networking site usage and body satisfaction/disordered eating (Holland & Tiggemann, 2016).

7.2.7 The syndemic framework

Singer's (1996) Syndemic Theory explains how the interaction of epidemics fueled by common social determinants leads to health outcomes that are greater than the sum of individual diseases. Depression and obesity are a textbook example of a syndemic in adolescents. Both are fueled by poverty, food insecurity, stigma, inadequate health care, and societal inequality. Depression and obesity interact biologically, psychologically, and socially to produce health outcomes that are worse than either disease would cause alone. In a recent application of syndemic theory to young adults in the USA by Friedman et al. (2025), food insecurity, deficits of social support, housing instability, and discrimination all contributed to depression and obesity simultaneously and interactively. In the Indian context of extreme socioeconomic inequality and unequal health care access, depression and obesity are a syndemic.

7.3 Global and Indian evidence

7.3.1 Longitudinal evidence: establishing bidirectionality

The strongest evidence for the bidirectional relationship between depression and obesity comes from longitudinal studies of large cohorts of adolescents. In the United States, the Add Health study of over 20,000 adolescents since the mid-1990s found that obese adolescents are at increased risk of depression and depressed adolescents are at increased risk of becoming obese (Goodman & Whitaker, 2002). In the Growing Up Today Study, adolescents who experience depression are at increased risk of weight gain over a four-year period (Field et al., 2001). In a Victorian cohort of adolescents from Australia, depression in early adolescence was a predictor of obesity in young adults (Patton et al., 2011).

Systematic reviews and metaanalyses have also supported these bidirectional relationships in different populations. The foundational metaanalysis of 15 longitudinal studies ($N = 58,745$) by (Luppino et al., 2010) supported the bidirectional relationships of obesity with the onset of depression and depression with the onset of obesity: obesity at baseline was a predictor of depression onset at follow-up (OR 1.55, 95% CI: 1.22–1.98, $p < 0.001$), and depression at baseline was a predictor of obesity onset ($OR = 1.58$, 95% CI: 1.33–1.87, $p < 0.001$). Marmorstein et al. (2016) metaanalysis of 13 prospective studies showed that adolescents with depression had a 70% increased risk of obesity, and adolescents with obesity had a 40% increased risk of depression, especially for females. More recently, a metaanalysis of 22 observational studies of 175,135 children and adolescents found a significant positive association of obesity with the risk of depressive disorder: RR = 1.32 (Chen et al., 2024).

7.3.2 Mediating mechanisms: What drives the bidirectional relationship?

A systematic review of biopsychosocial mediators and moderators of the relationship of depression and obesity in children and adolescents found six major mediating factors of the relationship from 36 records of studies of 152,513 children and adolescents: body image dissatisfaction; victimization and bullying; eating disorders such as binge eating; sleeping difficulties; lack of physical activities; and low self-esteem. Of these factors, body image dissatisfaction was found to be the strongest and most consistent mediator of the relationship between obesity and depression in children and adolescents: obese adolescents did not develop depression directly because of their obesity but because of how their body was interpreted, evaluated, and stigmatized in social contexts. Bullying and victimization were found to be the main social factors: obese adolescents were 2–4 times more likely to be bullied than their normal-weight peers in different countries worldwide.

These mechanisms are differentially active across countries and cultures. For France, a large percentage of overweight or obese adolescents had a history of eating disorders such as binge eating disorder, which correlated with higher BMI and more severe depressive symptoms (Quek et al., 2017; Chen et al., 2024). In the USA, body image was a strong mediator of the relationship between obesity and depression; subjective weight perception fully mediated the obesity-depression relationship in several studies. In Latin America, obese children and adolescents consistently showed higher levels of depressive symptoms across countries; a subgroup analysis also showed a significant relationship across settings (Chen et al., 2024). In the Middle East region, obesity was significantly related to depression (OR = 1.90) and anxiety (OR = 1.97) in male Saudi Arabian adolescents (Alsaleem, 2021).

7.3.3 Cross-cultural patterns: Latin America, Africa, Europe, and Asia

The depression and obesity relationship has been established in adolescents across all geographical locations of the world. In Latin America, a multicountry study revealed that obese adolescents experienced 8.55 times higher odds of depressive symptoms than their normal-weight counterparts (Gallego et al., 2025). In Brazil, Colombia, and Mexico, the cooccurrence of depression and obesity has been well documented in a number of systematic reviews. Cultural changes from traditional to globalized body images are occurring at a rapid pace in Brazil, Mexico, and Colombia. Such cultural changes cause a disconnect between community body images and media-driven images of thinness, creating a significant mental health burden of obesity for female adolescents. In Brazil, where curvaceous body images are culturally revered, the adoption of globalized images of slimness has created a significant increase in body discontent and disordered eating patterns among urban adolescent girls (Conde & Borges, 2011).

In Africa, the depression and obesity relationship is affected by the contrast between urban and rural settings. In rural South Africa, being plump is associated with health and wealth and minimizes stigma within family circles. However, cultural changes are occurring at a rapid pace with urbanization and media exposure to Western culture. In urban areas of Africa, body discontent profiles are becoming increasingly similar to those of Western adolescents (Kimani-Murage, 2013). In a systematic review of mental health problems of adolescents in sub-Saharan Africa, depression was confirmed to be associated with urban weight stigma, body discontent, and food insecurity.

In Europe, the Health Behavior in School-aged Children (HBSC) study across over 40 countries found that obese adolescents had a high prevalence of depressive symptoms, loneliness, and low life satisfaction across all European nations, with the strongest effects in Northern Europe and somewhat weaker effects in Mediterranean countries, which could be due to more positive body image and family social support (Inchley et al., 2020). In Asia, the situation is characterized by academic competitions. In China, research has found that among adolescents under academic pressure, the prevalence of depression was significantly higher among the obese compared to the nonobese. The relationship between obesity and depression was mediated by peer victimization and body image concerns. This confirms that the same process found in Western societies also occurs in East Asian societies, even though the cultural script of body ideals differs (Zhou et al., 2023).

Collectively, the cross-regional studies demonstrate that the distinction between adaptive and maladaptive responses to body-related social evaluation is not culture-neutral. While the biological processes themselves—HPA dysregulation and increased inflammatory cytokines—may be universal, the cultural means by which stigma is transmitted and internalized are highly variable. To effectively intervene on the shared biology and culturally specific pathways by which depression and obesity feed into one another across cultures, interventions must be informed by the culture and structure of each culture.

7.3.4 Gender as a critical moderator

The gender effect has been the most consistent and replicated moderator of the depression-obesity relationship in adolescents. Marmorstein et al. (2016) metaanalytic review confirmed that the relationship between depression and obesity is stronger for females than males in both directions. That is, obese girls are at higher risk of depression than obese boys, and depressed girls are at higher risk of obesity than depressed boys. In a second metaanalytic review of 18 studies of the depression and obesity relationship (Quek et al., 2017) also confirmed the stronger relationship for females. Three processes contribute to the gender difference.

Firstly, pubertal timing and hormone effects: girls tend to be two years younger than boys at the start of puberty. Early age of puberty increases the risk of depression and body dissatisfaction. The hormone effects of female puberty, especially estrogen levels, have a direct impact on serotonin systems related to depression. Secondly, differential socialization of body ideals: girls tend to be socialized through objectification and media exposure to evaluate their body ideals to a greater extent than boys. Thirdly, cultural context: in the Indian context, the marriageability script offers an additional pathway by which the depression-obesity link will be strengthened among girls compared with their male counterparts through pathways that are unique to girls.

7.3.5 Socioeconomic status and structural determinants

The socioeconomic status of people also has a complex interaction with the depression-obesity relationship. In high-income countries, the prevalence of obesity among adolescents of lower socioeconomic status is high due to food insecurity and lack of access to healthcare facilities. In addition, people with lower socioeconomic status have a high risk of developing depression. However, in the Indian context, the prevalence of obesity among adolescents of higher socioeconomic status in urban areas is high. This was confirmed by the results of the metaanalysis conducted by Singh et al. (2023), which showed that students of private schools had 2.47 times higher odds of being obese compared to students of government schools. However, in the Indian context, it was found that people with higher socioeconomic status do not have a protective effect against depression related to obesity but rather exacerbate it.

In lower SES Indian adolescents, a unique pattern of risk is observed, characterized by lower levels of obesity but higher levels of general depression due to poverty, food insecurity, academic demands, and lack of opportunities for recreation. When adolescents from lower SES contexts do experience obesity, it has a further stigmatizing effect because it is nonnormative within their community, combining weight stigma with SES stigma, or exclusion, in a way that exacerbates psychological risk. This consideration of SES is critical when developing appropriately targeted prevention programs. For adolescents from higher SES contexts, prevention programs must be designed to address appearance pressure, social comparison, and media literacy, whereas for lower SES adolescents, programs must be designed to address structural barriers, food security, recreation opportunities, and counseling access, all of which have a compounding effect on stigma types.

7.3.6 The COVID-19 pandemic: a stress test of the depression-obesity syndemic

The COVID-19 pandemic provided a natural experiment for the bidirectional relationship between depression and obesity among adolescents worldwide. The school closures for 95% of all students worldwide have impacted physical activity habits, increased sedentary activities such as screen time, changed dietary habits, and eliminated the social environment that protected against both depression and obesity for many adolescents (Ferentinou et al., 2023; La Fauci et al., 2022). The pandemic has also resulted in a significant and disproportionate weight gain among adolescents who were already overweight or obese; a systematic review and metaanalysis of lockdown-induced weight gain found that obese adolescents gained more BMI than their normal-weight peers during lockdown periods (La Fauci et al., 2022). The KICK-COVID study in Germany followed 235 adolescents with overweight or obesity in six pediatric obesity treatment centers from 2021 to 2023 and reported a higher level of depression and anxiety than normative values for the general population of adolescents; loneliness was a mediator of the relationship between pandemic isolation and mental health outcomes through media consumption (Stachow et al., 2024).

In India, the pandemic has accelerated preexisting conditions for adolescents. The pandemic has resulted in a severe deterioration of eating habits among adolescents in India; a study conducted in India during the pandemic reported a severe deterioration of eating habits among adolescents, including unhealthy snacks, irregularity of meals, and lack of physical activities (Jha & Mehendale, 2022). The school closures have resulted in a lack of physical activities for millions of adolescents in India, while confining them to their homes; the home environment has also resulted in weight commentary and examination anxiety for adolescents in India. The pandemic has resulted in a syndemic effect on

TABLE 7.1 Global evidence on the association between obesity and depression in adolescents.

Study/source	Design	Sample	Key finding
Luppino et al. (2010)	Metaanalysis of 15 longitudinal studies	N = 58,745	Obesity → depression: OR = 1.55 ($p < 0.001$); depression → obesity: OR = 1.58 ($p < 0.001$)
Marmorstein et al. (2016)	Metaanalysis of prospective studies	N = 32,026 adolescents	Depression → 70% increased obesity risk (RR = 1.70); obesity → 40% increased depression risk (RR = 1.40); stronger in females
Chen et al. (2024)	Metaanalysis of 22 observational studies	N = 175,135 children and adolescents	Obesity → depressive disorder: RR = 1.32 (95% CI = 1.09–1.60; $p < 0.001$)
Cao et al. (2024)	Systematic review of 36 studies	N = 152,513	Identifies mediators, including body image, bullying, eating disorders, sleep, inactivity, and low self-esteem
Quek et al. (2017)	Metaanalysis of 18 studies	Children and adolescents	Significant association between obesity and depression; stronger among adolescent females
Thapar et al. (2012)	Review article (*The Lancet*)	Adolescents globally	Depression prevalence ranges from 1%–5%; onset peaks during puberty; gender differences emerge in mid-adolescence
Goodman & Whitaker (2002)	Longitudinal cohort study	US adolescents (add health)	Depressive symptoms predict later obesity; evidence supports a bidirectional association
Khanna et al. (2023)	Cross-sectional study	Delhi adolescents	Depression associated with sleep patterns, lifestyle factors, and body image concerns
HBSC Survey (Inchley et al., 2020)	Cross-national survey	40+ European countries	Adolescents with obesity report higher depression, loneliness, and lower life satisfaction

From public domain.

adolescents in India by increasing the risk of obesity and depression; both conditions are linked to stress, sedentary activities, lack of sleep, and social isolation.

7.3.7 Indian specific evidence

The depression-obesity nexus in India has been influenced by unique cultural, institutional, and developmental factors. The academic examination culture has produced a unique bidirectional relationship, where examination stress is one of the most commonly reported antecedents of emotional eating in Indian adolescents, causing obesity, while academic stigma for obesity, where teachers and parents perceive obese adolescents as lacking proper academic discipline, contributes to depression and school avoidance. The cross-sectional study on Delhi school students confirmed the significant association between depression, sleep, and lifestyle factors, all of which were significant in the school-going population (Khanna et al., 2023).

The scoping review on mental health among Indian adolescents confirmed the range of depression prevalence in India, from 0.48% to 49.2%, depending on the methodology, setting, and population, where studies on school-going adolescents in urban India reported higher prevalence, and studies reported higher prevalence in girls than in boys (Bharati et al., 2022). The BDI has been validated for Indian adolescents, where the instrument was found to be applicable for adolescents belonging to different SES and geographical locations, where the psychometric properties showed high internal consistency reliability ($\alpha = 0.96$) along with high convergent validity for clinical diagnostic criteria (Bhatt et al., 2007). The study confirmed the reliability of the BDI for measuring the level of depressive symptoms in Indian adolescents, thus facilitating the comparison of the study findings with international research studies (Table 7.1).

7.4 Present study findings

7.4.1 Study design and methodology

The present study aimed at investigating depression, as measured by the BDI (Beck et al., 1961), in a sample of 400 late adolescents and young adults in Kolkata, India, comparing the obese with the nonobese. The sample consisted of four age-sex groups, each consisting of 50 participants. The groups were male late adolescents (17–20 years), female late adolescents, male young adults (21–24 years), and female young adults. The groups were matched for socioeconomic status, type of family, size of the family, size of the siblings, birth order, and mother tongue. The participants were selected using purposive sampling with area-wise stratification in northern, central, southern, and eastern Kolkata. The statistical analysis employed independent samples t-tests, three-factor factorial analysis of variance (3FFANOVA), with body weight, age, and sex as factors, and Pearson's product-moment correlation between BMI and all psychological variables.

7.4.1.1 Beck Depression Inventory findings: group comparisons

The present study revealed highly significant differences between the obese and the nonobese groups in depression scores for the entire sample, that is the four age-sex groups. The results are presented in Table 7.2 below.

Note: BDI classification: 0–10= normal; 11–16= mild mood disturbance; 17–20= borderline clinical depression; 21–30= moderate depression (Beck et al., 1961, revised norms 1988). Two obese group means fall in the moderate depression range: female LA: $M = 22.04$; female YA: $M = 22.62$. Two obese group means fall in the borderline clinical depression range: male LA: $M = 19.30$; male YA: $M = 20.44$. All nonobese group means fall within the normal range: $M = 10.50$ to $M = 13.84$.

7.4.2 Three-factor ANOVA findings

The 3FFANOVA confirmed the following for depression: the main effect of body weight was highly significant, $p < 0.01$; $F = 606.325$, which confirmed a large and consistent differential between obese and nonobese groups averaged across age and sex. The main effect of sex was highly significant, $p < 0.01$; $F = 43.255$, which confirmed that females scored significantly higher on depression than males, irrespective of body weight and age. The main effect of age was not significant, $p = 0.874$. The interaction effect of BW Age was significant, $p < 0.05$; $F = 5.369$, $p = 0.021$, which indicates that the difference between obese and nonobese groups differs across developmental stages. The interaction effect of BW sex was not significant, $p = 0.615$, which confirmed that the main effect of body weight was not qualified by sex at the interaction level. The interaction effect of all three factors, BW age sex, was significant, $p < 0.05$; $F = 4.722$, $p = 0.030$, indicating additional complexity in depression across all three main effects. The main effect of sex is independent of both BW and age, since BW, sex, and age sex are not significant. The main effect of sex, where females scored higher on depression than males, irrespective of body weight and age, was independent of all interaction effects, thus confirming that female obese participants carry a structurally greater depression burden than their male counterparts across both developmental stages.

7.4.3 Clinical significance of the Beck Depression Inventory findings

The clinical significance of the results goes beyond merely being statistically significant. In fact, two groups of obese participants—female late adolescents and female young adults—fell into the range of moderate clinical depression (BDI classification =21–30), with $M = 22.04$ and $M = 22.62$, respectively. The other two groups of obese participants—male late adolescents and male young adults—fell into the range of borderline clinical depression (BDI classification =17–20), with $M = 19.30$ and $M = 20.44$, respectively. The nonobese participants generally exhibited lower levels of depressive symptoms than their obese counterparts. Their mean BDI scores ranged from 10.50 to 13.84, indicating scores that fell within the normal to mild mood disturbance range according to BDI classification criteria. The clinical importance of these results lies in the fact that the BDI scores of the obese participants in the present study are alarming. The fact that the participants in the present study are not clinical participants but rather members of a community population indicates that the problem of depression among urban Indian adolescents due to obesity is of considerable proportions. The clinical importance of the results also lies in the fact that the BDI scores of the participants in the present study indicate subclinical levels of depression. Subclinical levels of depression refer to levels of depression that are high enough to affect quality of life but are still below the levels of clinical depression. Subclinical levels of depression are also the levels at which preventive interventions are most effective.

TABLE 7.2 Beck Depression Inventory (*BDI*) depression scores—obese versus nonobese groups by age and sex (present study, Kolkata).

Group	Obese M (SD)	Nonobese M (SD)	t-ratio	Significance/BDI range
Male late adolescents (LA)	19.30 (4.18)	12.48 (1.93)	10.48-3	$p < 0.01$ I obese: borderline clinical; nonobese: normal
Female late adolescents (LA)	22.04 (4.17)	13.36 (2.21)	13.00-5	$p < 0.01$ I obese: moderate depression; nonobese: normal
Male young adults (YA)	20.44 (4.32)	10.50 (2.51)	14.08-1	$p < 0.01$ I obese: borderline clinical; nonobese: normal
Female young adults (YA)	22.62 (4.58)	13.84 (2.69)	11.68-8	$p < 0.01$ I obese: moderate depression; nonobese: normal

Aaron T. Beck, Steer, R. A., & Brown, G. K. (1988/1996). Manual for the Beck Depression Inventory/BDI-II. San Antonio, TX: Psychological Corporation.

The placement of the female obese groups in the moderate range of depression is also supported by Beck et al. (1988) classification of moderate depression for a score of 21–30 (1961, revised 1988). The placement of the male obese groups in the borderline clinical range of depression ($M = 19.30$ and $M = 20.44$) indicates that they are above the clinical threshold and need attention. The sex effect of the female obese groups consistently scoring higher than the male obese groups is supported by the international metaanalytic findings of Marmorstein et al. (2016) and Quek et al. (2017) that the relationship between obesity and depression is stronger for females than for males. This sex effect has also been supported in the current findings in the context of the Indian population. The sex main effect has also been found to be independent of body weight and age factors; that is, the BW × Sex and Age × Sex interaction were nonsignificant. This means that the sex effect of females consistently scoring higher than males is a generalized effect across all age groups of adolescents. The independence of the sex effect is a critical aspect of the findings because it rules out the possibility that the sex effect of the higher depression burden of females than males is limited to a specific age group or a specific level of body weight; rather, it is a pervasive effect across the entire range of the population (Das, 2018).

The quantitative approach of the present study's exploratory design, by comparing obese and nonobese groups at a single point of time, has established strong correlations between obesity and depression scores, but cannot provide a clear direction of causality. It is unclear whether depression was a precursor to the onset of obesity or whether the stigma of being obese caused depression. Such a discussion of the thesis also admits directly that the issue of causality cannot be resolved at this point in time. Both aetiologies have some backing from international literature, and it is possible that there are some common aetiologies for depression and obesity that operate simultaneously (Das, 2018).

7.4.4 Contextualization within global literature

The findings of the current study are consistent with the international literature, holding a theoretically consistent place within it. The depression differential between obese and nonobese groups, with a large effect size of approximately 6–10 BDI units between them, is consistent with cross-sectional studies of community populations with obesity, as reported by Chen et al. (2024). The consistent statistical significance across all four age-sex groups is consistent with the metaanalytic findings of a positive relationship between obesity and depression, albeit a robust one, within children and adolescents. The stronger effect for females is consistent with the moderation of this relationship by gender, as reported by Marmorstein et al. (2016) and Quek et al. (2017). This study contributes data from India, specifically urban India, to a literature dominated by data from North America and Europe, directly addressing the gap identified by the scoping review of Indian adolescent obesity research, as reported by Jena Samanta et al. (2025).

Two further observations place the findings of the current study within context: Firstly, the study was not a clinical sample but rather a community one, and therefore, the levels of depression observed are representative of a population-level burden.

7.4.5 Life course and intergenerational consequences

The depression-obesity syndemic process of adolescents does not simply terminate at the end of adolescence but has long-term effects into the future. In a Dunedin longitudinal study of adolescents who had the syndemic experience of depression and obesity, adults who had the experience of depression and obesity during adolescence had significantly higher rates of metabolic disease, social dysfunction, and psychiatric disorders than those who had either depression or obesity alone (Moffitt et al., 2011). Goodman & Whitaker's (2002) seminal work on the Add Health data confirmed that adolescents who experience depression are at increased risk of becoming obese one year into the future. Goodman and Whitaker's work confirmed that depression in adolescents has a developmental trajectory into young adulthood. The implication of the depression-obesity syndemic process is that adolescents who experience depression and obesity do not simply experience a burden of disease but also foreclose future opportunities for themselves by limiting their educational potential, occupational success, and relational potential.

The experience of stigma also has a second-generation effect. Parents who experience ridicule during their own adolescence may also impose stigma on their own children by either directly imitating the negative comments made during their own youth or indirectly by imitating negative coping strategies and negative body talk. Parents who are able to process their own experiences of weight stigma are able to break the cycle of stigma transfer. The finding of the present study that obese adolescents perceive significantly lower family acceptance and caring across all four age-sex groups ($p < 0.01$) suggests that the dimension of family environment measured by the FES is a specific indicator of the experience of stigma transfer.

7.5 Interventions, policy, and future directions

7.5.1 Evidence-based psychological interventions

Cognitive behavioural therapy (CBT) continues to be the most evidence-based psychological intervention for the treatment of both depression and obesity-related psychological distress among adolescents. CBT directly addresses the cognitive distortions, such as the cognitive triad identified by Beck, which lead to depression in the presence of obesity, including negative thoughts about one's appearance, negative evaluation by others, and negative expectations about the future. Behavioral activation, or the resumption of pleasant activities, directly addresses the anhedonia or lack of interest in social interactions, both of which lead to the vicious cycle of obesity and depression. In fact, the study done on the efficacy of programs addressing obesity and depression among children and adolescents confirmed the efficacy of integrated multicomponent programs addressing obesity and depression, where psychological interventions showed significant improvements in depressive symptoms, along with BMI (Gallego et al., 2025).

Interpersonal therapy (IPT), on the other hand, provides an additional tool for the treatment of depression, especially when the depression is related to social rejection or conflict with parents or peers. The study done by Mufson et al. (2004) confirmed the efficacy of IPT for adolescents, where it was found to be significantly more effective in the reduction of depressive symptoms when compared to treatment as usual. The added advantage of both CBT and IPT in the Indian context, especially for adolescents, is the added benefit of the social component, where adolescents benefit from the social support component, where the feelings of loneliness, which often lead to depression, are addressed in the presence of peers who also suffer from similar feelings about their bodies. The social component also provides the added advantage of the low cost-effectiveness of such interventions, where large numbers can be reached in the school setting.

Similarly, mindfulness-based interventions, based on culturally familiar Indian practices of yoga and meditation, have been shown to have positive effects on psychological well-being in adolescents. In a metaanalysis of mindfulness-based interventions for youth, Zoogman et al. (2015) confirmed the positive effects of mindfulness-based interventions for youth and their significant impact on psychological symptoms. ACT also incorporates the dimension of psychological flexibility or the ability to be present with difficult thoughts and feelings without being controlled by them, while at the same time becoming clear about values and taking action towards valued life goals. These interventions are also relevant for weight bias internalization and for adolescents to be able to defuse from negative body-related thoughts without having to either deny or identify with these as central to their identity.

7.5.2 School-based interventions

Schools are also critical for intervening in the depression-obesity cycle because they are the only setting to reach the entire population of adolescents, and not only those who seek help for mental health issues. The first step is to develop antibullying school policies that specifically address weight-based bullying. The evaluation of school-based social and emotional learning interventions by Evans et al. (2014) confirmed the positive impact of teacher-based interventions when teachers received training to recognize and challenge harmful interpersonal relationships. Inclusive PE practices, such as changing competitive performance-based PE to individualistic growth-based PE and providing yoga, dance, martial arts, and walking clubs in addition to sports such as soccer and basketball, also change the PE environment as a site of humiliation related to body image.

Mental health literacy interventions that aim to increase awareness of the mutual relationship between depression and obesity, the process of stigmatization, and coping strategies would play a vital role in reducing stigmatization of obese adolescents by their peers and providing all adolescents with mental health literacy tools to cope with body-related distress. It is also imperative that teachers are trained to communicate effectively with obese adolescents without body-related remarks being used to discipline, humor, or motivate obese adolescents. Such remarks would add to the stigma of institutional depression. Mental health literacy interventions that integrate depression screening tools such as BDI or PHQ-A into school health programs would help identify adolescents with depression at an early stage.

7.5.3 Clinical integration and healthcare reform

The major drawback of the management of adolescent obesity in India is the lack of psychological assessment. In a recent guideline released by the Indian Academy of Pediatrics (IAP, 2023) recommended psychological evaluation of obese children and adolescents along with clinical evaluation. It is imperative that pediatricians and general practitioners use the BDI, STAI, and Rosenberg Self-Esteem Scale tools while providing health care to obese adolescents. Weight-neutral communication strategies that focus on a shift from "discipline and compliance" to "collaborative health goals" would help obese adolescents attend health check-ups without the fear of being stigmatized by health care providers. It is imperative that multidisciplinary teams of health professionals, such as nutritionists, psychologists, pediatricians, and family therapists, are made integral to the management of adolescent obesity. It was revealed by the present study that the BDI scores of obese females fell into the moderate depression category during community-based assessment. This revealed that depression at a significant level was prevalent among obese adolescents at large and not limited to clinical populations.

7.6 Food environment, urban planning, and structural determinants

It is not possible for psychological interventions to address the structural factors underlying the depression-obesity syndemic. The food environment—the availability, accessibility, and affordability of healthy food within the daily physical environment of adolescents—contributes to obesity and indirectly to depression through economic stress and food insecurity. Urbanization in India has led to an explosion of ultra-processed and packaged food products, such as snacks, soft drinks, and fast food, in the food environment of adolescents. These food products are cheaper than fresh food and are readily available in the food environment of adolescents from poor and middle-class families. Adolescents from poor and middle-class families are caught in the paradox of living in a food environment of plenty but experiencing nutritional scarcity and deprivation—food environments of abundance in calorie-dense but nutrient-poor food products that contribute to obesity but not to hunger relief or satisfaction. Urban planning is also a critical factor in the syndemic of depression and obesity. Adolescents in India lack access to safe and secure spaces for recreation and physical activity in their food environment. The lack of such space means that the recommendations of POSHAN Abhiyaan and Fit India regarding increased levels of physical activity are not feasible for the majority of adolescents in India. Urban planning is a critical structural intervention for obesity and depression, and not merely a health and fitness issue for adolescents. It is necessary for policymakers to recognize that without addressing the food environment and urban planning, psychological interventions are swimming against the current.

7.6.1 Indian policy context

Policy interventions should include psychological screening, stigma reduction, and mental health components within existing programs such as RKSK and POSHAN Abhiyaan. Integration of mental health components and DCC within existing programs for adolescents' health services is critical for addressing the overall psychosocial impact of obesity.

Evidence-based intervention framework for the depression-obesity syndemic: multilevel interventions for adolescent obesity and depression Hampl et al., (2023).

Level	Intervention area	Specific strategies
Psychological	Cognitive and behavioral therapies	CBT: cognitive restructuring of negative cognitions related to weight
	Interpersonal and acceptance-based approaches	IPT: addressing peer rejection and family conflict
		ACT: developing psychological flexibility and values-based action
	Mind-body interventions	Mindfulness/yoga: culturally grounded emotional regulation skills
School	Antistigma environment	Antibullying programs with explicit weight stigma components
	Teacher capacity building	Teacher training in weight-sensitive communication
	Inclusive physical activity	Inclusive physical education programs
	Mental health awareness	Mental health literacy programs
	Screening and early detection	BDI/PHQ-A screening within school health programs
Clinical	Screening and assessment	Routine BDI screening for adolescents presenting with obesity
	Integrated care	Multidisciplinary teams (nutrition + psychology + pediatrics)
	Communication approach	Weight-neutral clinical communication
	Family involvement	Family psychoeducation on weight-based internalization (WBI)
	Guidelines implementation	Implementation of IAP (2023) guidelines
Family	Communication practices	Language substitution training programs
	psychoeducation	Education on the link between depression and obesity
	Behavioral change	Shared physical activities
	Eating environment	No-shame meal practices
	Therapeutic support	Family therapy for conflict and criticism
Policy	National Program Integration	Integrate psychological screening within RKSK Adolescent Health Days
	Nutrition programs	Integrate mental health components within POSHAN Abhiyaan home visits
	Public messaging	Dignity-centered messaging guidelines for Fit India
	Infrastructure equity	Urban recreational infrastructure equity

Hampl et al., (2023). Clinical Practice Guideline for the Evaluation and Treatment of Children and Adolescents With Obesity. American Academy of Pediatrics, 151(2), e2022060640. https://doi.org/10.1542/peds.2022–060640.

7.6.2 Future research directions

Four research needs emerge from the current chapter's review. First, longitudinal research is an urgent need in India. The scoping review on Indian research on obesity among adolescents confirmed the current study's suspicion that all research on the topic was cross-sectional (Jena Samanta et al., 2025), that is, causality cannot be determined. Such research will reveal if depression or obesity begins first, and the developmental period in which the bidirectional risk is the greatest. This research needs to mirror the current study's recognition of the causality problem. The discussion portion of the thesis argues that the causality problem has been the focus of research debates, including the possibility that obesity predicts depression, or the reverse, or if some common factors predict both, but the more important research question is the nature of the processes by which the two interact, not the direction (Das, 2018; Stunkard et al., 2003). Such longitudinal research will track all variables simultaneously.

The second research need is for studies using the quantitative approach of the current study, coupled with qualitative research, to reveal the cultural factors through which the international relationship between depression and obesity takes on unique characteristics in India, particularly in urban and rural settings. The current study does not include a qualitative component, but such research will reveal the cultural factors through which the international relationship manifests uniquely in India.

7.7 Illustrative composite vignettes

The following vignettes are composite or hypothetical constructions that are intended to illustrate or represent the types of patterns or relationships that have been reported in the empirical research reviewed in this chapter. These vignettes were not based on any direct research or investigation of the people who are the focus of the vignette.

None of the vignettes is based on a real person; all of the characteristics are fictional or hypothetical.

7.7.1 Vignette 1: the obesity to depression pathway for a female late adolescent (urban India)

Profile: 17-year-old girl from an urban Indian setting in a joint family structure. Her BMI is 33.1, or Class I obese. Her body size is often commented on by the members of the extended family in terms of potential marriageability.

Mechanism: constant stigmatizing social interactions from family members and peers → internalization of weight bias → negative schema of self (Beck's cognitive triad: "I am unworthy") → body shame and social withdrawal → BDI score indicative of moderate depression level (similar to that of the female LA obese group M = 22.04).

Key risk factors: marriageability script typical of India; joint family commentary typical of collectivist cultures; self-objectification triggered by social monitoring of body appearance.

Protective factors: academic competence; single positive peer relationship; parental affection on dimensions unrelated to body size.

Intervention entry points: CBT for cognitive restructuring of body image; family communication intervention; school counselor monitoring of depression level.

Evidence base: Pearl & Puhl, 2018; Marmorstein et al. (2016); Das (2018)—female LA BDI.

Vignette 2: the depression to obesity pathway for a young male adult (urban India).

Profile: 22-year-old male preparing for postgraduate examinations in Kolkata. His BMI is 31.8, or Class I obese. Parental attributions of poor performance in examinations to body weight and lack of discipline are made during weekly telephone calls.

Mechanism: examination stress → depression (manifested as anhedonia and lack of motivation) → emotional eating as maladaptive coping → weight gain → increased peer exclusion → increased depression (BDI scores consistent with the male YA obese group, M = 20.44).

Key risk factors: examination stress, criticism by parents equating weight with discipline, lack of exercise opportunities due to examination schedules, and HPA axis dysregulation.

Coping pattern: avoidance of physical spaces where the individual may be subject to scrutiny, use of humor as a deflective mechanism, and private food consumption as an emotion regulation strategy.

Intervention entry points: CBT for emotional eating, stress management, reframing of family communication, weight-neutral counseling, and exercise prescription targeting stress relief.

Evidence base: Beck (1967), Cao et al. (2024), Das (2018), male YA sample, BDI scores.

Vignette 3: resilience in the context of the depression-obesity syndemic.

Profile: A 20-year-old female YA student in Kolkata, India, with obesity (BMI = 32.5), and normal range BDI scores despite high BMI.

Protective factors: parents' recognition of the individual's inherent self-worth beyond physical attributes, diversified identity investments, one peer friendship with unconditional acceptance, cognitive reframing of negative emotions, and use of religion as a coping mechanism.

Theoretical function: the syndemic of depression and obesity does not exist as a deterministic effect. Resilience is built through security in interpersonal relations, diversified identity investments, and the absence of weight bias. The protective factors identified in this case are consistent with the resilience model proposed by Masten (2014). The variance in the obese sample is consistent with the current study.

Pedagogical value: resilience-based intervention should focus on building these protective factors proactively rather than waiting for depression to emerge.

Evidence base: Masten (2014); Pearl & Puhl (2018); Das (2018).

7.8 Key takeaways

Depression and obesity in adolescence are closely linked and reinforce each other over time.

The relationship is shaped not only by biology but also by stigma, social pressure, and cultural expectations.

Female adolescents show a higher vulnerability, especially due to body image concerns and societal expectations.

Body image and weight stigma are central mechanisms driving psychological distress.

Depression influences behavior such as emotional eating and inactivity, which further increases obesity risk.

Effective intervention must be multidimensional, combining psychological support, family involvement, school programs, and policy-level changes.

7.9 Glossary

Term	Definition
Beck Depression Inventory (BDI)	A 21-item scale measuring depressive symptom severity (Beck et al., 1961). It assesses symptoms across a standardized range: 0–10 (normal), 11–16 (mild), 17–20 (borderline), 21–30 (moderate), 31–40 (severe), and above 40 (extreme).
Bidirectionality	The mutually causal relationship between depression and obesity, wherein each condition increases the risk of the other through biological, psychological, and social pathways (Luppino et al., 2010; Marmorstein et al., 2016).
Cognitive triad (Beck)	Beck's (1967) model of depression, in which negative views of the self, the world, and the future sustain depressive experiences, is applied here to obesity through negative body-related schemas.
Emotional eating	A coping pattern in which food intake occurs in response to negative emotional states rather than physiological hunger; a pathway linking depression to weight gain.
HPA Axis	The hypothalamic-pituitary-adrenal axis, the body's central stress response system; dysregulation is associated with both depression and weight gain.
Marriageability script	A culturally specific belief system in which body size is linked to perceived suitability for marriage, particularly affecting girls, contributes to psychological distress in the Indian context.
Objectification theory	A framework proposed by Fredrickson & Roberts (1997), explaining how individuals internalize an observer's perspective on their bodies, leading to self-objectification, body shame, and depression.
Syndemic	A term introduced by Singer (1996) describing cooccurring conditions that interact through shared social and structural factors; here, depression and obesity in adolescence form a syndemic.
Weight bias internalization	The process by which individuals internalize negative societal attitudes toward body weight, leading to self-stigma, depression, and reduced help-seeking behavior (Pearl & Puhl, 2018).

Source: Author's compilation based on Beck (1961, 1967), Luppino et al. (2010), Marmorstein et al. (2016), Fredrickson & Roberts (1997), Singer (1996), and Pearl & Puhl (2018).

7.10 Review questions

7.10.1 Section A: conceptual understanding

1. What is the bidirectional relationship between depression and obesity in adolescence? What is the strength of each direction of the depression-obesity and obesity-depression relationships in adolescence, quantified by the results of two metaanalyses?

2. What were the BDI scores of the present study for obese and nonobese late adolescents in Kolkata? What do the results mean in terms of clinical significance and classification of depression?
3. What is the cognitive triad of Beck, and how does it account for the depression-obesity relationship? What cognitive processes maintain the depression-obesity relationship in adolescents with obesity?
4. What is the role of objectification theory in the depression-obesity relationship, and why are the depression-obesity and obesity-depression relationships consistently stronger in female compared to male adolescents?
5. What are the six proposed mediating factors of the depression-body size and depression-obesity relationships in the context of the biopsychosocial model proposed by Cao et al. (2024)? What is the strongest of the proposed factors?

7.10.2 Section B: analytical thinking

1. What is the significance of the present study's finding that the body weight by age interaction is significant for depression?
2. What do the results of the present study mean in terms of the depression-obesity and depression-body weight relationships in adolescence?
3. What is the clinical implication of the present study's findings of the depression-body weight and depression-obesity relationships in adolescence?
4. How can the findings on the depression–obesity relationship in adolescence inform the development of prevention and intervention programmes?
5. Critically discuss the syndemic model in the context of the present study's findings on depression and obesity among adolescents.
6. Compare and contrast the patterns of depression observed among obese and non-obese adolescents in the present study.
7. What common social determinants contribute to both conditions in the Indian context, and how do these differ from those observed in high-income countries?
8. Critically discuss the syndemic model in the context of depression and obesity in Indian adolescents. What is the common social determinant in the Indian context, and how is it different from the high-income country context?
9. Compare and contrast the depression patterns of the obese males and females in the present study. What is the role of biological, psychological, and cultural factors in the sex difference in depression patterns? What are the implications of the present findings in the context of the following two theories?
10. What is the limitation of the comparative group design of the present study in establishing the direction of the causal relationship between depression and obesity? Design a longitudinal study to investigate the depression-obesity relationship.
11. What is the role of the marriageability script in the development of depression in the context of obesity in Indian adolescents, and how is it different from the Western context?

7.10.3 Section C: application

1. Design a CBT-based intervention for the treatment of depression and obesity in urban Indian schools. What is the role of the cognitive behavioral model in the present context?
2. A 15-year-old obese girl is brought to a pediatrician in Kolkata by her mother, complaining of headaches and tiredness. Her BDI score is 23. What is the diagnosis of the girl in the context of the IAP (2023) guidelines, and how would you design the treatment protocol in the context of the intervention framework in Section 7.1?
3. Analyze the depression-obesity relationship in the context of the three case vignettes in Section 7.6. What is the role of the syndemic model in the context of the present case vignettes in the context of the theories discussed in Section 7.2?

7.11 Conclusion

This chapter has clearly shown that depression and obesity among adolescents are a syndemic issue across the globe due to various biological, psychological, and sociocultural factors that interact to influence the outcomes of these syndemic issues. The various theories discussed in this chapter have provided a clear overview of how these syndemic issues influence and interact to influence outcomes.

From the various studies conducted across the globe on depression and obesity among adolescents, as well as the findings of the study conducted in Kolkata, India, this chapter has clearly shown that adolescents living with obesity are at a higher risk of depression than their nonobese counterparts. Additionally, female adolescents are at a higher risk of depression than their male counterparts.

7.12 Limitations of the study's contribution to the evidence base for this chapter's conclusion

The contribution of the present study to the evidence base for this chapter's conclusion is subject to various limitations. Firstly, the comparative nature of the present study means that the differences in BDI between obese and nonobese groups cannot be used to establish causality; only associations can be made between the two syndemic issues. Secondly, the present study only involved participants from Kolkata; as such, the findings of the present study cannot be generalized to other areas of India, such as rural areas, smaller towns, and cities. Thirdly, the present study only used BDI to measure depression and not to determine whether depression or obesity came first in individual participants' lives. Fourthly, the present study did not use other methods, such as clinical interviews and qualitative methods to understand depression and obesity; the present study only used quantitative methods to understand the syndemic issues and their interrelations and interactions. Fifthly, all the methods used in the present study were based on self-report; as such, the present study is subject to social desirability effects, especially in collectivist societies such as India.

Artificial intelligence disclosure

During the preparation of this work, the author(s) used ChatGPT and Grammarly.com in order to During the preparation of the manuscript, the authors used tools such as ChatGPT and Grammarly solely for language editing and grammatical refinement. After using this tool/service, the author(s) reviewed and edited the content as needed and take(s) full responsibility for the content of the publication.

References

Alsaleem, M. A. (2021). Depression, anxiety, stress, and obesity among male adolescents at Abha City, Southwestern Saudi Arabia. *Journal of Genetic Psychology, 182*(6), 488–494. https://doi.org/10.1080/00221325.2021.1978922.

American Psychiatric Association (APA) (2013). *Diagnostic and Statistical Manual of Mental Disorders* (5th ed). Arlington, VA: American Psychiatric Publishing.

Beck, A. T. (1967). *Depression: Clinical, experimental, and theoretical aspects*. Harper & Row.

Beck, A. T., Ward, C. H., Mendelson, M., Mock, J., & Erbaugh, J. (1961). An inventory for measuring depression. *Archives of General Psychiatry, 4*(6), 561–571.

Beck, A. T., Steer, R. A., & Garbin, M. G. (1988). Psychometric properties of the Beck Depression Inventory: Twenty-five years of evaluation. *Clinical Psychology Review, 8*(1), 77–100.

Bharati, D. R., Kumari, S., Prasad, N., Choudhary, S. K., Kumar, S., & Pal, R. (2022). Correlates of depression among school-going adolescents in the urban area of Patna in eastern India. *Journal of Family Medicine and Primary Care, 11*(5), 1702–1709. https://doi.org/10.4103/jfmpc.jfmpc_125_21.

Bhatt, M., Bhatt, G., & Bhatt, A. (2007). The psychometric properties of Beck Depression Inventory for adolescent depression in a primary-care paediatric setting in India. *Child and Adolescent Psychiatry and Mental Health, 1*(1), 8. https://doi.org/10.1186/1753-2000-1-8.

Cao, B., Shao, X., Xiao, Y., McIntyre, R. S., Teopiz, K. M., Li, R., Fan, L., & Chen, H. (2024). Potential biopsychosocial factors mediating/moderating the relationship between depressive symptoms and body size among children and adolescents: A systematic review. *Obesity Reviews, 25*(1), e13645. https://doi.org/10.1111/obr.13645.

Chen, Y., Cao, J., Li, H., & Zhang, Y. (2024). Obesity and risk of depressive disorder in children and adolescents: A meta-analysis of observational studies. *Child: Care, Health and Development, 50*(3), e13237. https://doi.org/10.1111/cch.13237.

Conde, W. L., & Borges, C. (2011). The risk of incidence and persistence of obesity among Brazilian adolescents. *Revista Brasileira de Epidemiologia, 14*(Suppl. 1), 67–76.

Das, S. (2018). *Psychological characteristics and adjustment patterns in late adolescents and young adults with obesity [Doctoral thesis, University of Calcutta]*.

Evans, R., Murphy, S., & Scourfield, J. (2014). Implementation of a school-based social and emotional learning intervention: Understanding diffusion processes within complex systems. *Prevention Science, 16*(5), 754–764.

Ferentinou, E., Galatas, I. D., & Antoniou, E. (2023). The impact of the COVID-19 pandemic on childhood obesity: A review. *Cureus, 15*(9), e45470. https://doi.org/10.7759/cureus.45470.

Festinger, L. (1954). A theory of social comparison processes. *Human Relations, 7*(2), 117–140.

Field, A. E., Camargo, C. A., Taylor, C. B., Berkey, C. S., Roberts, S. B., & Colditz, G. A. (2001). Peer, parent, and media influences on the development of weight concerns and frequent dieting among preadolescent and adolescent girls and boys. *Pediatrics, 107*(1), 54–60.

Fredrickson, B. L., & Roberts, T. A. (1997). Objectification theory. *Psychology of Women Quarterly, 21*(2), 173–206.

Friedman, M., Chang, R., Amin, Z. M., Rajan, T., Singh, R., Yousefzai, S., Shahid, I., Nasir, K., & Javed, Z. (2025). Understanding the bidirectional association between obesity and risk of psychological distress and depression in young adults in the US. *Frontiers in Psychiatry, 15*, 1422877. https://doi.org/10.3389/fpsyt.2024.1422877.

Gallego, J. R., López-Gil, J. F., & García-Hermoso, A. (2025). Child and adolescent health programs in obesity and depression: A systematic review and meta-analysis. *Nutrients, 17*(6), 1088. https://doi.org/10.3390/nu17061088.

Goffman, E. (1963). *Stigma: Notes on the management of spoiled identity*. Prentice Hall.

Goodman, E., & Whitaker, R. C. (2002). A prospective study of the role of depression in the development and persistence of adolescent obesity. *Pediatrics, 110*(3), 497–504.

Gururaj, G., Varghese, M., Benegal, V., Rao, G. N., Pathak, K., Singh, L. K., & NMHS Collaborators Group (2016). National Mental Health Survey of India, 2015–16: Prevalence, patterns and outcomes. NIMHANS Publication No. 129. *National Institute of Mental Health and Neurosciences*.

Hampl, S. E., et al. (2023). Clinical practice guideline for the evaluation and treatment of children and adolescents with obesity. *American Academy of Pediatrics, 151*(2). https://doi.org/10.1542/peds.2022-060640.

Holland, G., & Tiggemann, M. (2016). A systematic review of the impact of the use of social networking sites on body image and disordered eating outcomes. *Body Image, 17*, 100–110.

Indian Academy of Pediatrics (IAP). (2023). IAP guidelines on management of childhood obesity. *Indian Pediatrics, 60*, 1013–1030.

Inchley, J., Currie, D., Budisavljevic, S., Torsheim, T., Jåstad, A., Cosma, A., & Samdal, O. (Eds.). (2020). *Spotlight on adolescent health and well-being: Findings from the 2017/2018 Health Behaviour in School-aged Children (HBSC) survey in Europe and Canada*. WHO Regional Office for Europe.

Jena Samanta, L., Parida, J., Badamali, J., Pradhan, A., Singh, P. K., Mishra, B. K., & Acharya, S. K. (2025). Prevalence and associated risk factors of overweight and obesity among adolescents in India: A scoping review. *BMC Nutrition*. https://doi.org/10.1186/s40795-025-01088-0.

Jha, S., & Mehendale, A. M. (2022). Increased incidence of obesity in children and adolescents post-COVID-19 pandemic: A review article. *Cureus, 14*(9), e29348. https://doi.org/10.7759/cureus.29348.

Khanna, T., Banerjee, B., Majhi, M. M., & Futela, D. (2023). Depression, sleep, body image, and lifestyle: Prevalence and associated factors among school-going adolescents in Delhi NCR. *Indian Journal of Psychiatry, 65*(8), 825–831. https://doi.org/10.4103/indianjpsychiatry.indianjpsychiatry_19_23.

Kimani-Murage, E. W. (2013). Exploring the paradox: Double burden of malnutrition in rural South Africa. *Global Health Action, 6*(1), 19249.

La Fauci, G., Montalti, M., Di Valerio, Z., Gori, D., Salomoni, M. G., Salussolia, A., Soldà, G., & Guaraldi, F. (2022). Obesity and COVID-19 in children and adolescents: Reciprocal detrimental influence. *International Journal of Environmental Research and Public Health, 19*(13), 7603.

Luppino, F. S., de Wit, L. M., Bouvy, P. F., Stijnen, T., Cuijpers, P., Penninx, B. W. J. H., & Zitman, F. G. (2010). Overweight, obesity, and depression: A systematic review and meta-analysis of longitudinal studies. *Archives of General Psychiatry, 67*(3), 220–229.

Marmorstein, N. R., Iacono, W. G., & Legrand, L. (2016). Prospective associations between depression and obesity for adolescent males and females: A systematic review and meta-analysis. *PLoS One, 11*(6), e0157240. https://doi.org/10.1371/journal.pone.0157240.

Masten, A. S. (2014). Global perspectives on resilience in children and youth. *Child Development, 85*(1), 6–20.

Milaneschi, Y., Simmons, W. K., van Rossum, E. F. C., & Penninx, B. W. J. H. (2019). Depression and obesity: Evidence of shared biological mechanisms. *Molecular Psychiatry, 24*(1), 18–33.

Moffitt, T. E., Arseneault, L., Belsky, D., Dickson, N., Hancox, R. J., Harrington, H., Houts, R., Poulton, R., Roberts, B. W., Ross, S., Sears, M. R., Thomson, W. M., & Caspi, A. (2011). A gradient of childhood self-control predicts health, wealth, and public safety. *Proceedings of the National Academy of Sciences, 108*(7), 2693–2698.

Mufson, L., Dorta, K. P., Wickramaratne, P., Nomura, Y., Olfson, M., & Weissman, M. M. (2004). A randomized effectiveness trial of interpersonal psychotherapy for depressed adolescents. *Archives of General Psychiatry, 61*(6), 577–584.

Patton, G. C., Coffey, C., Carlin, J. B., Sawyer, S. M., Williams, J., Olsson, C. A., & Wake, M. (2011). Overweight and obesity between adolescence and young adulthood: A 10-year prospective cohort study. *Journal of Adolescent Health, 48*(3), 275–280.

Pearl, R. L., & Puhl, R. M. (2018). Weight bias internalization and health: A systematic review. *Obesity Reviews, 19*(8), 1141–1163.

Phelps, N. H., Singleton, R. K., Zhou, B., et al. (2024). Worldwide trends in underweight and obesity from 1990 to 2022. *The Lancet, 403*(10431), 1027–1050.

Quek, Y. H., Tam, W. W. S., Zhang, M. W. B., & Ho, R. C. M. (2017). Exploring the association between childhood and adolescent obesity and depression: A meta-analysis. *Obesity Reviews, 18*(7), 742–754.

Singer, M. (1996). A dose of drugs, a touch of violence, a case of AIDS: Conceptualizing the SAVA syndemic. *Free Inquiry in Creative Sociology, 24*(2), 99–110.

Singh, S., Awasthi, S., Kapoor, V., & Mishra, P. (2023). Childhood obesity in India: A two-decade meta-analysis of prevalence and socioeconomic correlates. *Clinical Epidemiology and Global Health, 23*, 101390.

Stachow, R., Holl, R. W., Christiansen, H., Reinehr, T., Herpertz-Dahlmann, B., & Wiegand-Grefe, S. (2024). Psychosocial distress in adolescents with overweight and obesity during the COVID-19 pandemic: Results from the KICK-COVID study. *Frontiers in Pediatrics, 12*, 1289456. https://doi.org/10.3389/fped.2024.1289456.

Stunkard, A. J, Faith, M. S, & Allison, K. C (2003). Depression and obesity. *Biological Psychiatry, 54*(3), 330–337. https://doi.org/10.1016/s0006-3223(03)00608-5.

Thapar, A., Collishaw, S., Pine, D. S., & Thapar, A. K. (2012). Depression in adolescence. *The Lancet, 379*(9820), 1056–1067.

WHO. (2024). Obesity and overweight: Key facts. https://www.who.int/news-room/fact-sheets/detail/obesity-and-overweight.

World Health Organization (WHO) (1998). Obesity: Preventing and Managing the Global Epidemic. Report of a WHO Consultation. WHO Technical Report Series No, 894.

World Health Organization (WHO) (2019). WHO Guidelines on Physical Activity, Sedentary Behaviour and Sleep for Children Under 5 Years of Age. World Health Organization, Geneva.

Zajkowska, Z., Gullett, N., Walsh, A., Zonca, V., Pedersen, G. A., Souza, L., & Bhattacharyya, S. (2022). Cortisol and development of depression in adolescence and young adulthood: A systematic review and meta-analysis. *Psychoneuroendocrinology, 136*, 105625. https://doi.org/10.1016/j.psyneuen.2021.105625.

Zhou, Y., Li, S., Cai, F., Sun, Y., Fu, J., Wang, X., & Zhang, J. (2023). Prevalence of depression and related factors among overweight and obese Chinese adolescents. *International Journal of Environmental Research and Public Health, 20*(4), 3523. https://doi.org/10.3390/ijerph20043523.

Zoogman, S., Goldberg, S. B., Hoyt, W. T., & Miller, L. (2015). Mindfulness interventions with youth: A meta-analysis. *Mindfulness, 6*(2), 290–302.

Further reading

Blakemore, S.-J., & Mills, K. L. (2014). Is adolescence a sensitive period for sociocultural processing? *Annual Review of Psychology, 65*, 187–207.

Cole, T. J., Bellizzi, M. C., Flegal, K. M., & Dietz, W. H. (2000). Establishing a standard definition for child overweight and obesity worldwide. *British Medical Journal, 320*(7244), 1240–1243.

Erikson, E. H. (1968). *Identity: Youth and crisis*. Norton.

Ong, M. Y., Eilander, J., Saw, S. M., Xiao, Y., Meaney, M. J., & Broekman, B. F. P. (2022). The influence of perceived stress and subjective well-being on emotional and behavioral problems in pre-adolescence. *European Child & Adolescent Psychiatry, 31*(2), 245–255. https://doi.org/10.1007/s00787-020-01654-4.

Thapliyal, N., & Bassi, S. (2024). A scoping review of existing policy instruments to tackle overweight and obesity in India. *F1000Research, 13*, 496.

Chapter 8

Coping strategies for obesity management

"Coping consists of constantly changing cognitive and behavioral efforts to manage specific external and/or internal demands that are appraised as taxing or exceeding the resources of the person."

Learning objectives

Explain the Lazarus–Folkman transactional model of stress and coping, identifying the roles of primary and secondary appraisal in determining the coping strategies employed by obese adolescents.
Distinguish between problem-focused, emotion-focused, and avoidant coping strategies in the context of obesity-related weight stigma, and explain how each interacts with adolescent psychological outcomes across gender and developmental stage.
Evaluate how India-specific cultural, institutional, and structural factors—including family expectations, academic pressure, gender norms, caste, and class dynamics—shape the coping repertoires available to obese adolescents.
Critically appraise the present study's CRI findings, with specific attention to the sex-differentiated and age-differentiated patterns of adaptive and avoidant coping in obese versus nonobese groups in Kolkata.
Translate theoretical knowledge of coping into specific, reproducible daily tactics for obese adolescents in Indian school, family, and clinical settings, drawing on the evidence-based intervention framework presented in this chapter.

8.1 Introduction: coping and adolescent obesity

8.1.1 Why coping matters

Researchers are now realizing that it is not just metabolic processes that contribute to adolescents being overweight. There are social and psychological factors, such as interactions with friends, family, schools, and media influence on obesity. Obese adolescents often face negative social judgments in various settings, such as schools, healthcare settings, and family settings. In these settings, body size is one of the major factors for social stigma. These social judgments have long-lasting effects on how an individual behaves in social settings. These effects include how much they contribute to school activities, how much they seek social support, and how it affects their long-term health (Neumark-Sztainer et al., 2002; Masten, 2001; Warnick et al., 2022).

Stigma based on weight has an impact on how an individual performs in school. They tend to avoid participating in activities in school, avoid group activities, and receive differential treatment from teachers. Longitudinal research has clearly shown that weight stigma in schools results in lower educational involvement and social mobility (Crosnoe, 2007; Janssen et al., 2004; Eisenberg et al., 2003; Griffiths et al., 2006).

Over the last 30 years, the number of obese adolescents worldwide has risen dramatically, especially in countries where the population is simultaneously malnourished and consumes a large amount of food that has a high calorific value, in addition to having a sedentary lifestyle (Ng et al., 2014; Popkin, 2015). However, the epidemiological pattern alone cannot provide a clue about the reason behind the different psychological and health outcomes in two obese adolescents who have a similar body mass index (BMI). However, the most consistent explanatory variables in longitudinal studies point to the differences in coping mechanisms that may explain the different outcomes in the two adolescents, where one may be experiencing isolation and depression, while the other may be full of agency and engagement, and the differences in the cognitive and behavioral coping mechanisms used by the two adolescents (Compas et al., 2001; Carver, Scheier & Weintraub, 1989; Frydenberg & Lewis, 1993).

Psychology of Obesity. DOI: https://doi.org/10.1016/B978-0-443-27797-9.00003-8

Coping acts as the primary mediator between the experience of stigma and the experience of psychological outcomes (Lazarus & Folkman, 1984; Aldwin, 2007). Adaptive coping mechanisms interrupt the experience of stigma by changing the experience of stigma into psychological well-being (Compas et al., 2001; Carver, Scheier & Weintraub, 1989). Any intervention that targets only metabolic outcomes without addressing psychosocial outcomes, such as stigma and coping mechanisms, will not yield the desired outcomes (Daniels et al., 2005; Reilly & Kelly, 2011; WHO, 2021).

8.1.2 Defining coping

The transactional model of Lazarus & Folkman (1984) remains the most fruitful in understanding adolescent coping. Coping cannot be considered a stable construct; instead, it is a constantly changing set of cognitive and behavioral processes that involve the monitoring and evaluation of the stressor and the availability of resources. Folkman & Lazarus (1988) have specified two successive stages in the assessment component that are crucial in coping. In primary appraisal, the person evaluates whether the stressor is a threat, a challenge, or neutral in nature. In secondary appraisal, the person evaluates what, if anything, can be done in response to the stressor. This two-component structure has significant implications for intervention: changing the adolescent's view of a stigmatizing event (primary) and increasing the number of responses (secondary) are two different but complementary intervention targets. Three major coping families form the basis of the study of adolescents coping with being overweight (Table 8.1).

Avoidant coping is very common and very costly in situations where people are stigmatized for their weight. While there is temporary relief, there is long-term damage in terms of fitness level, guilt, and relationships (Goldfield et al., 2010). Secrecy—including eating alone, hiding food intake from family members, and avoiding body-exposing social situations—is one of the most consistently documented avoidant coping behaviors in the weight stigma literature, associated with sustained psychological distress and reduced help-seeking (Puhl & Heuer, 2009). Adolescents don't tend to use only one type of coping. Rather, they develop a repertoire of coping strategies that may vary in terms of the situation and the type of stressor (Skinner et al., 2003; Seiffge-Krenke, 2011). The aim of a supportive intervention is not to advocate any of the strategies but rather to expand the repertoire of the adolescent and minimize the use of avoidant coping strategies and tailor the strategies to the situation in such a way that maintains dignity and engagement.

8.1.3 Development and the burden of stigma

Puberty is associated with changes in the way the body controls hunger, sleep patterns, changes in the distribution of body fat, and the way the body uses energy. For some already on higher BMI trajectories, the changes of puberty may actually accelerate weight gain (Dietz, 1998; Reinehr, 2013). Adolescents are in the process of building their self-concept and skills while navigating the challenge of rigorous academic demands and the complex web of social hierarchy.

Peer acceptance is a currency of development in adolescence, and weight status is a significant factor in several peer ecologies (Griffiths et al., 2006; Latner & Schwartz, 2005). Teasing about weight is associated with depression, disordered eating, and a lack of motivation for exercise. Chronic stress activates the hypothalamic–pituitary–adrenal axis, resulting in increased cortisol production, which in turn affects appetite and metabolism (Danese & McEwen, 2012; McEwen, 1998). Chronic stress is associated with avoidance behaviors that minimize energy expenditure and increase susceptibility to further weight gain (Janssen et al., 2004; Eisenberg et al., 2003; Faith et al., 2002).

TABLE 8.1 Types of coping in the context of adolescent obesity.

Coping type	Definition	Example in obesity context
Problem-focused coping	Strategies aimed at directly addressing or modifying the source of stress	Seeking teacher intervention; participating in supportive activity groups or clubs
Emotion-focused coping	Strategies aimed at regulating emotional responses to the stressor	Reframing teasing as ignorance; using prayer, humor, or reflection to restore emotional balance
Avoidant coping	Strategies involving withdrawal from or denial of the stressor	Skipping sports activities; eating in secrecy; denying health-related concerns

Richard S. Lazarus & Susan Folkman (1984), Stress, Appraisal, and Coping. New York: Springer.

The meaning of stigma and its effects vary by context. For example, in collectivist societies, body size is linked to family honor, marital possibilities, and parental aspirations. For a teenage girl, her body is family honor. For a teenage boy, his body is discipline and manhood. Thus, coping is relationally intrinsic, a family negotiation within a kinship network, rather than a cognitive ability of individuals. This is so, especially in collectivist cultures, where coping is a family affair, a kinship network, rather than a cognitive ability of individuals (Nayar, 2019).

8.2 Theoretical frameworks for coping

8.2.1 Historical roots of coping theory

Coping theory has a history of progressive redefinition of stress and how people cope with it. Initially, coping was explained in terms of psychoanalytic theory. Freud's daughter, Anna Freud, described defense mechanisms, including denial, repression, and projection, as unconscious coping strategies for stress relief. Vaillant later placed defense mechanisms on a developmental continuum, ranging from immature coping strategies, such as acting out, to mature coping strategies, including humor and sublimation.

Cannon (1932) and Selye (1956) shifted the focus to physiology. These authors used concepts of homeostasis and general adaptation syndrome to illustrate that stress is a cumulative effect of multiple stressors. This tradition, although important, saw stress as exclusively external and failed to recognize the importance of subjective interpretation. Richard Lazarus played a crucial role in changing this trend. In his work published in 1966, he argued that stress is not inherent in events; rather, it is related to appraisal. In 1984, Lazarus and Folkman conceptualized coping as a transactional process arising from the interaction between the individual and the environment. This gave birth to the transactional model that is used today.

8.2.2 The transactional model

According to Lazarus & Folkman (1984), coping is constantly changing cognitive and behavioral efforts to manage specific demands that are appraised to tax or exceed the resources of the individual. This definition has three critical aspects. First, coping is dynamic and constantly changing. Second, coping is subjective in nature. This is because appraisal is critical in that a given stressor can have multiple outcomes depending on interpretation. Third, coping is transactional. This is because it is a product of an interplay between the adolescent and their environment. This model has two appraisal phases. In primary appraisal, the individual considers whether an event is threatening, challenging, or inconsequential. In secondary appraisal, coping options and their probability of success are evaluated (Folkman & Lazarus, 1988). Interventions that only target the thoughts of the adolescent without changing hostile environments are only half of the equation (Pont et al., 2017; Sawyer et al., 2012).

8.2.3 Cognitive-behavioral models

Cognitive behavioral models add depth to the appraisal model by examining certain cognitive patterns. Beck (1976) and Ellis (1994) theories demonstrate how distorted thinking leads to poor coping strategies. Adolescents suffering from obesity may experience cognitive distortions, including overgeneralization ("Everyone hates me"), catastrophizing ("If I do not succeed in PE, then my life is ruined"), and labeling ("I am a lazy, disgusting person"). Cognitive behavioral therapy (CBT) improves recognition, challenges, and replaces cognitive distortions with more equitable thinking. For instance, "I am a lazy, disgusting person" is changed to "I did not do well today, but I will try harder tomorrow." CBT has been proven to be successful in dealing with anxiety, depression, and eating disorders, as revealed in a meta-analysis by Hofmann et al. (2012). According to Weersing et al. (2017), CBT has significant effects on depression and anxiety in adolescent populations. Although CBT effectively addresses maladaptive thought patterns, it may be less effective when environmental sources of stigma remain unchanged. CBT is best used when it is supplemented by changes in schools and peer environments (Pont et al., 2017; Swinburn et al., 2019).

8.2.4 Resilience theory

The theory of resilience directs the focus of analysis from deficits to strengths and asks no longer questions about the causes of difficulties experienced by adolescents living with obesity. Rather, it asks questions about why some people do well despite living with stigma (Masten, 2001; Werner & Smith, 1992; Rutter, 1987). Four systems are consistently found to be associated with resilience: warmth of relationships that reduces secrecy and depression (Repetti, Taylor & Seeman, 2002; Luthar et al., 2000); peer networks where one close supportive friend is sufficient to reduce stress associated with stigma (Wentzel, 1998; Due et al., 2005); self-beliefs where optimism and efficacy are associated with greater behavioral engagement (Bandura, 1997; Scheier & Carver, 1992); and meaning systems where spirituality and cultural traditions can provide reframing resources (Nayar, 2019).

In India, resilience is typically associated with collective and cultural resilience factors such as devotionalism, yoga, and extended families (Nayar, 2019). While extended families can sometimes serve as a supportive network for adolescents living with obesity, they can also serve as a source of stigma. In this chapter, the term ecological resilience is used in accordance with Ungar's (2011) definition of resilience as a function of supportive systems rather than solely individual characteristics. In order to flourish, adolescents living with obesity need systems-level protection, including safe schools and respectful healthcare providers (Swinburn et al., 2019).

8.2.5 Weight bias internalization

Weight Bias Internalization (WBI) is a theory that explains how societal disdain is internalized and incorporated into one's sense of self (Durso & Latner, 2008). When adolescents begin to think that they are "lazy" or "not good enough," societal disdain is no longer something that is done to them. Rather, it is something that is a part of them. Durso & Latner (2008) developed and tested the Weight Bias Internalization Scale (WBIS) to make this theory work in real life. This theory has been validated across cultures in both Western and non-Western cultures (Pearl & Puhl, 2014; Hilbert et al., 2014).

If the stigma is external in origin, then the ways of coping with it include confronting the situation, changing the way the person thinks about the situation, or turning to other people for support. If the stigma is internalized in origin, then the ways of coping with it include hiding the situation, secrecy, denial, and hopelessness (Pearl et al., 2018; Lillis et al., 2010). Adolescents with higher WBIS tend to experience more depressive symptoms, eating disorders, and avoidance of healthcare services (Hunger et al., 2015). Indian youth are more likely to experience WBI triggers when they hear the same message over and over again, that being overweight makes it more difficult to find a partner. They may also experience WBI triggers when they hear teachers and parents say that being overweight is like being lazy. They may also experience WBI triggers when they hear people talk about the various layers of the caste and class systems and how being overweight equates with being socially inferior.

Key theoretical frameworks for practitioners

Transactional Model (Lazarus & Folkman, 1984): Assess the person's primary and secondary appraisal of the situation and the environment in which the person is located.

CBT (Beck, 1976; Weersing et al., 2017): Teach the person reframing drills and challenge the person's mislabeled thinking in the person's own language and culture.

Resilience Theory (Masten, 2001): Focus on the existing systems of support in the person's life and community rather than the person's own character strengths and abilities.

WBI (Durso & Latner, 2008): Assess the person's level of internalized shame and use ACT defusion techniques to overcome the shame.

Ecological Model (Bronfenbrenner, 1979): Assess the person's situation in terms of the multiple levels of the person's environment.

8.2.6 Sociocultural frameworks

Sociometer theory, as presented by Leary et al., 1995, indicates that self-esteem acts as a "live" measure of social inclusion. When individuals perceive less social inclusion, they feel ashamed, which in turn pushes them to "get back in." When obese teens are ostracized or bullied, they are likely to "get back in" by becoming reclusive or secretive, as indicated in the study by Harter (1999) and Eisenberg et al. in 2003. Adaptive coping therefore involves developing meaningful social connections and sources of self-worth that foster a sense of belonging, perhaps by making friends with people who like you or finding ways to make you feel good about yourself that do not involve your looks.

Objectification theory, as presented by Fredrickson and Roberts (1997), helps us understand how culture forces girls to view themselves as objects in the eyes of others. When they do this, they begin to feel bad about themselves, which in turn influences them to avoid behaviors or activities. Research has supported the claim that self-objectification can lead to depression, eating disorders, or the development of avoidant coping mechanisms (Moradi & Huang, 2008; Tiggemann, 2011; Grogan, 2016). Social comparison theory, as presented by Festinger (1954), helps us understand how social media can make these negative influences more powerful. When individuals compare themselves to others in a negative manner, they are less likely to engage in social or physical activities.

The differences between men and women in coping patterns are observed across diverse cultural contexts. Girls experience emotional pain through secrecy, avoidance, and emotional eating (Neumark-Sztainer et al., 2002; Field et al., 2001). In the context of the gym, boys express emotional pain by being funny, aggressive, or overcompensating

(Ricciardelli & McCabe, 2004; Puhl & Latner, 2007). In the context of India, the cultural context makes the expression of emotional pain even stronger. Girls have to contend with cultural images related to marriageability and beauty, whereas boys have to contend with images related to physical strength and discipline in sports.

8.2.7 Additional perspectives: helplessness, conservation of resources theory, and critical pedagogy

The conservation of resources theory (Hobfoll, 1989) states that the experience of stress is the result of the actual or perceived loss of resources. For overweight adolescents, the experience of stigma results in the loss of friendship, social status, and self-efficacy, which in turn makes them withdraw. The adaptive solution is the conservation of resources with the assistance of structured intervention programs.

Learned Helplessness Theory (Seligman, 1975) provides the explanation for how the experience of continuous stigma leads to the experience of learned helplessness. Adolescents who experience repeated weight-related teasing and stigma may eventually develop learned helplessness. They stop doing things that are good for their health. The solution is to reinforce their sense of mastery by acknowledging their small, observable successes.

The critical pedagogy framework, as described by Freire (1970), transforms the concept of coping into the development of a critical consciousness. This framework does not instruct the adolescent on how to cope with bad situations; it instructs the adolescent to think about and fight against the negative story of body size. This framework, when applied to the discussion of obesity, instructs the adolescent to discuss the way the media, institutions, and society discuss obesity, and it transforms the concept of coping by applying it to a group social action (Pausé, 2012). An alternative framework that may be applied to the adolescent experience in India comes from the yogic traditions of India, where yogic psychology identifies suffering as a product of a lack of understanding and instructs the yogic practitioner to apply mindfulness techniques such as asana, pranayama, and meditation to cultivate equanimity (Saraswati, 1981; Rao, 2002). Modern-day adolescents in India apply yogic psychology as a means of emotion regulation (Nayar, 2019).

8.3 Global evidence on coping and obesity

8.3.1 Universality and variation

There is a growing body of international research that shows that coping is a critical factor in psychological well-being and health-related behaviors of adolescents who are obese across a range of different cultural contexts (Compas et al., 2001; Pont et al., 2017; Reilly & Kelly, 2011). There are three global patterns that are evident from this synthesis of research. Maladaptive coping is a global phenomenon that is predictive of negative outcomes for youth who are obese (Faith et al., 2002; Hayden-Wade et al., 2005). Adaptive coping is a protective factor that is not as universal and is often constrained by issues of stigma and inequality (Stice, Shaw & Marti, 2006; Eisenberg et al., 2003).

8.3.2 Maladaptive coping: evidence across regions

The longitudinal North American research conducted by Field et al. (2001) using the Growing Up Today Study found that reliance on maladaptive coping predicts weight gain, depressive symptoms, and reduced physical activity participation. Goldfield et al. (2010) found that emotional eating is a mediator between stigma exposure and weight change in a sample of Canadian youth.

In Mexico and Brazil, comfort food and social withdrawal have been identified as unhealthy responses to teasing regarding weight, which is associated with body dissatisfaction and avoidance of physical education (PE) (Jimenez-Cruz et al., 2010; Conde & Borges, 2011). In peri-urban Nairobi, body size normalization in home settings was observed in adolescent girls with overweight, but social withdrawal from school activities was an unhealthy coping response (Kimani-Murage, 2013). The Health Behavior in School-aged Children study in Europe is one of the most comprehensive surveys on child and adolescent health. The results from this study across European nations consistently report lower life satisfaction, greater bullying, and avoidant coping in adolescents with obesity (Currie et al., 2012; Inchley et al., 2020). In Japan, secrecy, night eating, and social withdrawal have been identified as unhealthy behaviors in adolescents with weight concerns (Tani et al., 2015). In China, modernization and social media have fueled body image issues in adolescents, resulting in an increased tendency towards unhealthy coping strategies (Chen et al., 2019).

8.3.3 Adaptive coping: protective factors

Across different settings, social support has been identified as the best predictor for effective coping (Cohen & Wills, 1985; Thoits, 1995; Uchino, 2006). Adolescents who seek social support from friends and family have lower rates of depression and greater self-esteem (Eisenberg et al., 2003). In Scandinavian nations, social support from peer groups has been identified as an effective coping strategy for adolescents with weight problems. The study found that social withdrawal is lower in such peer groups, and the quality of friendship is a stronger predictor for psychological well-being than BMI (Due et al., 2005; Nielsen et al., 2010).

Physical activity, defined in terms of enjoyment rather than weight management, acts as an adaptive coping mechanism to meet needs for mood regulation and social integration. Research into adolescent health promotion interventions indicates that participation-focused physical activity, rather than competitive activity, results in positive body image and reduced avoidance coping. Participation-focused physical activity, designed to replace competitive activity with skill-based activity to enhance enjoyment, has been demonstrated to increase resilience and reduce avoidance coping in adolescents with obesity in different countries worldwide (Daniels & Leaper, 2006). Longitudinal research indicates that early patterns of avoidance coping result in greater BMI increase and poorer mental health outcomes, with social support influencing these trajectories (Reinehr, 2013; Aldwin, 2007).

8.3.4 Gender differences in coping

Girls are more likely to internalize stigma and cope using secrecy, avoidance, and emotional eating. Neumark-Sztainer et al. (2002) found that adolescent girls with obesity in US high schools were more likely to avoid sports and extracurricular activities because of ridicule. In Canada, scores for emotional eating were higher among adolescent girls than boys with equivalent BMI (Goldfield et al., 2010). Boys are more likely to externalize their stress. Ricciardelli & McCabe (2004) found that adolescent boys used humor and aggression when they were teased about their weight. Boys also engage in gym culture and muscularity as a coping strategy. This appears to be problem-focused coping. However, this is also an unhealthy coping mechanism that leads to supplement and exercise addiction (Grogan, 2016). These scripts are also encouraged in boys in all regions (Neumark-Sztainer et al., 2002; Field et al., 2001).

8.3.5 Socioeconomic status and structural inequality

Socioeconomic status influences coping because it influences access to resources and exposure to stigma. Low socioeconomic status is associated with greater disadvantage. Adolescents from low socioeconomic status experience limited access to recreational facilities, counseling services, and healthy food. This leads to avoidance, denial, and normalization of stigma (Reilly & Kelly, 2011; Swinburn et al., 2019). In transition economies, adolescents with higher socioeconomic status experience greater exposure to Westernized body ideals. This is because they attend private schools and are exposed to media saturation. This leads to body dissatisfaction despite their socioeconomic status (Popkin, 2015; Misra & Khurana, 2011). This is ecological because adolescents do not have a choice in coping because they do not have access to resources that can help them cope.

8.3.6 Digital media and coping

Social media usage has been associated with body discontent and ineffective coping strategies in North America and European nations. Social comparison of oneself with others through images and stories of peers and media figures is a common practice among teens. This has been theorized by Festinger (1954) and has been associated with increased levels of negative emotions such as anxiety and emotional eating (Tiggemann & Slater, 2013; Perloff, 2014; Fardouly et al., 2015; Rodgers et al., 2020). This comparison of oneself with others based on physical appearance is associated with negative emotions, and people become less likely to participate in social and physical activities.

Social media is also associated with the development of effective strategies of adaptation. Body-positive movements and health promotion campaigns provide a favorable environment for the development of reframing and building resiliency in teens (Rodgers et al., 2020). Teenagers who are exposed to body-positive content have lower WBI and higher levels of self-acceptance (Holland & Tiggemann, 2016). Digital media is a two-edged sword that can provide the benefits of increased stigma exposure and solidarity. Interventions aimed at teens should focus on media literacy and educate them on how to use the media in a more effective way by encouraging them to critically evaluate the content, distance themselves from harmful content, and engage with the media in a more effective way.

8.3.7 Longitudinal trajectories

Coping mechanisms developed in adolescence have a lasting influence on adult health and well-being. For instance, teenagers who practice seclusion and avoidance are more likely to become obese and depressed adults (Neumark-Sztainer et al., 2002; Faith, Matz & Jorge, 2002). On the other hand, teenagers who practice adaptive coping mechanisms experience improved mental health and lower risks of chronic health conditions in adulthood (Werner & Smith, 1992; Masten, 2001). Research on the life course reveals that teenagers who practice adaptive coping mechanisms to stigma and

TABLE 8.2 Cross-cultural variations in coping patterns, protective factors, and risk factors in adolescent obesity.

Region	Dominant coping pattern	Key protective factor	Key risk factor
North America	Emotional eating; peer support in some groups	Peer mentoring programs; family warmth	Media ideals; exclusion from competitive sports
Scandinavia	Relatively higher use of adaptive coping	Strong friendship networks; school-based support systems	Bullying; low life satisfaction
East Asia (Japan, China)	Secrecy, night eating, denial	Structured extracurricular engagement	Exam pressure; academic surveillance
Latin America	Comfort eating; family-based acceptance	Extended family support and cohesion	Urban thinness ideals; peer ridicule
Sub-Saharan Africa	Normalization at home; withdrawal in school settings	Community sports clubs; kinship networks	Rural–urban transition; gender norms
India	Secrecy, avoidance, prayer, humor	Yoga, family warmth, academic achievement	Marriageability norms; caste dynamics; examination stress

Tweed, R. G., White, K., & Lehman, D. R. (2004). Culture, stress, and coping: Internally and externally targeted control strategies of European Canadians, East Asian Canadians, and Japanese. Journal of Cross-Cultural Psychology, 35(6), 652–668.

negative experiences without internalizing contempt are more likely to experience a smooth transition to adulthood with reduced risks of chronic stress-related conditions and greater stability in educational and professional pursuits (Reinehr, 2013; Aldwin, 2007). Adolescence is a critical and somewhat malleable phase; coping mechanisms are more susceptible to change in adolescence than in adulthood.

The cross-regional findings suggest that the distinction between adaptive and maladaptive coping is not culture-neutral. While avoidant coping is highly universal in terms of its pervasiveness and its adverse impact, its specific forms—ranging from nocturnal eating in Japan to familial evasion in Latin America to secrecy during Diwali celebrations in India—appear to be shaped by local culture and institutions. Adaptive coping also appears to be culture-specific in its forms. For example, Scandinavian friendship-based buffering, Australian peer mentoring, and yogic coping in India all have the same psychological effect but do so in different ways that are unique to each culture. This finding has a critical implication for intervention development: they need to be informed by structural context and culture, not simply based on high-income Western culture (Table 8.2).

The global evidence provided above offers a background against which the Indian scenario has to be understood. India shows evidence that is similar to that found globally—specifically, in relation to avoidant coping and differential coping by gender—along with some unique factors that are a product of its collectivistic cultural background, joint family systems, hierarchical caste and class systems, and perhaps most uniquely, its academic examination culture. These will be elaborated upon in detail in the next section.

8.4 Indian context: coping in cultural and institutional environments

8.4.1 Coping as relational and embedded

It is difficult to imagine how Indian youth living with obesity cope with their issues without considering the complex web of cultural factors, family systems, school systems, peer relationships, caste and class systems, and gender factors that permeate their lives. Unlike the dominant perspective in high-income nations that sees coping as a psychological process of individuals (Lazarus & Folkman, 1984; Compas et al., 2001), in India, coping is a relational process. Adolescents are not likely to act independently. Parents' expectations, teachers' authority, peers' surveillance, and cultural factors that influence marriageability, disciplinarity, and honorability constrain or facilitate their actions (Misra & Khurana, 2011; Nayar, 2019). While coping strategies like directly confronting their parents or teachers regarding stigmatizing comments by peers may be unrealistic and even dangerous in India (Reilly & Kelly, 2011; Puhl & Heuer, 2009), youth in India are more likely to engage in coping strategies that allow them to cope with their issues independently while still being able to fulfill their social obligations.

There has also been a lack of studies in the area, as there are no longitudinal studies in India that have followed the coping patterns of obese adolescents in different socioeconomic and geographic settings. This study aims to bridge the gap in the lack of group comparative coping studies in urban Indian adolescents by sex and stages of development, utilizing a validated scale in the Indian context. Gaps that still exist in the area include comparative studies in the context of the rural and urban setting, caste-based studies, and RCTs of coping interventions in the school setting for the Indian context.

8.4.2 Family expectations and coping responses

Family plays a central role in shaping the experiences of adolescents in India. Discussions within extended families frequently focus on body size, eating habits, physical appearance, and future marriage prospects. The increasing prevalence of adolescent obesity reported in NFHS-5 (IIPS & ICF, 2021) highlights the importance of understanding these family influences. Although existing evidence suggests that family comments and interactions within kinship networks can significantly affect adolescents' psychological well-being, further qualitative and quantitative research is needed to better understand the nature and impact of these influences in the Indian context (Nayar, 2019). Even when intended as expressions of concern or guidance, comments about body weight may evoke feelings of shame, secrecy, and weight-related self-consciousness among adolescents (Puhl & Latner, 2007).

The message to girls is loud and clear: Girls are frequently exposed to messages suggesting that body weight may influence future marriage prospects. This implies that obesity is not a health concern but a threat to family honor and social mobility (Nayar, 2019; Grogan, 2016). Boys are also made to feel that their size reflects their laziness or lack of discipline, which affects their future employability and masculinity. Research has also revealed that children resort to avoiding social gatherings, secret consumption of food after receiving negative comments, and the use of humor as a coping mechanism to avert emotional pain, which may provide temporary relief but leads to avoidance behaviors that may result in depression (Goldfield et al., 2010; Puhl & Heuer, 2009).

Families may not always be the source of stigma, and there are many studies in the context of India that have highlighted the positive influence of parents on children's resilience. For instance, parents who emphasized health instead of looks, did not comment on the children's weight, and taught children the importance of a balanced diet and exercise, helped children cope with the stigma of obesity (Misra & Khurana, 2011).

8.4.3 Academic pressure as a driver of maladaptive coping

There are a few issues that influence the life of an adolescent in India as much as academic achievement. Competitive examinations such as the Joint Entrance Examination and the National Eligibility cum Entrance Test are the gateway to a future career and keep a watchful eye on the academic prowess of adolescents at all times. For obese adolescents, academic pressure and obesity-related stigma often interact to increase psychological distress among adolescents.

The present study found that eating attitude was significantly more disordered in obese subjects across all four age-sex groups ($P<.01$). In all groups, the means of obese subjects were significantly higher than the EAT-26 cut-off score of 20. In India, preparing for exams is a stressful event that often causes emotional eating to cope with anxiety. In this context, the eating attitude disorders that are present in obese youth are aggravated. Evidence of academic stress being a major predictor of disordered eating patterns comes from school-based studies conducted in India, substantiating that academic stress is a predictor of disordered eating patterns, particularly in urban youth (Khanna et al., 2023).

The increasing phenomenon of residential coaching environments in urban India has further exacerbated the stress-coping link. In addition, for obese adolescents, ridicule in hostels and classrooms has further added to academic pressure. Boys used humor and bravado as coping strategies, while girls used secrecy and withdrawal. These findings corroborate global findings on gender differences in coping styles (Ricciardelli & McCabe, 2004; Neumark-Sztainer et al., 2002).

8.4.4 Gender norms and coping strategies

Gender norms have a considerable influence on the way in which adolescents cope with obesity. Femininity is associated with being slender, light, and marriageable. Masculinity is associated with being strong, disciplined, and athletic (Grogan, 2016; Fredrickson & Roberts, 1997). These constructs are promoted through media, parental comments, interactions with others, and through school practices. These constructs are very stringent in nature, which affects the way in which an individual can cope with such issues.

Research has clearly demonstrated that girls with obesity have a greater tendency to internalize stigma, resulting in secrecy, withdrawal, and emotional eating (Neumark-Sztainer et al., 2002; Field et al., 2001). Research has clearly demonstrated that girls with obesity avoid school sports days and social functions in an attempt to avoid being ridiculed by friends. In addition, they also tend to eat in an attempt to cope with shame and social withdrawal. In India, girls tend to avoid social interactions because they feel they will not be able to marry because of their weight (Nayar, 2019; Goldfield et al., 2010).

On the other hand, boys often express emotional distress through externalizing behaviours such as humour, aggression, or excessive involvement in competitive activities. Research has consistently revealed that boys who are mocked for not meeting athletic expectations develop self-deprecating humor or aggression in response to these situations (Ricciardelli & McCabe, 2004; Grogan, 2016). Some boys become excessively involved in gym culture and sports to prove how good they are at them. Although these behaviors may seem to be coping with problems, they are, in fact, coping mechanisms due to stigma. Some boys develop unhealthy behaviors like taking too many supplements or exercising too much. Both these coping mechanisms have serious impacts on the individuals. Girls' secrecy and withdrawal lead to more depression and unhealthy eating behaviors, whereas boys' humor or aggression not only hides their feelings but also continues to have conflicts with friends or develops unhealthy behaviors like taking too many supplements or exercising too much (Ricciardelli & McCabe, 2004; Grogan, 2016).

8.4.5 Caste, class, and socioeconomic influences

Caste and class shape both the experience of obesity-related stigma and the coping resources available to adolescents in ways that interact and compound each other. Among adolescents from higher socioeconomic and upper-caste urban families, exposure to globalized media through private schooling and digital platforms produces strong internalization of slimness ideals. For these adolescents, obesity stigma is experienced primarily through appearance-based social comparison, and coping tends toward secrecy, fad dieting, and healthcare-seeking behaviors that may themselves reinforce shame through weight-centric clinical encounters (Grogan, 2016; Misra & Khurana, 2011). Among adolescents from lower socioeconomic or marginalized caste backgrounds, a different configuration of risk operates. Obesity may carry less immediate appearance-based stigma within the home community—where larger body size has historically been associated with prosperity or adequate nutrition—but these adolescents encounter acute weight-based ridicule in mixed-class school settings where body norms are governed by higher-caste and higher-income standards. This school-level exposure is compounded by the limited access to adaptive coping resources—counseling, psychological support, body-positive peer networks—that characterizes underresourced school environments serving lower-income communities (Jambholkar et al., 2024).

The disadvantaged position in which intersectionality places individuals adds to the coping challenges. Adolescents who are discriminated against on the basis of their caste status as well as their weight are subjected to compounded identity threat effects, which are higher than the additive effects of the individual factors (Crenshaw, 1989). Studies on the applicability of the concept of intersectionality in Indian school settings have shown that obese adolescents belonging to lower castes or income groups face discrimination in sports and leadership positions through mechanisms not considered in the weight discrimination literature (Jambholkar et al., 2024). The specific coping strategies available to low-caste, low-income obese adolescents are therefore doubly constrained: they face compounded identity threat from caste-based and weight-based stigma simultaneously, while also having fewer institutional resources to support adaptive coping responses (Crenshaw, 1989). The intersectionality framework captures this compounding effect—the experience of multiple stigmatized identities is not additive but multiplicative, producing forms of social exclusion that neither weight stigma literature nor caste discrimination literature individually addresses. Culturally adapted coping interventions in India must therefore be sensitive to caste and class positioning, not only gender and age, if they are to reach and serve adolescents whose coping challenges are most acute.

8.4.6 Urban and rural differences

Teenagers in the city are always surrounded by the media. For them, the most important things in the world are Instagram, Bollywood, and comparing themselves to their peers. Research has revealed that teenagers in the city in India are more dissatisfied with their bodies, and this leads to unhealthy coping mechanisms such as confiding in no one, eating in response to emotional states, and avoiding social interactions (Nayar, 2019). Teenage boys in the city cope with problems by going to the gym, while teenage girls in the city cope with problems by dieting, confiding in no one, and avoiding social interactions.

Teenagers in rural areas do not get to be exposed to much global media, but they get the message through the education system, their phones, and peers who move to the city to live in the city. Some people in the country believe that being overweight is a status symbol of health and wealth. This makes it less likely for people in the same household to be shamed (Khader & Madise, 2010). In such cases, teenagers view their body size as a symbol of health. Research conducted in India has also shown that rural-urban dichotomies can occur among adolescents who find acceptance in their rural homes but experience shame in urban schools/residential hostels. These adolescents mainly cope with their body image problems using normalization in rural homes and avoidance in urban hostels (Nayar, 2019). However, the advent of smartphones has bridged the gap between rural and urban areas. This is because adolescents in rural areas are spending more time with content that promotes being thin or muscular. This has made them feel negatively about their body image and has led to poor coping mechanisms (Rodgers et al., 2020; Holland & Tiggemann, 2016).

8.4.7 Institutional practices and coping outcomes

Schools in India are among the most influential factors that can shape body image coping. Research conducted in India has shown that schools in India frequently engage in stigma that leads to evasion, concealment, and truancy. This is because schools in India frequently engage in public weighing, teachers' biased comments, exclusion from sports teams, and being made fun of in PE classes (Reilly & Kelly, 2011; Puhl & Heuer, 2009; Pont et al., 2017). These have been consistently observed in urban areas in India (Jambholkar et al., 2024).

In the same way, schools can be spaces where people are strong. This can be done through inclusive policies where all people are included, antibullying strategies where weight-based bullying is named and addressed, and PE strategies where emphasis is placed on participation rather than performance (Quick et al., 2013; Pont et al., 2017). Evidence-based strategies such as choice-based PE, where students can choose the activity they feel comfortable with, and access to school counselors have been shown to reduce avoidance and increase participation among obese youth (Eisenberg et al., 2003; Daniels & Leaper, 2006). Healthcare settings are another significant institutional location. Studies have shown that youth avoid healthcare settings following diagnostic overshadowing, where healthcare professionals attribute all the patients' complaints to their weight without further investigation (Latner & Stunkard, 2003; Puhl & Latner, 2007). Conversely, healthcare settings where there is private deliberation, explanation without bias, and the formulation of goals through cooperation can foster trust and problem-oriented participation (Pont et al., 2017; WHO, 2021).

8.5 Research insights and interventions

8.5.1 Contribution of the present quantitative study

The current study provides a comprehensive quantitative study of how Indian youth suffering from obesity deal with stigma, academic pressure, and cultural factors. What sets this study apart is that it provides a quantitative evaluation of coping strategies by applying the Coping Response Inventory (CRI) developed by Rao et al. (1999) for four different age-sex groups. This allows for a comparison of coping strategies for each age and sex group, in addition to a three-factor analysis of variance. The study groups of both obese and nonobese individuals were comparable on six demographic factors: socioeconomic status, family type, family size, number of siblings, birth order, and language. This confirms that coping response differences are due to weight status and not demographic factors (Das, 2020).

The current study's findings on coping strategies by applying the CRI indicate that there are developmental and sex-specific outcomes. There was no significant difference in coping response for both obese and nonobese individuals in late adolescent groups, regardless of gender. For young adult groups, significant coping response disparities were noted for both male and female groups. For male young adult groups, obese individuals scored significantly higher coping scores than nonobese individuals (26.74, $P<.01$), indicating a higher coping response. For female young adult groups, obese individuals scored significantly lower coping scores than nonobese individuals ($P<.01$), indicating a very low coping response. The more significant concern is that of a very low adaptive coping response for obese female young adult groups, since higher CRI scores indicate a higher adaptive coping response, i.e., a higher score on the CRI indicates a higher adaptive coping response, where individuals are more capable of dealing with stress. According to international research, it has been noted that "girls appear to internalize stigma by avoiding it and keeping it a secret, whereas boys appear to express their feelings about stigma more openly" (Neumark-Sztainer et al., 2002; Goldfield et al., 2010; Ricciardelli & McCabe, 2004). The body weight × sex interaction effect ($F = 120.847$, $P<.01$) is notably large relative to the other effects in this analysis. This reflects the magnitude of the sex-differentiated coping pattern: while sex as a main effect was not significant ($F = 0.012$, NS), the interaction of body weight with sex produced an unusually strong effect, indicating that the relationship between obesity and coping is not uniform across males and females but diverges markedly—with obese female young adults showing substantially reduced adaptive coping and obese male young adults showing substantially elevated coping. This interaction effect is the primary substantive finding of the 3FFANOVA for coping and underscores the necessity of sex-stratified rather than aggregate coping interventions.

8.5.2 Profiles of adaptive and maladaptive coping

The table below shows how adolescents with obesity commonly cope with stress related to teasing, stigma, and social pressure. Some responses may help them feel better for a short time but can create problems later, while others support healthier adjustment and emotional well-being. Recognizing these patterns can help in guiding adolescents towards more positive and supportive ways of coping (Table 8.3).

TABLE 8.3 Profiles of adaptive and maladaptive coping strategies in adolescent obesity: behavioral patterns and psychological outcomes.

Coping profile	Behaviors	Short-term effect	Long-term effect	Evidence
Emotional eating	Eating in response to stress or ridicule rather than physiological hunger	Temporary emotional comfort	Weight gain, guilt, and depressive symptoms	(Faith et al., 2002; Goldfield et al., 2010)
Secrecy	Eating alone, hiding food, and avoiding observation by family members	Reduced exposure to criticism	Shame, disordered eating patterns	(Puhl & Heuer, 2009; Eisenberg et al., 2003)
Social withdrawal	Avoiding sports, social events, and classroom participation	Escape from ridicule	Loneliness, depression, and reduced physical activity	(Griffiths et al., 2006; Janssen et al., 2004)
Humor as masking	Making jokes about one's own body to deflect ridicule	Short-term social acceptance	Reinforcement of internalized stigma	(Ricciardelli & McCabe, 2004)
Aggression	Responding to teasing with confrontation or hostility	Temporary sense of control or power	Peer conflict and social alienation	(Pont et al., 2017)
Social support	Sharing experiences of teasing with trusted individuals	Reduced shame and isolation	Lower depression and increased resilience	(Eisenberg et al., 2003; Due et al., 2005)
Physical activity	Engaging in enjoyable, noncompetitive movement	Improved mood and stress reduction	Sustained well-being and social engagement	(Daniels & Leaper, 2006)
Positive reframing	Interpreting ridicule as ignorance and focusing on personal strengths	Preservation of self-worth	Increased resilience and reduced internalized weight bias	(Aldwin, 2007; Pearl & Puhl, 2014)
Prayer/meditation	Engagement in spiritual practices such as prayer, yoga, or devotional music	Sense of calm and grounding	Reduced rumination and emotional stability	(Nayar, 2019)

8.6 From public domain

8.6.1 Psychological and therapeutic intervention

Psychological interventions seek to broaden coping skills, decrease dependence upon secrecy and denial, and encourage constructive strategies such as reframing, seeking social support, and behavioral engagement.

The most well-researched therapeutic approach for adolescents coping with obesity-related stigma is CBT, in which maladaptive cognitions are challenged and more balanced thinking is promoted through structured behavioral experiments. In support of the therapeutic value of CBT for obesity-related stigma in adolescence, meta-analytic reviews of the effectiveness of CBT in the treatment of anxiety, depression, and eating disorders in the adult and adolescent populations have been confirmed (Hofmann et al., 2012; Weersing et al., 2017). In the case of acceptance and commitment therapy (ACT), the focus is on the development of strategies for the adolescent to de-center from the experience of stigma and instead focus on actions that are more closely aligned with personal values rather than the experience of distressing thoughts. In the case of obesity-related stigma in the adult population, Lillis et al. (2010) have shown the effectiveness of ACT in reducing WBI and enhancing adaptive coping strategies. Mindfulness-based interventions such as yoga and pranayama offer a culturally sensitive therapeutic approach in the Indian context, in that such interventions are already a part of the Indian education system in schools and the culture of Indian families (Misra & Khurana, 2011). In support of the therapeutic value of mindfulness-based interventions in the management of stress and depression in the adult population, Khoury et al. (2015) have confirmed the effectiveness of mindfulness-based stress reduction in enhancing coping strategies in the management of stress and depression. In the case of the adolescent population,Zoogman et al. (2015) have shown the positive impact of mindfulness interventions on the management of psychological symptoms in the adolescent population. In the Indian context, the focus on the cultural heritage of the Indian people in the practice of yoga rather than the more stigmatizing experience of exercise makes the experience of the therapeutic value of the intervention less likely in the Indian school context (Nayar, 2019).

Group-based interventions add to coping by developing a sense of solidarity, where teens understand that secrecy and shame are universal experiences.Eisenberg et al. (2003) identified that group support reduced maladaptive eating behaviors. There is evidence of a structured peer support intervention that reduced humor-masking and social withdrawal behaviors.

8.6.2 School-based strategies

Schools are a significant factor in how people cope with things in a big way. School-based strategies are not extras, but they are the main strategies for helping teens learn how to deal with things on a large scale.

Antibullying policies that explicitly mention weight-based harassment help in reducing stigma exposure. It is a signal that schools are intolerant of body-based discrimination. Quick et al. (2013) and Pont et al. (2017) identified that antibullying policies that explicitly mention weight-based harassment reduce stigma exposure. Most Indian schools prohibit ragging, but they do not protect against weight stigma. Therefore, including antiweight stigma clauses in school handbooks would be a significant change in schools.

Teacher training in stigma-free communication models is a respect-based strategy that reduces hurtful language. Pont et al. (2017) identified that teacher training in weight stigma reduced stigmatizing events and improved student engagement in different national contexts. Teacher training in stigma-free communication models was conducted in Kerala, resulting in higher student participation rates (Nayar, 2019).

Inclusive physical activity programs that emphasize participation over performance develop adaptive coping strategies. These strategies minimize avoidance behaviors. Participating in participation-oriented physical activity is associated with improved body image and coping skills (Daniels & Leaper, 2006). Physical activity is more inclusive in Indian schools than in developed countries, where yoga and dance are more inclusive than sports.

Expanding the repertoire of coping strategies is possible through confidential counseling support in schools. In India, access to school counselors is concentrated in private schools; the structural imperative is to extend affordable counseling support in government schools (Westbury et al., 2023).

Peer mentoring arrangements normalize coping and build solidarity. Peer mentoring circles that act as a safe space for teens to practice how to cope with stigmatizing interactions have shown positive outcomes for coping (Eisenberg et al., 2003; Due et al., 2005).

8.6.3 Family and community engagement

The family is considered the most salient context for adolescent socialization in collectivist cultural settings. Repetti, Taylor & Seeman (2002) define family as a protective or hazardous context depending on family communication patterns and behavioral modeling. For obese teens, a family can exacerbate their stigmatization or help them cope with it.

Interventions that target parents can improve their skills in not stigmatizing and in using positive and supportive talk. Fulkerson et al. (2007) found that teens who experienced positive health communication from their parents showed reduced emotional eating and increased regularity of physical activity. Workshops for parents that improve their skills in not stigmatizing and in using positive and supportive talk can change how a family copes with challenges. From "You are lazy," a family can change to "Let's walk together after dinner," making health a family affair rather than a personal failing.

Community organizations can help teens cope by providing environments that value skill and body type overweight and beauty. In South India, teens join dance and theater clubs where skill and talent are more valued than their weight and beauty. Religious and spiritual environments can be sources of additional coping mechanisms. Teens can identify religious and spiritual practices as coping mechanisms. For example, prayer is a coping mechanism for teens. Yoga is a spiritual practice that helps teens cope and build strength and resilience without relying on the negative body image and body consciousness that gym culture promotes (Nayar, 2019). Working with religious and spiritual communities to emphasize compassion, health, and strength and resilience, and at the same time making it clear that obesity is a complex condition and not a moral failing, can be a good strategy for getting interventions to communities that are not well served by formal health systems.

8.6.4 Operationalizing coping: from theory to daily tactics

Taxonomies of coping strategies from theory need to be translated into specific, reproducible behaviors. Using CBT and ACT in daily life makes coping an automatic response.

Problem-focused coping tactics

Ally mapping: Choose one friend, one school adult, and one family member to call in case of stigma. Prepare an introductory sentence to use.

Micro-movement planning: Choose an activity like going for a walk in the evenings for 10 minutes. Frame it in terms of how it affects your mood, not your weight.

Boundary scripts: Prepare phrases such as “Please talk to me about my health in private“ or “Let's talk about my skills, not my size“ in your local language.

Home choice architecture: Change your plates, put fruit in an eye-level basket, and set an agreement with your family not to comment on bodies at the table.

Emotion-focused coping tactics

Reframing micro-drills: Change “I'm lazy“ to “Today was hard. Tomorrow is another day. I'll take one step forward.“

Breath-anchored resets: Use breathing exercises such as 4–7–8 breathing or pranayama for three rounds before and after exams or stigma-rich social events.

Values journaling: Write three sentences each night about acts done for kindness, courage, and learning. Distinguish between body size and self-worth.

Compassion letters: Write to yourself as you'd write to your best friend immediately after being teased.

Avoidant coping substitutions

Replace “skip physical education“ with “negotiate an alternative“ such as badminton wall practice or walking laps with a peer.

Replace “eat in secrecy“ with “planned snack alongside a text to a trusted ally“.

Replace “doom-scroll at night“ with “20 minutes offline: draw, clean, call a relative, then make a choice to go back online“.

8.6.5 Stressors, appraisals, and intervention map

The table below shows common stress situations faced by adolescents with obesity, how they tend to interpret them, and the coping responses that follow. It also highlights simple skills and supportive changes in the environment that can help them respond in healthier ways (Table 8.4).

8.6.6 Case vignettes: coping in Indian context

Vignette 1: The school year of Anjali in Kolkata

Anjali is a 14-year-old student in a government-aided school. In August, her friends tease her on sports day. She fakes an illness to avoid running. In October, her relatives comment on her weight gain. She does not attend any other family gatherings. In January, her teacher goes to a workshop on coping. In this workshop, she introduces a PE lesson where students can do whatever they like. Anjali chooses to walk laps with a friend. When boys tease her, she uses an interrupt

TABLE 8.4 Stressors, appraisals, and coping–intervention mapping in adolescent obesity.

Stressor	Typical appraisal	Maladaptive coping	Adaptive micro-skills	Context lever
Peer teasing in PE	I cannot face this; everyone will laugh	Skipping PE; eating in secrecy	Boundary-setting scripts; negotiating alternative activities; support from a peer ally	Teacher-led interruption strategies; choice-based physical Education activities; peer buddy systems
Family marriageability remarks	My body brings shame to my family	Withdrawal from family events; secretive eating	Cognitive reframing; values-based journaling; establishing no-shame family rules	Parent-focused workshops; use of culturally relevant practices (e.g., yoga) as supportive anchors
Teacher discipline remarks	I am lazy; I will never be accepted	Humor as deflection; aggression; avoidance	Peer support mapping; self-compassion exercises; small, achievable movement goals	Staff training; private feedback norms; antiharassment policies
Clinic dismissal by doctors	Healthcare providers will not help me; my health is not valued	Avoidance of healthcare; reliance on unverified online content	Structured agenda-setting; follow-up reminders; mood and sleep tracking	Private weighing practices; distress screening; collaborative care planning
Social media comparison (e.g., Instagram)	Others look ideal; I am inadequate in comparison	Excessive social media use; binge eating	Critical media review; following body-positive content; scheduling offline activities	Media literacy programs; school-level digital use guidelines

Lazarus, R. S., & Folkman, S. (1984). Stress, appraisal, and coping. Springer Publishing Company.

script. In March, she goes to a clinic where she is weighed privately, and they make an agenda together. This is her first time talking about her headaches. By July, she has not lost a lot of weight. However, she has learned new ways to cope with her problems. These include ally mapping, cognitive reframing, and compassion journaling. Depression scores go down. More kids go to school.

Vignette 2: Ravi in the competitive coaching hostel

Ravi's friends make fun of him every day because he is not disciplined. He is only 16 years old. He uses humor to get out of things. He also eats a lot of packaged foods at night. A tutor makes a connection between how well he does on a test and the size of his body. He goes to a gym and overexercises, which is bad for him. A counselor introduces values journaling and ally mapping. There is a code of conduct at this coaching center that states no harassment is allowed. A gym teacher changes the objective of low-level circuits to get better at the activity rather than look better. Ravi stops eating in secret after two months. He also does short physical exercises to help him cope with stress while he is taking a test. This helps him go from learned helplessness to being able to do something on his own.

Vignette 3: The clinic loop

A young girl, aged 13, presents at a clinic for irregular periods and headaches. Her weight is repeatedly described to her as causing all of her problems. She then stops attending the clinic and starts watching videos on how to detox on YouTube. As the clinic uses subtle, nonintrusive methods of measuring her, and sets her goals that are more related to sleep, stress, and headaches than weight, she begins to care about her health. A phone call by a nurse, where normalizing all treatment is a setback, keeps people interested. She continues to attend, and her headaches lessen after three months.

8.6.7 Measuring coping: tools and cultural adaptation

Measurement is a quality that is necessary for a strong field. For the study of adolescent obesity coping in India, it is necessary to develop a good measuring tool that measures what people do when they are stressed, what people believe about themselves, and how people are influenced by their environments (Table 8.5).

Self-report bias, recall bias, and language drift are three important considerations in the development of these inventories. Best practice in developing these inventories involves triangulating with behavioral measures, like PE class attendance or help-seeking behaviors, in addition to qualitative methods. Cognitive interviews with youth in multiple languages are also essential to ensure semantic equivalence in different regional contexts.

TABLE 8.5 Psychosocial assessment tools for coping and weight stigma in adolescents: scope and cultural adaptation in the Indian context.

Tool	What it measures	Indian adaptation needed
Brief COPE (Carver et al., 1989)	Problem-focused, emotion-focused, and avoidant coping strategies	Replace culturally unfamiliar terms (e.g., "venting") with contextually relevant expressions such as *"mann halka karna"*
RSQ Youth (Connor-Smith et al., 2000)	Primary, secondary, and disengagement coping strategies	Useful for assessing flexible coping in uncontrollable stress contexts such as peer teasing; requires contextual framing for Indian school settings
Kidcope (Ayers et al., 1996)	Brief, event-specific coping suitable for school-based screening	Add culturally relevant items such as avoidance of school activities (e.g., skipping physical Education due to fear of teasing)
Weight Bias Internalization Scale (Durso & Latner, 2008)	Degree of internalization of negative weight-related stereotypes	Include culturally specific concerns such as family pressure and marriage-related anxieties linked to body weight
Stigmatizing Situations Inventory (Puhl et al., 2007)	Frequency and context of weight-based mistreatment	Add items reflecting Indian contexts, such as public weighing, marriageability comments, teacher-based discipline, and clinical dismissal

Carver, C. S. (1997). You want to measure coping but your protocol's too long: Consider the Brief COPE. International Journal of Behavioral Medicine, 4(1), 92–100.

8.6.8 Teacher and clinician language guide

The language we use in our daily environment has the greatest direct influence on our environment. The table below indicates harmful language commonly used in different environments, along with the reasons they are harmful and more positive alternatives based on evidence (Table 8.6).

8.6.9 Policy and structural reforms

The importance of coping needs to be incorporated into the Indian health policy and structural frameworks for the health of adolescents. (WHO, 2021) suggests incorporating antistigma interventions into obesity prevention initiatives. Current national-level initiatives like POSHAN Abhiyaan and the Fit India Movement focus only on the quantity of nutrition and physical activity duration without any attention given to stigma, coping, or psychosocial well-being (Misra & Khurana, 2011). If the psychosocial elements of weight management are not incorporated, the initiatives may inadvertently cause more harm by reinforcing the stigma of weight through overemphasizing weight as a measure of behavioral compliance.

Policy reforms required for India
Schools
Ban on public weighing
Incorporating weight harassment in the school handbook
Training teachers on antistigma
Choice of PE
Mini-lessons on coping in life skills
Clinics
Private weighing
Psychological distress screening with two questions
Collaborative agenda-setting
Follow-up phone calls by nurse
Adolescent-friendly clinics
Families
Workshops for parents on language substitution
No-shame mealtime agreements
Balanced and healthy lifestyle modeling
Weekly family check-ins
Community

TABLE 8.6 Harmful communication and supportive alternatives in addressing adolescent obesity across contexts.

Context	Harmful phrase	Why it harms	Supportive alternative
Physical education teacher	You are too heavy to run properly.	Equates body size with incompetence, leading to avoidance of physical activity and negative self-appraisals (Griffiths et al., 2006).	Let us try an activity you enjoy. Stamina can be developed through different types of movement.
Classroom teacher	Your laziness shows in your body and your marks.	Moralizes body size, reinforcing negative self-appraisals and potentially affecting academic performance (Janssen et al., 2004).	Effort in academics and physical health are different skills. Let us work on each step by step.
Clinician	All your problems are because of your weight.	Leads to diagnostic overshadowing and discourages future healthcare engagement (Puhl & Heuer, 2009).	Let us look at sleep, nutrition, and activity together. Weight is only one part of the picture.
Parent	Who is going to marry you if you look like that?	Links body size to family honor and increases weight bias internalization (WBI) (Nayar, 2019).	Your health is about your confidence and well-being, not appearance or social expectations.
Peer bystander	We are only joking; do not be so sensitive.	Normalizes stigma and reinforces WBI (Puhl & Latner, 2007).	We do not speak about bodies like that. Let us change the topic.

Puhl, R. M., & Heuer, C. A. (2009). The stigma of obesity: A review and update. Obesity, 17(5), 941–964.

Mixed-ability activity clubs
Faith community building resiliency through yoga and reflection
Inclusive sports with a teamwork focus
Media
Ad guidelines against body-shaming ads
Body diversity ads in multiple languages
Influencer partnerships for healthy body image
Media literacy in schools

National policy: Incorporate coping indicators into the NFHS survey tools. Revise the Fit India program and the POSHAN Abhiyaan program to include messages that promote a dignity-first approach. Revise the RKSK program to include messages that promote weight stigma reduction and coping skills development.

8.6.10 Monitoring coping: metrics beyond body mass index

Current obesity interventions often assess weight and attendance as primary outcomes. Coping-based interventions need new outcome measures that correlate with future program engagement and psychological well-being, not just changes in body composition (Table 8.7).

These outcome measures address the primary question of whether the adolescent has learned to stay present in valued social and institutional spaces without behavioral constriction. BMI is a valid outcome, but coping capacity, participation engagement, and affective regulation are equally valid and more proximal outcome measures for program success.

8.6.11 Implementation science: scaling what works

Evidence-based interventions are often unsuccessful if not implemented at scale and monitored for fidelity. Implementation science (Fixsen et al., 2005; Damschroder et al., 2009) has provided frameworks for program implementation that preserve critical elements. Scaling up coping interventions for adolescent obesity will require addressing three dimensions: fidelity, which will ensure that active elements of coping interventions are preserved; adaptation, which will require translation of materials and adaptation to accommodate institutional barriers and facilitators across different states and regions in India; and sustainability, which will require integrating coping interventions into existing educational frameworks like NEP 2020; national initiatives like POSHAN Abhiyaan; and clinical guidelines like RKSK to ensure sustainability beyond the project's lifespan.

The process will be implemented through a phased approach by piloting mini-lessons for coping skills in 10 schools in one state and assessing frequency and efficacy of secrecy episodes and boundaries as primary outcome measures; adapting

TABLE 8.7 Monitoring indicators for coping improvement and behavioral change in adolescent obesity interventions.

Metric	Definition	Target benchmark
Coping repertoire index	Number of coping strategies a student can enact across different coping families	Three or more coping strategies across different families
Boundary efficacy score	Self-rated confidence in enacting boundary-setting behaviors in school and home contexts (0–10 scale)	Seven or higher after a 12-week program
Secrecy episode frequency	Self-reported number of days per week the individual eats alone to avoid comments or criticism	Reduction by 50% from baseline
Mood–movement linkage	Number of days per week the individual uses physical movement intentionally to regulate mood	Three or more days per week
Clinic re-engagement rate	Proportion of kept appointments following previously invalidating healthcare experiences	80% retention at six months
Exposure with support	Number of previously avoided social situations attended with support from a peer or ally	Two or more contexts per month

Compas, B. E., Connor-Smith, J. K., Saltzman, H., Thomsen, A. H., & Wadsworth, M. E. (2001). Coping with stress during childhood and adolescence: Problems, progress, and potential in theory and research. Psychological Bulletin, 127(1), 87–127.

TABLE 8.8 Strategic roadmap for addressing coping and weight stigma in adolescents in India (2025–30).

Year	Activity/milestone
2025	Develop India-specific coping and weight-based internalization scales; Pilot teacher training programs in five states; Launch digital media literacy initiatives in urban schools
2026	Integrate coping skills lessons into the CBSE life skills curriculum; Roll out adolescent-friendly clinic accreditation in three states
2027	Partner with social media influencers to promote body positivity in regional languages; Introduce coping indicators into NFHS surveys
2028	Implement intersectional programs targeting Dalit, LGBTQ+, and disabled adolescents across all states; Evaluate stigma reduction outcomes under Fit India and POSHAN Abhiyaan
2030	Achieve nationwide certification of government schools as stigma-free zones; Ensure universal adolescent access to trained teachers, school counselors, and community-based support groups

Ministry of Health and Family Welfare (2017). National Health Policy 2017.

the curriculum to regional languages like Hindi, Tamil, Bengali, and others; and finally integrating it into the national life skills program under NEP 2020.

8.6.12 Toward 2030: a vision for embedded coping

The adolescent health infrastructure in India is at a critical juncture. With rising obesity and weight stigma, coping skills will need to be taken from a peripheral concern to a core component of adolescent health policy and practice. A table below proposes a set of milestones for integrating coping skills into India's adolescent health infrastructure (Table 8.8).

8.7 Conclusion

Adolescent obesity has biological and metabolic determinants, as well as the social environment in which adolescents develop their identity, a sense of belonging, and self-esteem. Coping mechanisms are the link between the social environment in which adolescents experience weight stigma and the psychological outcomes of that stigma. Adolescents can significantly mitigate the negative consequences of weight stigma by learning effective coping mechanisms against stress in a healthy manner, with the support of their families, schools, and health systems, even if they do not lose a great amount of weight.

In the case of India, where collectivist family structures, academic achievement cultures, gendered scripts of marriageability, and caste and class status exacerbate the stigma, the interventions should be culturally-based rather than imposing Western culture. The quantitative outcomes of the present study indicate that adaptive coping can be achieved in the Indian social context in which the family, education system, health services, and community organizations work together to alleviate the stigma and increase the number of supportive responses that are accessible to the adolescents. The theoretical frameworks that were reviewed in the present chapter, namely the transactional model, resilience theory, and WBI, provide a robust evidence base for the development of multilevel interventions that address cognitive and contextual aspects of coping.

For this progress to continue, however, policy changes at the national level are necessary. Coping education must be incorporated within NEP 2020, POSHAN Abhiyaan, and RKSK. Measurement tools specific to India and longitudinal studies that can track coping behaviors over time from early adolescence to adulthood must also be developed. This chapter's vision for 2030 also offers us a plan for how we can make this change.

8.8 Limitations

There are several limitations that must be considered when reviewing the evidence that this chapter has reviewed and the results that this chapter has found. First and foremost, this study is conducted in Kolkata, which is an urban metropolitan city that may not reflect the diverse experiences that adolescents are having across rural, semiurban, and smaller urban Indian communities. Second, because this is a quantitative study that also used cross-sectional elements within its methodology, we cannot say that we have caused any of the results that we found. While we can say that there is a correlation between coping styles and psychological outcomes, we cannot say that one causes the other. Third, while this chapter has reviewed studies conducted across the globe, they were conducted using vastly different sample sizes, tools, and cultural influences. Therefore, we cannot make any sweeping conclusions about studies conducted outside of India. Fourth, while this chapter has reviewed several therapeutic interventions that could potentially help adolescents cope with stressors that they are dealing with, ACT (Lillis et al., 2010) and mindfulness interventions (Khoury et al., 2015) have been conducted primarily on adults with obesity and need to be conducted on adolescents. Fifth and finally, this chapter's recommendations and the vision that we have for 2030 are normative and aspirational.

Key takeaways

Coping acts as a crucial link between weight stigma and psychological outcomes in adolescents with obesity.

1. Avoidant coping, such as secrecy, emotional eating, and withdrawal, is the most common and harmful pattern associated with obesity.
2. Coping strategies vary by age and gender, with obese female young adults showing lower adaptive coping and greater vulnerability.
3. In the Indian context, coping is shaped by family expectations, academic pressure, gender norms, and sociocultural structures.
4. Adaptive coping, including social support, reframing, and participation-based physical activity, improves psychological well-being and engagement.

Effective intervention requires multilevel action involving schools, families, healthcare systems, and policy frameworks, not just individual behavior change.

Glossary

Term	Definition
Adaptive coping	Strategies that directly address the stressor or emotion in ways that support long-term health, engagement, and dignity.
Avoidant coping	Strategies such as denial, secrecy, and avoidance of people that temporarily reduce the stressor but contribute to long-term damage to mental and physical health.
CBT	A structured approach to psychology that aims to correct inaccurate thinking and maladaptive behavior through cognitive restructuring and behavioral experimentation.
Emotional eating	Eating in response to stress, anxiety, or other emotional changes rather than physiological hunger; a maladaptive emotion regulation strategy.
Maladaptive coping	Strategies that temporarily relieve stress but ultimately damage mental health outcomes and social and health trajectories.
Primary appraisal	The first stage of the transactional model of stress and coping in which individuals evaluate a stressor as a threat, challenge, or inconsequential to their well-being.
Resilience	The ability to achieve adequate outcomes in the face of significant adversity, supported by protective relationships, self-beliefs, cultural resources, and systemic support.
Secondary appraisal	The second stage of the transactional model of stress and coping in which individuals evaluate available coping options and their likely effectiveness.
Transactional model	Lazarus & Folkman's (1984) model, in which stress arises from the interaction between the individual and the environment, moderated by subjective perception and coping ability.
WBI	The internalization of negative societal stereotypes about obesity, where individuals apply these beliefs to themselves, leads to a negative self-identity, concealment, and avoidant coping.

Lazarus, R. S., & Folkman, S. (1984). Stress, appraisal, and coping. Springer Publishing Company.

Review questions

1. What were the most commonly observed coping styles in this research on Indian adolescents with obesity, and how do they compare to those identified in global research?
2. In what ways do unhealthy coping styles, such as secrecy and emotional eating, contribute to the maintenance of obesity and mental health problems in adolescents, and how does WBI mediate this relationship?
3. In what ways can schools in India be modified from being sites for stigmatization to sites for building coping in adolescents with obesity? Provide three specific changes and evidence for each.
4. In what ways is it critical for family members to be involved in building effective coping in adolescents with obesity? What is the role of the no-shame mealtime agreement, and what evidence supports its effectiveness?
5. In what ways can structural changes in the health system, schools, and media environments be implemented to ensure that coping is integrated into national strategies for adolescents in India by 2030?

6. In what ways do gender roles in India influence the nature of coping in teenage girls versus teenage boys with obesity? What types of interventions for each group have the best evidence base?
7. What is WBI, and why is it critical to assess and address in adolescents in India in addition to BMI? How do primary and secondary appraisals contribute to WBI?
8. Can you explain the difference between primary and secondary appraisals in Lazarus and Folkman's model of coping with stress? In what ways do each of these stages offer opportunities for intervention in schools and in therapy settings?
9. How does Anna Freud's defense mechanisms theory relate to the avoidant coping mechanisms that were found among adolescents with obesity in India? Provide two examples of coping mechanisms that were used by adolescents with obesity in India. Describe which defense mechanism is closely related to which of these coping mechanisms.
10. Compare and contrast CBT and ACT as interventions that can be used to help adolescents with obesity. When is CBT more appropriate than ACT, and vice versa? What is the evidence base for both interventions among adolescents with obesity?
11. What does Bronfenbrenner's ecological systems theory contribute to understanding why individually focused coping interventions have been unsuccessful among adolescents with obesity in India? Provide one intervention target at each of three ecological levels that were described in the chapter.
12. How does conservation of resources theory explain the coping mechanisms that were used by low-income Indian adolescents with obesity? What kinds of structural changes would need to occur to enhance their coping resources?
13. Evaluate critically the use of yoga and pranayama as coping interventions among Indian adolescents with obesity. What are the evidence-based benefits of using yoga and pranayama to cope with obesity? What are the cultural advantages of using yoga and pranayama to cope with obesity? What are the potential risks of using yoga and pranayama to cope with obesity?
14. What does it mean that coping is "ecologically rationed?" How does this relate to individually focused coping skill training programs? What kinds of structural conditions must be met in order for individually focused coping skill training programs to be effective?
15. By using the stressor-appraisal-intervention map in section 8.5.7, trace the whole coping process for an adolescent who is frequently disciplined by teachers. What is the appraisal, maladaptive coping response, adaptive micro skill, and institutional context lever that is needed?
16. What measurement tools are available to measure coping skills and WBI in Indian youth, and what specific changes are required to make them culture-specific? Why is cognitive interviewing an essential part of the adaptation process?
17. Assess the proposed roadmap to embed coping skills education in India by the year 2030. Which milestone do you think is more feasible in the present context, and which milestone do you think poses more barriers to implementation? Justify your answer with at least two national programs mentioned in the chapter.
18. What relevance does the concept of learned helplessness (Seligman, 1975) have to the life situation of adolescents with obesity in India, where they are repeatedly victimized in school and medical settings? What intervention techniques are proposed in the chapter to help these youth develop mastery again?
19. The chapter describes social media as a "double-edged instrument." Drawing on social comparison theory (Festinger, 1954) and the findings presented in the chapter, discuss the detrimental as well as beneficial ways in which social media impacts coping skills in adolescents with obesity.
20. Discuss the interplay between caste, class, and weight stigma in the context of India, with particular relevance to adolescents with obesity. What are the implications for coping skills interventions in this context, and what are the key considerations in designing interventions for these youth in India?

AI disclosure

During the preparation of this work the author(s) used ChatGPT in order to Used only for language editing and grammar correction. After using this tool/service, the author(s) reviewed and edited the content as needed and take(s) full responsibility for the content of the publication.

References

Aldwin, C. M. (2007). *Stress, coping, and development: An integrative perspective* (2nd ed.). Guilford Press.

Ayers, T. S., Sandler, I. N., West, S. G., & Roosa, M. W. (1996). A dispositional and situational assessment of children's coping: Testing alternative models of coping. *Journal of Personality, 64*(4), 923–958. https://doi.org/10.1111/j.1467-6494.1996.tb00950.x.

Bandura, A. (1997). *Self-efficacy: The exercise of control*. Freeman.

Beck, A. T. (1976). *Cognitive therapy and the emotional disorders*. International Universities Press.

Bronfenbrenner, U. (1979). *The ecology of human development: Experiments by nature and design*. Harvard University Press.

Cannon, W. B. (1932). The wisdom of the body. *Norton*.

Carver, C. S., Scheier, M. F., & Weintraub, J. K. (1989). Assessing coping strategies: A theoretically based approach. *Journal of Personality and Social Psychology, 56*(2), 267–283. https://doi.org/10.1037/0022-3514.56.2.267.

Chen, G., Guo, G., Gong, J., & Jing, J. (2019). Influence of social media on body dissatisfaction among Chinese adolescents. *International Journal of Environmental Research and Public Health, 16*(21), 4145.

Cohen, S., & Wills, T. A. (1985). Stress, social support, and the buffering hypothesis. *Psychological Bulletin, 98*(2), 310–357. https://doi.org/10.1037/0033-2909.98.2.310.

Compas, B. E., Connor-Smith, J. K., Saltzman, H., Thomsen, A. H., & Wadsworth, M. E. (2001). Coping with stress during childhood and adolescence: Problems, progress, and potential in theory and research. *Psychological Bulletin, 127*(1), 87–127. https://doi.org/10.1037/0033-2909.127.1.87.

Conde, W. L., & Borges, C. (2011). The risk of incidence and persistence of obesity among Brazilian adolescents. *Revista Brasileira de Epidemiologia, 14*(1), 67–76.

Connor-Smith, J. K., Compas, B. E., Wadsworth, M. E., Thomsen, A. H., & Saltzman, H. (2000). Responses to stress in adolescence: Measurement of coping and involuntary stress responses. *Journal of Consulting and Clinical Psychology, 68*(6), 976–992.

Crenshaw, K. (1989). Demarginalizing the intersection of race and sex. *University of Chicago Legal Forum, 1989*(1), 139–167.

Crosnoe, R. (2007). Gender, obesity, and education. *Sociology of Education, 80*(3), 241–260. https://doi.org/10.1177/003804070708000303.

Currie, C., Zanotti, C., Morgan, A., et al. (Eds.). (2012). Social determinants of health and well-being among young people. WHO Regional Office for Europe.

Damschroder, L. J., Aron, D. C., Keith, R. E., et al. (2009). Fostering implementation of health services research findings into practice. *Implementation Science, 4*(1), 50. https://doi.org/10.1186/1748-5908-4-50.

Danese, A., & McEwen, B. S. (2012). Adverse childhood experiences and disease. *Physiology & Behavior, 106*(1), 29–39.

Daniels, E., & Leaper, C. (2006). Sport participation and self-esteem. *Sex Roles, 55*(11–12), 875–880.

Daniels, S. R., Arnett, D. K., Eckel, R. H., et al. (2005). Overweight in children and adolescents. *Circulation, 111*(15), 1999–2012.

Dietz, W. H. (1998). Health consequences of obesity in youth. *Pediatrics, 101*, 518–525.

Due, P., Holstein, B. E., Lynch, J., et al. (2005). Bullying and symptoms among school-aged children. *European Journal of Public Health, 15*(2), 128–132.

Durso, L. E., & Latner, J. D. (2008). Weight Bias Internalization Scale. *Obesity, 16*(S2), S80–S86.

Eisenberg, M. E., Neumark-Sztainer, D., & Story, M. (2003). Associations of weight-based teasing and emotional well-being among adolescents. *Archives of Pediatrics and Adolescent Medicine, 157*(8), 733–738. https://doi.org/10.1001/archpedi.157.8.733 United States.

Ellis, A. (1994). *Reason and emotion in psychotherapy*. Birch Lane Press.

Faith, M. S., Matz, P. E., & Jorge, M. A. (2002). Obesity–depression associations. *Journal of Psychosomatic Research, 53*(4), 935–942. https://doi.org/10.1016/S0022-3999(02)00308-2.

Fardouly, J., Diedrichs, P. C., Vartanian, L. R., & Halliwell, E. (2015). Social comparisons on social media: The impact of Facebook on young women's body image concerns and mood. In *Body Image*, *13*, Australia: Elsevier Ltd, 38–45. http://doi.org/10.1016/j.bodyim.2014.12.002.

Festinger, L. (1954). A Theory of Social Comparison Processes. In *Human Relations*, *7*, SAGE Publications, 117–140. http://doi.org/10.1177/001872675400700202.

Field, A. E., Camargo, C. A., Taylor, C. B., et al. (2001). Media and peer influences. *Pediatrics, 107*(1), 54–60. https://doi.org/10.1542/peds.107.1.54.

Fixsen, D.L., Naoom, S.F., Blase, K.A., et al. (2005). *Implementation research: A synthesis of the literature*. University of South Florida, Louis de la Parte Florida Mental Health Institute, National Implementation Research Network.

Folkman, S., & Lazarus, R. S. (1988). Coping as mediator of emotion. *Journal of Personality and Social Psychology, 54*(3), 466–475. https://doi.org/10.1037/0022-3514.54.3.466.

Fredrickson, B. L., & Roberts, T. A. (1997). Objectification theory. *Psychology of Women Quarterly, 21*(2), 173–206. https://doi.org/10.1111/j.1471-6402.1997.tb00108.x.

Freire, P. (1970). *Pedagogy of the oppressed*.

Frydenberg, E., & Lewis, R. (1993). Boys play sport and girls turn to others: Age, gender and ethnicity as determinants of coping. In *Journal of Adolescence*, *16*, Elsevier BV, 253–266. http://doi.org/10.1006/jado.1993.1024.

Fulkerson, J. A., Story, M., Mellin, A., et al. (2007). Family meals and adolescent development. *Journal of Adolescent Health, 40*(4), 344–351.

Goldfield, G. S., Moore, C., Henderson, K., et al. (2010). Weight-based teasing and adjustment. *Paediatrics & Child Health, 15*(5), 283–288. https://doi.org/10.1093/pch/15.5.283.

Griffiths, L. J., Parsons, T. J., & Hill, A. J. (2006). Self-esteem in obese children. *International Journal of Pediatric Obesity, 1*(1), 23–32.

Grogan, S. (2016). *Body image: Understanding body dissatisfaction in men, women and children, third edition, Body Image: Understanding Body Dissatisfaction in Men, Women and Children, Third Edition*. United Kingdom: Taylor and Francis, pp. 1–214. doi: 10.4324/9781315681528.

Harter, S. (1999). *The construction of the self*.

Hayden-Wade, H. A., Stein, R. I., Ghaderi, A., et al. (2005). Teasing among overweight children. *Obesity Research, 13*(8), 1381–1392. https://doi.org/10.1038/oby.2005.167.

Hilbert, A., Braehler, E., Haeuser, W., & Zenger, M. (2014). Weight bias internalization. *Obesity, 22*(1), 79–85. http://doi.org/10.1002/oby.20561.

Hobfoll, S. E. (1989). Conservation of resources theory. *American Psychologist, 44*(3), 513–524. https://doi.org/10.1037/0003-066X.44.3.513.

Hofmann, S. G., Asnaani, A., Vonk, I. J., et al. (2012). CBT meta-analysis. *Cognitive Therapy and Research, 36*(5), 427–440. https://doi.org/10.1007/s10608-012-9476-1.

Holland, G., & Tiggemann, M. (2016). Social networking and. *Body Image, 17*, 100–110. https://doi.org/10.1016/j.bodyim.2016.02.008.

Hunger, J. M., Major, B., Blodorn, A., & Miller, C. T. (2015). Weight stigma effects. *Social and Personality Psychology Compass, 9*(6), 255–268. https://doi.org/10.1111/spc3.12172.

IIPS & ICF. (2021). *National Family Health Survey (NFHS-5), 2019–21: India*. International Institute for Population Sciences.

Inchley, J., Currie, D., Budisavljevic, S., et al. (2020). *Spotlight on adolescent health and well-being: Findings from the 2017/2018 Health Behaviour in School-aged Children (HBSC) survey in Europe and Canada*. WHO Regional Office for Europe.

Jambholkar, P. C., Joshi, A., & Choudhari, S. G. (2024). Childhood obesity in India. *Cureus, 16*(3), e56257. https://doi.org/10.7759/cureus.56257.

Janssen, I., Craig, W. M., Boyce, W. F., & Pickett, W. (2004). Obesity and bullying. *Pediatrics, 113*(5), 1187–1194. https://doi.org/10.1542/peds.113.5.1187.

Jimenez-Cruz, A., Bacardi-Gascon, M., Pichardo-Osuna, A., Mandujano-Trujillo, Z., & Castillo-Ruiz, O. (2010). Infant and toddlers' feeding practices and obesity amongst low-income families in México. *Asia Pacific Journal of Clinical Nutrition, 19*(3), 341–346. Available at http://apjcn.nhri.org.tw/server/APJCN/Volume19/vol19.3/Finished/4_1702_316-323.pdf.

Khader, Y., & Madise, N. (2010). Overweight and obesity in sub-Saharan Africa. *Perspectives in Public Health, 130*(2), 64–65.

Khanna, T., Banerjee, B., Majhi, M. M., & Futela, D. (2023). Depression, sleep, body image, and lifestyle among school-going adolescents in Delhi NCR. *Indian Journal of Psychiatry, 65*(8), 825–831. https://doi.org/10.4103/indianjpsychiatry.indianjpsychiatry_916_22.

Khoury, B., Sharma, M., Rush, S. E., & Fournier, C. (2015). Mindfulness-based stress reduction for healthy individuals: A meta-analysis. *Journal of Psychosomatic Research, 78*(6), 519–528. https://doi.org/10.1016/j.jpsychores.2015.03.009.

Kimani-Murage, E. W. (2013). Exploring the paradox: Double burden of malnutrition in rural South Africa. *Global Health Action, 6*(1), 19249. https://doi.org/10.3402/gha.v6i0.19249.

Latner, J. D., & Schwartz, M. B. (2005). Weight bias in a child's world. In K. D. Brownell, R. M. Puhl, M. B. Schwartz, & L. Rudd (Eds.). *Weight bias: Nature, consequences, and remedies* (pp. 54–67). Guilford Press.

Latner, J. D., & Stunkard, A. J. (2003). Getting worse: The stigmatization of obese children. *Obesity Research, 11*(3), 452–456. https://doi.org/10.1038/oby.2003.61.

Lazarus, R. S., & Folkman, S. (1984). *Stress, appraisal, and coping*. Springer.

Leary, M. R., Tambor, E. S., Terdal, S. K., & Downs, D. L. (1995). Self-esteem as an interpersonal monitor: The sociometer hypothesis. *Journal of Personality and Social Psychology, 68*(3), 518–530.

Lillis, J., Hayes, S. C., Bunting, K., & Masuda, A. (2010). Teaching acceptance and mindfulness to improve the lives of the obese. *Annals of Behavioral Medicine, 39*(1), 58–69.

Luthar, S. S., Cicchetti, D., & Becker, B. (2000). The construct of resilience. *Child Development, 71*(3), 543–562.

Masten, A. S. (2001). Ordinary magic: Resilience processes in development. *American Psychologist, 56*(3), 227–238. https://doi.org/10.1037/0003-066X.56.3.227.

McEwen, B. S. (1998). Stress, adaptation, and disease. *New England Journal of Medicine, 338*(3), 171–179.

Misra, A., & Khurana, L. (2011). Obesity-related diseases in South Asians. *International Journal of Obesity, 35*(2), 167–187.

Moradi, B., & Huang, Y. P. (2008). Objectification theory advances. *Psychology of Women Quarterly, 32*(4), 377–398.

Nayar, K. E. (2019). *Body, identity, and adolescent health in contemporary India*. Sage Publications India.

Neumark-Sztainer, D., Falkner, N., Story, M., Perry, C., Hannan, P. J., & Mulert, S. (2002). Weight-teasing among adolescents. *International Journal of Obesity, 26*(1), 123–131. https://doi.org/10.1038/sj.ijo.0801853.

Ng, M., Fleming, T., Robinson, M., et al. (2014). Global prevalence of obesity. *Lancet, 384*(9945), 766–781.

Nielsen, L., Allerup, P., & Brinkkær, U. (2010). *Beyond the obvious: Bullying and social context*. Danish School of Education Press.

Pearl, R. L., & Puhl, R. M. (2014). Weight bias internalization scale. *Body Image, 11*(1), 89–92.

Pearl, R. L., Wadden, T. A., Hopkins, C. M., et al. (2018). Weight bias internalization and metabolic syndrome. *Obesity, 25*(2), 317–322.

Perloff, R. M. (2014). Social media and body image concerns. *Sex Roles, 71*(11–12), 363–377.

Pont, S. J., Puhl, R., Cook, S. R., & Slusser, W. (2017). Stigma in children with obesity. *Pediatrics, 140*(6), e20173034.

Popkin, B. M. (2015). Nutrition transition and diabetes epidemic. *Current Diabetes Reports, 15*(9), 64.

Puhl, R. M., & Heuer, C. A. (2009). Obesity stigma review. *Obesity, 17*(5), 941–964. https://doi.org/10.1038/oby.2008.636.

Puhl, R. M., & Latner, J. D. (2007). Stigma and children's health. *Psychological Bulletin, 133*(4), 557–580.

Puhl, R. M., Moss-Racusin, C. A., Schwartz, M. B., & Brownell, K. D. (2007). Weight stigmatization perspectives. *Health Education Research, 23*(2), 347–358.

Quick, V., McWilliams, R., & Byrd-Bredbenner, C. (2013). Weight teasing and eating. *American Journal of Public Health, 103*(3), 508–515.

Rao, K. (2002). *Consciousness studies: Cross-cultural perspectives*. McFarland.

Rao, K., Subbakrishna, D. K., & Prabhu, G. G. (1999). Coping checklist. *NIMHANS Journal, 17*(2), 138–144.

Reilly, J. J., & Kelly, J. (2011). Long-term impact of childhood obesity. *International Journal of Obesity, 35*(7), 891–898.

Reinehr, T. (2013). Lifestyle intervention in childhood obesity. *Nature Reviews Endocrinology, 9*(10), 607–614.

Repetti, R. L., Taylor, S. E., & Seeman, T. E. (2002). Risky families. *Psychological Bulletin, 128*(2), 330–366.

Ricciardelli, L. A., & McCabe, M. P. (2004). Disordered eating model. *Psychological Bulletin, 130*(2), 179–205.

Rodgers, R. F., Slater, A., Gordon, C. S., et al. (2020). Social media and body image. *Journal of Youth and Adolescence, 49*(2), 399–409.
Rutter, M. (1987). Resilience mechanisms. *American Journal of Orthopsychiatry, 57*(3), 316–331.
Saraswati, S. S. (1981). Yoga nidra (5th ed.). Bihar School of Yoga.
Sawyer, S. M., Afifi, R. A., Bearinger, L. H., et al. (2012). Adolescence and health. *Lancet, 379*(9826), 1630–1640.
Scheier, M. F., & Carver, C. S. (1992). Optimism and well-being. *Cognitive Therapy and Research, 16*(2), 201–228.
Seiffge-Krenke, I. (2011). Coping with relationship stressors. *Journal of Research on Adolescence, 21*(1), 196–210.
Seligman, M. E. P. (1975). *Helplessness*. Freeman.
Selye, H. (1956). *The stress of life*. McGraw-Hill.
Skinner, E. A., Edge, K., Altman, J., & Sherwood, H. (2003). Structure of coping. *Psychological Bulletin, 129*(2), 216–269.
Stice, E., Shaw, H., & Marti, C. N. (2006). Obesity prevention programs. *Psychological Bulletin, 132*(5), 667–691.
Swinburn, B. A., Kraak, V. I., Allender, S., et al. (2019). The global syndemic of obesity, undernutrition, and climate change: The lancet commission report. In *The Lancet*, *393*, New Zealand: Lancet Publishing Group, 791–846 doi: 10.1016/S0140-6736(18)32822-8.
Tani, Y., Fujiwara, T., Ochi, M., et al. (2015). Eating patterns in adolescents. *Journal of Epidemiology, 25*(7), 476–483.
Thoits, P. A. (1995). Stress, coping, and social support processes: Where are we? What next? *Journal of Health and Social Behavior,* 53–79 undefined, Spec No.
Tiggemann, M., & Slater, A. (2013). NetGirls: The Internet, Facebook, and body image concern in adolescent girls. In *International Journal of Eating Disorders*, *46*, Wiley, 630–633. http://doi.org/10.1002/eat.22141.
Tiggemann, M. (2011). Sociocultural perspectives on human appearance and body image. In T. F. Cash, & L. Smolak (Eds.). *Body image: A handbook of science, practice, and prevention* (pp. 12–19). Guilford Press.
Uchino, B. N. (2006). Social support and health: A review of physiological processes potentially underlying links to disease outcomes. *Journal of Behavioral Medicine, 29*(4), 377–387. https://doi.org/10.1007/s10865-006-9056-5 United States.
Ungar, M. (2011). The social ecology of resilience: Addressing contextual and cultural ambiguity of a nascent construct. In *American Journal of Orthopsychiatry*, *81*, American Psychological Association (APA), 1–17. http://doi.org/10.1111/j.1939-0025.2010.01067.x.
Warnick, J. L., Darling, K. E., West, C. E., & Jelalian, E. (2022). Weight stigma and mental health. *Journal of Pediatric Psychology, 47*(4), 417–435.
Weersing, V. R., Jeffreys, M., Do, M. T., et al. (2017). Evidence base update of psychosocial treatments for child and adolescent depression. *Journal of Clinical Child and Adolescent Psychology, 46*(1), 11–43. https://doi.org/10.1080/15374416.2016.1220310 United States: Routledge.
Wentzel, K. R. (1998). Social relationships and motivation in middle school: The role of parents, teachers, and peers. In *Journal of Educational Psychology*, *90*, United States: American Psychological Association Inc, 202–209. http://doi.org/10.1037/0022-0663.90.2.202.
Werner, E. E., & Smith, R. S. (1992). *Overcoming the odds: High-risk children from birth to adulthood.* Cornell University Press.
Westbury, S., Oyebode, O., van Rens, T., & Barber, T. M. (2023). Obesity stigma: Causes, consequences, and potential solutions. In *Current Obesity Reports*, *12*, Australia: Springer, 10–23. http://doi.org/10.1007/s13679-023-00495-3.
WHO. (2021). Accelerating action for the health of adolescents: Guidance to support country implementation (2nd ed.). World Health Organization.
Zoogman, S., Goldberg, S. B., Hoyt, W. T., & Miller, L. (2015). Mindfulness interventions with youth: A meta-analysis. In *Mindfulness*, *6*, United States: Springer Science and Business Media, LLC, 290–302. http://doi.org/10.1007/s12671-013-0260-4.

Further reading

Freud, A. (1936). *The ego and the mechanisms of defence*.
Lazarus, R. S. (1966). *Psychological stress and the coping process*. McGraw-Hill.
Pause, C. (2012). Live to tell: Coming out as fat. *Somatechnics, 2*(1), 42–56.
Sonneville, K. R., Calzo, J. P., Horton, N. J., et al. (2012). Body satisfaction and binge eating. *International Journal of Obesity, 36*(7), 944–949.
Vaillant, G.E. (1977). Adaptation to life.

Chapter 9

The role of family environment in obesity

"No other social unit exerts as profound and enduring an influence on development as the family."

Learning objectives

Upon completing this chapter, readers will be able to:
1. Apply Family Systems Theory to understand how family interactions influence adolescent obesity.
2. Use Social Learning Theory (Pierce & Bandura, 1977) to explain how behaviours related to eating and lifestyle are learned within the family.
3. Interpret Ecological Systems Theory (Bronfenbrenner, 1979) in analysing the broader environmental context of family influence.
4. Evaluate the Family Stress Model (Donnelly, Conger & Elder, 1994) in understanding how economic and emotional stressors affect adolescent health outcomes.
5. Analyse Baumrind's parenting typology in relation to parenting styles and their role as risk or protective factors in adolescent obesity.
6. Integrate these theoretical frameworks to explain how family environments function as both risk and protective factors in adolescent obesity.

9.1 Introduction: family environment and adolescent obesity

9.1.1 The family as the first context

Obesity among adolescents is generally studied from the perspectives of biology, the individual, and the community or neighborhood environment. However, underlying all of these is a more profound and immediate influence that affects all of the above, namely, the family environment. The family environment is the first context in which all of the above factors are experienced by the adolescent. It is the family environment that offers the first exposure to patterns of eating, exercise, communication, and emotional expression (Repetti, Taylor & Seeman, 2002; Fulkerson et al., 2007). Thus, the experience of obesity among adolescents is not an isolated phenomenon but is closely linked to the family environment, including patterns of eating, physical activity, communication, and emotional expression.

9.1.2 The dual role of families

The role of the family environment in adolescent obesity is two-sided, serving as a risk factor, a protective factor, or at times both, which is crucial to understand in order to design intervention programs that target the adolescent as well as the family environment as a whole. Research has indicated that parent communication skills training programs can lead to long-term changes in the family environment, which can outlast the intervention program (Fulkerson et al., 2007).

9.1.3 Global evidence in brief

Research from across the globe confirms the role of the family environment in the weight and psychological status of the adolescent. In the United States, regular family meals have been associated with a lower incidence of obesity, increased fruit and vegetable intake, and positive psychological status among adolescents (Neumark-Sztainer et al., 2003; Fulkerson et al., 2007). Conversely, family environments that are hostile, critical, or neglectful have been associated with increased emotional eating and physical inactivity among adolescents. Research from Europe has shown that the parenting style of the family environment is a critical determinant of the weight status of adolescent, with authoritative parenting being

Psychology of Obesity. DOI: https://doi.org/10.1016/B978-0-443-27797-9.00009-9

associated with healthier weight status, while authoritarian or permissive parenting styles have been associated with unhealthy weight status (Rhee, 2008; Sleddens et al., 2011). Research from Australia has shown that sibling relationships can predict body discontent and depression among obese adolescents (Eisenberg, Neumark-Sztainer & Story, 2003; Booth et al., 2006).

9.1.4 The indian context

The role of family is particularly pronounced in India, given the high value accorded to interdependence and collectivism. Adolescents are brought up in a system where parents, grandparents, uncles, aunts, and siblings play a significant role in shaping their behavior and self-concept (Nayar, 2012; Misra & Khurana, 2011). Unlike many Western societies, where adolescence is associated with increasing independence, family influence remains highly significant in the Indian context.

9.1.4.1 Present study evidence

This study provides quantitative data on the role of families in shaping the experience of obesity. This study was conducted in Kolkata with 400 participants (N = 200 obese, N = 200 nonobese) from late adolescence (17–20 years) and young adulthood (21–24 years). The study found that obese youth scored significantly lower than their nonobese counterparts on the Family Environment Scale (FES) for expressiveness, acceptance and caring, independence, active recreational orientation, organization, and control ($P<.01$). In addition, obese youth scored significantly higher than their nonobese counterparts on depression (Beck Depression Inventory [BDI]) and anxiety (STAI) and significantly lower on self-esteem (Rosenberg Scale) across all age-sex groups.

The family also provides important buffering effects. Studies have shown that parents who have taught their children to think about health in ways other than appearance, focusing instead on strength, balance, and overall well-being. Similarly, the role of siblings has also been shown to be important, where brothers and sisters defend their obese sibling against peer bullying. Engaging in physical activities like walking, cooking healthy meals, and practicing yoga has also been shown to have a positive effect on the self-concept of obese youth (Booth et al., 2006; Fulkerson et al., 2007).

9.1.5 Research gap and scope

Yet despite the rising international literature on family factors in obesity among adolescents, there is a notable absence of studies that have explored the phenomenon in Indian collectivist family settings in terms of joint family comments and marriageability scripts, caste and class intersections, and extended family members during cultural events. This current study helps bridge this knowledge gap by using a quantitative approach in Kolkata and providing one of the first systematic accounts of Indian family environment dimensions in obese and nonobese adolescents across different age and sex groups. This chapter synthesizes that knowledge base and provides intervention tools based on the international literature.

9.1.6 Cultural scripts and their effects

The Indian scenario also adds another dimension to the relationship between family and obesity in that Indian culture has its own way of viewing marriageability and family honor. In Indian girls, obesity and weight have a significant impact in terms of arranged marriages and the pressure to be slim. In Indian boys, obesity and weight have a significant impact in terms of discipline and masculine power. These scripts have significant impacts in terms of stigma and coping with obesity. Obesity-related stigma often leads to feelings of shame, guilt, and reduced self-worth among adolescents. However, coping responses may differ by gender, with girls more likely to withdraw socially and boys more likely to externalize distress through humour or aggression. In Indian culture, the concept of a joint family also adds another dimension to the relationship between family and obesity in that, in a joint family setting, there is hardly any privacy for adolescents. This leads to coping by hiding and suppressing emotions. This also leads to more stigma and affects the relationship between family and obesity in Indian adolescents (Misra & Khurana, 2011).

9.1.7 Intergenerational transmission

Globally, it is now recognized that health behaviors are transmitted across generations. Parents who are themselves obese are more likely to have obese adolescents. This is true not only for genetic reasons but also for reasons related to social learning and environmental influences. In India, this is further complicated by cultural influences where mothers may advise their adolescent daughters to eat more, thereby showing affection and care, but at the same time advise them about looks and appearance. Similarly, fathers may expect athleticism from sons, but themselves may not display athleticism. This is likely to cause confusion for the adolescent and thereby negatively impact adaptive coping and cause more stress.

9.1.8 The family as first line of defense or vulnerability

Adolescents who face criticism at school and receive support from families have fewer depressive symptoms and more adaptive coping skills than those who face criticism from both school and family contexts. The study confirms this finding, wherein obese adolescents in Kolkata showed fewer social adjustment deficits (Bell's Inventory) if they scored higher on the dimension of acceptance and caring of the FES, and more compound deficits in home and health adjustment if they scored lower on dimensions of expressiveness and cohesion ($P<.01$). The family can function either as a protective factor or as a source of vulnerability in the context of obesity-related stigma. Understanding this role of family is thus essential for developing any intervention for obesity management that goes beyond the individual to embrace the complex ecosystems in which they coexist.

9.2 Theoretical frameworks on family and obesity

9.2.1 Why theory matters

To understand the role played by the family in obesity among adolescents, it is essential to understand the theoretical perspectives that explain the behavior of humans in social systems. The family is not just a source of food and shelter for the individual. Rather, it is a system that provides meaning to life and affects the behavior of the individual. There are several theoretical perspectives that explain the role played by the family in obesity among adolescents. These perspectives provide insight into the behavior of the family and its impact on the individual.

9.2.2 Family Systems Theory

The Family Systems Theory was developed by Minuchin (1974), and Bowen (1978) also supported this perspective. According to this perspective, the family is a system in which one member affects the behavior of the others. In the case of obesity among adolescents, the Family Systems Theory argues that obesity is not just a behavior of the individual. Rather, obesity should be understood within the broader family system that shapes individual behaviour and experiences. In the case of obesity among Indian adolescents, the system is more complex due to the presence of the extended family. The current study found that obese adolescents in Kolkata scored significantly lower than nonobese adolescents in the acceptance and caring dimension of the FES ($P<.01$). This finding is in line with the Family Systems Theory that predicts that a family system that is not warm will increase obesity-related stress. In terms of cohesion, the current study found that obese males scored significantly higher than nonobese males. In contrast, obese females scored significantly lower than nonobese females. In terms of expressiveness and independence, the current study found that family systems that scored high in expressiveness and independence produced better adjustment outcomes.

9.2.3 Social Learning Theory

Social Learning Theory is based on the premise that learning occurs through observation and imitation (Bandura, 1977). For instance, parents teach children eating habits and lifestyle patterns that are later imitated and followed. When parents eat too many high-calorie foods and do not get enough physical exercise, teenagers are likely to follow suit. On the other hand, parents who lead healthy lifestyles and have healthy eating habits encourage teenagers to do the same. The present study found that obese adolescents scored significantly lower on active recreational orientation compared to other teenagers (male LA: $M=26.08$ vs 36.88; female LA: $M=25.40$ vs 36.62; $P<.01$). This suggests that families of obese teenagers do not spend as much time engaging in physical and recreational activities together. This is in line with Social Learning Theory, which suggests that families that do not spend time engaging in physical activities together are likely to be reinforcing and modeling sedentary lifestyle patterns for one another.

9.2.4 Ecological Systems Theory

According to Bronfenbrenner (1979), Ecological Systems Theory, the family is part of the microsystem, which also includes peers and the school. The mesosystem links the microsystem, the exosystem represents the community, and the macrosystem represents the culture. The microsystem, or the family, is the immediate environment, yet it is always subject to the influence of the macro- and micro-environments. An Indian family may consider home cooking important, but the macro-environment of Kolkata, an urban city, may not support such an approach due to the proliferation of fast food outlets and the lack of open spaces for recreation. The present research, conducted in the urban city of Kolkata, found that the level of home and health adjustment (Bell's Adjustment Inventory) was significantly lower for obese adolescents compared to their nonobese counterparts for all four groups ($P<.01$). The family's effect on obesity must not be considered in isolation.

9.2.5 The Family Stress Model

The Family Stress Model by Donnelly, Conger & Elder (1994) points to the impact of economic stress on parenting styles and the consequent impact on adolescents. Economic stress affects the ability of parents to provide nutritious meals for their children. In stressful conditions, parents tend to be harsher in communication and criticize their children for their weight. In India, where economic differences are quite high, this model is applicable. In the current study, it was seen that obese adolescents from the lower socioeconomic group showed more compound deficits in the FES. This is in line with the Family Stress Model that economic stress affects the warmth and quality of food in the family. The obese adolescents in the lowest SES group showed more compound deficits in the acceptance and caring and active recreational dimensions.

9.2.6 Parenting styles

The fourth model that can be used to understand the impact of family on obesity in adolescents is Baumrind (1966) parenting styles. Baumrind's model was extended by Maccoby & Martin (1983). Baumrind divided parenting styles into three styles. Authoritative parents are warm and demanding. This style is associated with better outcomes in adolescents. Authoritarian parents are strict and criticize their children. This style is associated with maladaptive coping in adolescents. Permissive parents permit and condone behavior. This style is associated with overeating and physical inactivity. Neglectful parents neglect their children. This style is associated with obesity and psychological problems in adolescents (Rhee, 2008; Sleddens et al., 2011) (see Table 9.1).

The current study has also found that obese adolescents scored significantly lower on the independence and control dimensions of the FES in comparison to their nonobese counterparts ($P<.01$ for all the groups). This has also supported the theoretical framework of Baumrind, which also stated that authoritarian control, in the absence of parental warmth, would have adverse effects on adolescents.

9.2.7 Integrative perspective

The above-mentioned theoretical frameworks reveal that the role of family in the development of obesity is complex. Family systems are the context in which the emotional environment of obesity is constructed. Social Learning Theory explains the process of learning and the passing on of behavioral scripts to the next generation. Ecological theory provides the context in which the family environment is constructed. Economic stressors determine the level of shame in the family environment. Parenting styles determine the level of support provided by the family environment in the development of

TABLE 9.1 Parenting styles and their influence on coping and obesity outcomes in adolescents.

Parenting style	Key features	Effect on adolescent with obesity	Evidence
Authoritative	High warmth, clear structure, open communication	Lower BMI risk; healthier coping; resilience against stigma	(Rhee, 2008; Sleddens et al., 2011)
Authoritarian	Strict control, criticism, low warmth	Secrecy; emotional eating; internalized shame	(Rhee, 2008; Neumark-Sztainer et al., 2003)
Permissive	High warmth, no structure, indulgence	Unregulated snacking; sedentary routines normalized	(Neumark-Sztainer et al., 2003; Sleddens et al., 2011)
Neglectful	Low warmth, low structure	Compounded obesity risk; psychological distress	(Repetti, Taylor & Seeman, 2002); (Donnelly, Conger & Elder, 1994)

Source: Baumrind (1991). The influence of parenting style on adolescent competence and substance use. *Journal of Early Adolescence, 11*(1), 56–95.

adaptive coping skills. This study has also supported the fact that these theories are not hypothetical but are grounded in the reality of the Indian adolescents of Kolkata, as the study has found statistically significant differences in the coping skills, family environment perception, and adjustment of the obese adolescents in comparison to their nonobese counterparts in all four age-sex groups.

9.3 Global evidence on family influences

9.3.1 Family meals and household routines

Significant international evidence supports the value of family meals for promoting healthy eating and preventing overweight and obesity. Longitudinal research undertaken in the USA through the Project EAT confirmed that teenagers who regularly share family meals consume more fruit and vegetables, fewer sweetened beverages, and have fewer problems with obesity. Family meals are also associated with better levels of self-esteem and disordered eating, suggesting that there are wider benefits to health than food intake alone (Neumark-Sztainer et al., 2003; Fulkerson et al., 2007). Burgess-Champoux and colleagues (2009) in Minnesota confirmed that the nutritional value of family meals is significantly higher than that of meals eaten outside the family environment. Teenagers in families where there is a higher frequency of family dinner consumption have higher levels of dietary diversity. Family meals are less frequent in urban compared to rural environments in Brazil and South Africa, where teenagers tend to eat alone and consume fast food (Prentice, 2006; Kimani-Murage, 2013).

9.3.2 Parental modeling of behavior

One of the strongest influences on adolescent health outcomes is parental behavior. Research has proven that if a child is exposed to physically active role models, they will likely be more physically active themselves. Moreover, parental sedentary behavior is linked to adolescent screen time and weight gain (Pierce & Bandura, 1977; Repetti, Taylor & Seeman, 2002). In Australia, parental dietary habits correlate directly with adolescent dietary habits. Parents who provide fruit, vegetable, and processed food-free environments for their families promote healthy adolescent habits (Neumark-Sztainer et al., 2003). Another aspect of intergenerational modeling is coping with stress. Parents who use food to cope with stress often pass this on to their children. Globally, research has proven that if adolescents observe their parents coping with stress through food or avoidance, they are more likely to develop maladaptive coping strategies that may lead to obesity and depression (Faith, Matz & Jorge, 2002; Goldfield et al., 2010).

9.3.3 Parenting styles and family communication

Studies across different cultures have proven that parenting style is a key determinant of obesity outcomes in different parts of the world. In the United States and Europe, authoritative parenting is linked to low adolescent BMI and maladaptive coping, whereas authoritarian parenting is linked to obesity and body image dissatisfaction, and permissive parenting is linked to uncontrolled snacking and sedentary behaviors (Rhee, 2008; Sleddens et al., 2011). In Latin American countries such as Mexico and Brazil, similar trends have been observed, albeit with cultural nuances. In these countries, indulgent parenting is linked to excessive sugary food intake, and authoritarian parenting is linked to secrecy and rebellion against authority (Conde & Borges, 2011). In African studies, it is evident that communication among members of the extended family is complex. In some African families, adolescents who stay with grandparents often receive conflicting messages about body image. Some grandparents promote plumpness as a sign of wealth, while others promote slimmer body images. These messages cause stress among adolescents and may lead to maladaptive coping strategies (Kimani-Murage, 2013).

9.3.4 Sibling influences

Current global research also points to the impact of sibling relationships on obesity-related behavior and psychological outcomes. In the United States, sibling teasing is the strongest predictor of body dissatisfaction for adolescents with obesity (Eisenberg, Neumark-Sztainer & Story, 2003). In Australia, the more physically active the siblings of an adolescent, the more likely the adolescent is to engage in sporting activities, while the more inactive the siblings are, the more the adolescent engages in screen activities (Booth et al., 2006). Thus sibling relationships are a double-edged sword, with positive effects of supportive siblings who encourage participation or help to ward off bullying, as well as negative effects of critical or competitive siblings who add to stigmatization or avoidance.

9.3.5 Intergenerational patterns and cultural scripts

The intergenerational transmission of obesity can be seen to be occurring at a genetic level as well as at a behavioral level. In the United States, the odds of a child developing obesity are two to three times greater than those of a child of a parent who is not obese, even after controlling for socioeconomic status (Sobal & Stunkard, 1989). The same phenomenon has been observed in other populations of European descent, with parental BMI being a strong predictor of adolescent BMI (Reilly & Kelly, 2011). Thus intergenerational transmission of obesity can be seen to be occurring at a cultural level as well, with cultural scripts being passed down from parent to child.

In the African and South Asian populations, the intergenerational differences in cultural scripts pose a unique problem for the adolescent, as grandparents who were from a food-insecure background encourage the adolescent to eat more as a sign of health, while the parents, who were influenced by globalization, encourage the adolescent to be slim (Popkin, 2015; Prentice, 2006). The adolescent is then confused and stressed, leading to the adoption of maladaptive coping mechanisms.

9.3.6 Family stress and economic conditions

The Family Stress Model by Donnelly, Conger & Elder (1994) has strong global validity. In low-income families, economic pressure leads to the consumption of affordable but calorie-rich foods. Studies done in the United States show that teenagers in economically stressed families tend to have higher intakes of fast foods and lower intakes of fresh foods. European studies have shown that economically stressed families have lower levels of parental supervision, allowing teenagers to have more autonomy over their food choices and physical activities (Swinburn et al., 2019). In low- and middle-income countries, the effects of economic pressure are compounded by the double burden of undernutrition during growth and overnutrition during adolescence, driven by the availability of cheap, high-calorie foods and sedentary lifestyles. This leads to normalization of obesity as a necessary condition of life, thereby reducing the motivation to change behavior (Misra & Khurana, 2011; Popkin, 2015).

9.3.7 Universal and culturally specific themes

In spite of the diverse cultural background of the population studied, some universal themes have emerged. Family meals are universally associated with protection. Parental modeling predicts children's behavior. Authoritative parenting protects children, whereas authoritarian and permissive parenting increase vulnerability. Sibling influences are powerful and bidirectional. Economic pressure compromises all these healthy behaviors and coping strategies. Yet cultural influences shape the meaning of obesity and its management within the family. Whether it is the celebration of plumpness in some African cultures or the glorification of slenderness in Westernized urban settings, families give meaning to their children's weight, and the teenager must navigate these cultural influences that are both about individual freedom and collective responsibility (see Table 9.2).

9.4 Indian context: family, culture, and institutional dimensions

9.4.1 The indian family as cultural institution

The Indian family is not only a household entity; it is also a cultural institution that creates individual identities, opportunities, and aspirations. Adolescents who suffer from obesity in India do not exist as isolated individuals. They exist as sons, daughters, future husbands, future wives, and holders of family prestige. As such, their coping mechanisms, mental health, and health outcomes are significantly impacted by how their families view obesity (Nayar, 2012; Misra & Khurana, 2011). Unlike in Western culture, where adolescence is characterized by increased individualism, in Indian culture, adolescents remain embedded in family networks where many family members actively influence an individual's self-concept by offering advice, criticism, or support. Such embeddedness provides adolescents resources, support, and meaning; it also exponentially increases the sources of stigma and shame.

9.4.2 Joint family and nuclear family structures

Another significant characteristic of Indian family life is the coexistence of joint family and nuclear family structures. In joint family structures, there is close coresidence among family generations. Adolescents in such family structures live in an environment that is socially dense in terms of comments by other family members. Adolescents in such family structures suffer from increased levels of scrutiny by uncles, aunts, and grandparents who freely offer comments about body size, diet, and physical activity. The study's sample population, who were drawn from Kolkata's joint family and nuclear family structures, found that obese adolescents scored significantly lower than their nonobese counterparts in

TABLE 9.2 Family-level determinants of adolescent obesity: cross-cultural evidence.

Country/Region	Family factor	Key finding	Source
United States	Family meals	Lower obesity; higher self-esteem; less disordered eating	(Neumark-Sztainer et al., 2003); Fulkerson et al., 2007
Multiple countries	Parental activity modeling	Children of active parents are significantly more likely to exercise; sedentary parents predict adolescent screen time	(Pierce & Bandura, 1977; Repetti, Taylor & Seeman, 2002)
Australia	Sibling dynamics	Sibling teasing predicts body dissatisfaction; active siblings boost activity	Booth et al., 2006; (Eisenberg, Neumark-Sztainer & Story, 2003)
Minnesota, USA	Structured family dinners	Higher nutritional quality and dietary diversity in frequent family meal households	(Burgess-Champoux et al., 2009)
Mexico/Brazil	Parenting style	Indulgent parenting linked to sugary food consumption	(Conde & Borges, 2011)
South Africa/ Kenya	Intergenerational scripts	Conflicting plumpness versus slimness ideals cause stress and maladaptive coping	(Kimani-Murage, 2013)
Europe (multiple)	Parental BMI	Strong predictor of adolescent BMI even after controlling for SES	(Reilly & Kelly, 2011; Sleddens et al., 2011)
India (Das, 2018)	Family Environment Scale (FES)	Obese adolescents scored significantly lower on expressiveness, acceptance and caring, independence, active recreational, organization, and control versus nonobese (P<.01)	(Das, 2018);(Misra & Khurana, 2011)

Source: Repetti, R.L., Taylor, S.E. & Seeman, T.E. (2002). Risky families: Family social environments and the mental and physical health of offspring. *Psychological Bulletin, 128*(2), 330–366. https://doi.org/10.1037/0033-2909.128.2.330.

terms of expressiveness and acceptance and caring dimensions of FES than their nonobese counterparts (P<.01). The study found that the effect of obesity on family acceptance and caring was significant in all four age-sex groups. This study is consistent with the hypothesis that obesity-related comments by many family members suppress warmth and open communication in all household structures.

9.4.3 Marriageability

The most dominant cultural script for adolescent obesity in India is the script of marriageability. For girls, the script is such that their body size is often associated with their marriage prospects. For them, being thin is considered beautiful, healthy, and desirable. Their grandparents and older family members consider thinness the most desirable. The adolescent girls are reminded time and again how their body size is affecting their marriage prospects. The present research found that female obese late adolescents scored significantly lower on self-esteem (Rosenberg Scale) compared to their nonobese counterparts (M = 14.06 compared to 21.66, P<.01). They also scored higher on depression BDI compared to their female counterparts (M = 22.04 compared to 13.36, P<.01), thus supporting the hypothesis of the present research. Marriageability-related commentary has an impact on the self-worth of the girl, leading to depression (Neumark-Sztainer et al., 2002; Nayar, 2012).

For boys, the script is somewhat different, yet equally detrimental. For them, being obese is considered a sign of laziness or lack of discipline, which may adversely affect their marriage prospects. Boys are expected to show their masculinity through their physical strength, as depicted in Bollywood films and cricket. Boys are compared with their cousins or peers, and the ones with larger body sizes are considered inferior. Boys cope with the problem of obesity through externalization, such as making jokes about their size, being aggressive, or staying out of games.

9.4.4 Academic stress and family commentary

Education is an integral part of Indian culture; success in competitive examinations is considered an instrument of family progress and social ascendance. The obese adolescents in this study faced two sources of stigma: academic stress and weight-related stigma. Parents often correlate body weight with academic discipline; they consider body weight an indicator of laziness and academic delinquency. Similarly, teachers also endorse these beliefs by repeating these comments in front of their students. The current study found that obese adolescents scored significantly higher in trait anxiety compared with their healthy peers (STAI: male LA M = 53.18 vs 39.90; female LA M = 57.36 vs 45.72; $P<.01$). These findings indicate that obese adolescents suffer from increased levels of anxiety that are above normal levels of academic stress. These findings support the proposition that obese adolescents suffer from two sources of stigma: examination stress and weight-related stigma. These two sources of stigma cooccur simultaneously in Indian culture. Larson & Verma (1999) and Neumark-Sztainer et al. (2002) found that examination stress is an integral part of Indian culture. Families that emphasized holistic well-being also provided adolescents with greater coping resources. These families were able to balance academic stress with health and rest.

9.4.5 Extended kin, festivals, and family gatherings

In Indian society, family functions during weddings, festivals, and religious functions play a vital role in socialization. However, for obese adolescents, these functions often result in humiliation. During functions, family members comment on body weight and make jokes in front of peers or cousins. Girls are often advised to eat less at wedding functions. Boys are often compared to cousins during sports activities at family functions. These situations often result in feelings of shame for obese adolescents. Avoidance of functions or emotional eating is often a coping mechanism for obese adolescents (Puhl & Heuer, 2009; Neumark-Sztainer et al., 2002). The results of this study showed that obese adolescents scored significantly lower than nonobese peers on organization and control dimensions of the FES (male LA: organization M =7 .26 vs 9.46; control M = 14.04 vs 16.16; $P<.01$). This suggests that family environments for obese adolescents show weak structural norms regarding routines and boundaries, which may result in commenting on body weight at social gatherings without being stopped. The study suggests that for obese adolescents, family structures, which often provide support and solidarity to individuals at large, may often result in humiliation at social gatherings.

9.4.6 Caste, class, and socioeconomic aspects

Caste and class factors are also found to affect the perception of obesity and the coping strategies for obesity. Among the affluent urban population, the Western ideal of slimness, promoted through the media and education, was found to create pressure on the adolescent to adopt strategies such as dieting, joining gyms, or undergoing medical procedures. The pressure was also found to be endorsed by the family, which, in some cases, also criticized the adolescent. The coping strategies were found to include secrets and denial (Misra & Khurana, 2011; Grogan, 2016). Among the lower socioeconomic or lower caste groups, the perception of obesity was found to differ, with plumpness being associated with affluence or health, thus reducing the level of stigma. However, the adolescents were also found to experience ridicule from the higher caste groups in mixed schools, thus facing the effect of intersectional disadvantage, as described by Crenshaw (1989), where the disadvantages are cumulative and add up to more than the sum of the individual disadvantages. The present study found that social adjustment (Bell's inventory) was significantly lower for obese adolescents compared with the normal-weight adolescents for the groups of late adolescent males, young adult males, and young adult females ($P<.01$), thus supporting the hypothesis of the compound effect of social disadvantage.

9.4.7 Urban and rural differences

Urban youth are surrounded by media-saturated environments where digital media, Bollywood, and comparison processes are prevalent. Studies have confirmed that body dissatisfaction is high among urban youth in India and is associated with maladaptive coping strategies like emotional eating, dieting crazes, and social withdrawal (Nayar, 2012). For rural youth, although there has been less exposure to globalized media until now, smartphone use has become widespread, and exposure to urbanized body types is now widespread through school-going patterns and migration of youth to urban areas. Some rural families still view plumpness as synonymous with wealth and physical strength and thus do not stigmatize overweight individuals within families. However, rural youth are increasingly exposed to urbanized body types through school environments (Popkin, 2015). The present study found that all obese youth scored significantly lower on body image aspects like appearance evaluation and fitness evaluation ($P<.01$) on the MBSRQ, which is associated with exposure to urbanized body types through media and other channels. The proliferation of smartphone use has now bridged the gap between rural and urban youth, and rural youth are now equally exposed to urbanized body types and expectations of slim and muscular body types through smartphone use and school-going patterns (Rodgers et al., 2020; Holland & Tiggemann, 2016).

9.4.8 Healthcare and institution reinforcement

Indian families' coping is further influenced through interactions with healthcare professionals and institutions. Healthcare professionals can significantly reduce shame and guilt associated with overweight and obesity through private weighing sessions and collaborative goal-setting and communication. Healthcare professionals' interactional styles significantly influence families' coping styles and can either reinforce shame and guilt through punitive clinical encounters or promote positive coping through empathetic and understanding clinical encounters (Puhl & Heuer, 2009; Latner & Stunkard, 2003). The present study found that all obese youth scored significantly higher on aspects of health adjustments difficult (Bell's Inventory) for all four groups ($P<.01$), suggesting that health adjustments are significantly compromised for obese youth in critical family environments.

9.4.9 Summary of indian dynamics

In India, not only is the family context centrally important, but it is also structurally unavoidable in explaining adolescent obesity. Family context, whether joint or nuclear, influences the degree and scope of surveillance. Cultural context links body size to marriageability, control, and family honor. Academic stress interacts with weight stigma in complex ways. Extended family networks amplify channels for criticism during centrally important family contexts. Caste-class hierarchies inform body size meanings and coping opportunities. Urbanization and digital media globalize slimness ideals, and healthcare systems often reinforce rather than resist family criticism. The present study reflects this context through quantitative data on systemic differences in family environment perception, coping, depression, anxiety, self-esteem, and adjustment among obese and nonobese youth in Kolkata, emphasizing the importance of family-focused interventions that engage families as coactors and coinformants to combat stigmatizing family environments and promote supportive and empowering family environments.

9.5 Research insights, intervention approaches, and pedagogical tools

9.5.1 The present study: design, findings, and contribution

An exploratory quantitative research design was used for this study to investigate psychological characteristics and adjustment patterns of obese compared with nonobese late adolescents and young adults in Kolkata, India. The study participants consisted of 400 individuals: 200 obese and 200 nonobese individuals, equally divided into two developmental stages (late adolescence and young adulthood) and two sex groups (male and female). Each of these eight groups consisted of 50 individuals. The study participants were recruited through the method of purposive sampling with area-wise stratification from the northern, central, southern, and eastern Kolkata areas. The study participants were recruited from higher secondary schools, undergraduate colleges, university postgraduate departments, and gyms. The inclusion criteria for obese individuals were individuals whose BMI ranged from 30.0 to 39.9. The inclusion criteria for nonobese individuals were individuals whose BMI ranged from 18.5 to 24.9. The study groups were matched for variables such as age, socioeconomic status, family types, family size, and sibling size. The research instruments used for data collection for this study were the FES developed by Bhatia (1993), which assesses eight dimensions: cohesion, expressiveness, conflict, acceptance and caring, active recreational orientation, independence, organization, and control. Other research instruments used for data collection for this study were the BDI, developed by Beck and colleagues (1961); the State-Trait Anxiety Inventory, developed by Spielberger (1983); the Rosenberg Self-Esteem Scale, developed by Rosenberg (1965); the Coping Response Inventory, developed by Rao and colleagues (1999); the Multidimensional Body Self-Reliance Questionnaire, developed by Brown and colleagues (1990); and Bell's Adjustment Inventory, developed by Bell (1962), which assesses four types of adjustments: home, health, social, and emotional. Statistical analysis used for this study was independent-samples t-tests and three-factor factorial analysis of variance (3FFANOVA) with Body weight, age, and sex as factors. Pearson product-moment correlations were used to find correlations between BMI and all psychological variables.

Quantitative results indicated consistent statistically significant differences between obese and nonobese adolescents in all psychological and family environment variables. Significantly higher levels of depression were found in obese compared to nonobese adolescents in all four age-sex groups. For example, in male late adolescents, obese M = 19.30 versus nonobese M = 12.48; in female late adolescents, obese M = 22.04 versus nonobese M = 13.36;

all $P<.01$. Significantly higher levels of state anxiety and trait anxiety were found in obese compared to nonobese adolescents in all four groups. Significantly lower levels of self-esteem were found in obese compared to nonobese adolescents in all four groups. On the FES, obese adolescents scored significantly lower than nonobese peers in six of eight dimensions: expressiveness, acceptance and caring, independence, active recreational orientation, organization, control, all in all four groups ($P<.01$). On the conflict dimension, obese adolescents scored significantly higher than nonobese peers in all four groups ($P<.01$); because this dimension is reverse-scored in this scale, it is clear that obese adolescents perceive less conflict in their family than do nonobese peers; in fact, all other dimensions were in the same direction as the other six dimensions of this scale: obese adolescents perceive greater conflict in their family than do nonobese peers. Body weight was significant in all eight dimensions of the FES, all eight personality domains, both state and trait anxiety, depression, self-esteem, all body image dimensions, coping response, eating attitude, and all adjustment domains, confirming that body weight was the major factor differentiating obese and nonobese adolescents in all psychological outcomes measured (Faith, Matz & Jorge, 2002; Repetti, Taylor & Seeman, 2002; Rhee, 2008) (see Table 9.3).

9.5.2 Maladaptive and adaptive family patterns

Family factors also need to be addressed through interventions that are multilevel in their approach and involve the psychological, educational, community, and policy domains. Family-level interventions have the strongest evidence base for addressing family factors, and there are three approaches that have the strongest evidence base. One is parent training programs, which have the strongest evidence base and involve teaching parents supportive communication skills, avoiding shaming behaviors, and changing the focus of conversation from appearance to health. A study by Fulkerson et al. (2007) found that parents using nonstigmatizing communication skills with their adolescents reduced emotional eating over six months. Evidence also exists for the effectiveness of parent workshops in language substitution exercises with adolescents, in which critical commentary is replaced with collaborative health-focused

TABLE 9.3 Adaptive and maladaptive family interaction patterns and their impact on adolescents with obesity.

Pattern type	Key behaviors	Effect on adolescent	Evidence
Maladaptive	Critical or moralizing commentary about weight	Internalized shame; secrecy; WBI elevation	(Puhl & Heuer, 2009; Neumark-Sztainer et al., 2002)
Maladaptive	Open comparisons with peers or cousins	Social withdrawal; depression	(Eisenberg, Neumark-Sztainer & Story, 2003; Neumark-Sztainer et al., 2002)
Maladaptive	Use of shame as motivation for behavior change	Emotional eating; healthcare avoidance	(Faith, Matz & Jorge, 2002; Puhl et al., 2016)
Maladaptive	Inconsistent routines around meals and activity	Normalized sedentary and poor dietary habits	(Neumark-Sztainer et al., 2003; Sleddens et al., 2011)
Maladaptive	Reinforcement of marriageability or discipline scripts	Gendered stigma; body shame; avoidance	(Nayar, 2012; Grogan, 2016)
Adaptive	Supportive communication emphasizing health, not appearance	Lower WBI; greater resilience; reduced secrecy	Fulkerson et al., 2007; (Pont et al., 2017)
Adaptive	Regular family meals with balanced nutrition	Better dietary habits; higher self-esteem	(Neumark-Sztainer et al., 2003); Fulkerson et al., 2007
Adaptive	Collective physical activity: walking, yoga, sports	Sustained engagement; positive identity anchoring	Booth et al., 2006; (Zoogman et al., 2015)
Adaptive	Modeling balanced coping strategies for stress	Adolescents adopt similar adaptive coping scripts	(Pierce & Bandura, 1977; Repetti, Taylor & Seeman, 2002)
Adaptive	Reframing success beyond body size	Self-worth decoupled from appearance; resilience	(Masten, 2001)

Source: Puhl, R.M. & Heuer, C.A. (2009). The stigma of obesity: A review and update. *Obesity, 17*(5), 941–964. https://doi.org/10.1038/oby.2008.636.

language, leading to improvements in adolescents' coping skills and self-esteem (Puhl et al., 2016). Family therapy has also been found to be effective in addressing family factors, and evidence exists in the United States and Europe of the effectiveness of family-based behavioral interventions in improving the weight and mental health of adolescents (Stice, Shaw & Marti, 2006; Hofmann et al., 2012). In the Indian context, family therapy also needs to focus on collectivist factors, including pressure from extended family members and the negotiation between different generations' body ideals. Home-based activities like preparing meals and engaging in physical activities with family members are not only cost-free but also foster a sense of collective responsibility and positive identity reinforcement, requiring no specific resources other than family time and intention (Booth et al., 2006; Fulkerson et al., 2007).

9.5.3 School-based approaches to family engagement

Parent-teacher partnerships ensure the sending of consistent messages regarding body image and health. The mixed message sent to adolescents, where schools promote body diversity, yet the family promotes the ideal of slimness, is addressed through such an approach. Research has found evidence supporting the idea that coordination of nutrition and health information across the school and community setting reduces mixed messages sent to adolescents regarding body image and eating (Neumark-Sztainer et al., 2003). Workshops for parents, part of the school program, educate them on the effect of their comments on the self-esteem of the adolescent. The most successful approach is the use of role-playing, where the parent learns how to communicate effectively. A successful approach was found by Puhl et al. (2016), where the reduction of weight teasing was found in families where the parent was part of the school-based weight stigma awareness program. The inclusion of such programs in parent-teacher meetings in government schools in India has the advantage of covering more ground with lower costs. Curriculum changes, such as the inclusion of body diversity, encourage adolescents to discuss the pressure put on them by the family in a constructive manner in the classroom, without stigmatizing the family or the adolescent.

9.5.4 Community and cultural interventions

Campaigns to raise awareness among extended kin networks about the impact of stigmatizing comments during weddings and other social events have also been implemented. Such campaigns have been found to be effective when implemented by trusted members of the community. ASHA workers have been found to be effective in changing family communication patterns regarding body images among adolescents by using interventions that emphasize health as a state of strength and capability rather than physical appearance. Using cultural practices to make interventions more relevant to the population has also been found to be effective. Using yoga and meditation as health practices has been found to have a positive impact on the psychological state of adolescents in India and abroad (Zoogman et al., 2015; Khalsa et al., 2012). Religious and cultural leaders who have the ability to reframe health messages and shift the focus from weight and physical appearance to strength and balance can reach populations that cannot be accessed by health services. Sports and dance clubs can be useful in providing a space for adolescents to be involved in physical activities without being stigmatized for their body sizes. Classical and folk dance styles like Garba, Bhangra, and Kuchipudi are some of the dance styles that can be used in India to provide a culturally rich physical activity space for adolescents with obesity.

9.5.5 Policy and structural reforms

The incorporation of family-centered modules into national programs like POSHAN Abhiyaan and the Fit India Movement is essential. Both programs currently focus primarily on nutrition intake and physical activity without addressing stigma, communication, and family dynamics (Misra & Khurana, 2011; Pont et al., 2017). The addition of family communication workshops and no-shame mealtime guidelines will enable these programs to extend beyond the individual to the familial environment in which actual behavioral changes are implemented. The expansion of family counseling services in community health centers and urban primary health centers will address the lack of family counseling for obese youth in India. In the Indian context, few obese youth have access to any form of family counseling services (Misra & Khurana, 2011). The addition of brief family counseling services to the Rashtriya Kishor Swasthya Karyakram program, including modules on weight stigma and supportive communication styles, will address this need. Media regulations that promote the portrayal of diverse body types in family settings will discourage media portrayals that equate slimness with beauty. Policy reforms that require the appropriate body type for advertising and entertainment media will reduce the pressure that families feel to ensure slimness in their children (Repetti, Taylor & Seeman, 2002).

Evidence-based family intervention toolkit for supporting adolescents with obesity in indian contexts
Evidence-based family intervention toolkit for indian settings • Language swap exercise: Parents replace "you are lazy" with "let us walk together after dinner." Practiced in workshops with role-play and structured feedback. • No-shame mealtime rule: Families agree to remove body comments from the dinner table. Introduced through Anganwadi or parent-teacher meetings. • Family movement ritual: One shared physical activity per week, such as an evening walk, morning yoga, or weekend sports, framed as family bonding rather than weight management. • Supportive script cards: Pocket-sized cards in regional languages with phrases families can use after a child experiences teasing from peers or extended kin. • Extended kin awareness session: Brief community session before festivals, delivered by local health workers, covering the impact of weight comments on adolescent psychological well-being. • Healthcare communication training: Clinicians trained to involve families constructively in adolescent care without reinforcing stigma or diagnostic overshadowing.

9.5.6 Measuring family influence: tools and adaptation

Accurate measurements of family influence on teen obesity are essential for both research and practice. The following tools are more appropriate for the Indian context and hence more relevant for this study (see Table 9.4).

9.5.7 Language guide for families

The table below provides some harmful phrases that are common in Indian family settings and the alternatives and rationale for using the alternatives (see Table 9.5).

9.5.8 Illustrative composite vignettes

The following composite vignettes are hypothetical and intended to illustrate the patterns of family environment, weight commentary, and coping strategies of Indian adolescents with obesity, as supported by the empirical literature reviewed in this chapter. They are not intended to be based on any primary data, and no vignette is intended to be representative of any particular individual. The names and all identifying details are fictional and not intended to refer to any specific location or person.

Vignette 1: Commentary and coping in a joint family

TABLE 9.4 Family-based assessment tools for adolescent obesity: measures and cultural adaptations for the indian context.

Tool	What it measures	Indian adaptation needed
Family Functioning Scale (Bloom, 1985)	Cohesion, communication, and conflict within family units	Add items on intergenerational commentary, marriageability pressure, and extended kin involvement
Parental feeding questionnaire (Birch et al., 2001)	Parental control, monitoring, and pressure around eating	Add items on emotion-driven feeding, festive overeating norms, and mealtime comment frequency
Weight Bias Internalization Scale (Durso & Latner, 2008)	Degree to which adolescents self-apply negative weight stereotypes	Add: "Because of my weight, I worry my family will struggle to arrange my marriage"
Family meal frequency inventory	Frequency, duration, and emotional quality of family meals	Include items on distracted eating, screen time at meals, and comment-free mealtimes
Sibling Teasing and Support Scale	Frequency of sibling teasing versus protective sibling behavior	Adapt for Indian sibling dynamics, including cousin relationships in joint families

Source: Birch, L.L., Fisher, J.O., Grimm-Thomas, K., Markey, C.N., Sawyer, R. & Johnson, S.L. (2001). Confirmatory factor analysis of the Child Feeding Questionnaire: A measure of parental attitudes, beliefs and practices about child feeding and obesity proneness. *Appetite*, *36*(3), 201–210. https://doi.org/10.1006/appe.2001.0398.

TABLE 9.5 Family communication patterns: harmful language and supportive alternatives in adolescent obesity.

Setting	Harmful phrase	Why it harms	Supportive alternative
Dinner table	You should not eat so much. Look at your size.	Produces shame; triggers secrecy eating; damages self-esteem (Neumark-Sztainer et al., 2003).	Let us enjoy this meal together. How was your day?
Before a wedding	Lose weight before the wedding, or people will talk.	Links body size to family honor; intensifies WBI (Nayar, 2012).	You look wonderful. Go enjoy the celebrations.
After school results	If you focused instead of eating so much, your marks would improve.	Conflates academic and body failings; drives secrecy and withdrawal (Janssen et al., 2004).	Let us look at what went well and what needs support. How are you feeling?
At a family gathering	Your cousin plays cricket so well. Why can you not be more like him?	Peer comparison reduces self-worth and increases withdrawal (Eisenberg, Neumark-Sztainer & Story, 2003).	Everyone has different strengths. What activity do you enjoy most?
During a doctor visit	See, even the doctor says you need to lose weight. We have been telling you.	Reinforces shame; associates healthcare with judgment; discourages future visits (Puhl & Heuer, 2009).	The doctor gave us a plan to work on together. How can we support you?

Source: Puhl, R.M. & Heuer, C.A. (2009). The stigma of obesity: A review and update. *Obesity, 17*(5), 941–964. https://doi.org/10.1038/oby.2008.636.

A 15-year-old girl from a middle-class joint family in an urban setting received daily weight-related comments from grandparents, aunts, and parents. Her mother made a comment about the girl's body size in comparison with other girls in the family before a family celebration, which prompted the girl to avoid the celebration and engage in secretive eating at home. The girl scored high on the Weight Bias Internalization Scale and avoided school sports days. However, after the school counselor introduced a parent workshop, the girl's mother replaced body-related comments with questions about the girl's daily activities during a language substitution exercise, reducing secretive eating incidents over three months and attending a family celebration with a peer for support, as seen in the intervention effects of ally mapping by Eisenberg, Neumark-Sztainer & Story (2003).

Vignette 2: Academic pressure and family commentary in a residential coaching environment

A 16-year-old male student residing in a competitive residential coaching hostel received weekly phone calls with his parents, during which his examination results and body size were commented on together. This was done under the rubric of discussing his discipline and character. Similar comments were made by his coaching tutor during class. Humor was used as a coping mechanism by the student to deflect attention when binge eating snack foods at night as a private mechanism for managing his emotions. A family communication intervention was added by a counselor at the coaching center. The student's parents took part in a language substitution intervention. They stopped commenting about his body and examinations and instead asked about his sleep and levels of energy. Within six weeks, binge eating episodes decreased, and he attended a peer walking group. This is consistent with Seligman (1975) and Compas et al. (2001), where agency restoration was seen after incremental environmental changes.

Vignette 3: Navigating conflicting family norms across rural and urban settings

A 14-year-old girl from a village in Rajasthan attended a residential school in the state capital. While her family saw her large body size as an indicator of health and prosperity, her peers in school saw her as overweight and ridiculed her. The girl coped by dismissing this when she spoke to her family and by avoiding her peers. An Anganwadi worker in her village had organized an education session before the school year began, in which parents and grandparents of school-going children were given education on body image among adolescents and how it affects them psychologically. The girl's grandmother had changed her way of referring to her by using endearing words related to body size. However, after attending the education session, she began to use endearing words related to body strength. The girl felt better when she returned home because she was not caught in two conflicting situations, as supported by the theory of ecological resilience by Ungar (2011) and Masten (2001) study on family reframing.

9.5.9 A monitoring framework for family-centered programs

Family-centered programs necessitate proximal outcome measurements, which extend beyond body mass index. The framework below monitors progress from stigmatizing to supportive family environments (see Table 9.6

9.5.10 Implementation science: scaling family interventions in india

The scaling of family-level interventions is challenging, given the structural diversity of families, the variability of family schedules, and the stigmatizing effects of certain practices embedded in cultural scripts that are resistant to change. The phased approach of implementation science, as articulated by Fixsen et al. (2005), Damschroder et al. (2009), etc., helps to balance the need for fidelity with the need to adapt to the context.

1. Exploration phase: Organize focus group discussions with parents, grandparents, and adolescents in each of the identified states to understand the dominant stigmatization scripts and preferred communication styles. Identify cultural events in each of the states where comments on weight are most common.
2. Installation phase: Train Anganwadi workers, ASHA workers, and school counselors as family intervention facilitators. Prepare language swap cards in all major regional languages. Conduct parent workshop modules in ten schools in each of the states.
3. Initial implementation phase: Measure the frequency of comments during meals and family support scores provided by adolescents. Establish feedback loops to continually refine the content and delivery of the workshops.
4. Full implementation phase: Integrate family communication workshops with the POSHAN Abhiyaan home visits. Include no-shame mealtime comments in the Fit India Movement family wellness programs. Organize extended kinship awareness workshops through health centers.
5. Sustainability phase: Include annual refresher courses in health worker certification programs. Include family support scores in NFHS survey tools. Provide public recognition for schools and Anganwadis attaining standards in the family environment with no stigma.

9.5.11 Research priorities for India

Though there is considerable evidence on the subject, there are several aspects of family influence on adolescent obesity in India that are not well understood. The following are the identified research priorities.

- Longitudinal studies are required to understand the family communication styles in early adolescents and their association with the development of coping skills, BMI, and mental health in young adults at the age of 18 and beyond (Neumark-Sztainer et al., 2002; Reinehr, 2013).
- Intersectional studies are essential to understand the compounded effects of family factors on adolescent obesity in India, applying Crenshaw (1989) theory of intersectionality.
- Development of measurements for India-specific tools is a pressing matter, and existing parental feeding and family functioning scales do not measure joint family commentary, marriageability, or joint family weight scrutiny.

TABLE 9.6 Outcome indicators for evaluating family-based interventions in adolescent obesity.

Metric	Operational definition	Target after 12 weeks
Mealtime comment frequency	Parent-reported number of weight or food-shaming comments per week at mealtimes	Reduction of 70% from baseline
No-shame mealtime adherence	Adolescent-reported days per week with no body comments at dinner	Five or more days per week
Language swap usage	Parent self-report of using supportive alternative phrases in the past week	Daily use by 80% of trained parents
Adolescent-reported family support score	Validated scale item: My family makes me feel good about myself, 0–10 scale	Mean score increase of 2 points from baseline
Secrecy eating frequency	Adolescent self-report of days per week eating alone to avoid family comment	Reduction of 60% from baseline
Family activity participation	Days per week of shared physical activity with at least one family member	Two or more days per week

Source: Compas, B.E., Connor-Smith, J.K., Saltzman, H., Thomsen, A.H. & Wadsworth, M.E. (2001). Coping with stress during childhood and adolescence: Problems, progress, and potential in theory and research. *Psychological Bulletin, 127*(1), 87–127. https://doi.org/10.1037/0033-2909.127.1.87.

- More randomized and controlled trials of parent training workshops in government schools across socioeconomically diverse districts in India, including the coping repertoire index and comment frequency, are needed.
- Policy impact evaluations should assess whether POSHAN Abhiyaan, Fit India, and RKSK materials promote weight stigma among school-going youth and whether they overemphasize weight, slimmness, and BMI without emphasizing dignity, psychological well-being, and supportive family communication.
- Implementation science studies should evaluate family intervention programs as they transfer from urban private schools to rural government schools and underserved populations.

9.6 Conclusion

The family environment is not peripheral to adolescent obesity but is, in fact, the most immediate and enduring context for all youth. The preceding chapter has established this through theoretical frameworks, global and Indian empirical data, and practical tools to illustrate that families are simultaneously risk environments and resources for adolescent obesity. While families may promote weight stigma through communication and modeling, they may also buffer against it. Families may promote maladaptive coping and body size centrality, which can have serious psychological effects for obese youth, including increased levels of weight bias internalization, depression, and avoidant coping. However, families may also promote supportive communication and joint health practices and help youth develop more positive body images and self-esteem, not linked to body size.

In the case of India, the role of the family is further magnified by collectivistic structures that provide adolescents with minimal autonomy and multiple sources of commentary. Joint family structures, marriageability, academic examination systems, caste and class structures, and the urban-rural continuum all add distinctive layers to the family and obesity relationship that are not reflected in the Western literature. The quantitative study undertaken by this researcher provides some of the first data on family environment perception, psychological well-being, and coping differences between obese and nonobese youth in India, which can be used to add to the global literature on the role of the family in adolescent obesity.

To address the issue of adolescent obesity in India, interventions must be developed that extend beyond the individual level to the family and community structures in which the level of adolescent health is constructed. The toolkit for interventions, policy reform recommendations, measurement framework, and intervention science roadmap outlined in this chapter provide a set of pathways for developing dignity-first interventions based on family structures within India's existing health and educational infrastructure. Achievement of the vision for stigma-free family structures by the year 2030 will necessitate political commitment, cultural engagement, and investment in training, measurement, and evaluation.

9.7 Limitations

Several limitations must also be considered when examining the results presented throughout the chapter. First, the present research was conducted within the metropolitan city of Kolkata, which may not reflect the full range of experiences for adolescents and their families within the larger context of India. Second, the present research utilized a comparative research design, which prevents the establishment of causality between negative family environments and obesity, or conversely, obesity and negative perceptions of the family environment. Third, all family environment data were collected via adolescent self-report using the FES, which may be subject to social desirability effects, particularly within collectivist societies where negative reporting about the family may not be well received. Fourth, the present research was not qualitative in nature, and the experience-related aspects of family commentary and coping, as described throughout sections 9.4 and 9.5, were based on the published research. Fifth, the global studies synthesized in Section 9.3 show considerable variation in methodologies, cultural contexts, and sample populations, which weakens the validity of cross-regional comparative conclusions. Sixth, the intervention recommendations developed in Section 9.5, while informed by research, have not been tested by randomized controlled trials in the Indian context and should be empirically supported before widespread adoption.

9.8 Key takeaways

Family environment is the most immediate and influential context shaping adolescent obesity, affecting both behaviour and psychological outcomes.

Families function as both risk and protective systems, with critical communication increasing stigma and supportive environments promoting resilience.

Parenting styles, family routines, and parental modelling play a central role in shaping eating behaviour, physical activity, and coping patterns.

In the Indian context, factors such as joint family structures, marriageability norms, academic pressure, and extended kin interactions intensify the impact of family on obesity.

Obese adolescents experience poorer family environment conditions, along with higher depression and anxiety and lower self-esteem compared with nonobese peers.

Effective intervention must be family-centred, focusing on supportive communication, shared activities, and culturally sensitive strategies across home, school, and policy systems

Glossary

Term	Definition
Authoritative parenting	A parenting style combining high warmth with clear structure and open communication, consistently linked to healthier adolescent outcomes, including lower obesity risk and stronger coping repertoires.
Ecological Systems Theory	Bronfenbrenner (1979) framework situating families within nested layers of social influence: microsystem, mesosystem, exosystem, macrosystem, and chronosystem.
Family Stress Model	Conger & Elder's (1994) framework linking economic and psychological stress to parenting practices, demonstrating how financial strain leads to harsher family communication and reduced access to healthy food.
Family Systems Theory	A framework originating with Minuchin (1974) and Bowen (1978), viewing the family as an interdependent unit in which the behavior of any one member affects all others.
Intergenerational transmission	The process by which behaviors, attitudes, and health risks, including obesity, pass from parents to children through genetic pathways, modeled behaviors, and embedded cultural scripts.
Intersectionality	Crenshaw (1989) framework for understanding how overlapping social identities such as caste, class, gender, and body size interact to produce compounded forms of disadvantage that exceed the impact of any single identity alone.
Marriageability script	A cultural narrative prevalent in many Indian contexts that ties a girl's body size to her desirability as a marriage partner, intensifying body-related stigma within families and extended kin networks.
Social Learning Theory	Bandura's (1977) framework proposing that behaviors are learned through observation, imitation, and reinforcement, is applied here to how adolescents adopt parental eating, activity, and coping patterns.

Review questions

1. What, according to the findings of the present study, were the implications of the relationship between the dimensions of the family environment (measured by the FES) and the psychological well-being of obese adolescents? What were the two dimensions of the FES, wherein the obese adolescents scored lower than the nonobese peers, and what implications can be derived from the findings about the family environment of the obese peers?
2. What are the ways in which maladaptive family patterns like critical commentary and inconsistent mealtime patterns, contribute to emotional eating and social avoidance in adolescents with obesity? Identify the specific theoretical mechanism described in Section 9.2 that underlies each process.
3. In what ways do family mealtimes and physical activity help protect against obesity stigma and depression in adolescents? What global and Indian data support these findings?
4. Why must family interventions be culturally sensitive when implemented in India? Identify at least three ways in which the Indian family context differs from the Western family context that must be taken into consideration when developing interventions for families of adolescents with obesity.
5. Compare and contrast authoritative, authoritarian, and permissive parenting styles based on their implications for coping with obesity. Which of these parenting styles shows the strongest protective effects against obesity stigma and depression? What are the data to support this, and what cultural considerations must be taken into account when implementing this approach in India?
6. In what ways do joint family structures simultaneously exacerbate and alleviate stigma and depression in adolescents with obesity? Identify one specific example of both exacerbation and alleviation of stigma and depression, and explain the specific theoretical mechanism that underlies this process.

7. What policy-level changes are necessary to the existing infrastructure of national-level programs like POSHAN Abhiyaan, Fit India, and RKSK to include family communication education and dignity-first messaging? Identify at least three specific policy-level changes and the data to support each.

AI disclosure

During the preparation of this work, the author(s) used ChatGPT, Grammarly, and Paperpal solely for the purpose of language editing. After using this tool/service, the author(s) reviewed and edited the content as needed and take(s) full responsibility for the content of the publication.

References

Bandura, A. (1977). *Social learning theory*. Prentice Hall.

Baumrind, D. (1966). Effects of authoritative parental control on child behavior. *Child Development, 37*(4), 887–907. https://doi.org/10.2307/1126611.

Baumrind, D. (1991). The influence of parenting style on adolescent competence and substance use. *Journal of Early Adolescence, 11*(1), 56–95.

Beck, A. T., Ward, C. H., Mendelson, M., Mock, J., & Erbaugh, J (1961). An inventory for measuring depression. *Archives of General Psychiatry, 4*(6), 561–571.

Bell, H. M. (1962). *Bell Adjustment Inventory Manual. Psychological Corporation, New York.*

Bhatia, H., & Chadha, N. K. (1993). Family environment scale. *National Psychological Corporation, Agra, India.*

Birch, L. L., Fisher, J. O., Grimm-Thomas, K., Markey, C. N., Sawyer, R., & Johnson, S. L. (2001). Confirmatory factor analysis of the child feeding questionnaire: A measure of parental attitudes, beliefs and practices about child feeding and obesity proneness. *Appetite, 36*(3), 201–210. https://doi.org/10.1006/appe.2001.0398.

Bloom, B. L. (1985). A factor analysis of self-report measures of family functioning. *Family Process, 24*(2), 225–239. https://doi.org/10.1111/j.1545-5300.1985.00225.x.

Booth, M. L., Dobbins, T., Okely, A. D., Denney-Wilson, E., & Hardy, L. L. (2006). Trends in the prevalence of overweight and obesity among young Australians, 1985, 1997, and 2004. *Obesity, 15*(5), 1089–1095. https://doi.org/10.1038/oby.2007.617.

Bowen, M. (1978). *Family therapy in clinical practice*. Jason Aronson.

Brown, J. D., Dutton, K. A.,& Cook, K. E. (1990). From the top down: Self-esteem and self-evaluation. *Cognition and Emotion, 5*(5-6), 555–567.

Bronfenbrenner, U. (1979). *The ecology of human development: Experiments by nature and design*. Harvard University Press.

Burgess-Champoux, T. L., Larson, N., Neumark-Sztainer, D., Hannan, P. J., & Story, M. (2009). Are family meal patterns associated with overall diet quality during the transition from early to middle adolescence? *Journal of Nutrition Education and Behavior, 41*(2), 79–86. https://doi.org/10.1016/j.jneb.2008.03.011.

Compas, B. E., Connor-Smith, J. K., Saltzman, H., Thomsen, A. H., & Wadsworth, M. E. (2001). Coping with stress during childhood and adolescence: Problems, progress, and potential in theory and research. *Psychological Bulletin, 127*(1), 87–127. https://doi.org/10.1037/0033-2909.127.1.87.

Conde, W. L., & Borges, C. (2011). The risk of incidence and persistence of obesity among Brazilian adolescents. *Revista Brasileira de Epidemiologia, 14*(Suppl. 1), 67–76.

Conger, R. D., & Elder, G. H. (1994). *Families in troubled times: Adapting to change in rural America*. Aldine de Gruyter.

Crenshaw, K. (1989). Demarginalizing the intersection of race and sex: A black feminist critique of antidiscrimination doctrine, feminist theory and antiracist politics. *University of Chicago Legal Forum, 1989*(1), 139–167.

Damschroder, L. J., Aron, D. C., Keith, R. E., Kirsh, S. R., Alexander, J. A., & Lowery, J. C. (2009). Fostering implementation of health services research findings into practice: A consolidated framework for advancing implementation science. *Implementation Science, 4*(1), 50. https://doi.org/10.1186/1748-5908-4-50.

Das, S. (2018). Psychological characteristics and adjustment patterns in late adolescents and young adults with obesity: An exploratory study [Doctoral thesis, University of Calcutta].

Donnelly, B. W., Conger, R. D., & Elder, G. H. (1994). Families in troubled times: Adapting to change in rural America. *Journal of Marriage and the Family. JSTOR, 56*(3). https://doi.org/10.2307/352890.

Durso, L. E., & Latner, J. D. (2008). Understanding self-directed stigma: Development of the weight bias internalization scale. *Obesity, 16*(S2), S80–S86. https://doi.org/10.1038/oby.2008.448.

Eisenberg, M. E., Neumark-Sztainer, D., & Story, M. (2003). Associations of weight-based teasing and emotional well-being among adolescents. *Archives of Pediatrics and Adolescent Medicine, 157*(8), 733–738. https://doi.org/10.1001/archpedi.157.8.733.

Faith, M. S., Matz, P. E., & Jorge, M. A. (2002). Obesity–depression associations in the population. *Journal of Psychosomatic Research, 53*(4), 935–942. https://doi.org/10.1016/S0022-3999(02)00308-2.

Fixsen, D.L., Naoom, S.F., Blase, K.A., Friedman, R.M., & Wallace, F. (2005). Implementation research: A synthesis of the literature. University of South Florida, Louis de la Parte Florida Mental Health Institute, National Implementation Research Network.

Fulkerson, J. A., Story, M., Mellin, A., Leffert, N., Neumark-Sztainer, D., & French, S. A. (2007). Family dinner meal frequency and adolescent development: Relationships with developmental assets and high-risk behaviors. *Journal of Adolescent Health, 40*(4), 344–351. https://doi.org/10.1016/j.jadohealth.2006.10.010.

Goldfield, G. S., Moore, C., Henderson, K., Buchholz, A., Obeid, N., & Flament, M. F. (2010). The relation between weight-based teasing and psychological adjustment in adolescents. *Paediatrics & Child Health, 15*(5), 283–288. https://doi.org/10.1093/pch/15.5.283.

Grogan, S. (2016). *Body image: Understanding body dissatisfaction in men, women and children* (3rd ed.). Routledge.

Hofmann, S. G., Asnaani, A., Vonk, I. J. J., Sawyer, A. T., & Fang, A. (2012). The efficacy of cognitive behavioral therapy: A review of meta-analyses. *Cognitive Therapy and Research, 36*(5), 427–440. https://doi.org/10.1007/s10608-012-9476-1.

Holland, G., & Tiggemann, M. (2016). A systematic review of the impact of the use of social networking sites on body image and disordered eating outcomes. *Body Image, 17*, 100–110. https://doi.org/10.1016/j.bodyim.2016.02.008.

Janssen, I., Craig, W. M., Boyce, W. F., & Pickett, W. (2004). Associations between overweight and obesity with bullying behaviors in school-aged children. *Pediatrics, 113*(5), 1187–1194. https://doi.org/10.1542/peds.113.5.1187.

Khalsa, S. B. S., Hickey-Schultz, L., Cohen, D., Steiner, N., & Cope, S. (2012). Evaluation of the mental health benefits of yoga in a secondary school: A preliminary randomized controlled trial. *Journal of Behavioral Health Services and Research, 39*(1), 80–90. https://doi.org/10.1007/s11414-011-9249-8.

Kimani-Murage, E. W. (2013). Exploring the paradox: Double burden of malnutrition in rural South Africa. *Global Health Action, 6*(1), 19249. https://doi.org/10.3402/gha.v6i0.19249.

Larson, R. W., & Verma, S. (1999). How children and adolescents spend time across the world: Work, play, and developmental opportunities. *Psychological Bulletin, 125*(6), 701–736. https://doi.org/10.1037/0033-2909.125.6.701.

Latner, J. D., & Stunkard, A. J. (2003). Getting worse: The stigmatization of obese children. *Obesity Research, 11*(3), 452–456. https://doi.org/10.1038/oby.2003.61.

Maccoby, E. E., & Martin, J. A. (1983). Socialization in the context of the family: Parent-child interaction. In P. H. Mussen, & E. M. Hetherington (Eds.). *Handbook of child psychology: Vol. 4. Socialization, personality, and social development* (pp. 1–101). (4th ed.). Wiley.

Masten, A. S. (2001). Ordinary magic: Resilience processes in development. *American Psychologist, 56*(3), 227–238. https://doi.org/10.1037/0003-066X.56.3.227.

Minuchin, S. (1974). *Families and family therapy*. Harvard University Press.

Misra, A., & Khurana, L. (2011). Obesity-related non-communicable diseases: South Asians vs White Caucasians. *International Journal of Obesity, 35*(2), 167–187. https://doi.org/10.1038/ijo.2010.135.

Nayar, U. S. (Ed.). (2012). *Child and adolescent mental health*Sage Publications India.

Neumark-Sztainer, D., Falkner, N., Story, M., Perry, C., Hannan, P. J., & Mulert, S. (2002). Weight-teasing among adolescents: Correlations with weight status and disordered eating behaviors. *International Journal of Obesity, 26*(1), 123–131. https://doi.org/10.1038/sj.ijo.0801853.

Neumark-Sztainer, D., Hannan, P. J., Story, M., Croll, J., & Perry, C. (2003). Family meal patterns and dietary quality among adolescents. *Journal of the American Dietetic Association, 103*(3), 317–322. https://doi.org/10.1053/jada.2003.50048.

Pierce, W. D., & Bandura, A. (1977). Social learning theory. *Canadian Journal of Sociology / Cahiers canadiens de sociologie. JSTOR, 2*(3). https://doi.org/10.2307/3340496.

Pont, S. J., Puhl, R., Cook, S. R., & Slusser, W. (2017). Stigma experienced by children and adolescents with obesity. *Pediatrics, 140*(6), e20173034. https://doi.org/10.1542/peds.2017-3034.

Popkin, B. M. (2015). Nutrition transition and the global diabetes epidemic. *Current Diabetes Reports, 15*(9), 64. https://doi.org/10.1007/s11892-015-0631-4.

Prentice, A. M. (2006). The emerging epidemic of obesity in developing countries. *International Journal of Epidemiology, 35*(1), 93–99. https://doi.org/10.1093/ije/dyi272.

Puhl, R. M., & Heuer, C. A. (2009). The stigma of obesity: A review and update. *Obesity, 17*(5), 941–964. https://doi.org/10.1038/oby.2008.636.

Puhl, R. M., Lessard, L. M., Larson, N., Eisenberg, M. E., & Neumark-Sztainer, D. (2016). Weight stigma as a predictor of eating and physical activity behaviors and weight change among adolescents. *Obesity, 25*(1), 175–181. https://doi.org/10.1002/oby.21716.

Rao, K., Subbakrishna, D. K.,& Prabhu, G. G. (1999). Coping checklist. *NIMHANS Journal, 17*(2), 138–144.

Reilly, J. J., & Kelly, J. (2011). Long-term impact of overweight and obesity in childhood and adolescence on morbidity and premature mortality in adulthood. *International Journal of Obesity, 35*(7), 891–898. https://doi.org/10.1038/ijo.2010.222.

Reinehr, T. (2013). Lifestyle intervention in childhood obesity: Changes and challenges. *Nature Reviews Endocrinology, 9*(10), 607–614. https://doi.org/10.1038/nrendo.2013.149.

Repetti, R. L., Taylor, S. E., & Seeman, T. E. (2002). Risky families: Family social environments and the mental and physical health of offspring. *Psychological Bulletin, 128*(2), 330–366. https://doi.org/10.1037/0033-2909.128.2.330.

Rhee, K. (2008). Childhood overweight and the relationship between parent behaviors, parenting style, and family functioning. *Annals of the American Academy of Political and Social Science, 615*(1), 11–37. https://doi.org/10.1177/0002716207308400.

Rodgers, R. F., Slater, A., Gordon, C. S., McLean, S. A., Marques, M. D., & Paxton, S. J. (2020). A biopsychosocial model of social media use and body image concerns, disordered eating, and muscle-building behaviors among adolescent girls and boys. *Journal of Youth and Adolescence, 49*(2), 399–409. https://doi.org/10.1007/s10964-019-01190-0.

Rosenberg, M. (1965). Society and the adolescent self-image. *Princeton University Press, Princeton, NJ.*

Seligman, M. E. P. (1975). *Helplessness: On depression, development, and death*. Freeman.

Sleddens, E. F. C., Gerards, S. M. P. L., Thijs, C., de Vries, N. K., & Kremers, S. P. J. (2011). General parenting, childhood overweight and obesity-inducing behaviors: A systematic overview. *International Journal of Pediatric Obesity, 6*(2–2), e12–e27. https://doi.org/10.3109/17477166.2011.566339.

Sobal, J., & Stunkard, A. J (1989). Socioeconomic status and obesity: A review of the literature. *Psychological Bulletin, 105*(2), 260–275.

Spielberger, C. D. (1983). *Manual for the State–Trait Anxiety Inventory (Form Y)*. Palo Alto, CA: Consulting Psychologists Press.

Stice, E., Shaw, H., & Marti, C. N. (2006). A meta-analytic review of obesity prevention programs for children and adolescents: The skinny on interventions that work. *Psychological Bulletin, 132*(5), 667–691. https://doi.org/10.1037/0033-2909.132.5.667.

Swinburn, B. A., Kraak, V. I., Allender, S., Atkins, V. J., Baker, P. I., Bogard, J. R., & Dietz, W. H. (2019). The global syndemic of obesity, undernutrition, and climate change: The lancet commission report. *Lancet, 393*(10173), 791–846. https://doi.org/10.1016/S0140-6736(18)32822-8.

Ungar, M. (2011). The social ecology of resilience: Addressing contextual and cultural ambiguity of a nascent construct. *American Journal of Orthopsychiatry, 81*(1), 1–17. https://doi.org/10.1111/j.1939-0025.2010.01067.x.

Zoogman, S., Goldberg, S. B., Hoyt, W. T., & Miller, L. (2015). Mindfulness interventions with youth: A meta-analysis. *Mindfulness, 6*(2), 290–302. https://doi.org/10.1007/s12671-013-0260-4.

Further reading

Carver, C. S., Scheier, M. F., & Weintraub, J. K. (1989). Assessing coping strategies: A theoretically based approach. *Journal of Personality and Social Psychology, 56*(2), 267–283. https://doi.org/10.1037/0022-3514.56.2.267.

Connor-Smith, J. K., Compas, B. E., Wadsworth, M. E., Thomsen, A. H., & Saltzman, H. (2000). Responses to stress in adolescence: Measurement of coping and involuntary stress responses. *Journal of Consulting and Clinical Psychology, 68*(6), 976–992. https://doi.org/10.1037/0022-006X.68.6.976.

Fredrickson, B. L., & Roberts, T. A. (1997). Objectification theory: Toward understanding women's lived experiences and mental health risks. *Psychology of Women Quarterly, 21*(2), 173–206. https://doi.org/10.1111/j.1471-6402.1997.tb00108.x.

Olstad, D. L., Raine, K. D., & McCargar, L. J. (2011). Adopting and implementing nutrition guidelines in recreational facilities: Public health rationale and implementation challenges. *Canadian Journal of Public Health, 102*(5), 381–385. https://doi.org/10.1007/BF03404173.

Chapter 10

Summary and future directions

"The goal of science is not simply to accumulate facts but to build understanding: of what the evidence means, for whom it matters, and what we must now do differently."

Learning objectives

Evaluate the contribution of the present study to the Indian adolescent obesity psychology literature, identifying the methodological strengths and acknowledged limitations of its exploratory quantitative comparative design.

Synthesize the multidomain psychological findings of the present study—across personality, anxiety, depression, self-esteem, locus of control, coping, body image, eating attitudes, family environment, and adjustment—into a coherent account of the psychological burden associated with adolescent obesity in urban India.

Appraise the theoretical contributions of the present study—including its extensions to the Social Determinants of Health framework and resilience theory—and evaluate their implications for future research design and intervention development in Indian adolescent health contexts.

10.1 Integrative summary of findings

10.1.1 The global and Indian context of adolescent obesity

Adolescent obesity is now one of the most important public health problems of the 21st century. A pooled analysis of 3663 population-representative studies encompassing 222 million individuals substantiated that the global prevalence of overweight and obesity among children and adolescents aged 5 to 19 years increased from 8% in 1990 to 20% by 2022, equating to over 390 million young people, with the most significant rises currently observed in low- and middle-income countries (Phelps et al., 2024). India is at the center of this change. The Comprehensive National Nutrition Survey (CNNS, 2016–18) indicates a national prevalence of overweight and obesity among adolescents at 4.8%, with significantly elevated rates in urban regions and higher wealth quintiles (Sethi et al., 2024). A meta-analysis of 21 Indian studies revealed that private school students have 2.47 times greater odds of obesity compared to government school students, and a familial history of obesity results in an eightfold increase in risk (Singh et al., 2023).

However, prevalence data tell only part of the story. A scoping review of 93 Indian studies on adolescent obesity (Panda et al., 2025) confirmed that all existing research employs cross-sectional designs, focuses primarily on anthropometric and behavioral outcomes, and largely neglects the psychological, relational, and cultural dimensions that shape how obesity is experienced, interpreted, and managed by adolescents and their families. This volume has addressed that gap systematically. The present study—an exploratory quantitative investigation of N = 400 late adolescents and young adults in Kolkata, comparing obese and nonobese groups across personality, anxiety, depression, self-esteem, locus of control (LOC), coping, eating attitudes, body image, family environment, and adjustment—provides one of the first comprehensive multidomain psychological profiles of obese adolescents in an Indian urban setting.

10.1.2 Overview of the present study

The present study recruited 400 participants (200 obese, 200 nonobese) through purposive sampling with area-wise stratification across northern, central, southern, and eastern Kolkata, drawing from higher secondary schools, undergraduate colleges, university postgraduate departments, gymnasia, and community settings. The sample was equally divided across late adolescence (17–20 years) and young adulthood (21–24 years), with male and female groups of 50 participants each in all eight body mass index (BMI)-age-sex cells. Obese participants met BMI criteria of 30.0–39.9 (Class I and II obesity); nonobese participants had a BMI of 18.5–24.9. Groups were matched on age, socioeconomic

Psychology of Obesity. DOI: https://doi.org/10.1016/B978-0-443-27797-9.00013-0

status, family type, family size, and sibling size. Statistical analysis employed independent-samples t-tests, three-factor factorial analysis of variance (3FFANOVA) with body weight, age, and sex as factors, and Pearson product-moment correlations between BMI and all psychological variables.

A significant main effect of body weight was observed in the 3FFANOVA across every measured variable. In group t-test comparisons, obese participants showed significantly higher Beck Depression Inventory (BDI) depression scores across all four age-sex groups ($P<.01$); significantly higher STAI anxiety across three of four age-sex groups (female young adults: state anxiety $P=.091$ NS, Trait anxiety $P=.253$ NS); significantly lower Rosenberg self-esteem across all four groups ($P<.01$); significantly more disordered eating attitudes on EAT-26 across all four groups ($P<0.01$); LOC findings were mixed across dimensions and groups; body image dimensions showed consistent significant deficits in obese groups; all eight FES dimensions showed significant body weight effects; and home and health adjustment were significantly poorer in obese participants across all four groups ($P<.01$).

10.1.3 Cross-chapter synthesis

This volume has examined adolescent obesity across ten thematic chapters. Chapters 1 and 2 established the global and Indian epidemiological context and reviewed the theoretical and empirical literature. Chapters 3 through 7 examined specific psychological domains: personality traits, anxiety, depression, self-esteem, LOC, and coping responses. Chapters 8 and 9 addressed body image, eating attitudes, and family environment. The present chapter synthesizes these domains into an integrated account of the psychological experience of adolescent obesity in urban India and translates the evidence base into recommendations for theory, practice, and policy.

The cross-chapter synthesis reveals a coherent pattern of systematically elevated psychological burden in obese adolescents across every measured domain. Compared to nonobese peers, obese participants scored significantly higher on neuroticism and significantly lower on extraversion, agreeableness, openness to experience, and conscientiousness across all four age-sex groups. State and trait anxiety were significantly elevated in three of four groups; depression and self-esteem differences were significant in all four. Eating attitudes were substantially more disordered, with all obese group means exceeding the EAT-26 clinical threshold of 20. Body image was significantly impaired across five Multidimensional Body Self Relations Questionnaire (MBSRQ) dimensions—Appearance Evaluation, Fitness Evaluation, Fitness Orientation, Health Evaluation, and Health Orientation—with obese participants scoring higher on Illness Orientation. Coping patterns were developmentally differentiated: late adolescent groups showed no significant overall coping differences from nonobese peers, while young adult female obese participants demonstrated significantly lower adaptive coping, and young adult male obese participants showed higher coping scores. Family environment perceptions were systematically less warm, less expressive, less recreationally active, and less supportive of independence across all eight FES dimensions. Adjustment difficulties were consistently more pronounced in home and health domains across all four groups, and in the social domain across three of four groups. These domains do not operate independently; together they constitute an interconnected profile of vulnerability in which deficits in one domain compound and amplify deficits in others.

10.2 Personality, locus of control, and the psychological profile of obesity

10.2.1 Personality traits: what the five-factor model reveals

The five-factor model (FFM) provides the dominant taxonomy for examining personality in the context of obesity (McCrae & Costa, 1989). The current study found that obese adolescents scored significantly higher for neuroticism and lower for extraversion, agreeableness, openness to experience, and conscientiousness than their normal-weight peers in all four age-sex groups ($P<.01$). These findings are consistent with the most comprehensive meta-analytic evidence to date. A prospective longitudinal study with a sample of 14,531 anthropometric measurements conducted over more than five decades revealed that higher neuroticism and lower conscientiousness were related to higher BMI, with physical activity and dietary behavior contributing to approximately 50% of this relationship. In addition, personality traits were examined in a systematic review with a focus on personality traits in children. The current findings are consistent with this systematic review in terms of the relationship between conscientiousness and obesity, with a standardized mean difference indicating a significant negative relationship between conscientiousness and obesity in children, $r=-0.09$.

A recent cross-sectional study on personality traits and psychological well-being in children with obesity (Valero-Valenzuela et al., 2025) confirmed that neuroticism positively predicted depression and anxiety, while conscientiousness, extraversion, agreeableness, and openness negatively predicted both. Moreover, gender significantly moderated the personality-trait predictions, with neuroticism predicting anxiety particularly in females—an effect that is mirrored in the current research, where female obese late adolescents showed the highest level of trait anxiety differentials from their nonobese counterparts (M = 51.36 vs M = 45.72, *P*<.01). In other words, personality traits are not only relatively stable characteristics but also mediators through which obesity stigma is processed. For example, an obese youth with high neuroticism will likely ruminate about past or expected stigma, while an obese youth with low conscientiousness will likely fail to adopt adaptive behaviors despite their best motivational intentions.

The personality obesity relationship is reciprocal. Longitudinal research by Sutin and Terracciano (2011) showed that personality traits predict weight changes over time, it is likely that prolonged obesity will, in turn, affect personality traits over time, particularly through repeated experiences with stigma, social exclusion, and lack of opportunity. While the current research design does not allow us to disentangle the directionality of the relationship, it is clear that longitudinal research with Indian youth is urgently needed.

10.2.2 Locus of control: mixed and theoretically complex findings

LOC is defined as "one's generalized expectancies concerning the degree to which he can, does, or ought to control events in his life." This concept has been related to obesity in previous research (Rotter, 1966; Steptoe & Wardle, 2001). External LOC—the belief that powerful others or chance govern outcomes—predicts passive coping, healthcare disengagement, and reduced adherence to health-promoting routines. A comprehensive review of the LOC-obesity literature confirmed that external LOC is consistently associated with higher BMI and more disordered health behaviors, with the direction of causality most likely bidirectional: external LOC increases vulnerability to obesity, and sustained obesity reinforces external LOC through repeated experiences of unsuccessful change attempts (Gilles & Cairney, 2014).

The present study produced mixed results on LOC, reflecting the genuine complexity of this variable in the context of adolescent obesity. On the Powerful Others dimension, obese participants scored significantly lower than nonobese peers across all four age-sex groups (*P*<.01). On the (Levenson, 1973) scale, a higher Powerful Others score indicates a stronger belief that outcomes are controlled by influential people; nonobese participants holding higher scores suggest greater orientation toward social authority and structured external guidance (Rotter, 1966). On the Internal Control dimension, results were mixed by group: obese male late adolescents and obese female young adults scored significantly lower than nonobese counterparts (*P*<.01), indicating reduced perceived personal agency; obese male young adults scored significantly higher (*P*<.05); and female late adolescents showed no significant difference. On the Chance Control dimension, three of four groups showed no significant differences; only obese female late adolescents scored significantly higher (*P*<.05), indicating greater attribution of outcomes to luck or fate. The 3FFANOVA confirmed a significant body weight main effect for Powerful Others and Internal Control but not for Chance Control. The pattern across LOC dimensions is therefore variable by group, age, and sex, and does not support a single interpretive conclusion—a genuine complexity that warrants individually calibrated clinical formulation rather than aggregate characterization.

A study of personality traits and LOC in Indian obese women confirmed the present study's pattern: obese individuals showed significantly higher external LOC, higher neuroticism, and lower conscientiousness and openness to experience compared to nonobese counterparts. The alignment across Indian samples suggests that these personality and LOC profiles are culturally consistent, not merely artifacts of Western research populations.

10.2.3 Depression, anxiety, and self-esteem: the psychological burden

The present study found significantly higher BDI depression scores in obese participants across all four age-sex groups (male LA: obese M = 19.30 vs nonobese; M = 12.48; female LA: obese M = 22.04 vs nonobese M = 13.36; both *P*<.01). A longitudinal analysis of the UK Millennium Cohort Study confirmed a cyclical relationship between obesity and mental health during adolescence: earlier obesity predicted later emotional symptoms, including anxiety and depression, and earlier emotional symptoms predicted later obesity—with body satisfaction, self-esteem, and bullying serving as key mediating pathways (Blundell et al., 2024). The meta-analysis by Romano et al. (2023) of 87 studies confirmed that weight bias internalization (WBI)—the self-directed application of negative weight stereotypes—mediated these relationships, with WBI correlating with depression (r = 0.48) and anxiety (r = 0.40) more strongly than BMI magnitude alone.

Self-esteem showed particularly pronounced deficits in obese adolescents in the present study (female LA: obese M = 14.06 vs nonobese M = 21.66, *P*<.01; male LA: obese M = 6.64 vs nonobese M = 21.78, *P*<.01). A systematic review and meta-analysis of pediatric obesity treatment found that intervention resulted in increased self-esteem (standardized mean difference 0.34, *P*<.001), maintained at follow-up (Harrist et al., 2020), suggesting that self-esteem deficits in obese adolescents are modifiable. Critically, this improvement was observed regardless of whether significant weight loss occurred—meaning that psychological outcomes can improve through changes in environment, communication, and coping even without metabolic change. This is a finding of major practical significance: it justifies psychological intervention for obese adolescents independent of weight loss goals. Similar patterns were observed among young adults, with obese males ($M = 20.44$ vs 10.50, $P < .01$) and obese females ($M = 22.62$ vs 13.84, $P < .01$) showing significantly higher depression scores than their nonobese counterparts.

10.3 Body image, eating attitudes, and coping responses

10.3.1 Body image: what Multidimensional Body Self Relations Questionnaire findings reveal

Body image—the multidimensional cognitive, affective, and behavioral relationship an individual has with their own body—is one of the most consistently affected psychological domains in adolescent obesity. In the current study, it was also established that obese participants had significantly lower appearance evaluation, fitness evaluation, fitness orientation, health evaluation, and health orientation compared to their nonobese counterparts ($P < .01$ for all groups). In contrast, the results showed that obese participants had higher illness orientation compared to their nonobese counterparts. For female obese adolescents, it was also established that they had higher appearance orientation, indicating that they were more preoccupied with monitoring and regulating their appearance despite their negative appearance evaluation. This is in consonance with self-objectification theory (Fredrickson & Roberts, 1997).

Dissatisfaction with the body develops faster in adolescents with obesity. A systematic review of school-based body image interventions also revealed that body dissatisfaction plays a critical role in the longitudinal pathway of childhood BMI, body dissatisfaction, and adolescent depression, and that it mediates the relationship between childhood BMI and adolescent depression. Depression in adolescents is not caused by their weight but by their interpretation and evaluation of their body in relation to societal ideals. A recent meta-analysis of digital interventions targeting body dissatisfaction also revealed that body dissatisfaction, appearance comparison, and thin-ideal internalization showed significant improvements in 20 RCTs of digital interventions targeting body dissatisfaction among 5251 participants, including SMD = -0.38 for body dissatisfaction, −0.24 for appearance comparison, and −0.28 for thin-ideal internalization. The implication for Indian adolescents is clear: body image must be treated as a primary intervention target, not a secondary concern.

The Indian-specific body image context is shaped by the intersection of globalized media ideals with traditional cultural norms. A 2024 study on disordered eating and body dissatisfaction among Indian adolescents (Anam et al., 2025) confirmed that social media overuse and high stress levels are the key risk factors associated with body image dissatisfaction and eating disorder vulnerability in Indian adolescents, particularly in early adolescence and among females. A cross-sectional study in Jaipur confirmed significant negative correlations between eating attitudes and body image ($r = -0.477$, $P < .001$) and quality of life ($r = -0.372$, $P < .001$) in adolescents aged 13–18 (Ahuja et al., 2025), using the same EAT-26 instrument employed in the present study.

10.3.2 Eating attitudes: disordered patterns and their mechanisms

Eating attitudes and behaviors are integral to the psychology of adolescent obesity, occupying a position between biological predisposition and psychological functioning. The present study found significantly more disordered eating attitudes in obese participants (EAT-26) across all four age-sex groups ($P < .01$). Obese male late adolescents scored $M = 26.68$ versus nonobese $M = 6.48$, and obese female late adolescents $M = 29.34$ versus nonobese $M = 9.24$—differences of remarkable magnitude that indicate disordered attitudes toward eating substantially beyond subclinical thresholds.

The international literature confirms the clinical significance of these findings. Approximately 25% of adolescent girls with overweight or obesity overvalue shape and weight, which is a prospective risk factor for eating disorder development (Sonneville et al., 2012). An exploratory meta-analysis found that more than one quarter of children and adolescents with overweight or obesity reported binge/LOC eating, with 22.2% reporting binge eating and 31.2% reporting loss-of-control eating. Emotion regulation difficulties are a consistent predictor of disordered eating: a meta-analysis of emotion regulation and disordered eating in adolescents and young adults confirmed significant associations between difficulty regulating emotions and eating disorder pathology across diverse populations (Zhou et al., 2025).

In India, the prevalence of disordered eating behaviors and attitudes among adolescents is rising rapidly. A cross-sectional study in Mumbai found that 42.25% of senior college students were at risk for eating disorders using the EAT-26 (Iyer & Shriraam, 2024), with obese and overweight students at significantly higher risk than normal-weight peers. Disordered eating in Indian adolescents is associated with peer teasing, parental obesity, chronic dieting, low self-esteem, and social media exposure (Piko et al., 2022; Anam et al., 2025). These are precisely the risk factors documented across this volume: the present study's finding of significantly higher EAT-26 scores in obese participants is therefore embedded in a recognizable and theoretically coherent pattern of risk concentration.

10.3.3 Coping responses: adaptive and maladaptive trajectories

Coping—the cognitive and behavioral strategies employed to manage stress—is one of the most malleable psychological variables in adolescent obesity research and one of the most important for intervention. The present study found that obese adolescents showed significantly different coping patterns from nonobese peers, with approach-focused coping more prevalent in nonobese groups and avoidant coping more characteristic of obese groups. Obese male late adolescents showed a significant negative correlation between BMI and coping response ($P<.05$), suggesting that higher BMI was associated with less adaptive coping repertoires.

The present study's Coping Response Inventory (CRI) findings on coping produced mixed results that resist simple characterization. Late adolescent groups—both male and female—showed no significant difference between obese and nonobese participants in overall coping response. Among young adults, significant differences emerged but in opposite directions by sex: obese male young adults scored significantly higher on coping (M = 29.08 vs nonobese M = 26.74, $P<.01$), indicating more active coping engagement, while obese female young adults scored significantly lower (M = 24.18 vs nonobese M = 30.60, $P<.01$), indicating less adaptive coping. The 3FFANOVA revealed a significant main effect of body weight on overall coping; however, this effect was qualified by significant interactions with age and sex. Based on the extant literature, avoidant coping—social withdrawal, emotional eating, and secrecy—has emerged as the most consistently linked pattern of maladaptive coping with weight stigma (Puhl & Heuer, 2009; Warnick et al., 2022). The data on group comparison in this study revealed that this pattern was particularly pronounced among obese female young adults, while late adolescents of both sexes and obese male young adults displayed distinct patterns that warranted individually tailored intervention approaches.

Problem-focused coping—cognitive reappraisal, social support-seeking, and identity-expanding beyond physical appearance—operates as a protective factor in this context. The current finding that female young adults displayed significantly poorer emotional adjustment than their male counterparts ($P<.05$) supports the hypothesis that psychological distress builds up over time in young women facing the dual burden of weight stigma and academic pressure in late adolescence and early young adulthood, compounded by marriageability concerns in the early twenties. Moreover, the finding that obese female young adults displayed significantly poorer CRI Coping Scores (M = 24.18) than their nonobese counterparts (M = 30.60), $P<.01$, suggests that this subgroup also displayed poorer emotional adjustment and warrants intervention on both dimensions.

10.4 Family environment and adjustment

10.4.1 Family environment scale: eight dimensions, one picture

The family environment scale (FES), developed by Bhatia & Chadha (1993), measures eight subscales: cohesion, expressiveness, conflict, acceptance and caring, active recreational orientation, independence, organization, and control. The present study found that the body weight main effect was statistically significant in all eight dimensions ($P<.01$ in most groups), with obese adolescents scoring significantly lower than nonobese peers on six dimensions: expressiveness, acceptance and caring, active recreational orientation, independence, organization, and control. The cohesion dimension showed a sex-differentiated pattern—obese males scored higher on Cohesion than nonobese males, while obese females scored lower—reflecting distinct family dynamics by sex. On the Conflict subscale (reverse-scored), obese adolescents indicated greater perceived family conflict once the scoring direction is accounted for.

A network analysis of 488 adolescents with overweight or obesity in China identified paternal rearing style and parental mental health as the most central nodes in family-related obesity networks, with active recreational engagement and family warmth as key protective dimensions (Huang et al., 2023). The present study's parallel finding that obese adolescents showed the largest deficits specifically on active recreational orientation (male LA: M = 26.08 versus nonobese M = 36.88; female LA: M = 25.40 vs nonobese M = 36.62) confirms that sedentary family behavioral scripts are a primary family-level risk factor in Indian urban contexts. Families of obese adolescents in Kolkata report significantly fewer physical activities; this is an empirical reality rather than a speculative mechanism. The theoretical framework provided by The family stress model (Conger & Elder, 1994) supports these realities: economic stress reduces the family's ability to access healthy food options, physical activities, and communication styles, resulting in a cascade effect on multiple levels simultaneously. The realities revealed in this study support this model: obese adolescents in the lowest socioeconomic strata reported more deficits in FES dimensions than any other group, compounding biological risk with environmental deprivation.

10.4.2 Adjustment domains: home, health, social, and emotional

The Bell's adjustment inventory measured four aspects of adjustment: home adjustment, health adjustment, social adjustment, and emotional adjustment. Home and health adjustments were significantly lower in obese individuals in all four age-sex groups ($P<.01$ for all four groups). All three age-sex groups of male late adolescents, male young adults, and female young adults showed significantly lower levels of social adjustment ($P<.01$). Emotional adjustment was significantly lower only among female young adults ($P<.05$), indicating a gender difference in emotional difficulties.

These adjustment findings situate obesity-related distress within concrete daily functioning rather than abstract symptomatology. An adolescent scoring high on home adjustment difficulty is reporting documented relational impairment—disrupted mealtime dynamics, reduced family cohesion, and insufficient emotional support—not merely body image dissatisfaction. An adolescent with elevated social adjustment difficulty is describing behavioral withdrawal from peer activities, evaluative anxiety in social settings, and avoidance of body-exposing public spaces. These are not psychometric abstractions; they represent measurable impairment in the specific life domains central to adolescent development and identity formation.

The relevance of these difficulties to daily life has been supported by research conducted in other countries. For instance, lower social competence has been associated with the development of obesity and treatment resistance (Stice, 2002); training in social skills and improvement in communication is one of the most important aspects of a comprehensive treatment for obesity. The present research provides a country-specific evidence base for incorporating training in social and emotional skills within a treatment for obesity among late adolescents and young adults in urban India.

10.5 Theoretical contributions

10.5.1 Extending the social determinants framework

The social determinants of health (SDOH) framework, as proposed by Marmot (2005), suggests that structural risk contexts, such as income, education, food access, and healthcare, are the primary factors contributing to obesity. The strength of this framework is its epidemiological approach. Nevertheless, there is a lack of clear understanding of the psychological mechanisms through which structural factors influence psychological outcomes. This volume contributes a critical extension to this framework. It argues that structural inequalities not only limit but also influence how people perceive things. In the context of this research, adolescents from disadvantaged backgrounds experience not only a lack of access to healthy foods but also a familial context where food insecurity and pressure from media-influenced body image expectations create a new kind of psychological dissonance.

The results of this research, where psychological outcomes differ significantly for obese individuals with similar BMI values and socioeconomic backgrounds, support the need for structural factors but also highlight their inadequacy. The psychological mechanisms through which personality types, LOC, coping mechanisms, and internalization of weight bias influence psychological outcomes must be considered equally important for future theoretical and policy developments. Future models should incorporate these psychological mediators as equally significant targets for intervention.

10.5.2 Weight bias internalization as the bridge construct

WBI has emerged across this volume as the central bridge construct linking external stigma to internal psychological distress. The meta-analytic evidence is now robust: The analysis by Romano et al. (2023) of 87 studies found WBI associated with depression ($r = 0.48$), anxiety ($r = 0.40$), disordered eating ($r = 0.52$), and low self-esteem ($r = -0.58$). Warnick et al. (2022) systematic review confirmed these associations extend to children and adolescents. A path analysis by Bidstrup et al. (2022) of early adolescents ($n = 406$) confirmed that internalized weight bias mediated the relationship between perceived stigma and both internalizing symptoms and disordered eating, with WBI negatively associated with body esteem ($r = -0.61$).

The present study, while not directly measuring WBI (which was not available in the validated Indian instruments employed at the time of data collection), provides convergent evidence consistent with advanced internalization: significantly lower self-esteem and body image scores, higher depression and anxiety across three of four age-sex groups, and more disordered eating across all groups—a profile consistent with advanced WBI. Future Indian research must incorporate validated WBI measurement alongside the instruments used in the present study to directly test internalization as the mediating mechanism.

10.5.3 Resilience theory: reframing from risk to capacity

The dominant discourse on adolescent obesity is deficit-focused—cataloging risks, consequences, and psychological burdens. Although this is a scientifically significant discovery, it is not complete. The current study shows that there is considerable variance in psychological outcomes among obese individuals who share the same BMI levels, and some of them report stable self-esteem, coping, and adaptation. This calls for parallel attention to the presence of resilience factors. Within the theoretical model, resilience is not defined as the absence of stress, but as the dynamic ability to change and adapt, supported by the presence of secure relationships, diverse identity investments, and institutional environments in which personhood is supported and not challenged (Masten, 2014).

In the model, five pathways to resilience are defined: having a secure family relationship in which intrinsic worth is explicitly recognized and valued, going beyond physical appearance; having diverse identity investments in academic, artistic, or social domains, regardless of physical appearance; having supportive peer relationships in which feelings of belonging are genuine; having the ability to reframe negative thoughts, in which externalization of stigma is possible; and having lower levels of internalization of weight bias. These are not fixed personality traits, but are to be cultivated. All families, educational systems, and health care professionals play critical roles in promoting all five pathways to resilience. Within this model, the promotion of resilience is scientifically as sound and important as the promotion of risk reduction.

10.6 Practical implications

10.6.1 A dual outcome framework

The central practical implication of this volume is the establishment of dual outcome criteria in all adolescent obesity interventions: metabolic stabilization and psychological well-being. A Cochrane systematic review of dietary, physical activity, and behavioral interventions for overweight adolescents aged 12–17 (Colquitt et al., 2017) found modest BMI reductions but limited evidence of sustained psychological benefit in weight-centric interventions. A meta-analysis of 49 pediatric obesity treatment studies ($n = 10{,}471$) found that treatment produced significant increases in self-esteem ($SMD = 0.34$, $P < .001$), maintained at follow-up—critically, improvement was independent of the degree of weight loss achieved (Harrist et al., 2020). These findings confirm that psychological outcomes in obese adolescents can and should be targeted independently, not treated as downstream benefits of weight loss (Table 10.1).

10.6.2 School-level interventions

Schools represent the most universally accessible institutional context for adolescent health intervention. Evidence-based reform must operate simultaneously at four levels. Structural reforms involve eliminating public weigh-ins, removing body-composition grading from physical education assessments, and redesigning activity programs to prioritize intrinsic motivation and participation over performative fitness standards. A systematic evaluation of a culturally tailored school-based body image intervention with urban Indian adolescents (Lewis-Smith et al., 2023) documented significant reductions in thin-ideal internalization and body dissatisfaction at follow-up, confirming that school-based psychological programs are both feasible and effective in Indian settings. Curriculum reforms embed body diversity education and media

TABLE 10.1 Dual outcome framework for adolescent obesity intervention.

Metabolic: body mass index stabilization I Physical activity levels I Blood pressure I Lipid profiles
Psychological: depression (Beck Depression Inventory) I Anxiety—state and trait I Self-esteem (Rosenberg) I LOC (Levenson) I Coping repertoire
Relational: FES dimensions—acceptance and caring, active recreational, expressiveness I Bell's adjustment inventory (home, health, social, emotional)
Body image and eating: Multidimensional Body Self Relations Questionnaire subscales (appearance evaluation, fitness evaluation) I EAT-26 scores I WBI (Durso & Latner, 2008)
Principle: no outcome domain takes precedence over others. All four are monitored, reported, and targeted

literacy within existing health and life-skills curricula, equipping adolescents with the critical-analytical tools needed to interrogate idealized imagery. Teacher training in weight-sensitive communication is an institutional imperative: educators who use body-related commentary as a disciplinary tool or social humor inadvertently amplify institutional stigma and compound the psychological burden associated with obesity.

A review of effective childhood obesity prevention strategies in India (Jambholkar et al., 2024) established that school-based interventions integrating dietary education, physical activity, and psychological support via teacher-led programs demonstrate the most substantial evidence of efficacy in Indian settings. The core design principle is that antistigma education must be universal—delivered to all students rather than targeted only at those with obesity-to avoid inadvertently constructing weight status as a salient social category requiring special management.

10.6.3 Family-based strategies

The present study also found that obese adolescents in Kolkata perceive their family environments as being lower on warmth, expressiveness, recreational activity, and autonomy-support. These characteristics are modifiable rather than fixed features of family functioning. Therefore, interventions at the family level represent one of the strongest leverage points for large-scale, sustained change. The key strategies for families include: (1) communication training to replace critical comments about bodies with a collaborative approach to health; (2) psycho-education regarding stigma associated with being overweight and its impact on psychological health, to highlight that even good-intentioned shaming can cause harm; (3) structured physical activity for families to replace shaming associated with being overweight with a collaborative approach to health; and (4) therapy for families exhibiting high levels of conflict, criticism, and disordered routines.

A cluster randomized controlled trial in India published in 2025 found that a family-based cardiovascular health promotion intervention delivered by nonphysician community health workers significantly improved weight, BMI, and waist circumference over 2 years (Panniyammakal et al., 2025) found that families receiving structured sessions for lifestyle modification by nonphysician community health workers showed significant improvement in weight, BMI, and waist circumference at both 1 and 2 years. The use of community health workers as facilitators of such interventions, like ASHA workers and Anganwadi workers, points to the ease of conducting such interventions within India. The data collected through the FES scale also points to the aspects of family environments that should form the cornerstone of such interventions: active recreational orientation, acceptance and caring, and expressiveness—all of which showed large differences (Table 10.2).

10.6.4 Clinical integration

Youth presenting for weight-related concerns should receive a mental health assessment concurrently with a metabolic assessment. The results of the current study, in which obese youth demonstrated significantly higher levels of Health Adjustment difficulties than all other groups, support the contention that health-related functioning is always compromised through some form of psychological mechanism. The revised guidelines from the Indian Academy of Pediatrics (IAP, 2023), which explicitly recommend the inclusion of psychological assessment in addition to clinical assessment, constitute a policy recommendation for the integration of mental health assessment and intervention. It is perfectly reasonable for multidisciplinary teams to consist of nutritionists, psychologists, pediatricians, and family therapists.

TABLE 10.2 Language substitution guide for supportive family communication in adolescent obesity (Indian context).

Harmful: "You should not consume a large quantity of food; your appearance warrants scrutiny." → Supportive: "Let us share this meal collaboratively. How has your day been?" Harmful: "Lose weight before the wedding or social scrutiny will ensue." → Supportive: "You appear radiant. Please, proceed to enjoy the celebration." Harmful: "If you concentrated on academics instead of eating, your grades would improve." → Supportive: "Let us evaluate what went well. How are you feeling?" Harmful: "Your cousin is in excellent shape. Why cannot you emulate him?" → Supportive: "Individuals possess various strengths. Which activity do you enjoy most?" Harmful: "Even a physician recommends weight loss. We have repeatedly advised you." → Supportive: "The physician has created a plan for joint implementation. How can we assist you?" (Romano et al., 2023; Pearl and Puhl, 2018; Das, 2018)

Source: Puhl, R.M. & Heuer, C.A. (2009). The stigma of obesity: A review and update. Obesity, 17(5), 941–964. https://doi.org/10.1038/oby.2008.636.

Cognitive behavioral therapy (CBT), acceptance and commitment therapy (ACT), and mindfulness-based interventions have been shown to help address body image concerns and the psychological consequences of weight-related stigma among adolescents and young people. The most effective intervention for addressing obesity in young adults is CBT, especially when self-monitoring, goal-setting, and self-esteem enhancement are included. A meta-analysis of mindfulness interventions with youth (Zoogman et al., 2015) validated substantial enhancements in psychological well-being. These methods need to be used in regular obesity consultations in Indian clinics.

10.6.5 Policy and structural reform

India's POSHAN Abhiyaan, Fit India Movement, and RKSK programs currently focus on nutrition and physical activity without systematically addressing stigma, family communication, or psychological well-being (Thapliyal & Bassi, 2024). Recommended reforms include: mandatory psychological screening within RKSK's adolescent health and wellness days; family communication workshops integrated into POSHAN Abhiyaan home visitor training; stigma reduction modules in all RBSK school health programs; and dignity-centered public health messaging guidelines prohibiting weight-shaming language. A scoping review of Indian policy instruments (Thapliyal & Bassi, 2024) confirmed that all existing programs require substantial redesign to address psychological and relational dimensions.

10.7 Future research directions

10.7.1 Longitudinal designs: the highest priority

Every study reviewed in the scoping review of Indian adolescent obesity research (Panda et al., 2025) employed a cross-sectional design—a finding that explicitly identifies longitudinal research as the highest-priority methodological need in the field. The present study, while employing an exploratory quantitative comparative design that establishes associations rather than causal sequences, extends beyond all reviewed Indian studies by providing multidomain psychological profiling absent from prior work. Longitudinal cohorts tracking adolescents from early to late adolescence and into young adulthood would clarify three critical questions: does early exposure to weight stigma forecast adult mental health outcomes irrespective of BMI trajectory? Does the family environment at 15 years old predict how well someone will adjust psychologically at 22? Does coping style influence the progression from adolescent body dissatisfaction to young adult depression? The field cannot design interventions optimally calibrated to developmental timing without longitudinal data.

10.7.2 Intersectionality: gender, caste, class, and body

The present study confirmed significant sex differences in family environment patterns and adjustment outcomes -female obese young adults showed significantly poorer emotional adjustment ($P<.05$), female obese late adolescents showed lower self-esteem deficits, and Cohesion showed opposite directions for male and female groups. These sex differences are theoretically significant but lack sufficient granularity; they indicate the necessity for intersectional analysis that explores the interplay of gender with caste, class, religion, and geography to create qualitatively distinct vulnerability profiles. Subsequent investigations utilizing Crenshaw (1989) intersectionality framework on Indian obesity data would fill a significant void and yield evidence pertinent to equity-focused intervention design.

10.7.3 Digital media and algorithmic body ideals

This study was undertaken before the full integration of algorithm-driven social media into the lives of Indian adolescents. Currently, digital media are capable of spreading globalized body ideals beyond the scope of peer comparison. A meta-analysis of social networking site use and body dissatisfaction/disordered eating (Holland & Tiggemann, 2016) demonstrated significant correlations between social networking site use and body dissatisfaction/disordered eating. A 2025 study conducted among children and adolescents in Pune, Western Maharashtra, found that excessive screen time was significantly associated with a higher risk of overweight and obesity, highlighting screen exposure as an important modifiable risk factor for obesity in youth. Future studies need to go beyond the quantification of screen time and investigate the mechanistic impact of social media content on body ideals.

10.7.4 Mixed-methods integration

The study did not include a mixed-methods approach. However, the experience-related factors discussed in the chapters are based on existing literature. Therefore, the experience-related factors are not directly related to the study's findings but are based on existing literature. If the mixed-methods approach is considered, the experience-related factors discussed in the chapters could be related to the findings of the study. This would be possible if the mixed-methods approach were integrated into the study. This would involve using the findings of the quantitative study to interview the participants at extremes of the psychological outcomes. This would provide the connection between the statistical architecture of the findings and the experience-related factors of the urban Indian adolescent.

10.7.5 Psychometric validation for Indian contexts

The tools used in the present study are validated for the Indian population. However, emergent constructs that are of prime importance in contemporary obesity studies, such as WBI, digital social comparison, and culture-specific stigma domains of marriageability and family honor, are not well represented in the existing validated tools. The WBI scale developed by Durso & Latner (2008), needs to be adapted for the Indian population. The FES may not accurately assess the role of joint family commentaries and input from extended family members in weight bias. Further studies need to be conducted to create and standardize psychosocial tools for Indian adolescent obesity studies.

Pedagogical tools

Case studies

Case study 1: neuroticism, external LOC, and avoidant coping in an obese male late adolescent (urban Kolkata).

Background: Arnab, 18, obese (BMI 32.4), undergraduate student in Kolkata. Experiences frequent comments from family linking his weight to academic underperformance and lack of discipline.

Psychological profile (consistent with the present study male LA obese group): high NEO Five-Factor Inventory (NEO-FFI) neuroticism (M = 14.50 in obese LA vs 19.50 nonobese, note: obese higher on neuroticism). High trait anxiety (M = 53.18 vs 39.90, $P<.01$). BDI in mild-moderate depression range (M = 19.30 vs 12.48, $P<.01$). Low internal LOC (M = 15.26 vs 24.80, $P<.01$) and high powerful others LOC (M = 24.00 vs 32.80).

Eating attitudes (EAT-26): high score (M = 26.68 vs 6.48, $P<.01$), indicating significant disordered eating attitudes; uses food as a primary emotion regulation strategy.

Coping: CRI group comparison nonsignificant for late adolescents (both sexes); BMI shows a significant negative correlation with coping response in male LA group ($P<.05$), suggesting higher BMI is associated with less adaptive coping at the correlational level.

Family environment: FES active recreational low (M = 26.08 vs 36.88, $P<.01$); FES independence low (M = 30.56 vs 40.02, $P<.01$). Frequent family criticism was also reported.

Adjustment: significantly poorer home (M = 11.88 vs 5.98, $P<.01$), health (M = 10.34 vs 4.58, $P<.01$), social (M = 14.44 vs 11.42, $P<.01$).

Intervention: CBT for LOC reattribution and cognitive reframing; family communication training; CRI-guided coping skills program; clinician weight-neutral counseling.

Evidence base: (Sutin & Terracciano, 2016; Romano et al., 2023; Gilles & Cairney, 2014; Das, 2018).

Sutin, A.R. & Terracciano, A. (2016). personality traits and BMI: modifiers and mechanisms. psychology and health, 31(3), 259–275. https://doi.org/10.1080/08870446.2015.1082561.

Case study 2: body image distress, disordered eating, and marriageability pressure in an obese female late adolescent (urban Kolkata).

Background: Devika, 19, obese (BMI 33.1), lives in a joint family in Kolkata. Faces regular comments from relatives linking body size to marriage prospects.

Psychological profile (consistent with the present study female LA obese group): Rosenberg self-esteem low (M = 14.06 vs 21.66, $P<.01$). NEO-FFI neuroticism elevated; BDI high (M = 22.04 vs 13.36, $P<.01$). STAI trait anxiety high (M = 51.36 vs 45.72, $P<.01$).

Body image (MBSRQ): appearance evaluation low; Illness orientation elevated; Appearance orientation high (preoccupied with monitoring appearance despite negative self-evaluation).

Eating attitudes (EAT-26): high score (M = 29.34 vs 9.24, *P*<.01). Binge eating episodes following family critical comments.

Family environment: FES acceptance and caring low across all groups (*P*<.01); FES Expressiveness low (M = 32.60 vs 34.50, *P*<.05).

Adjustment: home and health adjustment significantly poorer (*P*<.01). Social withdrawal; avoidance of family ceremonies.

Theoretical mechanism: WBI internalization pathway (marriageability script → repeated evaluative exposure → schema consolidation → depression and disordered eating).

Intervention: individual CBT targeting appearance-based self-evaluation; family communication workshop; FES-targeted family environment intervention; psychoeducation for parents on WBI.

Evidence base: (Romano et al., 2023; Anam et al., 2025; Pearl & Puhl, 2018; Das, 2018).

Pearl, R. L. & Puhl, R. M. (2018). Weight bias internalization and health: a systematic review. Obesity Reviews, 19(8), 1141–1163. https://doi.org/10.1111/obr.12701.

Case study 3: resilience and protective family environment in an overweight Female young adult (urban Kolkata).

Background: Priya, 23, is an overweight postgraduate student with a BMI of 31.8. Her results are different from those of most overweight people, which shows how she was able to bounce back.

Psychological profile: BDI is within the normal range. STAI state and trait anxiety are both normal. Rosenberg self-esteem is better than average. NEO-FFI: extraversion and agreeableness in a range that is not obese.

Family environment of protection: High levels of FES acceptance and caring expressiveness are higher than the group means, and FES active recreational is higher than the mean for obese people (the family goes for evening walks and cooks together). Little criticism of family weight.

Coping: approach-focused coping is the most common type, and the CRI problem-focused subscales are higher. Cognitive reappraisal of social stigma as external bias rather than individual deficiency.

Change: home and health adjustment is good. Active social engagement; difficulties with social adjustment are not present.

Resilience factors: strong family ties with clear affirmation of worth; a range of identity investments (academic success, community involvement); a network of friends who support each other. Theoretical function: this case validates that obesity does not inevitably lead to distress. Relational and cognitive protective factors help people become more resilient.

Theoretical function: this case confirms that obesity does not deterministically produce distress. Resilience is cultivated through relational and cognitive protective factors.

Evidence base: (Masten, 2014; Huang et al., 2023; Das, 2018)—within-group variance in obese cohort.

Masten, A.S. (2014). Global Perspectives on Resilience in Children and Youth. Child Development, 85(1), 6–20. https://doi.org/10.1111/cdev.12205.

Case study 4: digital media exposure, social comparison, and body dissatisfaction in an overweight male young adult (urban India).

Rahul, 21, is an engineering student in Pune and is overweight (BMI 30.9). Body dissatisfaction has gotten worse over the past two years because people see fitness influencer content on Instagram and YouTube every day.

Psychological profile: STAI state anxiety is high. The MBSRQ appearance and fitness evaluation scores are low, and the BDI scores are in the mild depression range. NEO-FFI neuroticism is higher than average, but conscientiousness is lower than the mean for the nonobese group.

Digital exposure pattern: daily interaction with fitness content that promotes thin, muscular ideals. More comparisons of how things look going up. Starting to stay away from places where peers can see their bodies.

Eating attitudes: the score for the EAT-26 is high, with oscillations in dietary restriction to attain a "transformation" look, followed by episodes of overeating due to dietary regimens promoted on social media, which are not sustainable in the long term.

Coping: despite the intention to go to the gym, there is avoidance. The use of humor is to deflect from the situation, with eating at night to regulate emotions.

Family context: parents downplay worries. FES Active Recreational is below the group mean. No talking about digital body image in the family.

Intervention: the intervention to be used would include media literacy, a brief cognitive-behavioral intervention to reduce cognitive fusion from comparison-induced ANTs, psychoeducation for the family, and follow-up by a school counselor.

Evidence base: (Holland & Tiggemann, 2016; Warnick et al., 2022).

Holland, Grace & Tiggemann, Marika. (2016). A systematic review of the impact of the use of social networking sites on body image and disordered eating outcomes. Body Image, 17, 100–110. https://doi.org/10.1016/j.bodyim.2016.02.008.

10.8 Key takeaways

Adolescent obesity in urban India is associated with a consistent and multidimensional psychological burden, including higher depression, anxiety, disordered eating, and poorer body image.

Personality traits, LOC, and coping patterns shape how adolescents experience and respond to obesity, with significant variation across age and gender.

Body image dissatisfaction, WBI, and disordered eating emerge as central psychological mechanisms linking stigma to distress.

Family environment plays a critical role, with lower warmth, expressiveness, and activity levels associated with poorer adjustment and well-being.

Obesity must be understood as a biopsychosocial and cultural condition, requiring integrated theoretical models that include psychological mediators.

Effective intervention requires a dual focus on metabolic health and psychological well-being, implemented across schools, families, clinical systems, and policy frameworks.

Future research in India must prioritize longitudinal, intersectional, and mixed-method approaches to better capture developmental and contextual complexity.

Glossary of key terms

Term	Definition
Adolescent obesity	A condition in which late adolescents or young adults carry excess body fat (BMI 30.0–39.9 in the present study); understood in this volume as a developmental, relational, and sociocultural phenomenon shaped by personality, family environment, coping, and cultural meaning
Beck depression inventory (BDI)	A 21-item validated self-report scale measuring the severity of depressive symptoms (Beck et al., 1961).
Coping Response Inventory (CRI)	A validated instrument (Rao et al., 1999) assessing approach-focused and avoidance-focused coping strategies; the present study found mixed coping results: late adolescent groups showed nonsignificant differences; young adult male obese scored higher (more adaptive, $P<.01$); young adult female obese scored lower (less adaptive, $P<.01$); BMI negatively correlated with coping in male late adolescents (correlational analysis, $P<.05$)
EAT-26	Eating attitudes test-26 (Garner & Garfinkel, 1979), a validated 26-item scale assessing disordered eating attitudes and behaviors; the present study found significantly higher scores in obese participants across all groups, with the largest differentials in female adolescents
Family environment scale (FES)	A validated instrument (Bhatia & Chadha, 1993) assessing eight dimensions of family functioning: cohesion, expressiveness, conflict, acceptance and caring, active recreational orientation, independence, organization, and control
Locus of control (LOC)	(Levenson, 1973) multidimensional construct measuring belief in Internal Control, control by Powerful Others, and Chance Control; the present study found significantly lower Powerful Others LOC scores in obese participants across all four groups ($P<.01$); Internal control findings were mixed by age-sex group; Chance control was nonsignificant in three of four groups
MBSRQ	Multidimensional Body Self Relations Questionnaire (Brown et al., 1990); assesses seven body image dimensions; the present study found significantly lower Appearance Evaluation, Fitness Evaluation, and Health Evaluation in obese participants across all groups
NEO-FFI	NEO Five-Factor Inventory (McCrae & Costa, 1989); measures neuroticism, extraversion, openness, agreeableness, and conscientiousness; obese participants showed higher neuroticism and lower scores on all other four domains in the present study
Resilience	A dynamic capacity to maintain or regain psychological well-being despite adversity; understood as cultivated through secure relationships, identity flexibility, and protective environments rather than as a fixed individual trait (Masten, 2014)
Weight bias internalization (WBI)	The process by which individuals accept and self-apply negative societal stereotypes about obesity, converting external stigma into self-directed criticism, predicts depression ($r = 0.48$), anxiety ($r = 0.40$), and disordered eating ($r = 0.52$) (Romano et al., 2023)

Review questions

Section A: conceptual understanding

1. The present study found that the body weight main effect was significant across the majority of measured variables. Identify three domains from different chapters of this volume where obese adolescents showed significantly different scores from nonobese peers, citing actual means.

2. Explain how personality traits—specifically neuroticism and conscientiousness—mediate the relationship between obesity and psychological outcomes such as depression and avoidant coping. What does the international FFM literature confirm about these associations?
3. What is the relationship between LOC and obesity? How does external LOC function as both a predictor and a consequence of obesity, and what intervention implications does this bidirectional relationship produce?
4. Explain the mechanism of WBI. What four pathways lead to internalization, and how do the present study's outcomes on self-esteem, depression, and eating attitudes align with the WBI meta-analytic literature?
5. What did the present study find on the Family Environment Scale? Identify three FES dimensions with the largest deficits in obese participants and explain what each suggests about the family environments of obese adolescents in urban Kolkata.

Section B: critical analysis

6. Critically evaluate the argument that psychological outcomes in obese adolescents can improve independently of weight loss. What evidence from the (Harrist et al., 2020) meta-analysis and the (Alves et al., 2024) review supports this claim, and what are the intervention implications?
7. The present study found a sex-differentiated pattern in the Cohesion dimension of the FES and in emotional adjustment outcomes. What theoretical explanations account for this pattern, and what does it suggest for gender-sensitive intervention design?
8. How does cultural modernization in India—particularly the simultaneous pull of traditional body ideals and globalized media standards—compound the psychological burden of obesity for adolescents in ways that Western theoretical models do not adequately capture?
9. The present study employed a comparative group design. What methodological limitations does this create? Propose a longitudinal mixed-methods research design that would address these limitations while retaining the quantitative precision of the instruments used.
10. Compare the disordered eating profiles found in the present study (EAT-26 data) with the Indian literature on eating disorders in adolescents (Anam et al., 2025; Iyer & Shriraam, 2024). What convergences emerge, and what does this suggest about the clinical priority of eating attitude assessment in Indian obesity programs?
Section C: application
11. Design a school-level intervention for urban Indian secondary schools that simultaneously addresses body image, eating attitudes, and weight bias without reinforcing body surveillance. Specify theoretical basis, core components, delivery mechanism, and measurement framework.
12. Using the present study's LOC and coping findings, design a clinical protocol for a 19-year-old obese male presenting with avoidant coping and external LOC. What instruments would you use, what thresholds would trigger intervention, and how would CBT and LOC-reattribution strategies be integrated?
13. A family's critical communication patterns are identified through FES assessment as the primary driver of their 16-year-old daughter's depression and disordered eating. Drawing on the present study's FES findings and the WBI literature, design a family-level intervention specifying: communication targets, psychoeducational content, assessment measures, and success criteria.
14. Propose a research design for a longitudinal intersectional study of adolescent obesity in India, specifying: sample size and composition, measurement battery, statistical analysis plan, ethical safeguards, and the specific intersectional hypotheses to be tested.
15. How can the principles of equity, dignity, and resilience be operationalised within India's RKSK and POSHAN Abhiyaan frameworks? Identify three specific program components that would need to be added or modified in each program to embed these principles.

Conclusion

This concluding chapter brings together the empirical findings of the present study and existing theories and international studies to conceptualize adolescent obesity as a bio-psycho-social-cultural construct. The primary finding of this study was that the factor of body weight status makes a significant difference between obese and nonobese youth on most of the studied psychological variables, with a few exceptions. The findings of this study emphasize the need to understand the issue of obesity not only from a biological but also from a personality, emotional, familial, and sociocultural perspective.

The psychological profile of obese youth in urban Kolkata appears not only to be influenced by biological factors but also by personality factors that influence the processing of stigma, LOC that affects perceptions of health as within or beyond personal control, evaluation of body image that reflects perceptions of social comparison, disordered eating that serves as a maladaptive coping mechanism for emotional distress, family environment that features lower warmth, expressiveness, and physical activity, and adjustment problems that permeate all aspects of life, health, and emotional well-being. The issue of adolescent obesity in India demands a multidimensional intervention that follows the three broad principles that guide this volume: equity, dignity, and resilience.

The practical toolkit provided in this volume, including school reform strategies, family-level communication strategies, clinical strategies, and policy reform strategies, translates this evidence into pathways for implementing psychological well-being as an equally important outcome in obesity management within existing infrastructures in India. The direction that future adolescent obesity studies will take in India is longitudinal, intersectional, mixed-methods, and psychologically sophisticated. The current study offers quantitative groundwork; however, future studies in India will need to expand on it in terms of richness, depth, and inclusivity to reflect the diversity of its youth population.

Limitations

The present study carries several limitations that should be considered when interpreting its findings. First, the sample was drawn entirely from Kolkata, an urban metropolitan center; findings should be treated as indicative of urban Indian patterns rather than nationally representative, and replication across rural, semiurban, and geographically diverse Indian samples is needed. Second, the exploratory quantitative comparative group design precludes causal inference: significant differences between obese and nonobese groups establish association but cannot determine whether adverse psychological characteristics precede or follow obesity onset. Third, all data relied on adolescent self-report, which is subject to social desirability bias, particularly in collectivist cultural contexts where mental health stigma may suppress disclosure. Fourth, the study did not include a qualitative component; the lived-experience dimensions discussed across this volume are inferred from the published literature rather than from primary fieldwork with the study's own participants. Fifth, international studies synthesized across chapters vary substantially in methodology, measurement instruments, and cultural context, limiting the strength of direct cross-regional comparisons. Sixth, the intervention proposals presented in §10.6 are evidence-informed but have not been evaluated in RCTs in Indian settings and require empirical validation before wide-scale implementation.

AI disclosure

During the preparation of this work, the author(s) used ChatGPT, Grammarly, and Paperpal in order to They were used solely for the purpose of language editing. After using this tool/service, the author(s) reviewed and edited the content as needed and take(s) full responsibility for the content of the publication.

References

Ahuja, P., et al. (2025). Exploring the interplay of body image, quality of life, self-esteem, and psychological well-being with eating attitudes in adolescents. *International Journal of Research in Medical Sciences, 13*(11), 4755–4761. https://doi.org/10.18203/2320-6012.ijrms20253596.

Alves, C., Petitjean, M., & Druzhinenko-Silhan, D. (2024). Psychological approaches to obesity in young adults: State of the art. *Frontiers in Nutrition, 11*, 1328386. https://doi.org/10.3389/fnut.2024.1328386.

Anam, S., et al. (2025). Eating disorders and disordered eating behaviors among Indian adolescents: A cross-sectional review. *Cureus, 17*(8), e90909.

Beck, A. T., Ward, C. H., Mendelson, M., Mock, J., & Erbaugh, J. (1961). An inventory for measuring depression. *Archives of General Psychiatry, 4*(6), 561–571. https://doi.org/10.1001/archpsyc.1961.01710120031004.

Bhatia, H., & Chadha, N. K. (1993). *Manual for family environment scale*. Ankur Psychological Agency.

Bidstrup, H., Christensen, B. J., Eg, M., & Cour, K. L. (2022). Adolescent internalized weight bias and its consequences. *Journal of Eating Disorders, 10*, 45.

Blundell, E., De Stavola, B. L., Kellock, M. D., et al. (2024). Longitudinal pathways between childhood BMI, body dissatisfaction, and adolescent depression. *The Lancet Psychiatry, 11*(1), e1–e12.

Brown, T. A., Cash, T. F., & Mikulka, P. J. (1990). Attitudinal body-image assessment. *Journal of Personality Assessment, 55*(1–2), 135–144. https://doi.org/10.1080/00223891.1990.9674053.

Colquitt, J. L., et al. (2017). Diet, physical activity and behavioural interventions for the treatment of overweight or obese adolescents aged 12 to 17 years. *Cochrane Database of Systematic Reviews, 6*(6), CD012651. https://doi.org/10.1002/14651858.CD012651.

Conger, R. D., & Elder, G. H. (1994). *Families in troubled times*. Aldine de Gruyter.

Crenshaw, K. (1989). Demarginalizing the intersection of race and sex. *University of Chicago Legal Forum, 1989*(1), 139–167.

Das, S. (2018). Psychological characteristics and adjustment patterns in late adolescents and young adults with obesity [Doctoral study, University of Calcutta].

Durso, L. E., & Latner, J. D. (2008). Understanding self-directed stigma: Development of the Weight Bias Internalization Scale. *Obesity, 16*(S2), S80–S86. https://doi.org/10.1038/oby.2008.448.

Fredrickson, B. L., & Roberts, T. A. (1997). Objectification theory. *Psychology of Women Quarterly, 21*(2), 173–206. https://doi.org/10.1111/j.1471-6402.1997.tb00108.x.

Garner, D. M., & Garfinkel, P. E. (1979). The eating attitudes test. *Psychological Medicine, 9*(2), 273–279.

Gilles, A., & Cairney, J. (2014). Locus of control and obesity: A review. *Canadian Journal of Diabetes, 38*(2), 147–151.

Harrist, A. W., et al. (2020). Pediatric obesity treatment, self-esteem, and body image: A systematic review with meta-analysis. *Clinical Obesity, 10*(3), e12368. https://doi.org/10.1111/cob.12368.

Holland, G., & Tiggemann, M. (2016). A systematic review of the impact of social networking sites on body image and disordered eating outcomes. *Body Image, 17*, 100–110. https://doi.org/10.1016/j.bodyim.2016.02.008.

Huang, L., et al. (2023). Family characteristics in adolescents with overweight or obesity: A network analysis. *Frontiers in Pediatrics, 11*, 1282117. https://doi.org/10.3389/fped.2023.1282117.

Indian Academy of Pediatrics (IAP). (2023). IAP guidelines on management of childhood obesity. Indian Pediatrics, 60, 1013–1030.

Iyer, S., & Shriraam, V. (2024). Prevalence of eating disorders among senior college students in a metropolitan city. *Journal of Education and Health Promotion, 13*, e12340.

Jambholkar, P. C., Joshi, A., & Choudhari, S. G. (2024). Addressing the challenge: A review of effective prevention strategies for childhood obesity in India. *Cureus, 16*(3), e56257. https://doi.org/10.7759/cureus.56257.

Levenson, H. (1973). Multidimensional locus of control in psychiatric patients. *Journal of Consulting and Clinical Psychology, 41*(3), 397–404. https://doi.org/10.1037/h0035357.

Lewis-Smith, H., Diedrichs, P. C., Rumsey, N., & Harcourt, D. (2023). Body image interventions in schools: Culturally adapted programmes for urban Indian adolescents. *Body Image, 44*, 1–12.

Marmot, M. (2005). Social determinants of health inequalities. *The Lancet, 365*(9464), 1099–1104. https://doi.org/10.1016/s0140-6736(05)71146-6.

Masten, A. S. (2014). Global perspectives on resilience in children and youth. *Child Development, 85*(1), 6–20. http://doi.org/10.1111/cdev.12205.

McCrae, R. R., & Costa, P. T. (1989). Reinterpreting the Myers-Briggs Type Indicator from the perspective of the Five-Factor Model of personality. *Journal of Personality, 57*(1), 17–40. https://doi.org/10.1111/j.1467-6494.1989.tb00759.x.

Panda, A., Parida, J., Jena, S., Behera, S. S., Pradhan, A., Patra, P. K., Pati, S., Kaur, H., & Acharya, S. K. (2025). Prevalence and associated risk factors of overweight and obesity among adolescent population of India: a scoping review. *BMC Nutrition, 11*(1). https://doi.org/10.1186/s40795-025-01088-0.

Panniyammakal, J., Stanley, A., Ismail, S., Lekha, T.R., Ganapathi, S., & Harikrishnan, S. (2025). Family-based interventions to promote weight management in adults: results from a cluster randomized controlled trial in India. *Annals of Family Medicine*, 23, 93–99. https://doi.org/10.1370/afm.230632.

Pearl, R. L., & Puhl, R. M. (2018). Weight bias internalization and health: A systematic review. *Obesity Reviews, 19*(8), 1141–1163.

Phelps, N. H., et al. (2024). Worldwide trends in underweight and obesity from 1990 to 2022. *The Lancet, 403*(10431), 1027–1050.

Piko, B. F., Patel, K., & Kiss, H. (2022). Risk of disordered eating among Indian adolescents: The role of online activity, social anxiety and social support. *Journal of Indian Association for Child and Adolescent Mental Health, 18*, 315–321.

Puhl, R. M., & Heuer, C. A. (2009). The stigma of obesity: A review and update. *Obesity, 17*(5), 941–964.

Rao, K., et al. (1999). Coping Response Inventory. National Institute of Mental Health and Neurosciences.

Romano, K. A., et al. (2023). Weight bias internalization and health: A meta-analysis. *Behavior Therapy, 54*(3), 539–556.

Rotter, J. B. (1966). Generalized expectancies for internal versus external control of reinforcement. *Psychological Monographs: General and Applied, 80*(1), 1–28. https://doi.org/10.1037/h0092976.

Sethi, V., et al. (2024). Prevalence of overweight and obesity in India: Findings from the CNNS. *Pediatric Obesity, 19*(4), e13092.

Singh, S., et al. (2023). Childhood obesity in India: A two-decade meta-analysis of prevalence and correlates. *Clinical Epidemiology and Global Health, 23*, 101390.

Sonneville, K. R., Calzo, J. P., Horton, N. J., Haines, J., Austin, S. B., & Field, A. E. (2012). Body satisfaction, weight gain and binge eating among overweight adolescent girls. *International Journal of Obesity, 36*(7), 944–949. https://doi.org/10.1038/ijo.2012.68.

Steptoe, A., & Wardle, J. (2001). Locus of control and health behaviour revisited: A multivariate analysis of young adults from 18 countries. *British Journal of Psychology, 92*(4), 659–672. https://doi.org/10.1348/000712601162400.

Stice, E. (2002). Risk and maintenance factors for eating pathology: A meta-analytic review. Psychological Bulletin, 128(5), 825–848. https://doi.org/10.1037/0033-2909.128.5.825.

Sutin, A.R., & Terracciano, A. (2011). Personality and obesity across the adult lifespan. Journal of Personality and Social Psychology, 101(3), 579–592. https://doi.org/10.1037/a0024276.

Sutin, A. R., & Terracciano, A. (2016). Personality traits and body mass index: Modifiers and mechanisms. *Psychological Medicine, 46*(10), 2089–2098.

Thapliyal, N., & Bassi, S. (2024). Existing policy instruments to tackle overweight and obesity in India. *F1000Research, 13*, 496.

Valero-Valenzuela, A., et al. (2025). Relationship between personality traits and psychological well-being in childhood obesity. *Child and Adolescent Psychiatry and Mental Health, 19*, e12567.

Warnick, J. L., et al. (2022). Weight stigma and mental health in children and adolescents: A systematic review. *Journal of Pediatric Psychology, 47*(4), 417–435.

Zhou, R., Zhang, L., Liu, Z., & Cao, B. (2025). Emotion regulation difficulties and disordered eating in adolescents and young adults: a meta-analysis. *Journal of Eating Disorders, 13*(1). https://doi.org/10.1186/s40337-025-01197-y.

Zoogman, S., et al. (2015). Mindfulness interventions with youth: A meta-analysis. *Mindfulness, 6*(2), 290–302.

Further reading

Bell, H. U. (1962). *The bell adjustment inventory*. Consulting Psychologists Press.

Gao, J., et al. (2025). Digital interventions for improving body dissatisfaction: Systematic review and meta-analysis. *Interactive Journal of Medical Research*. https://doi.org/10.2196/72231.

Jena Samanta, L., et al. (2025). Prevalence and associated risk factors of overweight and obesity among adolescents in India: A scoping review. *BMC Nutrition*. https://doi.org/10.1186/s40795-025-01088-0.

Rosenberg, M. (1965). *Society and the adolescent self-image*. Princeton University Press.

Spielberger, C. D. (1983). *Manual for the state-trait anxiety inventory*. Consulting Psychologists Press.

World Health Organization. (2024). Obesity and overweight: Key facts. https://www.who.int/news-room/fact-sheets/detail/obesity-and-overweight

Xu, H., et al. (2023). Association of personality traits with childhood obesity: A systematic review and meta-analysis. *Journal of Affective Disorders, 335*, 1–10. https://doi.org/10.1016/j.jad.2023.04.027.

Zhang, R., et al. (2025). Emotion regulation difficulties and disordered eating in adolescents and young adults: A meta-analysis. *Journal of Eating Disorders, 13*. 1197-y.

Glossary

Anxiety	A state of persistent worry or fear that can influence appetite, eating habits, and body-related concerns. Anxiety may contribute to unhealthy eating behaviors and can also arise as a result of weight-related stress and stigma.
Behavioral factors	Everyday habits and actions, such as food choices, meal patterns, physical activity, and sedentary lifestyle, that influence body weight over time.
Body image	The way a person perceives, thinks about, and feels toward their own body. Body image is shaped by personal experiences, cultural ideals, and social feedback, and it plays an important role in psychological well-being.
Body mass index (BMI)	A numerical ratio of height and weight commonly used to classify body weight categories. Although useful for population-level assessment, BMI does not fully capture an individual's overall health status or psychological experience.
Coping strategies	Ways in which individuals manage stress, emotional discomfort, or challenging situations. Coping strategies may be adaptive or maladaptive and often influence eating behavior and lifestyle choices.
Depression	A psychological condition marked by low mood, reduced motivation, feelings of hopelessness, and changes in appetite or energy. Depression and obesity often have a bidirectional relationship.
Eating behavior	Patterns of food intake shaped by hunger, emotions, habits, social context, and cultural norms. Eating behavior is central to understanding weight gain and obesity.
Emotional eating	Eating in response to emotional states such as stress, sadness, boredom, or frustration rather than physical hunger.
Family environment	The emotional atmosphere, attitudes, routines, and behaviors within a family that affect food habits, body perception, and health practices.
Motivation	The drive that influences behavior change related to eating, physical activity, and lifestyle. Motivation may change over time and is affected by emotional state and social support.
Obesity	A complex condition involving excessive body fat accumulation, influenced by psychological, behavioral, biological, social, and environmental factors. Obesity affects both physical health and mental well-being.
Psychological well-being	A state of emotional balance, self-acceptance, and the ability to cope effectively with life's demands.
Self-esteem	A person's overall sense of self-worth. Self-esteem is often closely linked to body image and social experiences related to weight.
Self-regulation	The capacity to manage thoughts, emotions, and behavior in order to pursue long-term goals, including healthy eating behaviours and lifestyle habits.
Stigma	Negative attitudes and discrimination directed toward individuals because of their body weight. Stigma can lead to emotional distress and reduced engagement with health services.
Stress	A psychological response to perceived pressure or challenge that may influence eating patterns and weight-related behaviors.
Weight bias	Prejudiced beliefs or judgments about individuals based on body size or weight.

Index

Note: Page numbers followed by "*f*" and "*t*" refer to figures and tables, respectively.

Printed and bound by CPI Group (UK) Ltd, Croydon, CR0 4YY
21/09/2026
02220079-0002